Networks Resear(

Design and Applications

This edited volume demonstrates the potential of mixed methods designs for the research of social networks and the utilization of social networks for other research. Mixing methods applies to the combination and integration of qualitative and quantitative methods. In social network research, mixing methods also applies to the combination of structural and actor-oriented approaches.

The volume provides readers with methodological concepts to guide mixed method network studies with precise research designs and methods to investigate social networks of various sorts. Each chapter describes the research design used and discusses the strengths of the methods for that particular field and for specific outcomes.

Silvia Domínguez is an Associate Professor of Sociology and Human Services in the Department of Sociology and Anthropology at Northeastern University.

Betina Hollstein is Chair of Sociology at the University of Bremen.

Structural Analysis in the Social Sciences

Mark Granovetter, editor

The series *Structural Analysis in the Social Sciences* presents studies that analyze social behavior and institutions by reference to relations among such concrete social entities as persons, organizations, and nations. Relational analysis contrasts on the one hand with reductionist methodological individualism and on the other with macro-level determinism, whether based on technology, material conditions, economic conflict, adaptive evolution, or functional imperatives. In this more intellectually flexible structural middle ground, analysts situate actors and their relations in a variety of contexts. Since the series began in 1987, its authors have variously focused on small groups, history, culture, politics, kinship, aesthetics, economics, and complex organizations, creatively theorizing how these shape and in turn are shaped by social relations. Their style and methods have ranged widely, from intense, long-term ethnographic observations to highly abstract mathematical models. Their disciplinary affiliations have included history, anthropology, sociology, political science, business, economics, mathematics, and computer science. Some have made explicit use of social network analysis, including many of the cutting-edge and standard works of that approach, whereas others have kept formal analysis in the background and used "networks" as a fruitful orienting metaphor. All have in common a sophisticated and revealing approach that forcefully illuminates our complex social world.

Other Books in the Series

(continued after the index)

Mixed Methods Social Networks Research

Design and Applications

Edited by

SILVIA DOMÍNGUEZ
Northeastern University

BETINA HOLLSTEIN
Hamburg University

CAMBRIDGE
UNIVERSITY PRESS

CAMBRIDGE
UNIVERSITY PRESS

32 Avenue of the Americas, New York, NY 10013-2473, USA

Cambridge University Press is part of the University of Cambridge.

It furthers the University's mission by disseminating knowledge in the pursuit of education, learning, and research at the highest international levels of excellence.

www.cambridge.org
Information on this title: www.cambridge.org/9781107631052

© Cambridge University Press 2014

First published 2014

Printed in the United States of America

A catalog record for this publication is available from the British Library.

Library of Congress Cataloging in Publication data
Mixed methods social networks research / [edited by] Silvia Domínguez, Northeastern University, Betina Hollstein, Hamburg University.
    pages   cm. – (Structural analysis in the social sciences)
Includes bibliographical references and index.
ISBN 978-1-107-02792-3 (hardback)
1. Social networks – Research – Methodology.   I. Domínguez, Silvia, 1961–   II. Hollstein, Betina, 1965–
HM741.M59   2014
302.3–dc23   2013027222

ISBN 978-1-107-02792-3 Hardback
ISBN 978-1-107-63105-2 Paperback

In memory of our colleague and friend
Janet W. Salaff

Contents

ix

List of Tables

List of Figures

Contributors

Christine B. Avenarius, Dr. phil., Sociocultural Anthropologist, is an Associate Professor for Anthropology at East Carolina University. She attended the Universität zu Köln (Th. Schweitzer), Germany; Peking University, China; and the University of California, Irvine. Her research interests include social networks, legal anthropology, cognitive anthropology, ethnicity, integration, migration, conflict resolution, globalization, East Asia, and China. Her relevant publications include: Work and Social Network Composition among Immigrants from Taiwan to Southern California, *Anthropology of Work Review* 23 (3–4): 3–15 (2003); Conflict, Cooperation, and Integration among Subethnic Immigrant Groups from Taiwan, *Population, Space and Place* 13 (2): 95–112 (2007); The Role of Information Technology in Reducing Social Obligations Among Immigrants from Taiwan, *Journal of International Communication* 2008 14 (1) (2008); To Bribe or Not to Bribe: Comparing Perceptions About Justice, Morality, and Inequality Among Rural and Urban Chinese, *Urban Anthropology* 41 (2,3,4): 247–291 (2012).

Laura Bernardi, Prof. Dr., Demographer, is an Associate Professor for Life Course Research at the University of Lausanne and Deputy Director of the Swiss National Center for Competence in Research "Overcoming Vulnerability in the Life Course." She attended the University of Rome La Sapienza (Italy), the Catholic University of Louvain (Belgium), and Brown University (US). She has been the principal investigator of numerous projects about fertility and family in Europe funded by the Max Planck Gesellschaft, the U.S. National Institute for Health, and the European Community. Her main research interests include population fertility, family sociology, life course, social networks, anthropological demography, social research mixed methods. Her publications include: Channels of Social Influence on Reproduction, *Population Research and Policy Review* 22: 527–555

(2003); (with H. von der Lippe and A. Klaerner) Job Instability and Parenthood, *European Journal of Population* 24 (3): 287–313 (2008); (with A. Fuerrnkranz-Prskawetz, T. Fent, and B. Aparacio) Transition to Parenthood: The Role of Social Interaction and Endogenous Networks, *Demography* (2010).

Peter J. Carrington, Ph.D., is a Professor of Sociology and Legal Studies at the University of Waterloo and editor of the *Canadian Journal of Criminology and Criminal Justice*. His current research project, the Canadian Criminal Careers and Criminal Networks Study, combines his long-standing interests in social network analysis and the development of crime and delinquency. His articles have appeared in the *Journal of Mathematical Sociology, Social Networks, Criminology,* the *Canadian Journal of Criminology and Criminal Justice,* and *Criminal Justice Policy Review.* He is editor of *Applications of Social Network Analysis,* Thousand Oaks, CA: Sage Publications (forthcoming) and co-editor of *The SAGE Handbook of Social Network Analysis,* Thousand Oaks, CA: Sage Publications (2011) and *Models and Methods in Social Network Analysis,* Cambridge: Cambridge University Press (2005).

James A. Danowski, Ph.D., is an Associate Professor (ret.) of Communication at the University of Illinois at Chicago. His recent publications include: (with E. J. Yuan and M. Feng) Privacy in Semantic Networks on Chinese Social Media: The Case of Sina Weibo, *Journal of Communication* (forthcoming); Social Network Size and Designers' Semantic Networks for Collaboration, *International Journal of Organization Design and Engineering* 2 (4): 343–361 (2012); Mining Social Networks at the Organizational Level, in I-Hsien Ting, Tzung-Pei Hong, and Leon S. L. Wang (Eds.), *Social Network Mining, Analysis and Research Trends: Techniques and Applications* (pp. 205–30), Hershey, PA: IGI-Global; Counterterrorism Mining for Individuals Semantically-Similar to Watch List Members, in U. K. Wiil (Ed.), *Counterterrorism and Open-Source Intelligence: Models, Tools, Techniques, and Case Studies,* Lecture Notes in Social Networks, Vol. 2 (pp. 223–247), Berlin: Springer DOI: 10.1007/978-3-7091-0388-3_1 (2011); (with K. Riopelle and J. Gluesing) The Revolution in Diffusion Models Caused by New Media: The Shift from S-Shaped to Convex Curves, in G. A. Barnett and A. Vishwanath (Eds.), *The Diffusion of Innovations: A Communication Science Perspective* (pp. 123–144), New York: Peter Lang Publishing (2011); (with M. V. Duran, A. C. Diaz, and J. L. T. Jimenez) Semantic Networks for Corporate Communication Concepts and Crisis: Differences Based on Corporate Reputation, *Observatorio (OBS*)* 6 (2): 127–145 (2011); Inferences from Word Networks in Messages, in K. Krippendorff and M. Bock (Eds.), *The Content Analysis Reader* (pp. 421–430), Thousand Oaks, CA: Sage Publications (2011).

Silvia Domínguez, Ph.D., is an Associate Professor of Sociology and Human Services at Northeastern University, Boston. Her research interests include the social mobility of immigrants, transnational ties, the acculturation of host individuals, cultural identity, violence, mental health, and trauma as a neighborhood effect. She uses ethnographic and qualitative data on her studies and is the author of several articles on immigrants' networks, including: (with Celeste Watkins) Creating Networks for Survival and Mobility: Social Capital among African-American and Latin-American Low-Income Mothers, *Social Problems* 50 (1): 111–135 (2003) and (with Amy Lubitow) Transnational Ties, Poverty, and Identity: Latin American Immigrant Women in Public Housing, *Family Relations* 57 (4): 419–430 (2008). She is also the author of *Getting Ahead: Social Mobility, Public Housing and Immigrant Networks*, New York: New York University Press (2011). Silvia is the Past Chair of the Latino(a) or Latino/a Sociology Section and present Chair-Elect of the Race and Ethnic Minorities Section of the American Sociological Association.

Julia C. Gluesing, Ph.D., is a business and organizational anthropologist and Research Professor in Industrial and Manufacturing Engineering at Wayne State University, Detroit, Michigan, who specializes in global teaming and global product development. She was the principal investigator of an NSF grant to study the diffusion of innovation across the global enterprise by tapping into an organization's information technology infrastructure. She conducts research in global work practices, and in cross-cultural and organizational communication for companies such as Ford Motor Company, Nissan Motor Corporation, Aegon, EDS Corporation, and Sun Microsystems. She has published in: *Virtual Teams That Work: Creating Conditions for Virtual Team Effectiveness*, New York: Jossey-Bass (2003); *Handbook of Managing Global Complexity*, Oxford: Blackwell (2003); *Crossing Cultures: Lessons from Master Teachers*, New York: Routledge (2004).

Roger Häussling, PD Dr. phil., is a sociologist and Professor of Sociology at RWTH Aachen University, Germany. He is a Senior Research Fellow at the Research Center, Karlsruhe University of Arts and Design, and he has been a Fellow at the International Academy Schloss Solitude and a Dissertation Fellow at the Landesgraduiertenförderung Baden-Württemberg (Germany). He received is academic education at the Universities of Mannheim, Siegen, and Karlsruhe. He holds an M.A. (Magister Artium) in sociology and a Diploma in economics and engineering. His relevant publications include: (with Christian Stegbauer, Eds.) *Handbuch Netzwerkforschung* [*Handbook of Network Research*], Wiesbaden: VS Verlag (2010); Allocation to Social Positions in Class. Interactions and Relationships in First Grade School Classes and Their Consequences, *Current Sociology* 58 (1) (2010).

Betina Hollstein, Dr. phil., Sociology, at the Free University Berlin. She holds a Chair in Microsociology at the School of Economics and Social Sciences, University of Hamburg, Germany. She has been a lecturer and researcher at the University of Munich and Assistant Professor at Mannheim University and Humboldt-University Berlin. She has been a Simon Visiting Professor at the University of Manchester, UK (2012) and a Visiting Fellow at Yale University (2010). Her research interests include social networks, sociology of the life course, social inequality, and methods. Her relevant publications include: *Grenzen sozialer Integration. Zur Konzeption informeller Beziehungen und Netzwerke [Boundaries of Social Integration. A Simmelian Approach to Social Relationships and Networks]*, Opladen: Leske und Budrich (2001); *Soziale Netzwerke nach der Verwitwung [Changes in Social Networks after the Death of the Spouse]*, Opladen: Leske und Budrich (2002); Qualitative Approaches, in John Scott and Peter J. Carrington (Eds.), *Sage Handbook of Social Network Analysis* (pp. 408–417), London/New Delhi: Sage (2011).

Jeffrey C. Johnson, Dr. phil., Social Science, University of California, Irvine. He is a Senior Scientist at the Institute for Coastal Science and Policy, University Distinguished Research Professor of Sociology, and Harriot College of Arts and Sciences Distinguished Professor at East Carolina University, Greenville, NC. He has held adjunct positions in Anthropology, Biology, Biostatistics, and at The Institute for Software Research at Carnegie Mellon University, Pittsburgh, PA. His research interests include social networks, network visualizations, modelling indigenous ecological knowledge, small group dynamics at Antarctic research stations, and complex models of social and biological systems. He has published in more than 80 peer reviewed publications, including *The Journal of Mathematical Sociology, American Anthropologist, American Ethnologist, Primates, Aviation, Space, and Environmental Medicine, Journal of Computational and Mathematical Organization Theory, Human Ecology, Social Networks, The Journal of Theoretical Biology and Social Science and Medicine.* He is the founder of the *Journal of Quantitative Anthropology,* an Associate Editor of *The Journal of Social Structure, Social Networks,* and a Co-Editor of *Human Organization.* He is an editorial board member of *Field Methods,* the *Open Sociology Journal,* and the *Developing Qualitative Inquiry* series for Left Coast Press. He is also a co-author of *Analyzing Social Networks,* Thousand Oaks, CA: Sage (2013).

Sylvia Keim, Dr. rer. pol., is a sociologist and Assistant Professor at the Institute of Sociology and Demography, University of Rostock, Germany. Her research interests include sociology of the family and the life course, social networks, and qualitative research methods. Her relevant publications include: (with L. Bernardi and H. von der Lippe) Social Influence on Fertility: A Comparative Mixed Methods Study in Eastern and Western Germany, *Journal of Mixed Methods Research* 1 (1): 23–47; (with A. Klärner and L. Bernardi) Qualifying Social Influence on Fertility Intentions: Composition, Structure and Meaning of Fertility-relevant Social Networks in Western Germany, *Current Sociology* 57 (6): 888–907 (2009).

Andreas Klärner, Dr. phil., is a sociologist and Guest Professor at the University of Hamburg, and Assistant Professor at the University of Rostock, Germany. He received his academic education at the Technical University Darmstadt, and then held research positions at the Hamburg Institute for Social Research and the Max Planck Institute for Demographic Research. His research interests include social networks, social capital, sociological theory, and qualitative research methods. His relevant publications include: (with S. Keim and L. Bernardi) Tie Strength and Family Formation: Which Personal Relationships Are Influential? *Personal Relationships* 20: 462–78 (2012).

Carlos Lozares, is a Professor of Social Research Techniques and Methods at the Universitat Autònoma de Barcelona, Spain, and a co-founding member of the Centre d'Estudis Sociològics sobre la Vida Quotidiana i el Treball (QUIT). His research subjects and publications refer to data analysis, multivariate and stratified sampling and the methodology of large surveys, mathematical modelling and the methodology of social research; the analysis of social networks, social capital, and network analysis of discourse; social time and the interactions between productive and reproductive practices and time and, more extensively, to the sociology of everyday life. His current interests are also focused on ethnographic analyses, situated activity and socially distributed knowledge, and social complexity and simulation. His most recent publications include: (with Pedro López-Roldán) El Atributismo estructural y el Interaccionismo estructural en ciencias sociales: ¿concepciones alternativas, antagónicas o complementarias? *Metodología de Encuestas. Revista de la Sociedad Internacional de Profesionales de la Investigación en Encuestas* 14: 25–44 (2012); (with Joan Miquel Verd and Oriol Barranco) El potencial analítico de las redes socio-métricas y ego-centradas: una aplicación al estudio de la Cohesión-Integración de colectivos sociales, *Empiria* 26: 35–62 (2013); (with Mireia Bolíbar and Joel Martí) Aplicaciones de los métodos mixtos al análisis de las redes personales de la población inmigrada, *Empiria* 26: 89–116 (2013).

Isidro Maya-Jariego, Doctor in Psychology, is a Full Professor at the Department of Social Psychology at the University of Seville, Spain; Director of the Laboratory of Personal Networks and Communities; Assistant Dean of the Faculty of Psychology; and the Coordinator of the Master in Psychology of Social and Community Intervention and the Doctorate Program "Community and Social Intervention." He is also Editor of the journal *REDES, Revista Hispana para el Análisis de Redes Sociales*. His main interests are social network analysis, social and community intervention, and migration and cultural diversity. He has researched social support and personal networks of international immigrants. His most recent research compares the psychological sense of community in local, transnational, and on-line communities. His relevant publications include: (with S. Domínguez) Acculturation of Host Individuals: Immigrants and Personal Networks, *American Journal of Community Psychology* (2008); (with N. Armitage) Multiple Senses of Community in Migration and Commuting: The Interplay between Time, Space and Relations, *International Sociology* 22 (6): 743–766.

Christopher McCarty is Director of the Bureau of Economic and Business Research at the University of Florida and currently a rotating program officer at in the Cultural Anthropology Program at the U.S. National Science Foundation. His areas of research include the development of new methods and tools for studying personal networks in a transcultural framework, collaborative networks, and survey research methods. He is the author of the software package *Egonet*, a program for the collection and analysis of personal networks. His relevant publications include: (with Peter D. Killworth, H. Russell Bernard, Eugene Johnsen, John Domini, and Gene A. Shelley) Two Interpretations of Reports of Knowledge of Subpopulation Sizes, *Social Networks* 25 (2): 141–160 (2003); (with José Luis Molina, Claudia Aguilar, and Laura Rota) A Comparison of Social Network Mapping and Personal Network Visualization, *Field Methods* 19 (2): 145–162 (2007).

Cecilia Menjívar is the Cowden Distinguished Professor of Sociology in the School of Social and Family Dynamics at Arizona State University. Her research interests include family, gender, and intergenerational relations among immigrant populations; religion and the church; and immigrants' transnational ties, as well as similar substantive issues in non-immigrant contexts in Central America. She has used various methods in her work, including ethnographic and other qualitative methods. She is the author of several articles on immigrants' networks which have appeared in such journals as *International Migration Review, American Journal of Sociology, International Migration, Journal of Comparative Family Studies, Social Problems*, and *Sociology of Religion*, as well as the book *Fragmented Ties: Salvadoran Immigrant Networks in America*, Berkeley: University of California Press (2000).

José Luis Molina is head of the Department of Social and Cultural Anthropology (UAB) and Director of the Personal Networks Lab at Universidad Autónoma de Barcelona, Spain. His areas of interest are economic anthropology and social networks, especially the change among ethnics groups moving to other countries. Southeast Europe is his ethnographical area of interest. His recent publications include: (with Miranda Lubbers and Chris McCarty) Personal Networks and Ethnic Identifications: The Case of Migrants in Spain, *International Sociology* 22 (6): 720–740 (2007); The Development of Social Network Analysis in the Spanish-Speaking World: A Spanish Chronicle, *Social Networks* 29 (2): 324–329 (2007).

Kenneth R. Riopelle, Ph.D., is an educator, entrepreneur, management consultant, and retired research professor at the Department of Industrial & Systems Engineering, Wayne State University, Detroit, MI. His professional career spans more than 40 years in both the auto industry and academia. His primary research interests include "Accelerating the Diffusion of Innovations in Globally Networked Organizations," which was funded by a National Science Foundation (NSF) grant from 2005 to 2010; the study of Collaborative Innovation Networks or COINs; and the Science of Team Science using co-author and co-citation analysis as a method to visualize, measure, and understand scientific collaboration. His relevant publications include: Being There: The Power of Technology-Based Methods, in Brigitte Jordan (Ed.), *Advancing Ethnography in Corporate Environments: Challenges and Emerging Opportunities*, Walnut Creek, CA: Left Coast Press (2012); (with James Danowski and Julia Gluesing) The Revolution in Diffusion Caused by New Media, in Arun Vishwanath and George Barnett (Eds.), *The Diffusion of Innovations: A Communication Science Perspective* (pp. 123–144), New York: Peter Lang (2011); (with Willie L. McKether and Julia C. Gluesing) From Interviews to Social Network Analysis: An Approach for Revealing Social Networks Embedded in Narrative Data, *Field Methods* 21: 154–180 (2009).

Bruce Rogers was awarded his Ph.D. in Mathematics from Arizona State University in 2009 and considers himself a social scientist trapped in a mathematician's body. As such, much of his research is devoted to computational social science in the broadest sense using both computer simulation and data analysis. From 2009 to 2011, he was a post-doctoral Fellow at the Statistical and Applied Mathematical Sciences Institute in North Carolina. He is currently a statistical consultant in St. Louis, Missouri, and he loves dogs. His relevant publications include: (with David Murillo) Control of Opinions in an Ideologically Homogeneous Population, *Proceedings of Social Computation, Behavioral Modeling, and Prediction Conference*, 2009; (with Gregory K. Fricke and Devendra P. Garg) On the Stability of Swarm Consensus under Noisy Control, *Proceedings of the ASME Dynamic System and Control Conference*, pp. 291–298, 2011; (with Gregory K. Fricke and Devendra P. Garg) Aggregation and Rendezvous in an Unbounded

Domain without a Shared Coordinate System, *Proceedings of the IEEE Conference on Decision and Control and European Control Conference*, pp. 1437–1442, 2011.

Joan Miquel Verd, Graduate in Political Science and Sociology, Graduate in Economics and Business Studies, PhD in Sociology, is a member of the Centre d'Estudis Sociològics sobre la Vida Quotidiana i el Treball (QUIT) in the Department of Sociology at the Universitat Autònoma de Barcelona, Spain, and a Professor of Social Research Methods at the same university. His research activity focuses on the relationship between training and employment, labor market trajectories, and the links between social protection and employment. Methodologically, he is interested in discourse analysis, narrative analysis, social network analysis, and CAQDAS use. His recent publications include: (with Martí López-Andreu) Employer Strategies, Capabilities and Career Development: Two Case Studies of Spanish Service Firms, *International Journal of Manpower*, 34 (4): 292–304 (2013); (with Irene Cruz) La fuerza de los lazos: una exploración teórica y empírica de sus múltiples significados, *Empiria* 16: 149–174 (2013); (with Emanuela Abbatecola, Florence Lefresne, and Josiane Vero) Individual Working Lives through the Lens of the Capability Approach: Evaluation of Policies and Items for Debate, *Transfer* 18 (1): 83–89 (2012).

Claudius Wagemann, Ph.D., political scientist, works as a full professor for qualitative social science methods at the Goethe University, Frankfurt, Germany. Previously, he had held positions at the Istituto italiano di scienze umane (SUM) in Florence and at the Florence program of New York University. He received his education at the University of Konstanz (Diplom degree), the Max Planck Institute for the Study of Societies in Cologne, and at the European University Institute in Florence (Ph.D.). His research interests include comparative methodology (above all qualitative comparative analysis and fuzzy sets), political participation (political parties, interest groups, social movements), quality of democracy, and governance. His selected publications include: (with C. Q. Schneider) *Set-Theoretic Methods for the Social Sciences: A Guide to Qualitative Comparative Analysis*, New York: Cambridge University Press (2012); *Breakdown and Change of Private Interest Governments*, New York: Routledge (2011); (with M. Caiani and D. della Porta) *Mobilizing on the Extreme Right: Germany, Italy, and the United States*, New York: Oxford University Press (2011).

Andreas Wald is Dean of Research and Professor of Management and Strategy at the European Business School Paris and a Visiting Professor at the EBS Business School in Germany. He holds a Master's degree in Political Science and Business Administration and a PhD from the

University of Mannheim. His research interests include organizational networks, network analysis, innovation management, and project management. His relevant publications include: A Micro-Level Approach to Organizational Information-Processing, *Schmalenbach Business Review* 61 (July): 270–289; Effects of "Mode 2"-Related Policy on the Research Process: The Case of Publicly Funded German Nanotechnology, *Science Studies* 20 (1): 26–51 (2007); (with K. Franke and D. Jansen) Governance Reforms and Scientific Production: Evidence from German Astrophysics, in D. Jansen (Ed.), *New Forms of Governance in Research Organizations – From Disciplinary Theories towards Interfaces and Integration* (pp. 213–232), Dordrecht: Springer (2007).

Foreword

H. Russell Bernard

This book illustrates an important moment in social network analysis: the continued maturation of the field into a truly interdisciplinary science. The chapters represent the disciplines of anthropology, applied mathematics and statistics, communications research, demography, industrial engineering, management, political science, social psychology, and sociology.

The chapters also represent the continued maturation of social network analysis into a truly "normal science," in Thomas Kuhn's (1996:10) memorable phrase. In 1977, Samuel Leinhardt edited a volume titled *Social Networks: A Developing Paradigm*. The book had papers from social psychology, sociology, statistics and mathematics, and anthropology – the range of disciplines that, in 1977, was coalescing into what Leinhardt called a developing paradigm – that is, a normal science. Leinhardt was right. In 1993, Norman Hummon and Kathleen Carley analyzed the contents of the first 12 years of the journal *Social Networks* (1978–1989). The pattern of citations, they said, indicated the development of a normal science: The field was incremental (people "attend to each other's work") and there were "young scientists willing to base their careers on work in this field," suggesting that "social networks as a specialty is in a 'normal science' phase rather than an early developmental phase" (pp. 103–04).

One characteristic of a normal science is the easy, unpretentious use of qualitative and quantitative data and analysis. This is the salutary result of the mixed methods movement. I use the word "movement" deliberately. As of April 2012, there were 2,100 citations to the term "mixed methods" in the Social Science Citation Index. As shown in the figure, the first occurrence of the term dates from 1993, with more than 80 percent since 2008. There is a *Journal of Mixed Methods Research* (mmr.sagepub.com), several textbooks on mixed methods research

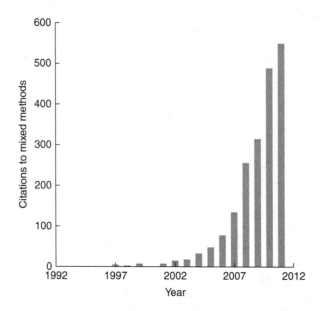

(Creswell and Plano Clark 2011; Greene 2007; Hesse-Biber 2010; Morse and Niehaus 2009), and a handbook of mixed methods research (Tashakkori and Teddlie 2010). What else could this possibly be if not a movement?

First, here is what it is not: It is not a discovery of the value of combining qualitative and quantitative data and analysis in the same study. In fact, the most normal thing about normal science is the uncomplicated, taken-for-granted mixing of qualitative and quantitative data and qualitative and quantitative analysis. That was the recipe for the conduct of science followed by Galileo in his observations about the surface of the moon (Galileo 1610). It was the recipe adopted by Adolphe Quételet, John Stuart Mill, and the other founders of social science in the nineteenth century. It was the recipe followed in the twentieth century by Donald Campbell in psychology, Franz Boas in anthropology, Paul Lazarsfeld in sociology, and so on. And what exercise in all of science is more of a mixing of the quantitative and the qualitative than poring over the results of a factor analysis and talking with one's colleagues – free-associating, really – about what to call a particular factor?

There is a well-known countercurrent, of course, an on-again, off-again "war between the quals and the quants," as Peter Rossi (1994) called it, marked by periods of rapprochement and vitriol. One of Franz Boas's students, Paul Radin, accused his mentor of being *naturwissenschaftlich eingestelt* or science minded – what a disgrace! – and warned that this would lead ethnologists to the quantification of culture

(Radin 1933:10). In contrast, one of my teachers, Oscar Lewis, a gifted and prodigious ethnographer, observed with approval in 1953 that an increase in the use of quantification had been "one of the most significant developments in anthropological field work in recent years" (Lewis 1953:454). And in 1973, Sam Sieber argued – in the *American Journal of Sociology*, no less – for the integration of "qualitative fieldwork and survey research." This "marriage of survey and fieldwork methodologies," said Sieber, would produce "a new style of research" (p. 1337). The new style that Sieber described in 1973 would be indistinguishable from what is called mixed methods today.

The bottom line: Mixed methods is the natural order of science. It has never gone away, but it comes in and out of style in the social sciences. Which brings us to the current phenomenon, shown in the figure, a phenomenon that begs to be explained.

In grappling with this same question, Johnson et al. (2007:117), in the first issue of the *Journal of Mixed Methods Research*, offered that the movement is a "reaction to the polarization between quantitative and qualitative research." I would take it a step further. It's a reaction against the all-too-successful effort by some colleagues in the humanistic, interpretive tradition in social science to define the word "qualitative" as meaning not-quantitative and to force students of social science to choose epistemological sides – humanism or science, understanding or explanation, qualitative or quantitative. The current mixed methods, a-plague-on-both-your-houses, movement makes no such pernicious claims on the lives of young scholars. It is the development of an intellectual safe space where the "qual–quant" war is ignored and the result is an explosion of creativity and collaborative research across disciplines – like that in this book.

References

Creswell, J. W. and V. L. Plano Clark . 2011. *Designing and Conducting Mixed Methods Research*. 2nd ed. Los Angeles: SAGE Publications.

Galileo, Galilei. 1610. The Starry Messenger. Venice. http://www.bard.edu/admission/forms/pdfs/galileo.pdf (accessed April 9, 2012).

Greene, J. C. 2007. *Mixed Methods in Social Inquiry*. San Francisco: Jossey-Bass.

Hesse-Biber, S. N. 2010. *Mixed Methods Research: Merging Theory with Practice*. New York: Guilford Press.

Hummon, N. P. and K. Carley. 1993. "Social networks as normal science." *Social Networks* 15:71–106.

Johnson, R. B., A. J. Onwuegbuzie, and L. A. Turner. 2007. "Toward a definition of mixed methods research. " *Journal of Mixed Methods Research* 1:112–33.

Kuhn, T. S. 1996. *The Structure of Scientific Revolutions*. 3rd ed. Chicago: University of Chicago Press.

Leinhardt, S. 1977. *Social Networks: A Developing Paradigm.* New York: Academic Press.

Lewis, O. 1953. "Controls and experiments in field work." Pp. 452–75 in *Anthropology Today*, edited by A. L. Kroeber et al. Chicago: University of Chicago Press

Morse, J. M. and L. Niehaus. 2009. *Mixed Method Design: Principles and Procedures.* Walnut Creek, CA: Left Coast Press.

Radin, P. 1933. *The Method and Theory of Ethnology.* New York: McGraw-Hill.

Rossi, P. H. 1994. "The war between the quals and the quants: Is a lasting peace possible?" Pp. 23–36 in *The Qualitative-Quantitative Debate: New Perspectives*, edited by C. S. Reichardt and S. F. Rallis. San Francisco: Jossey-Bass.

Sieber, S. D. 1973. "The integration of fieldwork and survey methods." *American Journal of Sociology* 73:1335–59.

Tashakkori, A. and C. Teddlie, eds. 2010. *Handbook of Mixed Methods in Social and Behavioral Research.* 2nd ed. Los Angeles: SAGE Publications.

Acknowledgments

The idea for putting together this volume on the use of mixed methods in studying social networks emerged from discussions that we, Silvia Domínguez and Betina Hollstein, had in our time organizing the qualitative and mixed method sessions for Sunbelt International Network Conferences. In fact, we are grateful to the International Network for Social Network Analysts (INSNA) for providing the context that brings together a wide international range of social network researchers from different traditions and disciplines. As is the way of such things, the project to produce this book turned out to be much larger and more complicated – and, of course, took much longer – than we or anyone could have foreseen. But we would have never embarked on this project if we had not received the encouragement of Janet W. Salaff and Julia Gluesing, who supported it from the very beginning. We are very thankful to the Berlin Graduate School of Social Sciences (BGSS) at the Humboldt University Berlin, especially the dean of the Faculty of Arts and Humanities at Humboldt University, Berlin, Bernd Wegener, as well as the Faculty Advancement Grant from the Provost's Office at Northeastern University for their financial and instrumental support in bringing the authors and us together for a conference at the European Academy in Berlin. The 2009 conference in Berlin allowed all contributors to present their work, provide and receive feedback, fine-tune the organization of the manuscript, and advance the development of a coherent book. We also thank Markku Lonkila, who served as discussant at this occasion.

We are especially thankful to Mark Granovetter and the two anonymous reviewers for their encouragement and their helpful comments on the draft manuscript. We are thankful to Robert Dreesen and Elise M. Oranges from Cambridge University Press, who provided assistance during production. We would also like to thank Mazhena Trypucka,

Liz Williams, and Tammi Arford for help during the production of the book. We are grateful to all the individuals who participated in the qualitative and mixed methods sessions and who provided feedback on many of the studies that are now chapters in the book. We owe a great debt of gratitude to the hundreds of respondents all over the globe who allowed us entry into their lives and provided us with the data for the studies in this volume. Finally, we also dedicate this book to our families. They lived with this project for a couple of years, reminding us of the need to balance work and family. We are thankful to Matias Ancelovi-Dominguez, Eric Brown, and Werner Rammert.

Silvia Domínguez and
Betina Hollstein

Part I

General Issues

1

Mixed Methods Social Networks Research: An Introduction

Betina Hollstein

Over the past 20 years there has been increasing recognition that focusing on *either* quantitative *or* qualitative research techniques alone leads researchers to miss important parts of a story. Researchers have found that better results are often achieved through combined approaches. In line with this observation, an increase in so-called mixed methods studies and research designs as well as in work providing overviews and systematic accounts of such research has been witnessed in various disciplines and fields of study since the early 1990s (Morse 1991; Creswell 2003 (first ed. 1994); Greene and Caracelli 1997b; Tashakkori and Teddlie 2003; Axinn and Pearce 2006; Bryman 2006; Creswell and Plano Clark 2007; Bergman and Bryman 2008; Teddlie and Tashakkori 2008). Of course, the combination of different methodical approaches is anything but a recent phenomenon in field research – one might think of the Marienthal study (Jahoda, Zeisel, and Lazarsfeld 1933), the Hawthorne studies (Roethlisberger and Dickson 1939), as well as of several studies by the Chicago School. In many areas of research, the combined application of different methods goes back a long time without being explicitly referred to as a mixed methods design.[1] However, the increased interest in and the systematic review of mixed methods designs and the results they yield are indeed new aspects in this development.

This interest in mixed methods designs can probably be explained in that their bringing together the strengths of both quantitative and qualitative strategies holds the promise of compensating for the respective weaknesses of both approaches. In view of the usually small sample

---

[1] Articles discussing the combination and integration of methods have been published in such journals as *Field Methods* and *International Journal of Social Research Methodology* right from the outset.

I am grateful to Johannes Huinink and the two anonymous reviewers for their helpful comments.

3

sizes, so-called qualitative (or interpretive, less standardized) research faces criticism for an allegedly arbitrary selection of samples and a lack of representativity, which in turn is said to raise questions as to the generalizability of results and to cause difficulties in the systematic comparison of cases and testing of causal models. Skepticism toward so-called quantitative (or quantifying, standardized) research, on the other hand, is mainly voiced with respect to its apparent neglect of the particular social context in which actors attribute meaning to their actions and to its potentially lower sensitivity to new, unexplored, or marginal social phenomena and developments. Mixed methods designs attempt at engaging quantitative and qualitative research strategies in an intelligent dialogue that benefits both sides. In their definition of mixed methods, Johnson and Onwuegbuzie aptly describe the aim and motivation underlying the mixed method approach: "Mixed methods research is the type of research in which a researcher or team of research-ers *combines* elements of qualitative and quantitative approaches (e.g., use of qualitative and quantitative viewpoints, data collection, analysis, inference techniques) *for the purpose of breadth and depth of under-standing and corroboration*" (Johnson and Onwuegbuzie 2007:123; emphasis added by BH).

Upon close inspection, a wide range of different approaches fall within this definition. Johnson and Onwuegbuzie asked 21 researchers for their definition of mixed methods and received 19 different responses. It seems safe to say that their definition represents the smallest common denominator of a variety of different definitions used to describe mixed methods. The various definitions offered by Johnson and Onwuegbuzie's respondents, which give a quite accurate picture of the definitions also found in the literature, can be distinguished as to what precisely is com-bined (methods, methodologies, or types of research), at what stages of the research process methods are combined (formulation of the research question, data collection, data analysis, data interpretation or infer-ence), and to what end methods are combined (e.g., to achieve breadth or for corroboration or triangulation). In any case, when we speak of *combining* approaches, we are referring to more than a simple process of mere *addition*. As Creswell et al. put it, "A mixed methods study involves the collection or analysis of both quantitative and/or qualita-tive data in a single study in which the data are collected concurrently or sequentially, are given a priority, and involve the *integration* of the data at one or more stages in the process" (Creswell 2003:212; emphasis added by BH). Instead of simple addition, the task is to systematically relate quantitative and qualitative strategies or data at at least one stage of the research process. Due to this systematic integration of qualita-tive and quantitative strategies, mixed methods designs create special opportunities for improving data quality, thereby increasing the significance of results (Greene, Caracelli, and Graham 1989; Tashakkori and Teddlie 2003; Axinn and Pearce 2006; Bryman 2006).

In the discussion to come, we speak of mixed methods studies when at least three conditions are met: (1) First, the studies make use of qualitative as well as quantitative *data*. This does not necessarily mean that both qualitative and quantitative data must actually be collected. Making use of the two types of data may also take the form of data conversion; for instance, qualitative data are collected and converted into quantitative data for analysis. (2) Second, both qualitative and quantitative *strategies of data analysis* are applied. (3) And, finally, at at least one stage of the research process, there must be some form of *integration* of either data, or of data analysis or of results (meta-inference).

In reviewing network research, we notice that there has been no systematic consideration of mixed methods studies so far, neither with regard to possible research designs nor their potential for the study of social networks. If we look at the relevant manuals and handbooks in the field, it is quite obvious that the methodical repertoire of current social network analysis for the most part consists of sophisticated, highly standardized, and formalized methods of analysis (cf. Wasserman and Faust 1994; Degenne and Forsé 1999; Scott 2000; Carrington et al. 2005; Scott and Carrington 2011).[2] Although there is a significant number of network studies that combine qualitative and quantitative methods of data collection and analysis (e.g., Wellman et al. 1988; Provan and Milward 1995; McLean 1998; Diani and McAdam 2003; Smith 2005; Small 2009), we still lack a compendium that provides a systematic account of the field. The present volume contributes to this end as it is the first systematic overview on the use of mixed methods for investigating social networks.

We will present different ways of mixing qualitative and quantitative strategies and discuss the challenges and benefits for research on social networks. The chapters assembled in this book illustrate that the application of such designs can improve the quality of data and enhance the explanatory power and generalizability of results. Moreover, with respect to social network research, mixed methods studies promise to provide empirically sound contributions to current

---

[2] The application of qualitative research methods in network studies is mentioned only with respect to the collection of relational data (such as interviews, observations, or archival records; Wasserman and Faust 2005). Mixed methods designs for data collection are not described in detail, and qualitative methods and mixed methods designs for analyzing network data are not considered. For the first English language review on qualitative network research, cf. Hollstein (2011).

issues, especially concerning the processes, dynamics, and consequences of social networks.

We will take a closer look at these issues later on. Before we do so, we will first give a brief overview of the objects, questions, and approaches of network research. We must also clarify what the terms "quantitative," "qualitative," and "mixed methods" actually mean in the context of social networks.

The Concept of Social Network

According to J. Clyde Mitchell's classic definition, networks can be described as a "specific set of linkages between a defined set of social actors" (Mitchell 1969:2), whereby both the linkages and the social actors can refer to quite different social entities. Actors can be organizations, political actors, households, families, or individuals. The linkages or relationships may, for instance, refer to interactions or relations defined by a specific content, such as power relations, information exchange, or emotional proximity.[3] Social networks are typically the subject matter of anthropology and sociology, of communication studies as well as political science, but they also play an increasingly prominent role in computer science, economics, history, and medical science. Research topics range from communication networks, the formation of subcultures, and social movements to networks of local power elites, informal networks within and between organizations, and on to personal or private networks, including virtual and semantic networks (cf. Scott 2000; Scott and Carrington 2011).

The particular attractiveness of the network concept lies in the fact that it focuses attention on the "totality" of social relations and their social context and hence on the "embeddedness" of social action (Granovetter 1985). Going beyond single relationships, network research investigates the relations between the various relationships of a network (e.g., the formation of clusters or cliques) and the influence of structural properties of networks and social relations on social integration. For instance, information flow is a lot faster and norms are more effectively established in dense networks where a large number

---

[3] Even though the linkages between actors are defined by their *content*, the network concept as such rather refers to the *formal structure* of those social relations, e.g., the size of a network, the frequency of interactions between its members (*alteri*), or its density (the number of actual as compared to potential relationships between alteri). Therefore, network concepts are often combined with concepts aimed at the functions or the content of relationships (e.g., concepts capturing social support or social capital; cf. Marsden 1990, 2011).

of people are acquainted with one another than in networks marked by a low density of relationships. At the individual level, dense networks provide more social support but also exert more social control (Coleman 1990). Another well-known structural property of networks are so-called "structural holes" (Burt 1992). Occupying such structural holes gives privileged access to information, power, and influence (Padgett and Ansell 1993).

Due to its relational perspective, the network concept integrates both the societal micro- and macro-levels and offers a specific starting point for tracing the mechanisms of social integration as well as the conditions and implications of social change. Moreno's sociometric studies in the 1930s and American community studies in the 1940s were early antecedents of contemporary network research in the social sciences. The term "social network" was first introduced in the 1950s by British cultural anthropologists who investigated small-scale social settings at the time, such as rural communities, neighborhoods, and subcultural environments (Barnes 1954; Bott 1957; Mitchell 1969). However, it was not until the 1970s that network analysis was established in the social sciences as a distinct empirical paradigm for analyzing systems of social relationships, parallel to the development of its mathematical foundations (cf. Freeman 2004; Knox et al. 2006; Carrington, this volume). Within the scope of this paradigm – known as "structural network analysis" – an extensive set of methodical instruments has been developed since then. Structural network analysis is characterized by the use of highly differentiated standardized methods of data collection (e.g., established name generators like Burt generator, position generator, resource generator, etc.), various measures of network structures (e.g., density and centrality measures), as well as sophisticated analytical procedures and calculation models, comprising block models, random graph models, and as of recently also advanced models for the analysis of longitudinal data (cf. Wasserman and Faust 1994; Carrington et al. 2005; Scott and Carrington 2011; Snijders 2011). As Peter J. Carrington (this volume) points out, precisely this "mathematization of social network analysis" can be assumed to have played a key role in rendering the network concept compatible across a wide range of academic disciplines, thus contributing to its remarkably widespread use.

In spite of the obvious strengths and benefits of the network approach, the structuralist paradigm that has dominated it has also attracted criticism since the early 1990s: Critics claim that the significance of action has been overlooked due to this preoccupation with structure. Such criticism is mainly directed against approaches that are either committed to "structural determinism" (Emirbayer and Goodwin 1994) or involve utilitarian models of action ("structural instrumentalism"; Emirbayer and Goodwin 1994).[4] According to these critics the challenge of network research is to link the structural level with the actors involved. This would particularly concern the systematic integration of their capacity to act and actively shape their (social) environment as well as their reference to norms, symbols, and cultural practices (Emirbayer and Goodwin 1994; Mizruchi 1994; Schweizer 1996; Emirbayer 1997). As Dorothea Jansen (1999) put it, "A significant theoretical problem [of network research; BH] lies in the sparsely reflected relation between concrete networks and interactions, on the one hand, and subjective attributions of meaning, norms, and institutions, [as well as] cultures and symbolic worlds, on the other. In their dispute with structural functionalism of the Parsonian kind, network researchers have possibly thrown out the baby with the bathwater in claiming absolute priority for concrete structures of interaction vis-à-vis norms and symbolic worlds of any kind" (p. 258 f.; translated from German by BH). However, in recent network research, work has been done that seeks to conceptually integrate agency and to take cultural symbols and norms into account. Research from the quarters of phenomenological network theory comes to mind (White 1992; Mische 2003; Gibson 2005; Yeung 2005).[5] As we will show, mixed methods studies can provide stimulating contributions in this respect as well.

What Do We Mean by "Mixed Methods" in Social Network Research?

Let us now turn to the question of how network research can be positioned in relation to both quantitative and qualitative methods and what

---

[4]   Emirbayer and Goodwin (1994) differentiate three theoretical positions with respect to how social structure, culture, and agency are conceptualized in network research: "The first of these implicit models, that of *structuralist determinism*, neglects altogether the potential causal role of actor's beliefs, values, and normative commitments – or, more generally, of the significance of cultural and political discourses in history. It neglects as well those historical configurations of action that shape and transform pregiven social structures in the first place. A second and more satisfactory – but still deeply problematic – approach is that of *structural instrumentalism*. Studies within this perspective accept the prominent role of social actors in history, but ultimately conceptualize their activity in narrowly utility-maximizing and instrumental forms. And finally, the most sophisticated network perspective on social change, which we term *structuralist constructivism*, thematizes provocatively certain historical processes of identity conversion and 'robust action.' It is the most successful of all of these approaches in adequately conceptualizing human agency and the potentially transformative impact of cultural idioms and normative commitments on social action" (Emirbayer and Goodwin 1994:1425f.; emphasis in the original).

[5]   Other approaches pointing in this direction are symbolic interactionism (Fine and Klineman 1983), Bourdieu's theory of practice, Latour's actor-network theory (cf. Knox et al. 2006), and Luhmann's theory of social systems (cf. Fuhse and Mützel 2010).

"mixed methods" means precisely in social network research. Clearly positioning network research in the spectrum of empirical methods is no easy task if we rely on the common systems for the classification of methodology offered in the literature. Or, in the words of Peter J. Carrington, "Social network analysis itself is neither quantitative nor qualitative, nor a combination of the two. Rather, it is structural"[6] (this volume; similarly Bellotti 2010). Like qualitative methods, network research places special emphasis on the contextuality or "embeddedness" of social action. Yet unlike qualitative methods, network research employs established standardized instruments to this end, and network structures are typically described in terms of measured values and numbers, thus in a formalized or quantified manner. Nevertheless, the concept of representativity usually cannot be applied to network studies – at least not without some restrictions. (For sociocentric or whole networks, it is impossible to determine the statistical population. And if egocentric[7] network data are collected within the scope of representative samples, representative conclusions can only be drawn about the attributes of ego but not about the relations existing with or between the alteri; cf. Belotti 2010). That, of course, rules out the use of inferential statistics, and reliable statements on the prevalence of networks and network structures can be made only to a limited extent. We also have to consider that we are often dealing with relatively small sample sizes, especially when investigating whole networks.

In the following we distinguish quantitative and qualitative network *data* and quantitative and qualitative *strategies of network analysis*. In line with a commonly made distinction, we understand by quantitative data numerical data and by qualitative data data in text form (cf. Bernard 1994). Accordingly, what we call *quantitative network data* refers to all data describing relations, interactions, and structures of networks in formal terms using numbers (e.g., the number of relationships between the members of a network). We speak of *qualitative network data* when aspects of networks are described in text form (e.g., when actors explain the strategies of action adopted vis-à-vis other members of a network).

---

[6] Or in the words of an anonymous reviewer, "There is an argument that social network analysis, as a method of formal analysis, is not quantitative but uses numbers in order to grasp the quality of social relationships. It is, at the very least, different from obvious quantitative approaches that focus on attributes rather than relations."

[7] Whole (sociocentric), complete, or "entire" networks – e.g., entire communities – are investigated less often. If so, the respondents can, for instance, be selected by means of snowball sampling (on sampling strategies, cf. Frank 2011). In contrast, so-called "ego-centered" (egocentric) networks refer to the networks of individual actors who are in most cases the only source of information about their networks (cf. Carrington, this volume; Wald, this volume). The present volume assembles studies on ego-centered as well as on whole networks.

Quantitative strategies of analysis are defined as strategies of data analysis to describe in quantitative terms empirical regularities, the frequency and prevalence of social phenomena, as well as causal mechanisms and processes. The basic strategies of data analysis consist of descriptive measures, statistical methods, and path or causal models. More recently, we are also observing an increasing trend toward computer simulations. In network research, quantitative methods are geared toward mathematical descriptions and analyses of interactions, relations, and network structures. Measured values and numbers, for instance, are density and centrality measures or the triad census (e.g., Gluesing, Riopelle, and Danowski, this volume). More sophisticated analyses apply formal models and statistical procedures, such as block model analysis, exponential random graph modeling, or regression analysis (cf. Wasserman and Faust 1994; Carrington et al. 2005; Scott and Carrington 2011). In this sense, we consider most of the methods used in social network analysis to be "quantitative."

Qualitative analysis refers to all those methods in empirical social research that aim at gaining an understanding of meaning and its frames of reference (cf. Hollstein 2011). Qualitative data will generally come as text and are meant to provide insight into contexts of action as well as systems of meaning. If no such data are readily available, researchers will turn to open-ended methods of data collection, such as interviewing or unstructured observation methods, and interpretive methods of data analysis. Interpretive strategies of data analysis allow one to reconstruct cultural practices and interaction patterns. Moreover, they are especially well suited for capturing the actors' own systems of relevance, perceptions, interpretations, and action orientations. With respect to network research, qualitative methods are therefore most appropriate for investigating network practices and network perceptions and interpretations (cf. Hollstein 2011). In principle, perceptions, attributions of meaning, and systems of relevance can also be investigated with standardized methods (e.g., Maya-Jariego and Dominguez; Gluesing et al., this volume). An open, inductive approach, however, is indicated in cases where the research question is of a more exploratory nature. The same holds true for settings where we expect great variations in individual meanings and/or systems of relevance (cf. Wald, this volume).

As we now have established a more precise understanding of what is meant by mixed methods, qualitative and quantitative data, and qualitative and quantitative strategies of analysis in network research, we can proceed to define more precisely mixed methods in network research. We will speak of mixed methods network studies when three conditions are satisfied:

- The studies are based on both *quantitative, numerical network data* – that is, data describing nodes and relations – and *qualitative textual data*. As mentioned earlier, this does not imply that both types of data actually must be collected; data may also be converted from one type into another (e.g., Verd and Lozares, this volume).
- In analyzing relations and networks, both *quantitative, mathematical strategies* and *qualitative, interpretive strategies* are used. While the former are tailored toward analyzing the structural dimensions of relationships and networks, the latter are designed to capture practices, meanings, and the social contexts of relationships and networks.
- And finally, at at least one stage of the research process, the data or strategies of analysis must be *integrated* in some form, at either the stage of data collection, data analysis, or interpretation of results (meta-inference). When we speak of integration in the following, we refer to systematically relating or linking qualitative and quantitative data or strategies of analysis.[8] Such integration is a key element in mixed methods studies. Were it not for this integrative component, these studies would be no more than the mere addition of qualitative and quantitative analyses.

Mixed Methods Research Designs

We now turn our attention to the ways in which qualitative and quantitative data and strategies can be integrated. Relating qualitative and quantitative data and analyses can take very different shapes depending on the research in question (Creswell et al. 2003; Greene and Caracelli 1997; Johnson and Onwuegbuzie 2004; Morgan 1998; Morse 1991, 2003). For instance, studies may differ in the *number of strands* or phases included (monostrand, multistrand). A strand of a research design is a phase of a study that comprises three main stages (steps, components): the conceptualization stage, the experiential stage (methodological/analytical), and the inferential stage (Tashakkori and Teddlie 2009:288). Most mixed methods designs are "multistrand designs" that consist of a complete quantitative cycle (including quantitative data collection, quantitative data analysis, and inference) and a complete qualitative cycle accordingly. Yet there are differences in *implementation*. For instance, the designs may differ in terms of chronological order, as

---

[8] In contrast, we may also speak of "combining" data or strategies of analysis in a broader sense to also include merely additive approaches.

quantitative and qualitative strands of a study can be employed either simultaneously or consecutively. Apart from simultaneous or consecutive implementation, we also observe conversion as a third mode in which either qualitative data are transformed or converted into quantitative data, or vice versa (Teddlie and Tashakkori 2006; Tashakkori and Teddlie 2009). When considering implementation, the sampling methods employed in mixed method research must also be taken into account: Are the samples identical; do they overlap – for instance is one a subset of the other – or are the sample compositions completely different (Tashakkori and Teddlie 2009; cf. Bernardi et al., this volume)? Whatever the case may be, an especially important aspect is at what stages and at how many different stages in the research process the *integration* of approaches takes place: during conceptualization, data collection, data analysis, and the interpretation of data (inferential stage). In some studies, the qualitative and quantitative strands of the research are given equal importance; in other cases, one strand has priority over the other. Finally, depending on the underlying logic guiding research, some studies place emphasis on exploratory forms of inquiry while others focus on the testing of hypotheses.

Drawing on the classifications suggested by Teddlie and Tashakkori (2006), Tashakkori and Teddlie (2009), Creswell et al. (2003), Creswell and Plano Clark (2007), and Greene et al. (1989), we differentiate between five families of mixed methods designs[9]: sequential designs (exploratory, explanatory), parallel designs, fully integrated designs, embedded designs, and conversion designs. This classification distinguishes designs mainly along the following dimensions: type of implementation process, stage of integration, and priority of one approach. It also takes into consideration the logic guiding the research (exploratory or explanatory sequential design) and the number of strands (monostrand conversion design or multistrand conversion design). All five of these families of designs and subtypes are represented in this volume.

Sequential Design

Sequential designs are multistrand designs. The characteristic feature of sequential designs is the consecutive use of quantitative and qualitative strands. Conclusions drawn based on the results of the first strand determine the questions, data collection, and analysis of the next strand (Teddlie and Tashakkori 2006:21). According to the underlying rationale of

---

[9]   A note is in order here that these design families are neither exhaustive nor completely non-overlapping. It has frequently been pointed out that developing an exhaustive typology of mixed methods designs is impossible (e.g., Teddlie and Tashakkori 2006).

research, we distinguish between "sequential exploratory" and "sequential explanatory" designs (Creswell et al. 2003).

A *sequential exploratory design* starts with a qualitative phase, which is then followed by a quantitative phase. In many studies, the qualitative part figures only as a prestudy to the actual quantitative research, for instance, if important issues and events or relevant actors and forms of cooperation have to be identified first, such as in investigations of political networks or cooperative research networks (cf. Baumgarten and Lahusen 2006; Wald, this volume). The primary purpose of the qualitative pretest is to support the development of instruments for the main (quantitative) study with the purpose of enhancing the validity of the collected data. Thorough qualitative prestudies or pretests are particularly advisable in advance of any standardized research into sociocentric networks. Since such studies typically require a massive effort in terms of data collection, a good knowledge of the field is a precondition for obtaining meaningful results (Baumgarten and Lahusen 2006).

The qualitative study, however, can also represent an independent element of inquiry in its own right. In that case, it may be used to explore new or yet unexplored types of networks and network practices, for instance, regarding networks of particular ethnic groups (Smith 2005), migrants (Menjivar 2000), or social movements (Mische 2008). Additional quantitative strands will then help to identify the prevalence of such types of networks and network practices. It can also help to obtain a more comprehensive picture of the conditions (e.g., institutional settings) under which such patterns have effects (Mische 2003, 2008; Smith 2005). Yet another option is to use a simulation to analyze network consequences. For instance, based on an ethnographic study, Rogers and Menjivar (this volume) use agent-based modeling to investigate the long-term development of social networks of Salvadorian migrants living in San Francisco. In this case, the qualitative analysis serves as input to create a computational model.

A *sequential explanatory design*, in contrast, starts with the collection and analysis of quantitative data, which is then followed by a qualitative strand. In some cases, the qualitative inquiry is meant to deepen and further elucidate the results obtained by the quantitative analysis (Bearman and Parigi 2004).[10] The quantitative strand can also lay the groundwork for selecting and locating cases to be examined more closely by qualitative means (so-called "mapping"; e.g., McLean 1998; Wong and Salaff 1998; Hollstein 2002). Cases can then be selected, for

---

[10] For instance, in a qualitative follow-up study to the General Social Survey, Bearman and Parigi (2004) examine what precisely the GSS respondents had in mind when declaring that they would talk to other people about "important matters" (Burt name generator question).

instance, using multidimensional scaling (McLean 1998) or based on the network structure (Maya-Jariego and Dominguez, this volume). Case selection can be guided by quite different criteria: Sometimes emphasis is placed on extreme cases or "outliers"; at other times it is more about identifying particularly typical cases. In their analysis of migrant acculturation, Maya-Jariego and Dominguez identify host individuals by a process of screening based on the structure of personal networks. The individuals thus selected are then studied from an ethnographic perspective for their relationships to migrants, attitudes, and the value systems they subscribe to.

On the whole, sequential designs consisting of two consecutive studies are generally a little less complex and easier to do than parallel designs, which we will discuss later. This is why Teddlie and Tashakkori (2006) recommend sequential designs to researchers who are just beginning to work with mixed methods designs. A disadvantage, however, is that because they require performing one step after another, sequential designs tend to be more time and thus cost intensive compared to parallel designs (Bernardi et al., this volume).

Parallel Design

Parallel designs are multistrand designs in which quantitative and qualitative strands are employed more or less simultaneously. This does not mean that the individual stages (data collection and data analysis) of the qualitative and quantitative strands necessarily have to be conducted at the same time; they can take place at different points in time just as well. In contrast to sequential designs, parallel designs allow for data to be collected synchronously since the data collected for one strand do not rely on the results of the other strand. For precisely this reason, it seems more appropriate to speak of "parallel" instead of "concurrent" design (Tashakkori and Teddlie 2009). Both parts are usually also analyzed separately. Only once the results from the individual strands of analysis are available are meta-inferences made. Parallel designs are a suitable means of pursuing both exploratory and confirmatory research questions. They are especially useful for triangulating data and checking for complementarity, that is, to gain a more complex and complete picture of the subject matter. Parallel designs with special emphasis on the triangulation of data are aimed at validating and at the same time corroborating results (cf. the methodological discussion by Wald, this volume, and the empirical study by Gluesing et al., this volume). Parallel designs can also be employed to increase the explanatory power as well as the generalizability of results by generating a broad, complex, and – to the greatest possible degree – comprehensive understanding of social phenomena. Such an approach thus looks for complementarity rather than convergence.

Empirical examples in this line of research are the longitudinal study by Bidart and Lavenu (2005) on changes in the networks of young adults and the study by Bernardi et al. (this volume) on the influence of social networks on family formation. A theoretically and empirically instructive case of a so-called *multilevel parallel design*[11] is Häussling's study (this volume) on the restructuring of a car manufacturer's sales department. He analyzes different levels of interaction: semantic contexts and networks of interaction as well as individual action orientations. He relates all of these levels and shows that the implementation of knowledge management systems fails because it is systematically undermined by the employees' informal network relationships.

Compared to sequential designs, parallel designs are less time consuming. The obvious drawback of parallel designs, however, is that studying the same phenomenon by applying two different approaches simultaneously yet separately requires considerable expertise. In this light, it comes as no surprise that most of the empirical contributions to this volume are collaborations between authors with different methodical backgrounds. Teddlie and Tashakkori (2006:21) direct attention to yet another kind of problem in this respect. The novice or the researcher working alone may face particular problems when the results of the qualitative and quantitative analyses yield discrepant results and the researcher is challenged to interpret or resolve these inconsistencies to draw inferences at the meta-level.

Fully Integrated Design

The fully integrated mixed design is a specific kind of multistrand parallel design or, in Teddlie and Tashakkori's (2006:23) words, "the 'Full Monty' of mixed methods designs." This is the variant that most closely meshes and integrates qualitative with quantitative approaches. The different approaches are integrated interactively and dynamically along all stages of the research process. In this way, the fully integrated design manages to combine the benefits of both the parallel and sequential designs, which makes it a potentially especially fruitful endeavor. Because of its complexity, however, it at the same time places the greatest demands on the researcher in terms of coordinating the various elements across the whole process. This type of design is illustrated by Avenarius and Johnson's study (this volume) on the acceptance of newly established legal institutions in rural China. The study not only combines survey and ethnographic data but manages to do so in such a way that the qualitative and quantitative approaches inform one another at several points

---

[11] In so-called *multilevel designs* (Tashakkori and Teddlie 2009), the qualitative and quantitative strands address different levels of analysis.

in the research process: at the points of sampling and collecting data, and in the course of analyzing and interpreting the findings. The study is also an instructive illustration of the fact that mixed methods studies are often initially not planned as such. At times it is seemingly contradictory phenomena, not clearly explicable observations, or the open questions of a previous study that motivate researchers to consider new paths in collecting and analyzing data involving different and complementary methods.

Embedded Design

In principle, the qualitative and quantitative parts can be given equal weight in the multistrand designs considered so far (both in terms of their significance for the research project and regarding the share of research activities devoted to the two strands). Of course, one approach may also be dominant or have priority over the other. Because this is an important aspect in planning the research process and the allocation of resources, we have included the "embedded design" (Creswell and Plano Clark 2007) in our collection. In the case of an embedded design, either the qualitative or the quantitative strand constitutes only a small part of the study, which may be conducted in parallel with, subsequent to, or as a prestudy to the major part of the research. Embedded designs are also referred to as *nested designs* (Creswell 2003). An example of a network study of this kind is the contribution by Gluesing et al. (this volume) on the patterns of communication and the effectiveness of innovation networks in multinational corporations. Apart from tens of thousands of e-mails, the data collection in this study also included in-depth interviews as well as participant observation of interactions between team members who were "shadowed" by the researchers for days. The observational data serve to validate the quantitative information and help classify and comprehend the relevance of the e-mail communication. The analysis of the different types of data reveals surprising differences in e-mail use between Americans and Germans. (The former handle many things by e-mail even if the addressee is located in the office next door while in that particular case Germans prefer face-to-face communication.) The chapter demonstrates how ethnographic methods provide both relevant content and context that can be incorporated into IT-based techniques for data mining.

An advantage of embedded designs is that they are often less costly than designs in which the qualitative and quantitative parts are given equal weight in terms of their significance for the research project and also regarding the share of research activities devoted to the two strands. The cost advantage results from the fact that the embedded part of the research is usually applied to objects and areas with well-defined boundaries. On the other side of the coin, the results that embedded designs yield are mostly limited to narrowly focused research questions.

Conversion Design

Conversion designs are designs that involve the transformation of data of one type into data of the other type for purposes of analysis: qualitative data are converted into numerical codes and re-analyzed quantitatively (quantitizing strategy), or quantitative data are transformed into data that can be analyzed qualitatively (qualitizing strategy).

Conversion mixed designs are a type of multistrand parallel design that involves mixing qualitative and quantitative parts at all stages while the data are either qualitized or quantitized and analyzed accordingly as the case may be (Teddlie and Tashakkori 2006; Tashakkori and Teddlie 2009). Hollstein and Wagemann (this volume) illustrate this approach with their study on the significance of network resources for young adults' successful transition to employment. Qualitative data on network support are converted into fuzzy sets, that is, numerical codes, and, in a dynamic interactive process, subjected to alternate rounds of qualitative analyses involving the reconstruction of individual cases, on the one hand, and quantitative analyses on the other (Ragin 2008). The chapter demonstrates how fuzzy set Qualitative Comparative Analysis (QCA; Ragin 2008) facilitates systematic case comparisons while it also enables developing typologies that strongly build on individual cases.

In Hollstein and Wagemann's chapter, network data are described in terms of individual attributes, which are used to explain individual behavior, in this case the successful transition to employment. While Verd and Lozares (this volume) also convert qualitative into quantitative data or, in other words, apply a "quantitizing strategy," their focus is on how biographical narrative interview data are used to derive data on network structures. Based on a thorough interpretive text analysis, Verd and Lozares transform interview data on the relationships of young adults into data on the structure of networks. They then use these data to perform further quantitative analyses. In essence, they apply what is called a *monostrand conversion design* or *simple conversion design* or a *quasi-mixed methods design*, as it is also sometimes referred to (Tashakkori and Teddlie 2009:288). This study is not a "typical" mixed methods design since data of one type are collected and converted while the data thus transformed are analyzed using only one type of method. We have included this study because it is an especially interesting strategy for studying networks: As opposed to procedures using automated coding, Verd and Lozares analyze textual data and extract network information using interpretive strategies of analysis.

Monostrand designs are generally less demanding in terms of time and cost compared to multistrand designs. The latter require closely coordinating the steps in converting and analyzing qualitative and quantitative data throughout the entire process. In this respect, they are similar to fully integrated mixed methods designs.

Benefits and Drawbacks of Mixed Methods Network Research

In a nutshell, the *benefits* of mixed methods designs can be summarized as follows: In general, mixed methods studies provide special opportunities for enhancing both the quality and explanatory power of data (cf. Greene et al. 1989; Tashakkori and Teddlie 2003; Axinn and Pearce 2006; Bryman 2006). They contribute to a broader and deeper understanding of social phenomena. In combining different perspectives on social phenomena, mixed methods studies support the development of measurement and improvement of implementation, the validation and confirmation of results, and contribute to a more comprehensive picture by giving a more complex account of social phenomena (Greene et al. 1989). As the chapters in this book illustrate, mixed methods designs facilitate the process of selecting individual cases and positioning them in social space while shedding light on the prevalence of patterns of social action and network practices, the conditions upon which they rest, as well as the consequences they entail. It should be added that the findings obtained by the different methods can relate to one another in a number of ways: Often they are complementary, sometimes they corroborate each other, but occasionally they can also be contradictory or lead to unexpected insights. Such observations can in turn initiate follow-up studies – which lead to a broader and deeper understanding of the subject matter and further enhance the explanatory power of results.

Apart from these general benefits, mixed methods studies can be expected to provide *specific contributions to investigating social networks*, especially in three areas. The first area is thick descriptions of networks, network practices, and interpretations. The second area is network effects, and the third is network dynamics.

Thick Descriptions of Networks, Network Practices, and Interpretations

Combining qualitative and quantitative approaches gives special insight into networking practices and the perceptions of networks. *Network perceptions and interpretations* are important factors, for example, in studying how individuals position themselves in relation to their social environment, as in analyses of the integration patterns of young adults (Verd and Lozares, this volume), the elderly (Hollstein 2002), members of social movements (Hofer et al. 2006), or of migrants (Molina et al.; Maya-Jariego and Dominguez, this volume). Network practices are relevant aspects, for instance, in exploring patterns of contact and cooperation between organizations (Wald, this volume) or workflows and interaction patterns within organizational networks (cf. Häussling; Gluesing et al., this volume). Other studies investigate exchange patterns in networks of migrants (Menjivar 2000; Maya-Jariego and Dominguez, this volume), the "art of networking" among Florentine nobility (McLean 1998), or discourse patterns and conversation dynamics in Brazilian youth movements (Mische 2008). Qualitative data can give a detailed account of individual cases by way of *"thick descriptions"* (Geertz 1973) that are geared toward tracing how actions or events unfold and the impact they have in order to make them comprehensible in terms of social meaning (*Verstehen*). It must be emphasized, however, that we cannot make valid statements about networks based on qualitative data alone without linking them with data on network structures. Formal descriptions of network structures are the prerequisite for making any kind of valid statements about social networks at all and not simply speaking of networks in a merely metaphorical sense (Johnson 1994).

Network Effects

Furthermore, combining qualitative and quantitative approaches can contribute to a better understanding of how networks matter and of what mechanisms and conditions figure in when producing certain network outcomes. Network perceptions, for instance, can be helpful in assessing the functioning of exchange relations or the effectiveness of networks, for instance, when investigating the reasons for a research group's success or failure (Wald, this volume), studying the departments of a company (Häussling, this volume), or examining the innovation networks of global players (Gluesing et al., this volume). Members of organizations can be considered as experts on the networks of which they are part, for instance, with regard to the reasons why cooperation between research teams failed or concerning the strategies and contexts of action, for example, when studying learning processes in decentralized systems (Lazer et al. 2011). Other studies are concerned with the effects of personal networks, for example, when studying decision-making about higher education and the role of personal networks (Fuller et al. 2011). Using both survey and ethnographic data, Avenarius and Johnson (this volume) show how network structures play a role in the decision of Chinese peasants to take a dispute to court or seek the assistance of a traditional mediator. Bernardi et al. (this volume) use qualitative and quantitative data from interviews to reconstruct how personal networks influence the decision to start a family. Hollstein and Wagemann (this volume) investigate what aspects of networks facilitate or impair the transition from school to work.

Network Dynamics

Apart from the question of how networks function, combining quantitative and qualitative approaches also helps to understand the formative conditions, dynamic processes, and change of networks. This concerns not only fluctuations or changes in networks over time but also fluctuations and changes in networks in physical space (e.g., migrant networks). How to deal with changes in networks was one of the major trouble spots of network research in the past (cf. Borgatti 2009). In the meantime, sophisticated quantitative methods for describing and analyzing network change have been developed (cf. Snijders 2011; Gluesing et al., this volume). On the other hand, qualitative social research provides special means for understanding (in the sense of *Verstehen*) network constitution and the mechanisms of network change (e.g., Hollstein 2002; Crossley 2009; Small 2009). Actor strategies can be one source of insights into network formation and change. However, since network dynamics always involve at least two actors, analyses of interaction and network practices are keys to understanding the dynamic side of network development. In cases where research on network dynamics also seeks to understand connections between network orientations and actual network changes, longitudinal data on social networks, changes in those networks, actor orientations, and shifts in such orientations are most suited. The study of dynamics in the social integration of young adults by Bidart and Lavenu (2005) is an example of such research. If the inquiry is concerned with the influence of concrete social interaction and actor practices on network dynamics, observation over lengthy periods of time can be expected to deliver the best data basis for this purpose. Ann Mische's (2003, 2008) studies of Brazilian youth movements or Gluesing et al.'s study (this volume) of innovation networks in global teams are cases in point. Finally, Rogers and Menjivar (this volume) demonstrate how computer simulations (agent-based modeling) based on a qualitative strand are a useful tool in predicting the prospective development and dissolution of Salvadorian immigrants' networks.

Relating data in this way also has theoretical implications. Since qualitative data are better attuned to capturing individual actors and their systems of relevance compared to relational data on the structure of relationships and networks, incorporating qualitative and quantitative network data provides a way of linking theoretical perspectives that focus on either structure or agency (Hollstein 2001; Häussling, this volume). Advocates of a relational sociology have been arguing to that effect since the early 1990s (White 1992; Emirbayer and Goodwin 1994; Mizruchi 1994). We can thus expect empirical studies along such lines to also yield theoretically inspiring insights.

Drawbacks of Mixed Methods Designs

Last but not least, it needs to be pointed out that all the benefits notwithstanding, mixed methods designs also have drawbacks compared to monomethod studies (cf. also Wald, this volume; Bernardi et al., this volume). The main downside is resource intensity: It is not unusual for mixed methods studies to require considerably more time and thus more research funds than monomethod studies. This can have methodological consequences. For example, applying the qualitative and the quantitative strands to the same sample to enhance validity limits the sample size, which in turn limits the possibility of running statistical tests (Wald, this volume).[12] A key issue, however, is that mixed methods studies are very demanding in terms of the skills required to apply both approaches at equally high levels of sophistication and integrate them at the meta-level. This is reflected in the contributions assembled in this volume. The empirical studies on which the chapters in Parts II and III are based are all the product of collaboration, mostly of the interdisciplinary kind. Conducting a mixed methods study requires a huge coordination effort and presupposes not only the knowledge but also the readinesses of researchers to embark on mixed methods research as well tackle the practical questions of data management (Wald, this volume; Bernardi et al., this volume). With this in mind, it seems fair to say that mixed methods designs are generally not well suited for the novice researcher. As we have shown, there are of course differences in the complexities and resource intensities of the designs. Parallel designs and especially fully integrated designs are particularly demanding in terms of coordinating the qualitative and quantitative strands. The advantage of sequential designs is that they allow conducting the research consecutively one stage at a time. On the other hand, this limits the ability to make adjustments at later stages. Moreover, sequential designs are generally less time and cost intensive compared to parallel designs. For well-defined aspects of the research question, it may therefore make good sense to use embedded designs.

Due to the resource intensity of mixed methods studies, the researcher should carefully consider whether to employ a mixed methods design or

[12] For the challenges connected to mixed methods sampling, confer Bernardi et al. (this volume), Maya-Jariego and Dominguez (this volume), and Avenarius and Johnson (this volume).

qualitative or quantitative methods only. As Andreas Wald (this volume) elaborates, the selection of a mixed methods design should be guided by the research question, the research objective, and the nature of the phenomenon under study. Mixed methods designs are best suited for highly complex research questions (partly predetermined, partly open), for confirmatory and exploratory research objectives, objectives where "individual meaning, perception, frameworks of relevance and additional context factors play an important role" (Wald, this volume) while mathematical evidence is called for at the same time, and finally, for research phenomena for which prior knowledge of the field and of relevant context factors exists but is incomplete (Wald, this volume).

Organization of the Book

This book is the first to give an overview of research strategies that make use of mixed methods in studying social networks. It provides the reader with detailed accounts of the research designs and methods used in investigating social networks of various sorts. The chapters discuss the strengths of the different mixed methods designs and the specific methods they employ for particular fields and considering the kinds of results they can be expected to achieve. The chapters address important questions and engage in cutting-edge debates in the different areas on which they focus, thus making a substantial contribution to the field of social networks.

The contributions in this volume have been assembled to represent the most important types of mixed methods designs (sequential, parallel, fully integrated, embedded, and conversion designs). Furthermore, they illustrate how new methodological approaches can be employed in mixed methods network studies (like network visualizations and simulations). Finally, they provide excellent illustrations of how a variety of research questions are implemented in network research and the insights such research can be expected to yield in terms of network descriptions, network effects, and network dynamics (cf. Table 1.1).[13]

The book consists of four parts. The chapters in Part I, "General Issues," acquaint the reader with social network research as such (Carrington, Chapter 2) and discuss fundamental theoretical and methodological

---

[13] Table 1.1 gives an overview of the specific contribution provided by each chapter: the specific methodological contribution (mixed methods design and methodological approach) and the specific contribution to the respective field or topic under study made possible by integrating qualitative and quantitative approaches (thick network description, network effects, or network dynamics). In addition, Table 1.1 provides an overview of the different research topics of the chapters, the different network types investigated, as well as the methods and data used.

questions, such as triangulation and validity of network data (Wald, Chapter 3) and the theoretical perspectives that might be employed in mixed methods network research (Häussling, Chapter 4). The contributions in Part II, "Applications," demonstrate the use and the potential of the different mixed methods research designs for the investigation of social networks: a parallel design (Bernardi et al., Chapter 5), a sequential explanatory design (Maya-Jariego and Dominguez, Chapter 6), a fully integrated design (Avenarius and Johnson, Chapter 7), and an embedded design (Gluesing et al., Chapter 8). The contributions in Part III apply "New Methodological Approaches" in mixed methods network studies: Qualitative Comparative Analysis (QCA; Hollstein and Wagemann, Chapter 9), semantic network analysis and data mining (Verd and Lozares, Chapter 10), as well as mixed methods designs that make use of network visualizations (Molina, Maya-Jariego, and McCarty, Chapter 11) and computational modeling (Rogers and Menjivar, Chapter 12). They also make use of other types of designs, such as the sequential exploratory design (Rogers and Menjivar, Chapter 12) and conversion designs (Verd and Lozares, Chapter 10; Hollstein and Wagemann, Chapter 9).

In order to illustrate the wide spectrum of possible uses of mixed methods designs in investigating social networks and, at the same time, encourage the discussion of – the partially similar – methodical problems across different subjects, the book comprises studies from diverse areas of application. The empirical studies thus represent various fields of network research, such as organizational and innovation research; socialization and life-course research; family and migration research; and research on intercultural relations, cultural change, and modernization processes. To complete the picture, the studies focus on different kinds of social networks, including egocentric and whole networks, social networks within and between organizations, informal and formal networks, as well as personal networks (cf. Table 1.1). The substantive chapters all follow the same outline: They start with a set of empirical questions and then argue why using mixed methods is a promising way of addressing these questions. This is followed by a review of the literature on the subject, a description of the data and methods, and then the results of the research. The conclusion summarizes what the study contributes to our understanding of the topic in question and reflects on the research design and choice of methods, including their advantages and limitations.

The Contributions

The first part of the book discusses general issues relevant to mixed methods network research. It starts out with an introduction by Betina Hollstein, followed by an overview of social network analysis by Peter

Table 1.1. *Overview of the book*

Part	I. General issues			II. Mixed methods applications	
Authors	Carrington	Wald	Häussling	Bernardi et al.	Maya-Jariego/ Dominguez
Focus/MM design	Social network analysis	MM methodological issues (triangulation, validity)	Theoretical concepts	Parallel design MM sampling, data collection	Sequential explanatory design
NW aspects	NW descript. NW effects	NW effects NW dynam.	NW effects	NW effects (NW dynam.)	NW descript.
Topic	Various	Innovation/ cooperat.	Innovation/ cooperat.	Life-course/ fertility	Migration/ acculturat.
NW type	Various	Organizational NW	Organizational NW	Pers. NW	Pers. NW
	Various	Ego NW	Whole NW	Ego NW	Ego NW
Samples		Same	Same	Same	Different
Data					
Observations	-	x	-	x
Survey	x	x	x	x
Interviews	x	x	x	x
Documents	x	x	-	-
NW chart	x	x	x	x
NW grid	x	-	x	-
Strategies of Analysis					
Descriptive NW measures	x	x	x	x
Ethnography	-	-	-	x
Qual. text anal./ thematic coding	x	x	x	x
Quant. content analysis	-	-	-	-
Quantitizing strategy	x	-	x	x
Visualization	x	x	-	-
Other				Grounded Theory	Psychometric scales

		III. New methodological approaches used in MM designs			
Avenarius/ Johnson	*Gluesing et al.*	*Hollstein/ Wagemann*	*Verd/ Lozares*	*Molina et al.*	*Rogers/ Menjivar*
Fully integrated design	Embedded design	Fuzzy set QCA (Conversion /integrated design)	Semantic network analysis (Conversion design)	Visualization (Parallel design)	Simulation (Sequential exploratory design)
NW effects	NW dynam. NW effects	NW effects	NW descript.	NW descript.	NW dynam.
Moderniz./ culture	Innovation/ cooperat.	Life-course	Life-course	Migration/ acculturat.	Migration
Pers. NW/ local comm.	Organizational NW	Pers. NW	Pers. NW	Pers. NW	Pers. NW
Ego/Whole NW	Whole NW	Ego NW	Ego NW	Ego NW	Ego NW
overlap	Multi-level	Same	Same	Same	-
x	x	-	-	-	x
x	-	-	-	x	-
x	x	x	x	x	x
-	E-mail	-	-	-	-
-	-	x	-	x	-
-	-	-	-	x	-
x	x	x	x	x	x
x	x	-	-	-	x
x	x	x	x	x	x
x	x	-	-	-	-
x	-	x	x	-	-
x	x	-	x	x	x
Cultural consensus analysis	Quant. Semantic network analys. Triad census	QCA	Qual. Semantic network analys. Component analysis	Clustered graphs	Simulation Agent-based modeling

J. Carrington (Chapter 2). Carrington introduces the reader to social network research, its origins, principal concepts, and contributions to the different fields of research. He outlines the historical development of social network analysis and introduces the reader to the main concepts, such as graphs, ego-centered and socio-centered networks, concepts of social cohesion, social status and roles as applied in network research, and centrality. Research questions and major contributions of social network research are illustrated using examples of how it is applied in various fields of study.

Chapter 3, by Andreas Wald, connects the general introduction to social networks with mixed methods: Wald discusses triangulation as a methodological concept at the heart of mixed methods research and outlines its potential for network research. He argues that triangulating quantitative and qualitative methods in data collection and analysis can enhance the validity of network data and the explanatory power of network studies. Based on a study concerned with networks of research groups, Wald demonstrates how triangulation can be applied systematically in collecting and analyzing network data. Finally, he presents a set of criteria to assist in deciding whether to employ a single method or a mixed methods design.

In the fourth chapter devoted to general issues, Roger Häussling addresses theoretical strands to guide mixed methods network research. He distinguishes four different theoretical levels for capturing and interpreting the socially multidimensional nature of human interaction. These different and – as he shows – complementary levels of social interaction are (a) the context of interaction (cultural symbols, norms, and established roles), (b) the network of interlaced interactions, (c) the interventions of the actors involved, and (d) the expression of emotions accompanying the transformation of relationships. Based on a case study of the social network and the processes of communication and knowledge transfer in the sales department of an auto manufacturer, he demonstrates how this theoretical concept can be applied and the kinds of results it can be expected to yield.

The chapters in Part II illustrate applications of different mixed methods research designs for studying social networks of various sorts: In Chapter 5 Laura Bernardi, Sylvia Keim, and Andreas Klärner employ a *mixed methods parallel design* to investigate how network effects and social influence affect the fertility behavior of young adults in West and East Germany. The chapter shows how qualitative interviews and standardized methods of collecting network data (using network charts, network grids, and a network questionnaire) are applied simultaneously to the same sample. The mixed methods analysis then allows identifying relevant (influential) relationships as well as analyzing their structural characteristics and how the social influence may vary in networks with different structural characteristics.

In Chapter 6 Isidro Maya-Jariego and Silvia Domínguez describe a *mixed methods sequential explanatory design* to assess the acculturation of host individuals based on ethnographic and psychometric research of Latina immigrants in Boston (US) and Latin American immigrants in Andalucía (Spain). Assuming a contingent relationship between the kind of acculturation experience and the type of personal network, data on the structure of personal networks are used to identify individuals (screening) and are then combined in an iterative process with data from interviews, participant observation, and surveys using psychometric scales. This design allows understanding the complexity of the acculturation process while taking into account both the topology of the intergroup situation and the interactive nature of the intercultural contact.

Applying a *fully integrated mixed methods design*, in Chapter 7 Christine Avenarius and Jeffrey C. Johnson investigate the adaptation to new legal procedures in rural China; the complex relationship between social networks, beliefs, and perceptions of Chinese citizens regarding notions of justice and fairness; and preferred conflict resolution strategies. Despite efforts by the Chinese government to establish the rule of law and construct a new legal system, the rule of relationships continues to influence the daily reality of Chinese citizens. Integrating qualitative data from the peasants' narratives about justice and fairness as well as the preferred means of dispute resolution – analyzed by cultural consensus analysis – with quantitative data depicting their personal network structures and their structural position within the village network helps us to understand why some peasants prefer to take a case to court rather than just settle outside of court instead.

In Chapter 8 Julia Gluesing, Kenneth Riopelle, and James A. Danowski use an *embedded design* to study innovation networks in global organizations. In analyzing tens of thousands of e-mails, the authors show how social network analysis techniques that tap into the flow of electronic communication reveal much about how innovation networks are structured, how they evolve, and what kinds of messages flow through the communication networks. Supplementary ethnographic research (interviews, participant observation) was conducted to validate the quantitative measures of network dynamics and help uncover emerging roles, the different meanings of a particular innovation within the global networks, and the different patterns of collaboration. For instance, the interviews testify to different patterns of e-mail use in Europe and in the United States. (In the primary European location, managers did not engage in e-mail exchange with those whose offices were nearby; interpersonal communication was the norm instead.)

Part III presents new methodological approaches to mixed methods social network research. In Chapter 9 Betina Hollstein and Claudius Wagemann demonstrate how *fuzzy set analysis*, a new variant of Qualitative Comparative Analysis (QCA; Ragin 2000, 2008), can be employed to investigate the impact of personal networks on the successful entry into the labor market. Since it integrates qualitative and quantitative steps of analysis, fuzzy set analysis itself can be seen as a mixed method. Drawing on set-theoretical considerations, fuzzy set QCA facilitates systematically comparing cases and developing typologies from individual case analyses. This allows enhancing the explanatory power of studies based on medium-sized samples. Because qualitative data on network relations are transformed into numerical data (fuzzy sets of individual attributes), the chapter also provides a good illustration of a *conversion mixed design*.

An increasingly important issue in social network research is the extraction of data on network structures from qualitative text sources based on, for example, narrative data or digital communication – a procedure referred to as data mining (cf. Gluesing et al., this volume). In Chapter 10, Joan Miquel Verd and Carlos Lozares review various methods aimed at transforming textual data into relational and network data (so-called *quantitizing strategy of data conversion*). As opposed to procedures using automated coding, Verd and Lozares present an approach that analyzes textual data and *extracts network information using interpretive strategies of analysis*. Interpretive strategies allow analyzing texts with an eye to semantic structures, social meaning, and context. The procedure is applied to the analysis of narrative biographical interviews on education and employment careers.

In the subsequent Chapter 11, José Luis Molina, Isidro Maya-Jariego, and Christopher McCarty evaluate the potential of personal *network visualizations* as a tool in conducting and analyzing interviews. Network visualization is not only an important instrument in presenting data; it can also be a valuable tool in exploring and analyzing data. Moreover, visualizing networks in the form of diagrams, charts, or maps is a technique frequently used in collecting network data (e.g., Häussling; Bernardi et al.; Hollstein and Wagemann, this volume). Molina et al. show how the combination of computer-assisted visualizations of personal networks and qualitative interviews based on those visualizations allows researchers to obtain a special kind of information about the social world of informants (social circles, social support, etc.). The particular strength of visualizations lies in their ability to trigger cognitive responses that are difficult to obtain by other means. The chapter draws on methods of data collection and analysis utilized in two research projects targeting immigrants in Spain and the United States.

As computer technology evolves, this creates growing opportunities for the use of computer simulations in analyzing complex social phenomena. This is particularly interesting with regard to social networks. Using agent-based modeling, Bruce Rogers and Cecilia Menjívar simulate a social network in a poor economic environment and analyze the effects of reciprocal exchange on the network structure in Chapter 12. A qualitative ethnographic study on poor and legally marginal Salvadoran immigrants living in the San Francisco area serves as input for creating a computational model (sequential exploratory mixed methods design). In the ethnographic part of the study, Menjívar identifies the mechanism of expected reciprocity to explain the weakening and dissolution of social relationships. In the following simulation, the notion is formalized in such a way as to allow for a wide range of different individual behaviors. Using computer simulations allows one to carefully track network evolution and to study the dynamic behavior of social networks.

Table 1.1 provides an overview of the chapters; their methodological focus; and the topics, network aspects, and network types investigated in the studies. The table provides a summary for readers who are interested in a particular approach to the combination of data, of strategies of analysis, or a particular type of mixed methods design. It intends to help identify the chapter to read if one wants to learn more about a particular kind of design.

References

Axinn, William G. and Lisa D. Pearce, eds. 2006. *Mixed Method Data Collection Strategies*. Cambridge: Cambridge University Press.

Barnes, John A. 1954. "Class and committees in a Norwegian island parish." *Human Relations* 7:39–58.

———. 1969. "Networks and political process." Pp. 51–77 in *Social Networks in Urban Situations: Analyses of Personal Relationships in Central African Towns*, edited by J. C. Mitchell. Manchester: Manchester University Press.

Baumgarten, Britta and Christian Lahusen. 2006. "Politiknetzwerke – Vorteile und Grundzüge einer qualitativen Analysestrategie." Pp. 177–99 in *Qualitative Netzwerkanalyse: Konzepte, Methoden, Anwendungen*, edited by B. Hollstein and F. Straus. Wiesbaden: VS Verlag für Sozialwissenschaften (GWV).

Bearman, Peter S. and Paolo Parigi. 2004. "Cloning headless frogs and other important matters: Conversation topics and network structure." *Social Forces* 83(2):535–57.

Belotti, Elisa 2010. "Comment on Nick Crossley/ 1." *Sociologica* 1.

Bergman, Manfred M. and Alan Bryman, eds. 2008. *Advances in Mixed Methods Research: Theories and Appications.* Los Angeles: Sage.

Bernard, H. Russell 1994. *Research Methods in Anthropology: Qualitative and Quantitative Approaches.* Thousand Oaks, CA: Sage.

Bickman, Leonard and Debra J. Rog, eds. 2009. *The SAGE Handbook of Applied Social Research Methods.* Los Angeles: Sage.

Bidart, Claire and Daniel Lavenu. 2005. "Evolutions of personal networks and life events." *Social Networks* 27(4):359–76.

Borgatti, Steve P. et al. 2009. "Network analysis in the social sciences." *Science* 323(5916):892–95.

Bott, Elizabeth. 1957. *Family and Social Network: Roles, Norms, and External Relationships in Ordinary Urban Families.* London: Tavistock.

Bryman, Alan. 2006. *Mixed Methods.* London: Sage.

Burt, Ronald S. 1992. *Structural Holes: The Social Structure of Competition.* Cambridge, MA: Harvard University Press.

Carrington, Peter J., John Scott, and Stanley Wasserman, eds. 2005. *Models and Methods in Social Network Analysis.* New York: Cambridge University Press.

Coleman, James S. 1990. *Foundations of Social Theory.* Cambridge, MA: Belknap Press of Harvard University Press.

Creswell, John W. 2003. *Research Design: Qualitative, Quantitative, and Mixed Methods Approaches.* 2nd ed. Thousand Oaks, CA: Sage.

Creswell, John W. and Vicki L. Plano Clark, eds. 2007. *Designing and Conducting Mixed Methods Research.* Thousand Oaks, CA: Sage.

Creswell, John W. and Vicki L. Plano Clark et al. 2003. "Advanced mixed methods research designs." Pp. 209–40 in *Sage Handbook of Mixed Methods in Social & Behavioral Research*, edited by A. Tashakkori and C. Teddlie. Los Angeles: Sage.

Crossley, Nick. 2009. "The man whose web expanded: Network dynamics in Manchester's post-punk music scene 1976–1980." *Poetics* 37(1):24–49.

Degenne, Alain and Michel Forsé, eds. 1999. *Introducing Social Networks.* London: Sage.

Diani, Mario and Doug McAdam, eds. 2003. *Social Movements and Networks: Relational Approaches to Collective Action.* Reprint. Oxford: Oxford University Press.

Emirbayer, Mustafa. 1997. "Manifesto for a relational sociology." *American Journal of Sociology* 103(2):281–317.

Emirbayer, Mustafa and Jeff Goodwin. 1994. "Network analysis, culture, and the problem of agency." *American Journal of Sociology* 99(6):1411–54.

Fine, Gary Alan and Sherryl Kleinman. 1983. "Network and meaning: An interactionist approach to structure." *Symbolic Interaction* 6:97–110.

Frank, Ove. 2011. "Survey sampling in networks." Pp. 389–403 in *Sage Handbook of Social Network Analysis*, edited by J. Scott and P. J. Carrington. London/New Dehli: Sage.

Freeman, Linton C. 2004. *The Development of Social Network Analysis: A Study in the Sociology of Science.* Vancouver, BC: Empirical Press.

Fuhse, Jan A. and Sophie Mützel, eds. 2010. *Relationale Soziologie: Zur kulturellen Wende der Netzwerkforschung.* Wiesbaden: VS Verlag für Sozialwissenschaften.

Fuller, Alison, Sue Heath, and Brenda Johnston, eds. 2011. *Rethinking Widening Participation in Higher Education: The Role of Social Networks.* New York: Routledge.

Geertz, Clifford. 1973. *The Interpretation of Cultures: Selected Essays.* New York: Basic Books.

Gibson, David R. 2005. "Taking turns and talking ties: Networks and conversational interaction." *American Journal of Sociology* 110(6):1561–97.

Granovetter, Mark S. 1985. "Economic action and social structure: the problem of embeddedness." *American Journal of Sociology* 91(3):481–510.

Greene, Jennifer C. and Valerie J. Caracelli. 1997a. "Defining and describing the paradigm issue in mixed-method evaluation." Pp. 5–17 in *Advances in Mixed-Method Evaluation: The Challenges and Benefits of Integrating Diverse Paradigms*, edited by J. Greene and V. Caracelli. San Francisco: Jossey-Bass.

———, eds. 1997b. *Advances in Mixed-Method Evaluation: The Challenges and Benefits of Integrating Diverse Paradigms.* San Francisco: Jossey-Bass.

Greene, Jennifer C., Valerie J. Caracelli, and Wendy F. Graham. 1989. "Toward a conceptual framework for mixed- method evaluation designs." *Educational Evaluation and Policy Analysis* 11:255–74.

Häussling, Roger. 2006. "Interaktionen in Organisationen. Ein Vierebenenkonzept des Methodologischen Relationalismus und dessen empirische Anwendung." Habilitation. Universität Karlsruhe.

Hofer, Renate, Heiner Keupp, and Florian Straus. 2006. "Prozesse sozialer Verortung in Szenen und Organisationen: Ein netzwerkorientierter Blick auf traditionale und reflexiv moderne Engagementformen." Pp. 267–95 in *Qualitative Netzwerkanalyse: Konzepte, Methoden, Anwendungen*, edited by B. Hollstein and F. Straus. Wiesbaden: VS Verlag für Sozialwissenschaften (GWV).

Hollstein, Betina. 2001. *Grenzen sozialer Integration: Zur Konzeption informeller Beziehungen und Netzwerke.* Opladen: Leske + Budrich.

———. 2002. *Soziale Netzwerke nach der Verwitwung: Eine Rekonstruktion der Veränderungen informeller Beziehungen.* Opladen: Leske + Budrich.

———. 2011. "Qualitative approaches." Pp. 404–16 in *Sage Handbook of Social Network Analysis*, edited by J. Scott and P. J. Carrington. London/ New Dehli: Sage.

Hollstein, Betina, and Florian Straus, eds. 2006. *Qualitative Netzwerkanalyse: Konzepte, Methoden, Anwendungen.* Wiesbaden: VS Verlag für Sozialwissenschaften (GWV).

Jahoda, Marie, Hans Zeisel, and Paul F. Lazarsfeld, eds. 1933. *Die Arbeitslosen von Marienthal: Ein soziographischer Versuch über die Wirkungen langdauernder Arbeitslosigkeit.* Leipzig: Hirzel.

Jansen, Dorothea. 1999. *Einführung in die Netzwerkanalyse: Grundlagen, Methoden, Anwendungen.* Opladen: Leske + Budrich.

Johnson, Jeffrey C. 1994. "Anthropological contributions to the study of social networks: A review." Pp. 113–51 in *Advances in Social Network Analysis,* edited by S. Wasserman and J. Galaskiewicz. Thousand Oaks, CA: Sage.

Johnson, R. Burke and Anthony J. Onwuegbuzie. 2004. "Mixed methods research: A research paradigm whose time has come." *Educational Researcher* 33(7):14–26.

———. 2007. "Toward a definition of mixed methods research." *Journal of Mixed Methods Research* 1:112–33.

Knox, Hannah, Mike Savage, and Penny Harvey. 2006. "Social networks and the study of social relations: networks as method, metaphor and form." *Economy and Society* 35(1):113–40.

Lazer, David, Ines Mergel, Curtis Ziniel, Kevin M. Esterling, and Michael A. Neblo. 2011. "The multiple institutional logics of innovation." *International Public Management Journal* 14(3):311–340.

Marsden, Peter V. 1990. "Network data and measurement." *Annual Review of Sociology* 16:433–63.

———. 2011. "Survey methods for network data." Pp. 370–88 in *Sage Handbook of Social Network Analysis,* edited by J. Scott and P. J. Carrington. London/New Dehli: Sage.

McLean, Paul D. 1998. "A frame analysis of favour seeking in the Renaissance: Agency, networks, and political culture." *American Journal of Sociology* 104(1):51–91.

Menjivar, Cecilia. 2000. *Fragmented Ties: Salvadoran Immigrant Networks in America.* Berkeley: University of California Press.

Mische, Ann. 2003. "Cross-talk in movements: Rethinking the culture-network link." Pp. 258–80 in *Social Movements and Networks: Relational Approaches to Collective Action.* Reprint. Oxford: Oxford University Press.

———. 2008. *Partisan Publics: Communication and Contention across Brazilian Youth Activist Networks.* Princeton, NJ/Oxford: Princeton University Press.

Mitchell, J. Clyde, ed. 1969. *Social Networks in Urban Situations: Analyses of Personal Relationships in Central African Towns.* Manchester: Manchester University Press.

Mizruchi, Mark S. 1994. "Social network analysis: Recent achievements and current controversies." *Acta Sociologica* 37(4):329–43.

Morgan, David L. 1998. "Practical strategies for combining qualitative and quantitative methods: Applications to health research." *Qualitative Health Research* 8:362–76.

Morse, Janice M. 1991. "Approaches to qualitative-quantitative methodological triangulation." *Nursing Research* 40(2):120–23.

———. 2003. "Principles of mixed methods and multimethod research design." Pp. 189–208 in *Sage Handbook of Mixed Methods in Social & Behavioral Research,* edited by A. Tashakkori and C. Teddlie. Los Angeles: Sage.

Padgett, John F. and Christopher K. Ansell. 1993. "Robust action and the rise of the Medici, 1400–1434." *American Journal of Sociology* 98(6):1259–1319.

Provan, Keith G. and H. Brinton Milward. 1995. "A preliminary theory of inter-organizational network effectiveness: A comparative study of four mental health systems." *Administrative Science Quarterly* 40(1):1–33.

Ragin, Charles C. 2008. *Redesigning Social Inquiry: Fuzzy Sets and Beyond.* Chicago and London: University of Chicago Press.

———. 2000. *Fuzzy-Set Social Science.* Chicago: University of Chicago Press.

Roethlisberger, Fritz J. and William J. Dickson, eds. 1939. *Management and the Worker.* Cambridge, MA: Harvard University Press.

Schweizer, Thomas. 1996. *Muster sozialer Ordnung. Netzwerkanalyse als Fundament der Sozialethnologie.* Berlin: Reimer.

Scott, John. 2000. *Social Network Analysis: A Handbook.* 2nd ed. London/New Dehli: Sage.

Scott, John, and Peter J. Carrington, eds. 2011. *Sage Handbook of Social Network Analysis.* London/New Dehli: Sage.

Small, Mario L. 2009. *Unanticipated Gains: Origins of Network Inequality in Everyday Life.* Oxford: Oxford University Press.

Smith, Sandra S. 2005. "'Don't put my name on it': Social capital activation and job-finding assistance among the black urban poor." *American Journal of Sociology* 111(1):1–57.

Snijders, Tom A. 2011. "Network dynamics." Pp. 501–513 in *Sage Handbook of Social Network Analysis.* London/New Dehli: Sage.

Tashakkori, Abbas and Charles Teddlie, eds. 2003. *Sage Handbook of Mixed Methods in Social & Behavioral Research.* Los Angeles: Sage.

Tashakkori, Abbas and Charles Teddlie. 2009. "Integrating qualitative and quantitative approaches to research." Pp. 283–317 in *The Sage Handbook of Applied Social Research Methods.* 2nd ed., edited by L. Bickmand and D. J. Rog. Los Angeles: Sage.

Teddlie, Charles and Abbas Tashakkori. 2006. "A general typology of research designs featuring mixed methods." *Research in the Schools* 13(1):12–28.

———. 2008. "Quality of inference in mixed methods research." Pp. 101–20 in *Advances in Mixed Methods Research: Theories and Appications.* Reprint. Los Angeles: Sage.

Wasserman, Stanley and Katherine Faust, eds. 2005. *Social Network Analysis: Methods and Applications.* Cambridge: Cambridge University Press.

Wasserman, Stanley and Joseph Galaskiewicz, eds. 1994. *Advances in Social Network Analysis*: Thousand Oaks, CA: Sage.

Wellman, Barry and Stephen D. Berkowitz, eds. 1988. *Social Structures: A Network Approach.* Cambridge: Cambridge University Press.

Wellman, Barry, Peter J. Carrington, and Alan Hall. 1988. "Networks as personal communities." Pp. 130–84 in *Social Structures: A Network Approach,* edited by Barry Wellman and Stephen D. Berkowitz. Cambridge: Cambridge University Press.

White, Harrison C. 1992. *Identity and Control: A Structural Theory of Social Action*. Princeton, NJ: Princeton University Press.

Wong, Siu-lun and Janet W. Salaff. 1998. "Network capital: Emigration from Hong Kong." *British Journal of Sociology* 49(3):358–74.

Yeung, King-To 2005. "What does love mean? Exploring network culture in two network settings." *Social Forces* 84(1):391–420.

2

Social Network Research

Peter J. Carrington

The basic insight of social network analysis is that social structure is an emergent property of the networks of relationships in which individuals (and other social actors, such as organizations) are embedded (Simmel [1922] 1955; Radcliffe-Brown 1940). Therefore, if one wants to understand social structure, one should study social networks. While research on social networks may use quantitative or qualitative or mixed methods, social network analysis itself is fundamentally neither quantitative nor qualitative, nor a combination of the two. Rather, it is structural. That is to say, the basic interest of social network analysis is to understand social structure, by studying social networks. Observing or calculating quantitative aspects of social networks, such as the average number of individuals with whom an individual is directly connected, or qualitative aspects, such as the nature of social ties among individuals, can be useful analytic techniques, but the fundamental quest is to understand the structure of the network, which is neither a quantity nor a quality.

As it has developed, social network analysis has become increasingly mathematical: That is, it employs formalisms and analytic techniques taken from mathematics and developed further for social network analysis by mathematicians. Many people think of social network analysis as primarily a quantitative approach to social science, because they mistakenly equate "quantitative" and "mathematical." But, as Harrison White (1963a:79) pointed out, "Mathematics has grown much 'beyond' quantity ...," and the branch of mathematics principally used by social network analysis – graph theory – represents structures (or the lack thereof), not quantities. The same point was made much earlier by Radcliffe-Brown (1957), in his lecture series given at the University of Chicago in 1937:

Relational analysis, even if not metrical, may be mathematical, in the sense that it will apply non-quantitative, relational mathematics. The kind of mathematics which will be required ultimately for a full development of the science of society will not be metrical, but will be that hitherto comparatively neglected branch of mathematics, the calculus of relations, which, I think, is on the whole more fundamental than quantitative mathematics. (p. 69)

In social network analysis, a real-life social network, consisting of people (or organizations, or other social actors) and their connections, is represented by the mathematical object called a graph, in which a set of points, or "nodes," represents the social actors, and lines, or "edges," between pairs of nodes represent the presence of a given relationship between pairs of actors. A graph is an abstraction with no particular visual representation, but it is usually visualized by a graph drawing (often, confusingly, just called a graph) (Figure 2.1a) and/or an adjacency matrix (Figure 2.1b), which contains exactly the same information as the graph drawing: John is tied (adjacent) to Dick and Harry; Dick is tied to John, Harry, and Jane, etc. There are no quantities or qualities in the graph depicted in Figure 2.1: The symbols "1" and "0" in the matrix could be replaced by any codes representing presence and absence, such as "X" and " [blank]." The graph drawing is usually more amenable to visual analysis, but the adjacency matrix has the advantage that it can be analyzed using matrix algebra.

Quantitative and qualitative aspects of real-life social networks can be represented by generalizing mathematical graphs: For example, the nodes and/or lines of the graph may be assigned numbers representing size, weight, strength, and so on, of the actors or their relationships, and the nodes and/or lines may be assigned labels representing qualitative attributes of the actors and their relationships, even difficult-to-measure attributes such as meanings (Hollstein 2011; Hollstein, this volume). The term "network" is often used in mathematics to denote a generalization of the graph, in which multiple types of lines, directed as well as undirected, and values on the lines and nodes are all permitted. Nevertheless, the fundamental interest remains the structure of the network. Indeed, during the early years, the terms "structural analysis," "structural sociology," and "structuralism" were often used interchangeably with "social network analysis" to refer to this field. For example, the chapter on social network analysis in Mullins' (1973) book on modern American social theories is called "The Structuralists," and the titles of several of the early books in this area referred to "(social) structure" instead of or in addition to "networks" (e.g., Nadel 1957; Burt 1982; Berkowitz 1982; Marsden

	John	Harry	Dick	Jane
John		1	1	0
Harry	1		1	0
Dick	1	1		1
Jane	0	0	1	

Figure 2.1. Representations of a hypothetical social network: (a) graph drawing; (b) adjacency matrix

and Lin 1982; Hage and Harary 1983; Wellman and Berkowitz 1988), as did the famous articles published in 1976 by Harrison White and his students (White et al. 1976; Boorman and White 1976). Other early books, however, referred only to "social networks" in their titles (e.g., Mitchell 1969a; Leinhardt 1977; Knoke and Kuklinski 1982; Burt and Minor 1983). The more recent practice is to refer to the field as "social network analysis"; presumably the terms "structuralism," and so on, fell out of favor because of confusion with the European school of social theory and research also called structuralism, which developed in a very different direction from the structuralism based on social networks.

Early Research in Social Networks[1]

A recent account of the development of social network analysis (Freeman 2004) has illuminated its diverse and fragmented origins in the nineteenth and twentieth centuries, in fields such as anthropology, geography, mathematical biology, sociology and social theory, political science, communication studies, management science, mathematics, and physics, and in countries including the United States, Great Britain, France, the Netherlands, and Sweden. Most writers on the development of social network analysis, such as Marsden and Lin (1982), Wellman (1988), Wasserman and Faust (1994), Scott (2000), Freeman (2004), and Knoke and Yang (2008), identify two or three major streams of thought, and groups of researchers, that laid the foundations of social network analysis: (i) sociometry, (ii) the organizational research done at Harvard in the 1930s and 1940s, and (iii) the structural research of British social anthropologists of the Manchester School in the 1950s. My own view is that the genius of early social network analysis lay in the marriage of a powerful new tool developed in sociometry – the sociogram – with a new theoretical development in social anthropology: the conceptualization of social structure as a web of actual human relations. Until it was taken up by anthropologists, sociometric analysis was limited in scope to the social psychology of small groups; until they discovered the sociogram, would-be structural anthropologists and sociologists were limited to using the concept of the "web" of human relations in a metaphorical sense, with no analytic leverage. Social network analysis can be seen, then, as having developed from the application of the sociogram to the problem of social structure.

Sociometry

"Sociometry" is a term coined by its founder, Jacob Moreno (1934), who also referred to it as "psychological geography" (Moreno 1937a:207). Originally, it involved the use of data on interpersonal choices made by the members of a small group to understand and manipulate for therapeutic purposes the social structure of the group and the positions of individuals within it.

The sociometric methods of data collection, data analysis, and therapeutic intervention were first developed by Moreno and his collaborator Helen Jennings in their research and clinical work in Sing Sing prison (Moreno 1932) and the New York State Training School for Girls, in

---

[1] Although the interpretations are my own, much of the historical information used in this section is drawn from Scott (2000) and Freeman (2004).

Hudson, NY (1934). In these and other sociometric studies, Moreno and Jennings were interested in social psychological processes such as leadership, isolation, rejection, reciprocity, popularity, and the dynamics of group structure. Their research was also clinical and experimental, as they used their research findings to make changes in group structures, for example re-assignments of inmates to different prison cottages, both as experimental manipulations and as individual- and group-therapeutic interventions. (Remarkably, Moreno is credited with founding not only sociometry but also American group psychotherapy and psychodrama [Marineau 1989].)

The fundamental contribution of sociometry to the development of social network analysis was the invention of the sociogram. In sociometric research, the researchers ask each group member to report their interpersonal choices – for example, with whom she would prefer to sit to eat – and then construct and analyze diagrams of the choices, or "sociograms" (e.g., Jennings 1937:114). Figure 2.1a is a sociogram. Jennings also constructed tables in which the rows represented individuals making choices, the columns represented individuals chosen, and a check mark in the cell indicated a choice, and did simple quantitative operations on them, such as summing the number of choices received by each individual (e.g., Jennings 1937:124).

Later writers made the obvious (in retrospect) connections with mathematical models. Dodd (1940a, 1940b) showed how the tables created by Jennings could be interpreted as matrices (later called "sociomatrices") and analyzed using matrix algebra. Figure 2.1b is a sociomatrix corresponding to the sociogram in Figure 2.1a. Others (e.g., Harary et al. 1965:2–3) realized that sociograms can be interpreted as drawings of mathematical graphs, which can be analyzed using graph theory, thus greatly expanding the analytic power of the sociometric approach to studying social structure.

Moreno (1953:440–50) used the term "network" in the same sense as it is used today, discussed rudimentary techniques for analyzing networks, and foresaw the possibility of the wide application of sociometric methods and insights in many branches of the social sciences other than social psychology, such as political economy, and to human groups of all sizes, up to "the psychological totality of human society itself" (Moreno 1937a:215). He founded a journal – *Sociometry* – and served as its editor until 1955, thus providing a peer-reviewed forum for publishing research in all areas of the social sciences that utilized his approach (Moreno 1937b). While it can be said that with their invention of sociometry, and in particular the sociogram and sociomatrix, Moreno and Jennings laid the groundwork for social network analysis, their work and that of their followers remained largely confined to the social psychology of small groups.

Social Structure as a Network of Human Relations

During the early twentieth century, a particular conceptualization of social structure was developed in which it was seen as the patterning, or configuration, of actual relationships among a defined set of human beings. Early influential exponents of this view of social structure were Georg Simmel ([1922] 1955), whose writings referred to the "web of group affiliations," and Alfred Radcliffe-Brown, who had been advocating what came to be called a "structuralist" view of society since the 1920s (Freeman 2004) and whose public lectures delivered in 1937 and 1940 referred explicitly to a "network of social relations" and "social morphology" (Radcliffe-Brown 1940, 1957). However, in the work of these pioneers of structural sociology and anthropology the concept of a web or network of human relations remained metaphorical.

Two major groups of researchers pioneered the use of the sociogram and/or sociomatrix to model social structure. At Harvard in the 1930s and 1940s, W. Lloyd Warner – an anthropologist who had been influenced by Radcliffe-Brown – and his collaborators applied ethnographic methods to the study of the social structure of a modern industrial society, namely the United States. Two famous studies by this group – the Yankee City study of a small industrial city in Massachusetts (Warner and Lunt 1941) and the Hawthorne studies of an electrical equipment factory outside Chicago (Roethlisberger and Dickson 1939) – utilized sociograms to visualize and analyze social structure, and their subsequent Deep South study of a segregated city in Mississippi (Davis et al. 1941) used both sociograms and sociomatrices.[2] The rudimentary network analyses of those studies were further developed in George Homans' (1950) re-analyses of data from the Deep South and Hawthorne studies.

In the 1950s, a group of British social anthropologists, often called the Manchester School, applied ethnographic methods and Radcliffe-Brown's concept of social structure to the study of urban life in Britain, Africa, and elsewhere. Unlike the Harvard researchers, they were definitely aware of Moreno's work and explicitly employed sociometric methods of graph visualization and analysis. Typical examples of their work include John Barnes' (1954) study of a Norwegian fishing village; Elizabeth Bott's (1957) research on marriage and family life in London; and the studies by researchers such as Epstein, Wheeldon, Kapferer, Boswell, and Harries-Jones of urban social relations in African towns in Clyde Mitchell's (1969a) edited collection. Mitchell (1969b) in

---

[2] Although, according to Scott (2000), there is no evidence that they were aware of Moreno's development of sociometry.

particular showed a strong interest in using concepts from graph theory to model social structure, and cited the applications of graph theory that had developed from sociometry, by writers such as Anatol Rapoport (Rapoport and Horvath 1961; Foster et al. 1963), James Davis (1963), Claude Flament (1963), Fararo and Sunshine (1964), and Frank Harary and his collaborators (Harary et al. 1965).

The anthropologists of the Manchester school confined their network researches for the most part to small-scale ethnographic research on the social networks of individuals living in modern urban settings, and interpreted them using rudimentary tools from graph theory. Their analyses remained close to the data, representing what Wellman (1988:22) calls "resolute British empiricism." In contrast, the French anthropologist Claude Lévi-Strauss ([1949] 1969) – also influenced by Radcliffe-Brown – and his collaborator André Weil concerned themselves with the kinship-based social structures of entire "primitive" societies. Lévi-Strauss used various kinds of diagrams and graphs to represent structures of kinship relations, and Weil ([1949] 1969) constructed algebraic models of kinship structures. This approach was generalized from kinship-based social structure to a general algebraic theory of social structure as a system of social roles by the Austro-British anthropologist Siegfried Nadel (1957). Algebraic modeling of social structure as a system of social positions and roles occupied by structurally equivalent actors – whether of kinship systems (e.g., White 1963b; Boyd 1969) or of general social structure (e.g., Lorrain and White 1971; White et al. 1976; Boorman and White 1976; Pattison 1993) – has developed into a powerful extension of the graph-theoretic analyses that are more characteristic of mainstream social network analysis.

Expansion Since the 1960s

There are two major themes in the development of social network analysis from the 1960s to the present. One theme is the huge expansion in its scope: in the volume of published work, and in the scope of its application in different disciplines in the social sciences and to substantive areas within these disciplines. Social network analysis is now used not only by sociologists, anthropologists, and psychologists, but also by political scientists, economists, historians, epidemiologists, gerontologists, criminologists, ethologists, organizational scientists, mathematicians, computer scientists, information scientists, and physicists. It has been used in the study of small group dynamics, personal networks, marriage, family, urban and rural community, social support, social mobility, culture, cognition, attitudes, identity, meaning, market organization and behavior, social capital, kinship and kinship-based social structure, animal behavior, online communication and communities, social stratification, political and corporate power, social movements, historical elites, terrorism, crime, criminal justice, intra- and interorganizational structure and behavior, the spread of disease, information and innovations, the organization of science, and world capitalism.

The other theme in the past 50 years of development of social network analysis is the increasing use of mathematical models and methods of analysis, aided by the increasing availability of computer programs and packages designed specifically for social network analysis (Huisman and van Duijn 2005, 2011; INSNA 2010). Beginning with finite graph theory, semigroup algebra, and multidimensional scaling, mathematical methods of social network analysis have been extended to include stochastic models (Wasserman and Robins 2005; Robins 2011; van Duijn and Huisman 2011), longitudinal stochastic models (Snijders 2011), and sophisticated visualization tools (de Nooy et al. 2005; Krempel 2005, 2011). There are now an increasing number of textbooks or compendia of mathematical models and methods for social network analysis (Wasserman and Faust 1994; Brandes and Erlebach 2005; Carrington et al. 2005).

These two characteristics of the development of social network analysis – the huge increase in scope and the increasing use of mathematical models – are not, in my view, unrelated. As Harrison White and many others have pointed out, one of the great utilities of mathematical structural models is that they are unencumbered by details of the specific situation, and therefore allow one to see structural similarities across radically different contexts. Thus, in the classic opening words of his essay on the "Uses of Mathematics in Sociology," White (1963a:77) writes, "Subinfeudation reminds one of industrial decentralization" – a medieval system of land tenure and political allegiance is structurally similar to modern corporate organization. Perceiving similarities in structure allows one to perceive similarities in behavior and its explanation:

> The same conundrums that baffled them baffle us. Just as William the Conqueror insisted on submission directly to himself from the chief vassals of his loyal lords ... so a wise President seeks loyalty of subcabinet officers directly to himself. (White 1963a: 78)

Thus, the use of mathematical models in social network analysis supports incredible cross-fertilization across substantive areas: a structural property of the Internet (it is "scale-free") is also true of citation networks of scientific papers, social influence networks among American physicians, and disease transmission networks (Barabási 2002).

Principal Concepts in Social Network Research

I have suggested previously that the genius of social network analysis lies in its use of structural mathematical concepts – mainly taken from graph theory – to model key concepts in the study of social structure. The brief review of substantive research in social network analysis that follows is organized under headings that represent, in my view, the main aspects of social structure that have been studied using network analysis, and the main network concepts that have been used to model them.

Social Relations, Graphs, and Networks

Fundamental to social network analysis is the representation of a social relation by a graph. Examples of social relations include parenthood, friendship, influence, social support, share ownership, having a common board member, citation, collaboration, voting for, and so on. Each of these relations can be represented by a graph in which there is a line between points a and b if actors a and b have the relation; otherwise not. Multiple relations among the same set of actors can be represented by a network, in which there are as many types of lines as there are relations, or "types of ties" among the actors.

Relations, or ties, among actors may be conceptualized as symmetric or asymmetric. If, for the relation R, aRb (a has the relation with b) logically implies bRa, then the relation is symmetric. If not, it is asymmetric. For example, in modern Western kinship, "sibling of" and "married to" are symmetric, and "parent of" is asymmetric. Liking is (conceptually) asymmetric, since "a likes b" does not logically imply "b likes a," but, like many asymmetric relations, it is often reciprocated, so that it may be empirically symmetric, or close to it. Conceptually symmetric relations may result in asymmetric data, due to the contingencies of data collection; for example, "belongs to the same gang as" is conceptually symmetric, but failure of memory, differences of opinion, and other measurement problems may result in teenagers a and b that provide conflicting accounts of whether they belong to the same gang. Symmetric relations are represented in a graph by unordered pairs of points, and in a graph drawing by undirected lines, as in Figure 2.1. Asymmetric relations are represented by ordered pairs of points in a directed graph, or digraph, and by lines with arrowheads in a graph drawing, as in Figure 2.2.

The decision as to what actors constitute the population to be represented by points in the network is partly a matter of the conceptual orientation of the research: egocentric or sociocentric. Research on the effects

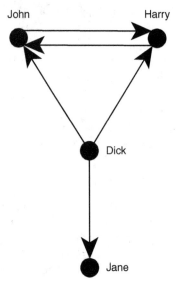

Figure 2.2. Directed graph for asymmetric relation

on individual actors (whether persons or otherwise) of their social environments (and vice versa) generally uses an egocentric (or ego-centered) approach. An egocentric network, or ego network, is centered on one social actor, or ego, and includes all actors, or alters, who (or which) are directly connected to ego by one or more type(s) of tie. Ego networks may also include the alters of ego's alters – termed second-order alters – the alters of second-order alters, and so on. In practice, this is fairly rare, for several reasons: the difficulty of collecting such data, the rapidly increasing number of actors, and the likelihood that the salience of higher-order alters for ego is attenuated by their social distance from ego. Egos – each one of which has its own egocentric network – may be selected purposively, randomly, and so on. The egocentric network is defined by ego, but it does not include ego (although often the drawing of the network includes ego, as an orienting point). The lines in the network are the ties among the alters, and the alters and their ties represent ego's immediate social environment. An early example of egocentric network analysis is Elizabeth Bott's (1957) study of the relationship between the conjugal roles adopted by a married couple and the extent to which the alters of the couple are connected with one another. The egocentric network approach has also been used extensively in the study of personal networks (e.g., Wellman et al. 1988), social support (e.g., Song et al. 2011), social capital (e.g., Lin 2001), and community (e.g., Wellman 1979, 1999; Wellman and Wortley 1990). It is used in social and community psychology, gerontology, addiction research, and criminology, where it has been found that the structure and composition of an individual's personal network affect his or her probability of committing a crime (Carrington 2011). It is applied clinically as network therapy, in which the client's personal network is therapeutically adjusted.

In contrast, in sociocentric, or whole-network research, no individual is focal. Rather, a population of actors is defined by some inclusion criteria, and the actors and the ties among them constitute the network. It is not always straightforward to specify the inclusion criteria and to include all actors, and their ties, who fulfill the criteria. Examples of sociocentric network analyses include network studies of industrial market structures, which include all corporations or other business units involved in a particular market, or in a set of related markets, or in the entire economy of a nation (e.g., Carrington 1981; Burt 1983), network studies of economic and/or political elites that include all members of the elite (e.g., Soref and Zeitlin 1987) and/or all the corporations through which elites exert power (e.g., Carroll 1986), network studies of the social organization of science that include all scientists working in a given topic area or sub-discipline (e.g., Breiger 1976), network studies of small group dynamics that include all members of the small group (e.g., Homans 1950:chapters 3, 6), network analyses of interorganizational relations among all organizations involved in a given organizational field (e.g., Knoke and Rogers 1979), and so on. Sometimes it is not feasible to include all members of a theoretical population, and sampling must be used (e.g., Frank 2011), but the approach is still sociocentric and not focused on particular egos. In many fields of network research, and even in single studies, both the egocentric and sociocentric approaches are used. For example, Carlo Morselli (2005) has used the egocentric personal network approach to study the careers and contacts of selected organized crime figures, and he has also used the sociocentric approach to study the structures of organized-crime groups (Morselli 2009). Similarly, the network study of diffusion (of ideas or of diseases) uses both approaches: attributes of the personal (egocentric) network predict the probability of ego's being infected or influenced; attributes of the whole network predict the parameters of the transmission of the disease or information through the population (Valente 1995).

Social Cohesion: Density, Connectivity, Embeddedness, Structural Holes, and Bridging

One of the most fundamental attributes of the social group is its cohesion. For the present purposes, a vague definition of social cohesion will suffice, as the "glue" or bond that holds the group together. Social cohesion has been studied extensively using social network research, and several network concepts have been used to represent social cohesion; all assume that the tie or ties between two actors are the basic elements of the social bond, and that measuring or modeling social cohesion involves summarizing the cohesive nature of the ties in the network.

Density. The simplest – and least "structural" – conceptualization of cohesion in a social network is the overall density of ties in the network, defined as the ratio of the number of actual lines to the maximum number of possible lines. In general, the more lines there are – that is, the more pairs of actors that are directly tied – the greater the cohesion in the network. The density of ties in real-life networks tends to decrease as the network becomes larger, as the number of theoretically possible ties increases with the square of the number of actors, but there are practical limits on how many actual ties an actor can maintain. Mayhew and Levinger (1976) show that constraints on the time and energy available for tie formation and maintenance limit the number of most types of ties that each human being can have, implying a decrease in density as the number of others in the network increases. Overall density of ties has been used to measure social cohesion or its equivalent for the type of ties studied, in research in substantive areas such as small group dynamics (Homans 1950; Sanders and Nauta 2004), interlocking directorates (Burris 2005), industrial organization (Carrington 1981), and scientific communities (Crane 1972). If the ties in a network represent flow, or the potential flow, of information, disease, and so on, then a denser network predicts increased flow (Valente 1995).

Density is measured in the same way for ego networks, omitting the focal actor (ego) and its ties. For ego networks, the density of ties represents the cohesion of ego's immediate social environment. Elizabeth Bott (1957) found that conjugal roles varied according to how "close-knit" the couple's social network was: that is, how dense the ties among their alters were (although Bott did not use the term "density" or measure it quantitatively). Barry Wellman's (1979, 1999; Wellman et al. 1988) research on community solidarity or cohesion analyzed the personal networks of a sample of residents of a neighborhood in Toronto. He found that the personal networks were relatively sparse (i.e., low in density) and that their density varied with the proportion of kin in the network, among other things.

Mark Granovetter's (1973, 1974) famous theory of "the strength of weak ties" proposes that ties among alters who are connected to ego by strong ties – such as close family members and close friends – tend to be more dense than weak ties, such as acquaintanceship, colleagueship, neighbor, and so on. One's close family and friends tend to be tied directly to one another, whereas one's acquaintances, colleagues, neighbors, and so on, are less likely to be directly connected to one another. In network terms, strong ties tend toward transitive closure and weak ties tend to be more open. Furthermore, following the principle of homophily (McPherson et al. 2001) strongly tied alters are more likely to be similar to one another and to ego in various ways, whereas weakly tied alters tend to be more heterogeneous. The important implication of this distinction is that it is the alters to whom one is weakly tied who are more likely to be sources of new information, ideas, attitudes, and so on, since the information held by one's strongly tied alters tends to overlap substantially with one's own.

Connectivity and Cohesive Subgroups. Ties are generally not distributed uniformly over a network. Therefore, the overall density of ties in the network – like the overall mean of a quantitative variable – may not reveal much about cohesion in the network. A conceptualization of cohesion that is more sensitive to the structure, and not just the number of ties in the network, is based on the idea of connectivity. A line is a direct connection between two nodes, but nodes are also indirectly connected by paths consisting of lines passing through intermediary nodes. For example, in Figure 2.3b, there is a (shortest) path of length 2 between nodes e and g, and in Figure 2.3c, we see paths of length 2 between i and j, j and k, and so on. Indirect connections (paths) between nodes can also contribute to social cohesion. In graph theory, a graph is called *connected* if all the nodes are directly or indirectly connected to one another. In Figure 2.3, only graph 2.3c is connected. In a *disconnected* graph, each (internally connected) part is called a component. In each of Figures 2.3a, 2.3b, and 2.3d, there are two components. Evidently, a connected network will have more cohesion than a disconnected network: In fact, a disconnected network will, in most cases, suffer from a fundamental lack of cohesion, because, by definition, there are no bonds whatsoever between its components. Thus, a simple characterization of the social cohesion in a network is whether it is connected, and – if it is disconnected – a basic operation on the network is to identify its connected components.

Apart from determining whether a network is connected, and identifying connected components of disconnected networks, the main application of the concept of network connectivity to social cohesion has been in the identification of cohesive subgroups within connected networks or their components. Cohesive subgroups are subsets of nodes that are in some sense more interconnected, directly or indirectly, than nodes outside the subgroup.[3] The "ideal" cohesive subgroup is one in which all

---

[3] Cohesive subgroups have been conceptualized in more ways than just their connectivity: Many different conceptualizations, measures, and procedures have been developed to capture and measure them (see, e.g., Wasserman and Faust 1994: chapter 7).

(a)

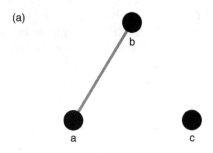

(b)

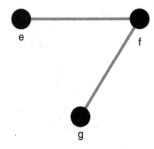

(c)

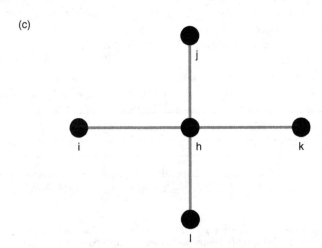

Figure 2.3. Example graphs showing connectivity

(d)

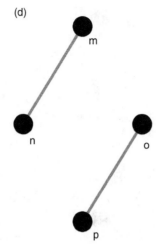

Figure 2.3. (*Continued*)

the nodes are directly tied (i.e., adjacent) to one another, which is the definition of a clique in graph theory. In Figure 2.1, John, Harry, and Dick form a clique. Since this too-restrictive criterion is rarely satisfied in real-life cohesive subgroups, the definition has been relaxed in various ways: For example, an n-clique is a subset of nodes in which every node is connected to every other node by a path consisting of no more than n lines (or, equivalently, by a path passing through no more than n − 1 intermediate nodes).

Moody and White (2003) argue that cohesiveness in a subgroup depends not on path lengths between nodes but on the vulnerability of the subgroup to becoming disconnected. This can be measured by the minimum number of nodes that must be removed to disconnect the subgroup. For example, the graph in Figure 2.4b is more cohesive, using Moody and White's definition, than the graph in Figure 2.4a, because it would require the removal of 2 nodes (e.g., nodes a and c) to disconnect graph 2.4b, whereas removing only 1 node (g) would disconnect graph 2.4a. In graph-theoretic terminology, Figure 2.4a is 1-connected and Figure 2.4b is 2-connected. However, Figure 2.4a has a higher density than Figure 2.4b, suggesting the superiority of a connectivity-based conceptualization of cohesiveness.

Cohesive subgroups in networks have been used to represent many sociological and social psychological concepts, such as cliques, social circles, gangs, factions, and teams (Knoke and Yang 2008), employed in the study of homophily, attitude formation, social support, adolescent peer groups, schoolrooms, prisons, workplaces, the family,

(a)

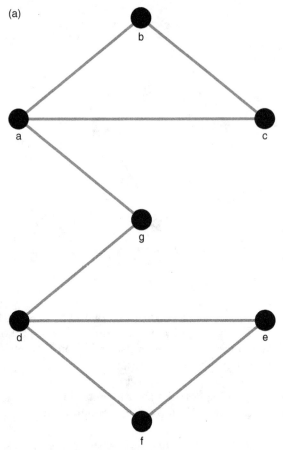

Figure 2.4. Example graphs for k-connectivity calculations: (a) 1-connected graph; (b) 2-connected graph

kinship groups, criminal and terrorist groups, military organization, sports organization, industrial organization, elites, the organization of science and scientists, and the transmission of information and of diseases.

Embeddedness. Membership in a cohesive subgroup also implies constraint: The more cohesive one's alters are, the more similar they are likely to be in attitudes, beliefs, and so on, and the more they are able to coordinate their efforts to exert influence on one's own behavior, attitudes, access to information, and so on. The concept of embeddedness

(b)

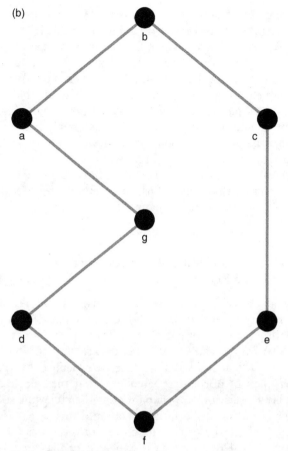

Figure 2.4. (*Continued*)

(Granovetter 1985, 1992) draws attention to the constraints on an actor that are due to its position in a social network. This concept has been used in the study of economic organization, social stratification, social support, sociology of health, and criminal networks (Moody and White 2003:111–12).

Structural Holes, Bridging, Betweenness, and Brokerage. Identifying cohesive subgroups of nodes in a network also directs attention to the areas of relatively sparse ties between those subgroups. These areas are called "structural holes" (Burt 1992) and are important as opportunity structures in social entrepreneurship (Thornton 1999). An actor that is positioned so as to bridge a structural hole is non-redundant;

has high betweenness (Shaw 1954; Freeman 1977) and superior access to network-based resources, or social capital (Lin 2001:71); and may serve as a broker or mediator between or among cohesive subgroups (Marsden 1982, 1983; Gould and Fernandez 1989). For example, in Figure 2.4a, actor g bridges the structural hole between the two cohesive subgroups, so all exchanges of information or other valuables between the two groups must pass through g. That is not the case in Figure 2.4b. The concept of structural holes in networks has mainly been employed in research on organizational behavior (reviewed in Burt 2000). The concepts of bridging and brokerage in networks have also been used in research on personal networks (Blok 1974; Boissevain 1974), animal networks (Williams and Lusseau 2006), community elites (Galaskiewicz and Krohn 1984; Knoke and Laumann 1982), and criminal networks (Morselli 2005, 2009).

Social Statuses and Roles: Block Modeling, or Positional and Role Analysis

The term "social status" is used here in the sense of a discrete position in the social structure, not in its other common sense, of an actor's place in a continuous scale of social stratification. Examples of social statuses in modern American social structure are "father," "police offi-cer," "friend," and "leader." Social statuses are defined by the social roles, or repertoires of normative behaviors, that their occupants are expected to play in relation to occupants of other relevant social sta-tuses. A father is necessarily a father of a child; his status is defined in terms of the biological role that he played in the conception of the child and/or the social role that he is expected to play in relation to the child in the family, kinship, and other relevant social subsystems. The status of father also implies expected behaviors toward the child's mother, schoolteachers, playmates, and so on – toward all the members of statuses that constitute the role-set of the status of father in this society. Similarly, the occupational and legal status "police officer" is defined by expected behaviors toward such other relevant statuses as other police officers, including specific others such as the immediate superior, the "partner," suspected or apprehended lawbreakers, persons in need of emergency help, witnesses to crimes, apparently law-abiding citizens, and so on. Similarly, "friend," "neighbor," "grandparent," and "student" are all defined by normative relationships with occupants of other relevant statuses. Thus, social structure can be conceptualized as a system of interlocking social statuses and their associated behavioral roles (Linton 1936; Park 1955).

Social network models of social statuses and roles began with the formal modeling in anthropology of systems of kinship and were generalized to non-kin relations by Nadel (1957) and White and his associates (Lorrain and White 1971; White et al. 1976; Boorman and White 1976). That development was discussed earlier under the heading "Social Structure as a Network of Human Relations." Social statuses or positions and social roles are modeled in social network analysis by positional and role analysis, also known as *blockmodeling*. A blockmodel of a social network is a model of the system of positions and roles. It consists of an image graph, in which each position is represented by a single point and the characteristic relations among the positions are represented by lines, and a mapping of the actors in the original social network into the positions in the model, that is, an assignment of each actor to a position in the model. All the actors in a given status or position – for example, all fathers, all police officers, all leaders, all friends – are, in terms of the social structure, equivalent.

It is rare that a researcher can posit a system of positions and roles a priori. The common approach to blockmodeling is inductive: Some criterion of equivalence and some clustering procedure are applied to the social network data to find subsets of equivalent or close-to-equivalent actors that constitute the points in the image graph; then the characteristic patterns of ties between occupants of positions are somehow summarized to produce the lines in the image graph. The important distinction between clustering actors in clique analysis (discussed under "Social Cohesion" earlier) and in blockmodel analysis is that in the former actors are clustered if they are tied to one another, but in the latter they are clustered if they are tied in similar ways to other actors. In principle, blockmodeling includes a second step, called role analysis – often, however, omitted in empirical research – which is the algebraic analysis of relationships among social roles that give rise to compound roles: for example, "sister of mother of... [i.e., aunt of...]," "friend of friend of ...," or "subordinate of the same manager as...."[4]

Blockmodeling, or positional analysis, has been used to model status and role structures in many areas of research: for example, the study of kinship (White 1963b; Boyd 1969), community interorganizational relations (Knoke and Rogers 1979; Knoke and Wood 1981; Knoke 1983; Galaskiewicz and Krohn 1984), industrial market organization (Burt 1983, 1992), corporate power and economic elites (Scott 1986), the world system (Snyder and Kick 1979; Alderson and Beckfield 2004; Kick et al. 2011), social mobility (Breiger 1981, 1982), the social organization

---

[4] A complete discussion of the theory and practice of blockmodeling can be found in Wasserman and Faust (1994); recent developments and extensions are in Doreian et al. (2005).

of science (Breiger 1976; Burt and Doreian 1982), adoption of innovations (Anderson and Jay 1985; Burt 1987; Galaskiewicz and Burt 1991), social influence (Friedkin 1984; Mizruchi 1989, 1990), social cognition (Pattison 1994), and animal social structure (Pearl and Schulman 1983; Flack et al. 2006).

Importance: Centrality

The importance of an actor by virtue of its location in a network is generally conceptualized in social network analysis as the actor's centrality. Importance, and hence centrality, can mean many different things, depending on the context, or the type of relation(s) in the network: for example, power, prestige,[5] popularity, dominance, prominence, or visibility. Social network analysis is often used to measure the relative importance or centrality of each actor in a network, to identify the most important or central actors, and to identify the correlates of importance, or centrality. While (actor) centrality is an attribute of an individual actor, centralization, or graph centrality, refers to the degree to which a network has central actors. Due to limitations of space, research on centralization is not discussed here.

The relative centrality of actors in a network is occasionally obvious from visual inspection of the graph drawing, especially if the network is small and highly centralized: for example, the "star" configuration in Figure 2.3c. This is not usually the case, however, especially in larger networks, and many definitions and measures of centrality have been proposed (see, e.g., Wasserman and Faust 1994: chapter 5, for a review). The most widely used definitions of centrality are the three reviewed in Freeman's (1979) seminal paper – degree, closeness, and betweenness centrality – and eigenvector centrality (Bonacich 1972, 1987).

Degree centrality is simply a normalized measure of the number of other actors to which the focal actor is directly tied, or adjacent: in graph-theoretical terminology, the degree of the point. Degree centrality has been used to study influence, leadership, efficiency, personal satisfaction and information flow in small task-oriented groups (e.g., Bavelas 1948, 1950; Jennings 1937; Moreno 1934), personal communities (Wellman 1979), community power structures (Wheeldon 1969; Laumann and Pappi 1976), intraorganizational power and influence (Krackhardt and Brass 1994:210–211), interorganizational power and influence (Mizruchi and Galaskiewicz 1994:239), dominance in primate networks (Sade and Dow 1994:156–157), and so on.

---

[5] "Prestige" is also used in a particular sense based only on ties received, in reference to directed graphs; see Wasserman and Faust (1994: 174–75).

Closeness centrality measures how "close" an actor is to all other actors in the network. Closeness is the inverse of distance, which is the number of lines in the shortest path between a pair of points: For example, two points that are directly tied have a distance of 1; a pair separated by one intermediary point (and therefore 2 lines) has a distance of 2, and so on. An actor with high closeness centrality is connected to other actors in the network by relatively short paths. Closeness centrality has been used especially in the study of power and influence in organizations that is related to the control of information or communication networks (e.g., Leavitt 1951; Brass and Burkhardt 1993; Krackhardt and Brass 1994:210–11) and to power and influence in trade networks (Hage and Harary 1983:35).

Betweenness centrality measures the extent to which an actor is "between" other actors in the network, that is, the number of shortest paths between pairs of other actors on which the focal actor is located. Some applications of betweenness centrality were discussed previously in the context of social capital and bridging between cohesive subgroups, under the title "Structural Holes, Bridging, Betweenness and Brokerage." Apart from providing opportunities for brokerage, betweenness centrality also confers upon its possessor access via multiple paths and from multiple sources to resources such as information. Thus, betweenness centrality has been used in research on organizational power, influence, and information control (e.g., Krackhardt 1990).

Finally, eigenvector centrality measures the extent to which an actor is tied to other actors that are central, using the same definition (Bonacich 1972, 1987). Due to its recursive nature, this definition is less easy to operationalize, but also more sensitive to global network structure, than the other definitions. As its alternative name, power centrality, suggests, it is believed to be particularly appropriate for measuring power (or prestige or prominence) in networks (Knoke and Burt 1983) and has been used particularly in analyzing power in organizational settings (Friedkin 1993) and corporate power in networks of interlocking directorates (Mizruchi and Galaskiewic 1994:239; Scott 2000:96–98).

Conclusion

In this chapter, I have tried to give a sense of the origins and development of social network analysis, and a brief overview of the range of social network research, grouped within what seem to me to be the most frequently referenced conceptual themes in social network analysis: social cohesion, social status and role, and centrality. This survey has necessarily been both abbreviated and selective: There are a large number of other concepts and operationalizations in social network analysis, which are reviewed in detail by Wasserman and Faust (1994). For a more comprehensive review of social network research in different subject areas, the reader is referred to the handbook by Scott and Carrington (2011).

Social network analysis originated in the early twentieth century with the application of the sociometric method developed by Moreno (1934) to the sociological and anthropological theory of social structure as a web of human relations (Simmel [1922] 1955; Radcliffe-Brown 1940, 1957). By the 1970s, social network analysis had become a recognizable paradigm

> that guides the selection of the social behavior data that are studied, influences the way these data are organized for analysis, and specifies the kinds of questions addressed. (Leinhardt 1977: xiii)

Social network analysis has a clearly defined and generally accepted theoretical and conceptual framework and an even more clearly defined and accepted methodology. Social network analysis is also a scientific community, or invisible college, with a recognizable intellectual lineage and clusters of researchers based in several centers and loosely linked by cross-cutting collaborations and intercitations. It is also a scientific institution, with dedicated journals (*Social Networks, Journal of Social Structure*, and *Connections*), textbooks and handbooks (e.g., Degenne and Forsé [1994] 1999; Wasserman and Faust 1994; Scott 2000; Knoke and Yang 2008), dedicated computer software (see, e.g., Huisman and van Duijn 2005, 2011), and an association (the International Network for Social Network Analysis; see http://www.insna.org/).

Although a well-defined paradigm, social network analysis is firmly embedded within traditional disciplines such as social psychology, social anthropology, communication science, organizational science, and, especially, sociology, as attested to by the many citations in this chapter to social network research published in the central sociological journals such as the *American Journal of Sociology* and the *American Sociological Review*. Since its "take-off" in the 1970s, the volume of published research in social networks has grown exponentially (Knoke and Yang 2008:1–2), while the number of subject areas in which it is being employed has experienced "almost linear" growth, from a handful to almost 60 by the year 1999 (Freeman 2004:5). Neither the volume of published research nor the expansion of social network analysis into diverse subject areas shows any sign of leveling off.

The brief account in this chapter may have left the impression that the major theoretical and methodological developments in social network analysis had been completed by the mid-twentieth century. Nothing could be further from the truth. Major developments occurred in the later twentieth century, and are still occurring – including the increasing use and formalization of statistical theory and methods in a field that was previously largely non-stochastic, the introduction of theory and methods for change over time in networks, the development of qualitative and mixed methods (Hollstein 2011; Hollstein, this volume), and the so-called "invasion of the physicists" (Bonacich 2004; Freeman 2011; Scott 2011). Ironically, these last two developments – the development of qualitative and mixed methods and the increasing contributions by physicists – represent for social network analysis a return to its roots. Much of the foundational work in social network analysis was done by ethnographers associated with the Manchester School, doing field work and using qualitative and mixed methods (e.g., Bott 1957; Mitchell 1969a), and the man who is often credited with the creation of modern social network analysis – Harrison White – was trained as a theoretical physicist (Freeman 2004).

References

Alderson, Arthur S. and Jason Beckfield. 2004. "Power and position in the world city system." *American Journal of Sociology* 109:811–51.

Anderson, James G. and Stephen J. Jay. 1985. "Computers and clinical judgment: The role of physician networks." *Social Science and Medicine* 20:969–79.

Barabási, Albert-László. 2002. *Linked: The New Science of Networks*. Cambridge, MA: Perseus.

Barnes, John A. 1954 "Class and committees in a Norwegian island parish." *Human Relations* 7:39–58.

Bavelas, Alexander. 1948. "A mathematical model for group structure." *Human Organization* 7:16–30.

––––––.1950. "Communication patterns in talk-oriented groups." *Journal of the Acoustical Society of America* 22:271–82.

Berkowitz, Stephen D. 1982. *An Introduction to Structural Analysis*. Toronto: Butterworths.

Blok, Anton. 1974. *The Mafia of a Sicilian Village, 1860–1960*. New York: Harper and Row.

Boissevain, Jeremy. 1974. *Friends of Friends: Networks, Manipulators, and Coalitions*. Oxford: Basil Blackwell.

Bonacich, Philip. 1972. "Factoring and weighting approaches to status scores and clique identification." *Journal of Mathematical Sociology* 2:113–20.

––––––. 1987. "Power and centrality: A family of measures." *American Journal of Sociology* 92:1170–82.

––––––.2004. "The invasion of the physicists." *Social Networks* 26:285–88.

Boorman, Scott A. and Harrison C. White. 1976 "Social structure from multiple networks II: Role structures." *American Journal of Sociology* 81:1384–1446.

Bott, Elizabeth. 1957. *Family and Social Networks*. London: Tavistock.

Boyd, John P. 1969 "The algebra of group kinship." *Journal of Mathematical Psychology* 6:139–67.

Brandes, Ulrik and Thomas Erlebach, eds. *Network Analysis: Methodological Foundations*. Berlin: Springer.

Brass, Daniel J. and Marlene E. Burkhardt. 1993 "Potential power and power use: An investigation of structure and behavior." *Academy of Management Journal* 36:441–70.

Breiger, Ronald L. 1976. Career attributes and network structure: A block-model study of a biomedical research specialty." *American Sociological Review* 41:117–35.

———. 1981 "The social class structure of occupational mobility." *American Journal of Sociology* 87:578–611.

———. 1982 "A structural analysis of occupational mobility." Pp. 17–32 in *Social Structure and Network Analysis*, edited by P. V. Marsden and N. Lin. Beverly Hills, CA: Sage.

Burris, Val. 2005. "Interlocking directorates and political cohesion among corporate elites." *American Journal of Sociology* 111:249–83.

Burt, Ronald S. 1982. *Toward a Structural Theory of Action*. New York: Academic Press.

———. 1983. *Corporate Profits and Cooptation*. New York: Academic Press.

———. 1987. "Social contagion and innovation: Cohesion versus structural equivalence." *American Journal of Sociology* 92:1287–1335.

———. 1992. *Structural Holes: The Social Structure of Competition*. Cambridge, MA: Harvard University Press.

———. 2000. "The network structure of social capital." *Research in Organizational Behavior* 22:345–423.

Burt, Ronald S. and Patrick Doreian. 1982. "Testing a structural model of perception: Conformity and deviance with respect to journal norms in elite sociological methodology." *Quality and Quantity* 16:109–50.

Burt, Ronald S. and Michael J. Minor, eds. 1983. *Applied Network Analysis*. Beverly Hills, CA: Sage.

Carrington, Peter J. 1981. *Horizontal Co-optation through Corporate Interlocks*. Doctoral dissertation, University of Toronto.

———. 2011. "Crime and social network analysis." Pp. 236–55 in *The SAGE Handbook of Social Network Analysis*, edited by J. Scott and P. J. Carrington. London: Sage.

Carrington, Peter J., John Scott, and Stanley Wasserman, eds. 2005. *Models and Methods in Social Network Analysis*. Cambridge: Cambridge University Press.

Carroll, William K. 1986. *Corporate Power and Canadian Capitalism*. Vancouver: University of British Columbia Press.

Crane, Diana. 1972. *Invisible Colleges*. Chicago: University of Chicago Press.

Davis, Allison, Burleigh B. Gardner, and Mary R. Gardner. 1941. *Deep South*. Chicago: University of Chicago Press.

Davis, James A. 1963. "Structural balance, mechanical solidarity and interpersonal relations." *American Journal of Sociology* 68:444–62.

De Nooy, Wouter, Andrej Mrvar, and Vladimir Batagelj. 2005. *Exploratory Social Network Analysis with Pajek*. Cambridge: Cambridge University Press.

Degenne, Alain and Michel Forsé. ([1994] 1999). *Introducing Social Networks*. London: Sage. Originally published as *Les réseaux sociaux. Une approche structurale en sociologie*. Paris: Armand Colin.

Dodd, Stuart C. 1940a. "The interrelation matrix." *Sociometry* 3:91–101.

———. 1940b. "Analyses of the interrelation matrix by its surface and structure." *Sociometry* 3:133–43.

Doreian, Patrick, Vladimir Batagelj, and Anuška Ferligoj. 2005. *Generalized Blockmodeling*. Cambridge: Cambridge University Press.

Fararo, Thomas J. and Morris H. Sunshine. 1964. *A Study of a Biased Friendship Net*. Syracuse, NY: Syracuse University Youth Development Center.

Flack, Jessica C., Michelle Girvan, Frans B.M. de Waal, and David C. Krakauer. 2006. "Policing stabilizes construction of social niches in primates." *Nature* 439:426–29.

Flament, C. 1963. *Applications of Graph Theory to Group Structure*. Englewood Cliffs, NJ: Prentice-Hall.

Foster, Caxton C., Anatol Rapoport, and Carol J. Orwant. 1963. "A study of a large sociogram II. Elimination of free parameters." *Behavioral Science* 8:56–65.

Frank, Ove. 2011. "Survey sampling in networks." Pp. 389–403 in *The SAGE Handbook of Social Network Analysis*, edited by J. Scott and P. J. Carrington. London: Sage.

Freeman, Linton C. 1977. "A set of measures of centrality based on betweenness." *Sociometry* 40:35–41.

———. 1979. "Centrality in social networks: I. Conceptual clarification." *Social Networks* 1: 215–39.

———. 2004. *The Development of Social Network Analysis*. Vancouver: Empirical Press.

———. 2011. "The development of social network analysis – With an emphasis on recent events." Pp. 26–39 in *The SAGE Handbook of Social Network Analysis*, edited by J. Scott and P. J. Carrington. London: Sage.

Friedkin, Noah E. 1984. "Structural cohesion and equivalence explanations of social homogeneity." *Sociological Methods and Research* 12:235–61.

———. 1993. "Structural bases of interpersonal influence in groups: A longitudinal case study." *American Sociological Review* 58:861–72.

Galaskiewicz, Joseph and Ronald S. Burt. 1991. "Interorganization contagion in corporate philanthropy." *Administrative Science Quarterly* 36:88–105.

Galaskiewicz, Joseph and Karl R. Krohn. 1984. "Positions, roles, and dependencies in a community interorganizational system." *Sociological Quarterly* 25:527–50.

Gould, Roger V. and Roberto M. Fernandez. 1989. "Structures of mediation: A formal approach to brokerage in transaction networks." *Sociological Methodology* 19:89–126.

Granovetter, Mark. 1973. "The strength of weak ties." *American Journal of Sociology* 78:1360–80.

———. 1974. *Getting a Job*. Cambridge, MA: Harvard University Press.

————. 1985. "Economic action and social structure: The problem of embed-dedness." *American Journal of Sociology* 91:481–510.

————. 1992. "Problems of explanation in economic sociology." Pp. 25–56 in *Networks and Organizations: Structure, Form, and Action*, edited by N. Nohria and R. G. Eccles. Boston: Harvard Business School Press.

Hage, Per and Frank Harary. 1983. *Structural Models in Anthropology.* Cambridge: Cambridge University Press.

Harary, Frank. 1969. *Graph Theory.* Reading, MA: Addison-Wesley.

Harary, Frank, Robert Z. Norman, and Dorwin Cartwright. 1965. *Structural Models: An Introduction to the Theory of Directed Graphs.* New York: Wiley.

Hollstein, Betina. 2011. "Qualitative approaches." Pp. 404–16 in *The SAGE Handbook of Social Network Analysis*, edited by J. Scott and P. J. Carrington. London: Sage.

Homans, George C. 1950. *The Human Group.* New York: Harcourt, Brace.

Huisman, Mark and Marijtje van Duijn. 2005. "Software for social net-work analysis." Pp. 270–316 in *Models and Methods in Social Network Analysis*, edited by P. J. Carrington, J. Scott, and S. Wasserman. Cambridge: Cambridge University Press.

————. 2011. "A reader's guide to SNA software." Pp. 578–600 in *The SAGE Handbook of Social Network Analysis*, edited by J. Scott and P. J. Carrington. London: Sage.

INSNA. 2010. "Member listed software." Website of the International Network for Social Network Analysis. Retrieved March 2, 2010 (http://www.insna.org/software/index.html).

Jennings, Helen. 1937. "Structures of leadership – Development and sphere of influence." *Sociometry* 1:99–143.

Kick, Edward, Laura A. McKinney, Steve McDonald, and Andrew Jorgenson. 2011. "A multiple-network analysis of the world system of nations, 1995–1999." Pp. 311–27 in *The SAGE Handbook of Social Network Analysis*, edited by J. Scott and P. J. Carrington. London: Sage.

Knoke, David. 1983. "Organization sponsorship and influence reputation of social influence associations." *Social Forces* 61:1065–87.

Knoke, David and Ronald S. Burt. 1983. "Prominence." Pp. 195–222 in *Applied Network Analysis*, edited by R. S. Burt and M. J. Minor. Beverly Hills, CA: Sage.

Knoke, David and James H. Kuklinski. 1982. *Network Analysis.* Beverly Hills, CA: Sage.

Knoke, David and Edward O. Laumann. 1982. "The social organization of national policy domains." Pp. 255–70 in *Social Structure and Network Analysis*, edited by P. V. Marsden and N. Lin. Beverly Hills, CA: Sage.

Knoke, David and David L. Rogers. 1979. "A blockmodel analysis of interorga-nizational networks." *Sociology and Social Research* 64:28–52.

Knoke, David and James R. Wood. 1981. *Organized for Action.* New Brunswick, NJ: Rutgers University Press.

Knoke, David and Song Yang. 2008. *Network analysis.* 2nd ed. Beverly Hills, CA: Sage.

Krackhardt, David. 1990. "Assessing the political landscape: structure, cognition, and power in organizations." *Administrative Science Quarterly* 35:342–69.

Krackhardt, David, and Daniel J. Brass. 1994. "Intraorganizational networks: The micro side." Pp. 207–29 in *Advances in Social Network Analysis*, edited by S. Wasserman and J. Galaskiewicz. Thousand Oaks, CA: Sage.

Krempel, Lothar. 2005. *Visualisierung komplexer Strukturen*. Frankfurt: Campus Verlag.

———. 2011. "Network visualization." Pp. 558–77 in *The SAGE Handbook of Social Network Analysis*, edited by J. Scott and P. J. Carrington. London: Sage.

Laumann, Edward O. and Franz Pappi. 1976. *Networks of Collective Action: A Perspective on Community Influence Systems*. New York: Academic Press.

Leavitt, Harold J. 1951. "Some effects of communication patterns on group performance." *Journal of Abnormal and Social Psychology* 46:38–50.

Leinhardt, Samuel, ed. 1977. *Social Networks: A Developing Paradigm*. New York: Academic Press.

Lévi-Strauss, Claude. [1949] 1969. *The Elementary Structures of Kinship*. Reprint. Rodney Needham, ed. Boston: Beacon Press. Originally published as *Les Structures élémentaires de la Parenté*. Paris: Mouton, 1949.

Lin, Nan. 2001. *Social Capital*. Cambridge: Cambridge University Press.

Linton, Ralph. 1936. *The Study of Man*. New York: Appleton-Century-Crofts.

Lorrain, Francois P. and Harrison C. White. 1971. "Structural equivalence of individuals in social networks." *Journal of Mathematical Sociology* 1:49–80.

Marineau, René F. 1989. *Jacob Levy Moreno, 1889–1974: Father of Psychodrama, Sociometry, and Group Psychotherapy*. London: Routledge.

Marsden, Peter V. 1982 "Brokerage behavior in restricted exchange networks." Pp. 201–18 in *Social Structure and Network Analysis*, edited by P. V. Marsden and N. Lin. Beverly Hills, CA: Sage.

———. 1983. "Restricted access in networks and models of power." *American Journal of Sociology* 88:686–717.

Marsden, Peter V., and Nan Lin, eds. 1982. *Social Structure and Network Analysis*. Beverly Hills, CA: Sage.

Mayhew, Bruce H. and Roger L. Levinger. 1976. "Size and the density of interaction in human aggregates." *American Journal of Sociology* 82:86–110.

McPherson, Miller, Lynn Smith-Lovin and James M. Cook. 2001. "Birds of a feather: Homophily in social networks." *Annual Review of Sociology* 27:415–44.

Mitchell, J. Clyde, ed. 1969a. *Social networks in urban situations*. Manchester: Manchester University Press.

———. 1969b. "The concept and use of social networks." Pp. 1–50 in *Social Networks in Urban Situations*, edited by J. C. Mitchell. Manchester: Manchester University Press.

Mizruchi, Mark S. 1989. "Similarity of political behavior among large American corporations." *American Journal of Sociology* 95:401–24.

———. 1990. "Cohesion, structural equivalence, and similarity of behavior: An approach to the study of corporate political power." *Sociological Theory* 8:16–32.

Mizruchi, Mark S. and Joseph Galaskiewicz. 1994. "Networks of interorganizational relations." Pp. 230–53 in *Advances in Social Network Analysis*, edited by S. Wasserman and J. Galaskiewicz. Thousand Oaks, CA: Sage.

Moody, James and Douglas R. White. 2003. "Structural cohesion and embeddedness: A hierarchical concept of social groups." *American Sociological Review* 68:103–27.

Moreno, Jacob L. 1932. *Application of the Group Method to Classification.* New York: National Committee on Prisons and Prison Labor.

———. 1937a. "Sociometry in relation to other social sciences." *Sociometry* 1: 206–19.

———. 1937b. "Editorial foreword." *Sociometry* 1:5–7.

———. 1953. *Who Shall Survive?* Beacon, NY: Beacon Press.

Morselli, Carlo. 2005. *Contacts, Opportunities, and Criminal Enterprise.* Toronto: University of Toronto Press.

———. 2009. *Inside Criminal Networks.* New York: Springer.

Mullins, Nicholas C. 1973 *Theories and Theory Groups in Contemporary American Sociology.* New York: Harper & Row.

Nadel, S. F. 1957. *The Theory of Social Structure.* London: Cohen & West.

Park, Robert E. 1955. *Society.* New York: Free Press.

Pattison, Philippa. 1993. *Algebraic Models for Social Networks.* Cambridge: Cambridge University Press.

———. 1994. "Social cognition in context: Some applications of social network analysis." Pp. 79–109 in *Advances in Social Network Analysis*, edited by S. Wasserman and J. Galaskiewicz. Thousand Oaks, CA: Sage.

Pearl, Mary C. and Steven R. Schulman. 1983. "Techniques for the analysis of social structure in animal societies." *Advances in the Study of Behavior* 13:107–46.

Radcliffe-Brown, Alfred R. 1940. "On social structure." *Journal of the Royal Anthropological Institute of Great Britain and Ireland* 70:1–12.

———. 1957. *A Natural Science of Society.* Chicago: University of Chicago Press.

Rapoport, Anatol and William J. Horvath. 1961. "A study of a large sociogram." *Behavioral Science* 6:279–91.

Robins, Garry. 2011. "Exponential random graph models for social networks." Pp. 484–500 in *Models and Methods in Social Network Analysis*, edited by J. Scott and P. J. Carrington. Cambridge: Cambridge University Press.

Roethlisberger, Fritz J. and William J. Dickson. 1939. *Management and the Worker.* Cambridge, MA: Harvard University Press.

Sade, Donald S. and Malcolm M. Dow. 1994. "Primate social networks." In *Advances in Social Network Analysis*, edited by S. Wasserman and J. Galaskiewicz. Thousand Oaks, CA: Sage.

Sanders, Karin and Aukje Nauta. 2004. "Social cohesiveness and absenteeism: the relationship between characteristics of employees and short-term absenteeism within an organization." *Small Group Research* 35:724–41.

Scott, John. 1986. *Capitalist Property and Financial Power.* Brighton, UK: Wheatsheaf.

———. 2000. *Social Network Analysis: A Handbook.* 2nd ed. London: Sage.

———. 2011. "Social physics and social networks." Pp. 55–66 in *The SAGE Handbook of Social Network Analysis*, edited by J. Scott and P. J. Carrington. London: Sage.

Scott, John and Peter J. Carrington, eds. 2011. *The SAGE Handbook of Social Network Analysis.* London: Sage.

Shaw, Marvin E. 1954 "Group structure and the behavior of individuals in small groups." *Journal of Psychology* 38:139–49.

Simmel, Georg. [1922] 1955. "The web of group affiliations." Pp. 125–95 in *Georg Simmel, Conflict and the Web of Group Affiliations*, edited by K. H. Wolff and R. Bendix. Reprint. New York: Free Press. Originally published as "Die Kreuzung sozialer Kreise." In Georg Simmel, *Soziologie.* Munich: Duncker & Humblot, 1922.

Snijders, Tom A. B. 2005. "Models for longitudinal network data." Pp. 215–47 in *Models and Methods in Social Network Analysis*, edited by P. J. Carrington, J. Scott, and S. Wasserman. Cambridge: Cambridge University Press.

———. 2011. "Network dynamics." Pp. 501–13 in *The SAGE Handbook of Social Network Analysis*, edited by J. Scott and P. J. Carrington. London: Sage.

Snyder, David and Edward L. Kick. 1979. "Structural position in the world system and economic growth 1955–70: A multiple network analysis of transnational interactions." *American Journal of Sociology* 84:1096–1126.

Song, Lijun, Joonmo Son, and Nan Lin. 2011. "Social support." Pp. 116–28 in *The SAGE Handbook of Social Network Analysis*, edited by J. Scott and P. J. Carrington. London: Sage.

Soref, Michael and Maurice Zeitlin. 1987. "Finance capital and the internal structure of the capitalist class in the United States." Pp. 56–84 in *Intercorporate Relations: The Structural Analysis of Business*, edited by M. S. Mizruchi and M. Schwartz. Cambridge: Cambridge University Press.

Stephenson, Karen and Marvin Zelen. 1989. "Rethinking centrality: Methods and examples." *Social Networks* 11:1–27.

Thornton, Patricia H. 1999. "The sociology of entrepreneurship." *Annual Review of Sociology* 25:19–46.

Valente, Thomas W. 1995. *Network Models of the Diffusion of Innovations.* Cresskill, NJ: Hampton Press.

van Duijn, Marijtje and Mark Huisman. 2011. "Statistical methods for ties and actors." Pp. 459–83 in *The SAGE Handbook of Social Network Analysis*, edited by J. Scott and P. J. Carrington. London: Sage.

Warner, W. Lloyd and Paul S. Lunt. 1941. *The Social Life of a Modern Community.* New Haven, CT: Yale University Press.

Wasserman, Stanley and Katherine Faust. 1994. *Social Network Analysis: Methods and Applications.* Cambridge: Cambridge University Press.

Wasserman, Stanley and Joseph Galaskiewicz, eds. 1994. *Advances in Social Network Analysis.* Thousand Oaks, CA: Sage.

Wasserman, Stanley and Garry Robins. 2005. "An introduction to random graphs, dependence graphs, and p*." Pp. 148–16 in *Models and Methods in Social Network Analysis,* edited by P. J. Carrington, J. Scott, and S. Wasserman. Cambridge: Cambridge University Press.

Weil, André. [1949] 1969. "On the algebraic study of certain types of marriage laws (Murngin system)." Chapter 14 in Claude Lévi-Strauss, *The Elementary Structures of Kinship,* rev. ed., edited by Rodney Needham. Reprint. Boston: Beacon Press. Originally published in Claude Lévi-Strauss, *Les Structures élémentaires de la Parenté.* Paris: Mouton, 1949.

Wellman, Barry. 1979. "The community question." *American Journal of Sociology* 84:1201–31.

———. 1988. "Structural analysis: From method and metaphor to theory and substance." Pp. 19–61 in *Social Structures: A Network Approach,* edited by B. Wellman and S. Berkowitz. Cambridge: Cambridge University Press.

———. 1999. *Networks in the Global Village.* Boulder, CO: Westview Press.

Wellman, Barry and Stephen D. Berkowitz, eds. 1988. *Social Structures: A Network Approach.* Cambridge: Cambridge University Press.

Wellman, Barry and Scot Wortley. 1990. "Different strokes from different folks." *American Journal of Sociology* 96:558–88.

Wellman, Barry, Peter J. Carrington, and Alan Hall. 1988. "Networks as personal communities." Pp. 130–84 in *Social Structures: A Network Approach,* edited by B. Wellman and S. Berkowitz. Cambridge: Cambridge University Press.

Wheeldon, Prudence D. 1969. "The operation of voluntary associations and personal networks in the political processes of an inter-ethnic community." Pp. 128–80 in *Social Networks in Urban Situations,* edited by J. C. Mitchell. Manchester: Manchester University Press.

White, Harrison C. 1963a. "Uses of Mathematics in Sociology." Pp. 77–94 in *Mathematics and the Social Sciences,* edited by J. C. Charlesworth. Philadelphia: American Academy of Political and Social Science.

———. 1963b. *An Anatomy of Kinship.* Englewood Cliffs, NJ: Prentice-Hall.

White, Harrison C., Scott A. Boorman, and Ronald L. Breiger. 1976. "Social structure from multiple networks I: Blockmodels of roles and positions." *American Journal of Sociology* 81:730–81.

Williams, Rob and David Lusseau. 2006. "A killer whale social network is vulnerable to targeted removals." *Biology Letters* 2:497–500.

3

Triangulation and Validity of Network Data

Andreas Wald

Introduction

This chapter deals with the potentials of triangulation of qualitative and quantitative data and methods in network analysis by pursuing two inter-related aims: first, to clarify under which circumstances a triangulation-based research strategy should be pursued and, second, to demonstrate how triangulation can be applied for network data collection and analysis. The relevance of the topic is due to the observation that a narrow focus on either a qualitative or a quantitative research strategy does not capitalize on the full explanatory potential as it systematically excludes certain insights and aspects of the phenomenon under investigation. For certain research questions and phenomena it can be useful and necessary to overcome these limitations (Hesse-Biber 2010). This approach follows the assumption that a method is not wrong or right per se. However, it can be more or less appropriate for specific research aims and settings. Different methodological approaches elaborate on different aspects of reality and are therefore dependent upon the research question (Bryman 2007). Therefore, I will not refer to the fundamental debate between quantitative and qualitative purists (Johnson and Onwuegbuzie 2004). Likewise, I do not discuss the relationship between research methodology, ontology, and epistemology in greater detail. From an ontological point of view, the necessary precondition for applying data triangulation is a very moderate positivistic position that is also in line with the assumptions of Grounded Theory and moderate (social) constructivist

Support for this research was provided by the German Research Foundation (DFG), grant no. JA 548/5–1. The project was carried out under the supervision of Dorothea Jansen at the German Research Institute for Public Administration, Speyer. I am grateful to Dorothea Jansen for her support and advice, and to Karola Barnekow for her contribution to earlier versions of this chapter.

approaches (Sale et al. 2002). Triangulation can be used to learn more about an objective reality, but also for investigating the social construction of meaning and perceptions.

The concept of triangulation originates from geodesy, a science dealing with the measurement of the Earth. In this discipline, triangulation describes a procedure to measure the position of a point C. If the distance between point A and point B is known and the angles between A and C as well as between B and C are given, the position of C and the distances A–C/B–C can be determined by means of trigonometry. In social science research triangulation means the combination of different methods in data collection and data analysis and for the interpretation of data with the purpose to gain more precise and broader insights compared to the use of only one method and/or source of data (Denzin 1978; Straus 2002; Creswell 2009). This definition is similar to several definitions of mixed methods research (Johnson et al. 2007). The critical part of this definition refers to the purpose: Through the triangulation of two or more methods and/or sources of data, the respective weaknesses will be overcome by a combination of the specific strengths of each approach. Triangulation combines several data sources and/or research methods for cross-validation. The aim is to come to a more encompassing and valid understanding of the phenomenon. Greene et al. (1989:259) provide a classification scheme for mixed methods designs. They identify different rationales behind mixed methods designs: triangulation, complementarity, development, initiation, and expansion. Triangulation in mixed methods designs is mainly used to increase the validity of measurement and inference.

In quantitative research, validity refers to the question of whether a research instrument actually measures what it is supposed to. A measurement instrument is valid, if it is precise, accurate, and relevant (Sarantakos 2005). For instance, internal validity is about the validity of causal inference (e.g., can the effect observed in the statistical model really be attributed to the explanatory variables and not to other causes?) whereas construct validity refers to the question to which extent operationalizations correspond to the theoretical construct. Commensurate to the concept of validity in quantitative studies, qualitative research uses a set of criteria for evaluating the quality of empirical research. Although there are no generally accepted labels, "dependability," "transferability," "confirmability," and "credibility" are among the most prevalent ones (Onwuegebuzie and Johnson 2006). Credibility, for instance, is equivalent to internal validity in quantitative research.

To avoid an association with either qualitative or quantitative research, Onwuegebuzie and Johnson (2006) use different labels for their criteria for assessing mixed methods studies. They term these criteria "legitimation types," which comprise "sample integration," "inside-outside," "weakness-minimization," "sequential, conversion," "paradigmatic mixing," "commensurability," "multiple validities," and "political." For the triangulation of network data and methods, sample integration legitimation, inside-out legitimation, conversion legitimation, and multiple validity legitimation are particularly important. The meanings and the applications of these criteria will be discussed further in the empirical part of this chapter.

The concept of data triangulation has a long tradition in social science and has been used with a focus on the validity of data (Campell and Fiske 1959). However, triangulation is neither restricted to data nor does it only comprise the triangulation of qualitative and quantitative methods. Denzin (1978) identified four different types of triangulation: data triangulation, theory triangulation, investigator triangulation, and methodological triangulation. Analytically, these types are separate entities; that is, one can imagine a triangulation in data collection combined with a purely quantitative approach in data analysis. In practice, the more prevalent form is a combination of several types of triangulation, for example, data triangulation along with methodological triangulation. In the following I will focus on triangulation of quantitative and qualitative network data and method.

Due to the broad and extensive use of network analysis in social science, a clarification of the underlying concept is necessary to avoid misunderstandings (Wellman 1988). From a network perspective, three dimensions can be distinguished: network phenomenon, network theory, and network method. Although this chapter uses examples of networks as phenomenon (i.e., networks of cooperation between research groups) and network theories (i.e., theories of social capital), I concentrate on network analysis as a research method for analyzing social structures. This method is not about individual attributes such as age, gender, or income, but rather about the patterns of relationships between individual, collective, or corporate actors (Emirbayer 1997). Therefore only such methods qualify as network analysis, which have been explicitly designed to examine the patterns of relationships (see Carrington, this volume).

Potentials and Limitations of Quantitative Network Analysis

In the following I distinguish the phases of data collection, data analysis, and interpretation. In practice, the phases of the research process often overlap and a myriad of interdependencies exists. For instance, the selection of a specific survey instrument (data collection) restricts the methods that can be applied in the phase of the analysis.

Data Collection

There are two prevalent approaches for collecting network data for individual and corporate actors: "egocentric networks" (personal networks) and "complete networks" (whole networks) (Wasserman and Faust 1994; Marsden 2005). In addition, social network data can be obtained by observation and archival records. The goal of a complete network is to survey a network between all actors of an explicitly defined area. This approach usually follows two steps. First, system delineation identifies the relevant actors. This is a very crucial and often problematic procedure (Lauman et al. 1989). Second, the relation content(s) of the network(s) has to be determined. Once the actors and relation contents are identified, data collection uses standardized lists including the complete set of actors. The interviewees are asked to mark all actors with whom they have a relationship. The relation content also determines if there are undirected (family ties, friendship) or directed (support, information) graphs in the networks.

Collecting data of complete networks requires comprehensive a priori knowledge of the system under investigation. The subjective meanings attached to the relations and their content must be known and/or be relatively stable as the relation content is predefined by the researcher. Dealing with networks between corporate actors, these necessary preconditions usually are given to some extent. For instance, in policy network studies, the actor set is composed of political agents and interest groups that can easily be identified on the basis of formal criteria such as legal documents or membership in a parliament (Pappi and Henning 1999). When it comes to the definition of the relation content, things become more difficult as it is the key informant answering the questionnaire on behalf of the organization. The question on the informant's interpretation of the relation content is hardly considered. Needless to say, people differ in their perceptions, frameworks of relevance, and subjective meanings regarding network relations and their content. Formulating the relation content before data collection is always ad hoc and therefore prone to measurement errors, random errors, equivocal findings, and validity problems (Burt and Schøtt 1985).

If only little prior knowledge about the system under investigation exists and the frameworks of relevance and subjective meanings of the actors differ significantly, the a priori delineation of the system and the definition of relation contents can lead to the systematic exclusion of relevant context factors and fundamental explanatory factors. Quantitative designs for collecting network data may particularly encounter problems of validity, especially when collecting data of complete networks. A typical validity problem for complete networks results from a difference between the definition of the relation content by the researcher and the individual perception and relevance of the relation content of the respondent. Respondents fill out the network lists of information flows or friendship but have a different understanding of what to consider a friendship tie or what to consider important flow of information. In this case, the data-collection procedure leads to a single network of information that in fact comprises different relation contents and may not measure information flow as intended by the researcher. This problem can be reduced but not entirely eliminated by precisely defining and explaining the relation content to the interviewees and by using only "confirmed" network data for the analysis. This method increases face validity. A relation between two units i and j is considered to exist only if in the interview i and j separately confirm that the relation exists (Krackhardt 1990).

The collection of egocentric (personal/focal) networks allows for accounting for some of these problems. Egocentric networks delineate the system on a personal basis. With the help of name generators, relevant actors for ego as the focal player (the interviewee) are identified. Respondents are asked to compile a list with all other persons (the alteri) with whom they have a (specified) relation. In a second step, name interpreters help to characterize the quality of the relationships between ego and alteri and also between the alteri (Marsden 2005). The name generator is the functional equivalent to the system delineation for complete networks. The number of actors is not defined a priori but it is the respondent who actively sets the boundaries. As a consequence, network size and the alteri usually vary among the egos in the sample. As an example, Burt in his study on the social capital of managers accounted for different frameworks of relevance of the respondents. Interviewees were asked to list persons with whom they discuss important personal matters. It was left open, if it were job-related or private matters (Burt 1992). The networks could vary regarding their specific relation content (business vs. private communication), as well as the quantity and quality of alteri (colleagues, friends, or family), although the general relation content "communication of personally important things" was predefined. In an earlier study, Pfenning (1995) compared different standardized name generators regarding their reliability and validity. He found that, in general, established name generators bring about sufficiently valid and reliable network data. Nonetheless, the validity of egocentric network data remains problematic for the alteri-to-alteri relations.

In contrast to complete networks, the survey instrument for egocentric networks is more open but limits, as it will be shown in the next section, the possible range of structural analysis. In case of even more explanatory research questions, more unstructured settings, complex context factors, and highly subjective meaning and perception (Hollstein 2003), standardized surveys with egocentric instruments may still be inappropriate for capturing all relevant aspects of the situation.

Data Analysis and Interpretation

Network analysis provides a set of powerful tools for the study of egocentric networks and complete networks. The methods allow for a precise description of network properties and for testing hypotheses on the coherence between relation properties and the actors' attributes. In addition, the existing procedures also offer a wide range for explorative, that is, hypothesis-generating, analyses. For the analysis of complete networks, the entire spectrum of methods is available. These range from simple indexes on the actor level (e.g., centrality), the level of single relationships (e.g., multiplexity), and the network level (e.g., density) to more advanced procedures of position and role analysis, in which complex, multiple network structures can be reduced to underlying macro-structures. More recently, quantitative network analysis developed more advanced methods for simulating network dynamics (Carley 2003; Snijders et al. 2010) and random graphs models (Koehly and Pattison 2005).

Compared to complete networks, egocentric networks limit the possible range of methods. The focus is on simple measures to describe the network structure such as network size or average tie-strength. On the other hand, egocentric networks allow for applying sample techniques and statistical analysis. In many studies, network-analytical measures for ego are treated like individual attributes and used as independent or dependent variables.

For both kinds of network data, certain research settings limit the explanatory power of purely quantitative research methods. Again, the predefined categories may not fit to the real situation. The established network-analytical measures deliver figures that may result in artifacts. As an example, a name generator may distinguish two networks, information exchange and cooperation, but interviewees may consider this relation content as identical. This results in a high multiplexity of the networks, a finding that could be misinterpreted if the subjective meanings were disregarded. Another pitfall for the interpretation of quantitative results is the motivation for network behavior which is often (implicitly) assumed but not empirically validated (Burt et al. 1998; Kadushin 2002). The interpretation of results is then based on these theoretical assumptions. This can be especially difficult in the light of deviant findings leading to ad hoc hypotheses because actor motivations and relevant context factors were not considered explicitly.

In short, quantitative network analysis offers a set of sophisticated tools for structural analysis. The two crucial steps in network data collection, system delineation and the definition of the relation contents, require extensive prior knowledge about the field of investigation. In more exploratory, hypothesis-generating research, a purely quantitative research strategy is not appropriate. Due to its high degree of standardization, quantitative methods may systematically neglect subjective meanings, individual frameworks of relevance, and context factors. In principle, one could raise a similar critique against quantitative network analysis as against quantitative methods in general (Lamnek 1993). Following Hollstein (2011), the specific traits of qualitative social research are the understanding of meaning, the openness of the survey instruments, and the interpretative character of the data analysis (see Hollstein in the introduction to this volume). This results in the question of how to compensate for the weaknesses of quantitative methods by triangulation with qualitative approaches.

Specific and Generic Qualitative Methods

For the methods of quantitative network analysis a variety of systematic introductions and textbooks exists (e.g., Wasserman and Faust 1994; Degenne and Forsé 1999; Scott 2000). A significant amount of publications on network analysis in different social science disciplines demonstrates the maturity of this field. With very few exceptions (e.g., Hollstein and Straus 2006) this is not the case for qualitative network analysis. This might be due to the fact that qualitative network studies have only recently become more prevalent. For the German-speaking countries, Straus (2002) identified only 12 articles published in the period from 1987 to 1999. The more generic character of the qualitative methods used in network studies is an alternative explanation for this finding. The use of qualitative methods in network analysis usually takes the form of cognitive, interpretative, and explanatory approaches that serve as a complement for quantitative methods. With a few exceptions, these methods have not been specifically designed for the analysis of relational data.

Qualitative methods for collecting network data can be found in the fields of social psychology (Straus 2002), political sociology (Broadbent 2003), sociology of the family (Hollstein 2003), and ethnology (Trotter 1999). Kahn and Antonucci (1980) introduced the method of "concentric circles" which demonstrates the openness of qualitative instruments.

The collection of the egocentric network data starts with a diagram of concentric circles where the name of the person interviewed stands in the innermost circle. During the interview, the interviewee is asked to place people with whom he feels emotionally connected in the outer circles. A position on an outer circle represents a lower emotional intensity than a position close to the center. At this stage, it is left open as to which kind of relations (relation content) ego has to the alteri. This kind of information is considered at a later stage of the interview. The method of concentric circles and related tools like network cards (Straus 2002; Bernardi et al., this volume) are functional equivalents to the more standardized name generators and name interpreters often used in quantitative designs. Instead of a list, respondents enter the contact persons in different circles. Compared to name generators, network cards are kept more open, that is, they do not predefine the relation content. The latter can be defined by the respondents by dividing the circles in several segments corresponding to different types of relations (friends, family, and work). The interviewees are asked to place the contact persons in the relevant sectors (Straus 2002). On this basis, the respondents further characterize their contacts and the respective relations. Additional symbols on the contact persons can be used to visually indicate certain characteristics (Straus and Höfer 1998). The distinction between quantitative and qualitative approaches for collecting network data is often blurred. At least to some extent, triangulation seems to be prevalent for data collection in egocentric network studies.

Network visualization is another prevailing tool in qualitative studies (see Bernardi et al.; Molina et al., this volume). It proved very helpful for exploratory analysis. These tools also have a long tradition in quantitative network research. Starting with simple sociograms drawn by hand (Whyte 1943) visualization techniques have progressed tremendously over the last couple of years (Brandes et al. 2001; Moody et al. 2005; Freeman 2005). Using mathematical transformation rules, quantitative information is converted into graphics. The position and shape of the network nodes, their size, and the strength of the lines are drawn depending on the nodes' position in the network and on several other characteristics of nodes and lines. Additional characteristics of the network and its environment, for example, clusters and cliques, can be marked in terms of variations in background color. Compared to the quantitative visualization techniques, qualitative network graphs usually are relatively simple.

To sum up, qualitative methods specifically designed for network analysis have developed tools for data collection and visualization. They can be considered as more open and less formalized counterparts of quantitative tools. Further methods, like expert interviews, narrative interviews, and content analysis, are more generic and their application is not restricted to applications within the scope of network studies. The next section demonstrates with a practical example how quantitative network methods and more generic qualitative methods can be combined.

Potentials of Triangulation in Network Analysis

Fundamental Prerequisite

Triangulation of qualitative and quantitative methods is complicated by the fact that researchers from both proveniences have grown out of their particular scientific communities and paradigms (Sale et al. 2002). The prevailing epistemological, ontological, and methodological assumptions may result in the incommensurability of the results. Every method has a specific approach toward reality and therefore can only analyze a particular aspect of it. Moreover, the application of a specific method to a large extent predefines the process of data analysis and interpretation. Data obtained from a large-scale standardized survey cannot be analyzed by means of content analysis, and data from narrative interviews can hardly be entered in structural equation models. The same is true for the underlying theoretical approaches. This "lack of consensus" may only be reduced but not completely eliminated with a triangulating research design (Denzin 1978; Howe 1988; Morse and Niehaus 2009).

As a necessary precondition for a successful triangulation, the members of the research teams should mutually reveal their (implicit) interpretation schemes and their pre-structuring of the research object and problem. Furthermore, it must be specified how to combine the different methods and instruments in order to broaden the perspective and to deliver more complete results. The successful combination of different epistemological, methodological, and axiological beliefs pertains to "paradigmatic mixing legitimation" as one criterion for the validity of mixed methods research (Onwuegbuzie and Johnson 2006). Triangulation does not simply mean to simultaneously use several methods and data but to purposefully integrate them (Caracelli and Greene 1993). Finally, researchers must be aware of the fact that triangulation may bring about discrepant findings. Contradicting results of the qualitative and quantitative elements of a study can be both a source of conflict and an opportunity to enhance the robustness of a study (Moffatt et al. 2006).

Triangulation in a Research Project on Network Strategies and Network Capacity

The research project "Networking Strategy and Network Capacity of Research Groups" was part of an interdisciplinary research group founded by the German Research Foundation (DFG JA-548/5–1). The project dealt with the effects of reforms in the governance of German research institutions on the research group as the unit of analysis. A research group is defined as the smallest stable unit in an organization that conducts research (Wald 2007). The focus was on networks between research groups in the fields of astrophysics, nanotechnology, and microeconomics. The research questions were, (a) How do individual groups systematically build up research cooperations and maintain them (network strategy)? (b) How are these networks composed and structured? (c) Which individual relevance do these cooperations have for research and how are they managed (network capacity)? and (d) What impact do the networks have on the performance of the research groups (network effects). For further details regarding the research design, theoretical foundations, research questions, and results see Franke et al. (2006), Wald et al. (2007), Jansen (2007, 2008, 2010), Jansen et al. (2007, 2010), and Wald (2007).

On an abstract level, a common code (true/false) exists for all scientific research regardless of the discipline or institution (Luhmann 1994). On a more concrete level, there is a huge variance in the logic of knowledge production in different disciplines, different institutional settings, and different national science systems. These differences intensify if we consider individual researchers or research groups. Different subjective meanings, frameworks of relevance, and context factors influence the logic of knowledge production. These factors had to be taken into account when analyzing the effects of governance reforms, but little prior knowledge existed on the specific logics of knowledge production in the different disciplines (Franke et al. 2006). Therefore, a qualitative approach seemed to be the appropriate research strategy. However, the findings should not be restricted to very few cases but rather be representative for the three fields of research. Therefore a quantitative approach based on a random sample and a standardized survey seemed to be appropriate. Finally, a triangulation of qualitative and quantitative methods for data collection and for data analysis was chosen. The assumption was that regardless of the research field, institutional affiliation, and other context factors, the researchers could specify their networks of cooperation and information exchange and also provide additional information on the composition of the research group and the research output measured in terms of publications. This part of the data could be collected with a standardized instrument for egocentric networks. For the analysis of subjective meanings, context factors, and perceptions of the individual partners as well as the entire network, a more open instrument was required. Following the typology of mixed methods designs discussed by Hollstein in the introduction to this volume, the research design of the study at hand can be classified as a parallel design that also includes elements of a conversion design.

Data Collection

The empirical basis consisted of a random sample of 75 research groups in the field of nanotechnology, astrophysics, and microeconomics (25 for each field) in the publicly funded part of the German research system. In this aspect, the study differs from many mixed methods research where we often find purposive sampling techniques (Teddlie and Yu 2007). Using exactly the same groups for the qualitative and the quantitative parts of the study enhances validity in the sense of "sample integration legitimation." This positively affects the generalizability of the results, which are not restricted to the sample but can be extended to a larger population (Owuegbuzie and Johnson 2006).

Data were collected in personal interviews with the heads of the research groups. All interviews were recorded and transcribed. The qualitative and the qualitative data were simultaneously collected (parallel/concurrent design). Semi-structured, qualitative expert interviews were complemented by a standardized questionnaire covering data on size, input factors, and output of the group. In addition to the qualitative data, a formalized inventory was used to collect data on the egocentric networks. A name generator served to identify the relevant partners for two networks: cooperation and information exchange. Respondents were asked to name all important cooperation and information partners on a list. The following question was asked as a name generator:

> In the following we would like to ask you about the network embeddedness of your research group. The aim is to identify and describe those relationships which are important for your research activities. First, we would like to ask you to list all the relevant actors with whom you cooperate or share information within the scope of your research activities.

Two separate name interpreters for the network of information exchange and cooperation served to collect the data on ego–alteri relations as well as alteri–alteri relations. Using a triangular matrix, respondents could indicate two different intensities for the relations (1 = regular, 2 = very intense). Figure 3.1 provides an example of the name generator and name interpreter used in the study. In the original questionnaire, the name interpreter comprised additional space to provide information on the partner's attributes (institutional affiliation, age of the relation, etc.) which is not shown in the figure. In the example in the figure, the research group (ego) maintains 11 collaborative relationships, of which 5 are very intense. Among the alteri 10 relationships exist.

															ego	
														1	2	1. Partner
													2		2	2. Partner
												3	1		1	3. Partner
											4				1	4. Partner
										5		1		2	2	5. Partner
									6						1	6. Partner
								7	2						2	7. Partner
							8	2	2						2	8. Partner
						9									1	9. Partner
					10	1	1					1	1		1	10. Partner
				11											1	11. Partner
			12													12. Partner
		13														13. Partner
	14															14. Partner
15																15. Partner

Figure 3.1. Name generator and name interpreter

The name generator and name interpreter represented the standard-ized quantitative part of the data-collection process. In the next step, an open question asked for describing the role of the individual cooperation and for providing more information on the partners:

> Could you please further describe your cooperation?
> Which partners are of particular importance and why?

Answering to these questions, the interviewees revealed their individual perceptions, subjective meanings, and frameworks of relevance. They also explained how and why specific context factors have an impact on their networks. This kind of data triangulation helped to avoid a poten-tial misinterpretation of network relations and enhanced the validity of the data (Burt and Schøtt 1985). It led to an improvement of the crite-ria of "weakness minimization legitimation" and "multiple validities legitimation." Weakness minimization corresponds to the question of how the weaknesses of one approach are compensated by the strengths of the other approach, and multiple validities is "the extent to which addressing legitimation of the quantitative and qualitative components of the study result from the use of quantitative, qualitative, and mixed validity types, yielding high quality inferences" (Owuegbuzie and Johnson 2006:57).

In research on the coherence between network embeddedness and individual action/individual outcome, measures of the individual's position in the network are often treated as independent variables and outcome measures (e.g., number of publications) as dependent variables. Although a variety of studies was able to show network effects in different contexts (e.g., Burt 1992; Uzzi 1996), the question of whether a favorable position in the network was purposefully chosen or was a rather emergent phenomenon was hardly considered. In the study on networks among research groups, another open question was asked about the motivation for building and maintaining relationships (network strategy) and about the success and failures in doing so (network capacity). In combination with the network data, this information was used to better interpret the findings of the statistical analysis and to test common-held assumptions on actor motivations (multiple validities legitimation).

> Please describe how your collaborative relationships have emerged.
> What are the contents and goals of the relationships?

Due to a sample size of 75 cases, the pre-definition of relation contents and a standardized collection of the network data and additional attributive data were necessary. Nonetheless, several open questions left room for the respondents to add as much individual information as they considered relevant. In general, the optimal share of qualitative and quantitative instruments for data triangulation must be chosen on a case-by-case basis and depends on the research question and objectives.

A challenge for triangulation is to adequately combine quantitative and qualitative elements in the instruments and in the interview situation. In the study at hand, the interviewer guided the interview and decided when to ask the open questions and when to fill out the standardized questionnaire and network matrixes. As all interviews were recorded, there was no need to take notes during the interview. This gave the interviewer flexibility to respond to the interviewee's reactions and to create an atmosphere of a conversation instead of an inquiry. Filling out the name generator and name interpreter often caused breaks in the conversation in which the interviewee had time to reflect. The respondents were sometimes surprised about how much information they came up with and often mentioned important details about their networks while filling out the form. In a different research situation this might not be possible and the interviewees might be forced to keep more strictly to the sequence of the questionnaire.

Data Analysis and Interpretation

To avoid a loss of information, triangulation on the level of data collection needs to be continued in the phase of data analysis. However, triangulation does not mean to separately analyze the quantitative and the qualitative data but to combine both sources of data. Similar to the process of data collection, the share of qualitative and quantitative elements has to be determined for the analysis of data. In the study at hand, the quantitative part played a dominating role for reasons of the relatively large sample size and of statistical evidence.

A computer-based content analysis was applied to the qualitative interview data, using the software package ATLAS.ti (Krippendorff 2003). To avoid a subjective bias, three persons separately examined the entire text material. The textual information was categorized by developing empirical categories that could be matched with the different research questions. Each person assigned the categories of the coding frame to different parts of the transcripts. In a further step, the results of the separate analyses were consolidated. For the most part, the results of the three investigators were identical. In case of discrepant categorizations an intensive discussion led to a common assignment of textual parts to the categories. To demonstrate the coding procedure, I consider the category about the influence factors/mechanisms of network building. It comprises several subcategories which are shown in Table 3.1.

The coding procedure is based on a multilevel process. In a first step, all parts in the text were marked, which had the topic "network building" and/or "network development." The codes were defined in a content-semantic and not in a formal-syntactic way (Früh 2001). In a second step, all codes of a category were compared to each other and their meanings were identified and described. Finally, the codes were assigned to a subcategory. For instance, a nanotechnologist mentioned that he predominantly selects his research partners strategically:

> This was a strategic decision [...] which kind of information do we need and how do we get access to this information in the best possible way [...]. I started to get in touch with potential [...] colleagues. Of course, I knew them before. We are in a small field of research. We know each other.

This statement falls in the subcategory "Strategic based on a limited pool of partners." Each relevant part in relation to a specific category was coded only once per case, even if a statement was repeated several times in similar words and/or different words. As a consequence, all categories have a dichotomous data format. Special attention was paid to the development of a code book. It covers not only the indices but also the abstractions of individual statements to the subcategories and to the main categories.

Table 3.1. *Category and subcategories*

Category: Influence on network building					
Subcategory 1	Subcategory 2	Subcategory 3	Subcategory 4	Subcategory 5	Subcategory 6
Emergence/ path dependency	Strategic based on a limited pool of partners	Strategic based on an open search for partners	External incentives	Internal incentives	Other reasons

As mentioned earlier, the study's goal was to provide statistical evidence for the effects of governance reforms on the individual research group. Therefore, the qualitative data were transformed into standard variables on a nominal or ordinal scale (Caracelli and Greene 1993). "Conversion legitimation" is the validity criteria for mixed methods research that measures the extent to which the quantitizing of qualitative data or the qualitizing of quantitative date improves the quality of inferences (Owuegbuzie and Johnson 2006). Table 3.2 shows the results of this transformation for the category "network building" and the discipline of astrophysics.

The integrated analysis of qualitative and quantitative data contributes to a better understanding and produces more valid results. It not only allows for the testing of theoretically derived hypotheses, but, in the case of an empirical rejection, may help to reformulate and refine theoretical postulates. As an example I use two well-known hypotheses on social capital: The first hypothesis postulates that social capital is generated in dense networks (network closure), whereas the second hypothesis assumes that occupying a broker position in sparse networks (structural holes) is a source of social capital (Burt 2005). Exemplarily, Figure 3.2 shows the networks of cooperation of two research groups, EGO 1 and EGO 2, in the field of astrophysics. From the visual analysis it is obvious that the upper network has a high density (88%) while the network below has a comparatively low density (21%). Moreover, the structure of EGO 2 resembles the ideal type of a network rich in structural holes (with the exception of several redundant relations). The research group of EGO 2 bridges holes in the network structure and, according to theory, should generate social capital out of it. In contrast, the network of the research group of EGO 1 exhibits the ideal type of a high network closure. Standard procedures of quantitative network analysis can identify these structural properties and test the two hypotheses on social capital (Franke et al. 2006). Empirical results may support theory or lead to the rejection of the hypotheses. The interpretation of results, in particular those that contradict theory, can be improved by adding qualitative information. For the two networks in Figure 3.2, information on the underlying motivations of actors for network building (Table 3.2)

Table 3.2. *Network building in the field of astrophysics*

| | Subcategories | | | | | |
	Emergence/ path dependency	Strategic based on a limited pool of partners	Strategic based on an open search for partners	External incentives	Internal incentives	Other reasons	Total
Cases (n = 25)	22	6	17	0	6	1	52
% of cases	88.0%	24.0%	68.0%	0.0%	24.0%	4.0%	208.0%
% responses	42,3%	11.5%	32.7%	0.0%	11.5%	1.9%	100.0%

Multiple responses

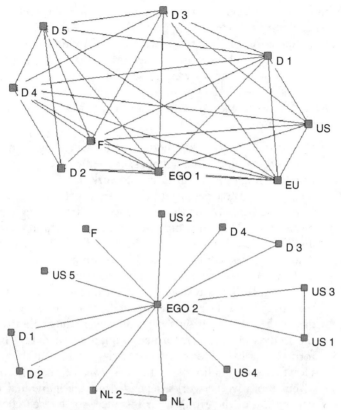

Figure 3.2. Networks of cooperation in astrophysics

is relevant. It is possible that both network structures are the result of strategic choices. In this case there is a high probability that both structures are appropriate means in achieving the targeted goals and therefore clear (positive) network effects should be observable. Alternatively, the network could be the result of path-dependency and chance and may therefore not fulfill a specific purpose. Accordingly, network effects may either not occur or may be rather weak. This kind of information related to actor motivations and differing frameworks of relevance can hardly be obtained with standardized surveys.

Additional Value and Additional Effort of Triangulating Research Strategy

In the example presented in the previous section, the additional insights gained by combining qualitative and quantitative methods outweighed the additional efforts in data collection and data analysis. The study allowed for a comprehensive and integrated analysis of quantitative data on the egocentric networks, the groups' attributes (size, age research output, composition of the group, etc.), and of qualitative data on the motivation, subjective meanings, frameworks of relevance, and context factors. In particular, the answers to several research questions would have been less precise, incomplete, and less valid by not using triangulation. The following examples illustrate the additional value gained by using triangulation:

- Question: Do network structures differ according to the orientation of research (fundamental vs. applied)? Answering this question by using only quantitative network data and a quantitative measure for the orientation of research would have resulted in a distorted picture of the coherence of structure and research orientation. Not only did the definition of fundamental and applied research differ across the three fields, but also within a field like nanotechnology, the distinction between fundamental and applied research was often not clear-cut.
- Question: Is there a relationship between the network strategy of the groups and their performance? Data on the network strategies of the research groups were collected in the qualitative part of the study and then transformed to quantitative data. This transformation allowed for statistical testing of the causal hypothesis. However, the qualitative data also revealed that the relevance of collaborative networks depended on the individual research orientation of the groups. For instance, some researchers in the field of economics were able to successfully (success measured with publication output) conduct research without any external network partner, whereas for most groups in nanotechnology and in astrophysics collaboration was vital. In addition, context factors like the resource endowment, the size of the group, the institutional affiliation, or the specialization were found to have an influence on network strategy. Therefore, the qualitative information not only enhanced the understanding of the logic of knowledge production in the different fields, but also served to better interpret the results of the quantitative analysis.

To sum up, triangulation in data collection, analysis, and interpretation contributed to a higher validity of the egocentric network analysis. In addition to testing theoretically derived hypotheses with statistical methods, contradicting and equivocal results could be further analyzed and explained. A purely quantitative or a purely qualitative network analysis would not have been able to adequately answer these questions. The former would have neglected important information revealed only in the expert interviews. For the latter, results would have been restricted to a few singular cases and not be representative for the entire research field.

However, the advantages of triangulating research designs do not come for free and triangulation is not an end in itself. The combined application of qualitative and quantitative methods poses a challenge in terms of methodological knowledge, time, coordination effort, and financial means (Creswell 2009). This additional effort must be carefully weighed up against the additional value. The integration of qualitative and quantitative methods usually requires a research team composed of experts in both fields. This leads to a higher effort for co-coordinating the activities. Combining quantitative data collection with expert interviews is also more time consuming and severely limits the sample size. In the study presented in this chapter the sample size was 75 cases, which is close to the lower limit for running statistical tests, but at the same time it entailed a considerable effort for conducting expert interviews. Triangulation also results in higher costs of the research infrastructure, for example, software packages for both kinds of data and analysis must be acquired and administered.

Conclusion

The aim of this chapter was to elaborate on the potentials of triangulation of qualitative and quantitative data and methods in network analysis. Special attention was paid to data collection and the problem of validity. A study on the networks of cooperation of research groups served to demonstrate how triangulation can be applied in practice.

Due to the large variety of different research questions and of potential context factors in the different social science disciplines, no detailed decision support can be provided for deciding on when to use a triangulating research strategy and on how to combine qualitative and quantitative elements of a study. However, a generic framework with three criteria may guide the decision about a single method or a mixed methods design (Table 3.3). These criteria are the research question, the research objectives, and the nature of the phenomenon (Johnson and Onwuegbuzie 2004; Bryman 2007; Greene 2007; Hesse-Biber 2010).

A triangulating research strategy should be chosen if there is a highly complex research question (Morse and Niehaus 2009). Complexity in this sense does not only pertain to the content of the question (e.g., many different questions in parallel, a complex set of potential interrelationships) but also to the purpose of the study (e.g., gaining in-depth knowledge about the phenomenon and simultaneously obtaining results that can be generalized). The purpose is directly related to the second criterion, the research objectives. A triangulation of qualitative and

Table 3.3. *Framework for the selection of a triangulating research design*

Quantitative	Triangulation	Qualitative
Research question: Rather simple and clear-cut	Research question: Highly complex, partly clear-cut and partly open.	Research question: Simple or complex, relatively open
Objectives: Confirmatory Testing of hypothesis derived from an established theoretical base, extension of existing theory based on empirical results	Objectives: Confirmatory and exploratory Testing of hypothesis derived from an established theoretical base, extension of existing theory based on empirical results and development of new theory	Objectives: Exploratory Development of theory and hypothesis
Research field/phenomenon:	Research field/ phenomenon:	Research field/ phenomenon:
Well structured, extensive knowledge of the field and on relevant context factors	Well structured elements and unstructured elements, prior knowledge of the field and on relevant context factors exists but is incomplete	Unstructured, little prior knowledge of the field and on relevant context factors
Subjective meanings and frameworks of relevance of the actors do not differ significantly and are rather stable	Subjective meanings and frameworks of relevance of the actors differ significantly and/ or are unstable	Subjective meanings and frameworks of relevance of the actors differ significantly and are unstable
Networks: System can be clearly delineated and the definition of relation content is straightforward	Networks: No clear delineation of the system; definition of relational content depends on subjective meaning and frameworks of relevance	Networks: No clear delineation of the system, definition of relational content depends on subjective meaning and frameworks of reference relevance

quantitative methods in network studies should be pursued if individual meaning, perception, frameworks of relevance, and additional context factors play an important role, and at the same time statistical evidence from a representative sample should be obtained. The third criterion is related to the research field and the nature of the phenomenon. If little prior knowledge on the phenomenon exists or if this knowledge is incomplete, the qualitative part of the study may reveal differences in subjective meanings and frameworks of reference. Once discovered and accounted for, this information can be integrated into the quantitative analysis.

The choice of a triangulating research strategy is also contingent on a variety of context factors which should be carefully considered on a case-by-case basis. This also applies to the subsequent decisions on the share of qualitative and quantitative elements and their integration in the research design (Caracelli and Greene 1993; Creswell and Plano Clark 2007). A very practical but highly important context factor is the (non-) availability of the necessary resources. First of all, researchers involved in the study must be able – in terms of their knowledge of both qualitative and quantitative methods – and willing – in terms of their readiness to embark on a mixed methods research – to conduct a triangulating study. Second, the additional financial resources and the additional time needed to collect and to analyze qualitative and quantitative data must be available. Third, additional context factors such as the expectations of important stakeholders (e.g., funding agencies), the methodological orientation of targeted outlets for the research results (e.g., qualitative vs. quantitative oriented scientific journals), or the research strategy of the institution to which the researchers are affiliated may influence the decision on the use of a triangulating research design. Provided that all the necessary preconditions for triangulation are given, this research strategy leads to a more valid and more insightful understanding of complex social phenomena.

References

Barnekow, Karola and Andreas Wald. (2014). "Triangulation." In *Qualitative Netzwerkanalyse. Konzepte, Methoden, Anwendungen*, edited by B. Hollstein and F. Straus. Wiesbaden: VS Verlag.

Brandes, Ulrik, Jörg Raab, and Dorothea Wagner. 2001. "Exploratory network visualization: Simultaneous display of actor status and connections." *Journal of Social Structure* 2.

Bryman, Alan. 2007 "The research question in social research: What is its role?" *International Journal of Social Research Methodology* 10:5–20.

Broadbent, Jeffrey. 2003 "Movement in context: Thick networks and Japanese environmental protest." Pp. 204–29 in *Social Movements and Networks. Relational Approaches to collective Action*, edited by Mario Diani and Doug McAdam. Oxford: Oxford University Press.

Burt, Ronald S. 1992. *Structural Holes. The Social Structure of Competition.* Cambridge, MA: Harvard University Press.

———. 2005. *Brokerage and Closure. An Introduction to Social Capital.* Oxford: Oxford University Press.

Burt, Ronald S. and Thomas Schøtt. 1985. "Relation contents in multiple networks." *Social Science Research* 14:287–308.

Burt, Ronald S., Joseph E. Jannotta, and James T. Mahoney. 1998. "Personality correlates of structural holes." *Social Networks* 20:63–87.

Campbell, Donald T. and Donald W. Fiske. 1959. "Convergent and discriminant validation by the multitrait-multimethod matrix." *Psychological Bulletin* 56:81–105.

Caracelli, Valerie J. and Jennifer C. Greene. 1993. "Data analysis strategies for mixed-method evaluation designs." *Evaluation and Policy Analysis* 15:195–207.

Carley, Kathleen. 2003. "Dynamic network analysis in dynamic social network modeling and analysis: Workshop summary and papers." Pp. 133–45 in *Committee on Human Factors, National Research Council*, edited by Ronald Breiger, Kathleen Carley, and Philippa Pattison. Washington DC: The National Academies.

Creswell, John W. 2009. *Research Design. Qualitative, Quantitative, and Mixed Method Approaches*. Los Angeles: Sage.

Creswell, John W. and Vicki L. Plano Clark. 2007. *Designing and Conducting Mixed Methods Research*. Thousand Oaks, CA: Sage.

Degenne Alain and Michel Forsé. 1999. *Introducing Social Networks*. London: Sage.

Denzin, Norman 1978. *The Research Act. A Theoretical Introduction to Sociological Methods*. New York: Aldine.

Emirbayer, Mustafa. 1997. "Manifesto for a relational sociology." *American Journal of Sociology* 103(2):281–317.

Franke, Karola, Andreas Wald, and Katinka Bartl. 2006. *Die Wirkung von Reformen im Deutschen Forschungssystem. Eine Studie in den Feldern Astrophysik, Nanotechnologie und Mikroökonomie*. Speyerer Forschungsberichte Nr. 245, Deutsches Forschungsinstitut für öffentliche Verwaltung. Speyer.

Freeman, Linton C. 2005. "Graphic techniques for exploring social network data." Pp. 248–69 in *Models and Methods in Social Network Analysis*, edited by John Scott and Peter J. Carrington. Cambridge: Cambridge University Press.

Früh, Werner 2001. *Inhaltsanalyse. Theorie und Praxis*. Konstanz: UVK.

Greene, Jennifer C. 2007. *Mixed Methods in SocialIinquiry*. San Francisco: Jossey-Bass.

Greene, Jennifer C., Valerie J. Caracelli, and Wendy F. Graham. 1989. "Toward a conceptual framework for mixed- method evaluation designs." *Educational Evaluation and Policy Analysis* 11:255–74.

Hesse-Biber, Sharlene N. 2010. *Mixed Methods Research: Merging Theory with Practice*. New York: Guilford Press.

Hollstein, Betina. 2003. "Netzwerkveränderung verstehen. Zur Integration von struktur- und akteurstheoretischen Perspektiven." *Berliner Journal für Soziologie* 13:153–74.

———. 2011. "Qualitative approaches." Pp. 404–16 in *Models and Methods in Social Network Analysis*, edited by John Scott and Peter J. Carrington. Cambridge: Cambridge University Press.

Hollstein, Betina and Florian Straus, eds. 2006. *Qualitative Netzwerkanalyse. Konzepte, Methoden, Anwendungen.* Wiesbaden: VS Verlag.

Howe, Kenneth R. 1988. "Against the quantitative-qualitative incompatibility thesis or dogmas die hard." *Educational Researcher* 17:10–16.

Jansen, Dorthea, ed. 2007. *New Forms of Governance in Research Organizations. Disciplinary Approaches, Interfaces and Integration.* Dordrecht: Springer.

Jansen, Dorthea. 2008. "Research networks – Origins and consequences: First evidence from a study of astrophysics, nanotechnology and micro-economics in Germany." Pp. 209–30 in *Scientific Competition,* edited by Max Albert, Dieter Schmidtchen, and Stefan Voigt. Tübingen: Mohr Siebeck.

Jansen, Dorthea, ed. 2010. *Governance and Performance in the German Public Research Sector: Disciplinary Differences.* Dordrecht: Springer.

Jansen, Dorthea, Richard Heidler, and Regina von Görtz. 2010. "Knowledge production and the structure of collaboration networks in two scientifc fields." *Scientometrics* 83:219–41.

Jansen, Dorthea, Andreas Wald, Karola Franke, Ulrich Schmoch, and Torben Schubert. 2007. "Drittmittel als Performanzindikator der wissenschaftlichen Forschung. Zum Einfluss von Rahmenbedingungen auf Forschungsleistung." *Kölner Zeitschrift für Soziologie und Sozialpsychologie* 59:125–49.

Johnson, R. Burke and Anthony J. Onwuegbuzie. 2004. "Mixed methods research: A research paradigm whose time has come." *Educational Researcher* 33(7):14–26.

Johnson R. Burke, Anthony J. Onwuegbuzie, and Lisa A. Turner. 2007. "Toward a definition of mixed methods research." *Journal of Mixed Methods Research* 1:112–33.

Kadushin, Charles. 2002. "The motivational foundations of social networks." *Social Networks* 24:77–91.

Kahn, Robert L., and Toni C. Antonucci. 1980. "Convoys over the life course: Attachment, roles, and social support." Pp. 383–405 in *Life-Span Development and Behavior,* edited by Paul B. Baltes and Orvile G. Brim. New York: Academic Press.

Koehly, Laura M. and Philippa Pattison. 2005. "Random graph models for social networks: Dependence graphs, and p*." Pp. 162–91 in *Models and Methods in Social Network Analysis,* edited by Peter J. Carrington, John Scott, and Stanley Wasserman. New York: Cambridge University Press.

Krackhardt, David. 1990. "Assessing the political landscape: structure, cognition, and power in organizations." *Administrative Science Quarterly* 35:342–69.

Krippendorff, Klaus. 2003. *Content Analysis: An Introduction to Its Methodology.* Beverly Hills, CA: Sage.

Lamnek, Siegfried 1993. *Qualitative Sozialforschung.* Weinheim: Psychologie Verlags Union.

Laumann, Edward O., Peter V. Marsden, and David Prensky. 1989. "The boundary specification problem in network analysis." Pp. 61–87 in *Research Methods in Social Network Analysis,* edited by Linton C. Freeman, Douglas W. White, and Kimball Rommey. Fairfax, VA: George Mason University Press.

Luhmann, Niklas 1994. "The Modernity of Science." *New German Critique* 61: 9–23.

Marsden, Peter V. 2005. "Recent developments in network measurement." Pp. 8–30 in *Models and Methods in Social Network Analysis*, edited by Peter J. Carrington, John Scott, and Stanley Wasserman. New York: Cambridge University Press.

Moffatt, Suzanne, Martin White, Joan Mackintosh, and Denise Howel. 2006. "Using quantitative and qualitative data in health services research – What happens when mixed methods findings conflict?" *BMC Health Service Research* 8:6–28.

Moody, James, Daniel McFarland, and Skye Bender-deMoll. 2005. "Dynamic network visualization." *American Journal of Sociology* 110:1206–41.

Morse, Janice M. and Linda Niehaus. 2009. *Mixed Method Design. Principles and Procedures*. Walnut Creek, CA: Left Coast Press.

Onwuegbuzie, Anthony J. and R. Burke Johnson. 2006. "The validity issue in mixed research." *Research in the Schools* 13:48–63.

Pappi, Franz U. and Christian Henning. 1999. "The organization of influence on the ec's common agricultural policy: A network approach." *European Journal of Political Research* 36:257–81.

Pfenning, Uwe 1995. *Soziale Netzwerke in der Forschungspraxis: Zur theoretischen Perspektive, Vergleichbarkeit und Standardisierung von Erhebungsverfahren sozialer Netzwerke. Zur Validität und Reliabilität von egozentrierten Netz- und Namensgeneratoren*. Darmstadt: DDD.

Sale, Joanna E. M., Lynne H. Lohfeld, and Kevin Brazil. 2002. "Revisiting the quantitative-qualitative debate: Implications for mixed-methods research." *Quality and Quantity* 36:43–53.

Sarantakos, Sotirios. 2005. *Social Reseach*. Houndmills: Palgrave.

Scott, John. 2000. *Social Network Analysis: A Handbook*. 2nd ed. London/ New Dehli: Sage.

Snijders, Tom A., Christian E.G. Steglich, and Gerhard G. van de Bunt. 2010. "Introduction to actor-based models for network dynamics." *Social Networks* 32:44–60.

Straus, Florian 2002. *Netzwerkanalysen. Gemeindepsychologische Perspektiven für Forschung und Praxis*. Wiesbaden: Deutscher Universitätsverlag.

Straus, Florian and Renate Höfer. 1998. "Die Netzwerkperspektive in der Praxis. " Pp. 77–95 in Netzwerkinterventionen, edited by Bernd Röhrle, Gert Sommer, and Frank Nestmann. Tübingen: dgvt-Verlag.

Teddlie, Charles and Fen Yu. 2007. "Mixed methods sampling. A typology with examples." *Journal of Mixed Methods* 1:77–100.

Trotter, Robert T. 1999. "Friends, relatives and relevant others: Conducting ethnographic network studies." Pp. 1–50 in *Mapping Social Networks, Spatial Data, and Hidden Populations. Ethnographers Toolkit*, edited by Jean J. Schensu, Magaret D. LeCompte, Robert T. Trotter, Ellen K. Cromley, and Merril Singer. Walnut Creek, CA: Altamira Press.

Uzzi, Brian 1996. "The sources and consequences of embeddedness for the economic performance of organizations: The network effect." *American Sociological Review* 61:674–98.

Wald, Andreas 2007. "Effects of 'Mode 2'-related policy on the research process. The case of publicly funded German nanotechnology." *Science Studies* 20:24–49.

Wald, Andreas, Karola Franke, and Dorothea Jansen. 2007. "Governance reforms and scientific production. Evidence from German Astrophysics." Pp. 213–32 in *New Forms of Governance in Research Organizations. Disciplinary Approaches, Interfaces and Integration*, edited by Dorothea Jansen. Dordrecht: Springer.

Wasserman, Stanley and Katherine Faust. 1994. *Social Network Analysis: Methods and Applications*. Cambridge: Cambridge University Press.

Wellman, Barry. 1988. "Structural analysis: From method and metaphor to theory and substance." Pp. 19–61 in *Social Structures: A Network Approach*, edited by Barry Wellman and S. Berkowitz. Cambridge: Cambridge University Press.

Whyte, William F. 1943. *Street Corner Society: The Social Structure of an Italian Slum*. Chicago: University of Chicago Press.

4

A Network Analytical Four-Level Concept for an Interpretation of Social Interaction in Terms of Structure and Agency

Roger Häussling

Introduction

This contribution proposes a four-level concept[1] for network analysis designed for adequately capturing and interpreting the socially multidimensional nature of human interaction. Specifically, the concept serves to link the actor perspective of an interaction-oriented sociology with a structural perspective on prevailing constellations of interaction and overall framework conditions. Both perspectives are warranted and stand more in a complementary than in a rival or even a mutually exclusive relationship. On the empirical side of methodology, this insight is mirrored by employing a combination of qualitative methods of collecting network data and formal methods of network analysis. The analysis itself follows a multilevel parallel design strategy (cf. Introduction). Exploiting the advantages of both approaches requires a conceptual framework capable of pinpointing what each approach can be expected to accomplish and where its limits is.

This conceptual framework is outlined in the following section. Its application is demonstrated afterwards drawing on a case study. The findings from a study on processes of communication and knowledge transfer in the sales department of an auto manufacturer are presented. Special attention is paid to ways of linking the results obtained through different methods of network analysis. The chapter concludes by underscoring that, when using mixed methods designs, method triangulation should be based on a conceptual framework defining the range and function of the individual methods applied. In case of network analysis, the concept of interaction is especially suited for this purpose.

---

[1] This four-level concept of interaction is not at all related to empirical multilevel analysis (see, inter alia, Engel 1998). For an alternative to the concept of levels proposed here see Haller (1999:603 ff.).

The Conceptual Framework of Interpretation:
A Four-Level Concept of Interaction

In accordance with common sociological definitions, here "interaction" is conceived of as "mutually related actions" where ego in the presence of alter orients action by taking alter's expectations and the common definition of the situation into account (see, e.g., Hillmann 1994:381). Viewed in this way, the sociological conception of interaction has always been a relational and procedural one. The concept of interaction proposed in this chapter is basically in line with this tradition. The specific objective is to link the view of the individual actor with the perspective that arises when we shift attention to the emergent level of interaction with its rules, resources, and own momentum. To accomplish this goal, four levels are analytically distinguished. This distinction intends to capture the multiperspectivity and multidimensionality of social interaction. The operationalization of the concept then leads to four corresponding levels of analysis, each of which calls for its own specific instruments of data collection. In the following, those four levels are introduced separately and some basic considerations are given as to how they might be approached empirically:

(1) The level of semantic context: Any interaction is part of a context and can be grasped properly only if this context is taken into consideration. However, the context to be considered is much more comprehensive than what Erving Goffman had in mind when speaking of framing. The context of interaction is more than the schemes of interpretation that actors rely on in making sense of concrete interactions (see Goffman 1977:36). It also involves tacit decisions that predetermine the perspective and cannot be detected by a situation analysis no matter how careful it is conducted; rather, such predetermining factors can only be grasped with reference to framework conditions that are either specific to the social entity in question or society in general. The societal framework also includes, for instance, those perspectives, possible interpretations, and modes of distinction that are established within a societal figuration at a certain time. Analytically, we may thus distinguish two types of framework conditions: The first type pertains to the conditions specific to the situation that have to be presupposed for a concrete interaction to take place. Following Anthony Giddens (1984:17–25; 254–55), we may speak of rules and resources in this case. This includes, for instance, role patterns, means of power, routines, and standards of behavior tailored to specific instances of concrete interaction. The second type refers to framework conditions that exert a major external influence on interaction. This involves conditions that affect interaction from superordinate levels. For instance, the legal, moral, and normative demands individual actors face fall into this category. We will draw on Niklas Luhmann's notion of semantics to characterize these

heterogeneous context factors: The notion of semantics refers to the totality of forms of meaning considered worth preserving in a certain temporal, spatial, and social context (see Luhmann 1997:200).[2] Cultural symbols, concepts, common language, expert or scene-related jargon, patterns of interpretation and action, norms, values, and logics that shape perception and determine the connections made, as well as established role sets all form the semantic context of an interaction. In a concrete situation such elements make up a semantic network, in which the interaction network is embedded. Also, the semantic network can be analyzed by formal network analysis methods. Depending on the case in question, data collection on such semantic contexts can involve a mix of observation methods, document analyses, interview analyses, and/or analyses based on an open-ended questionnaire.[3]

(2) The level of interaction network: The interaction level can also be analytically approached in two ways: by focusing either on its dynamic aspects or on its structural dimension. Following Harrison C. White (1992), it is assumed that in the structural dimension network dynamics and constellations assign each member its position in the network and identity respectively. Actors thus take specific network positions that for the most part are socially constructed. Somewhat overstated, those positions may be viewed as interpretive constructs of a "community of interpretation" (Lenk 1995:155 f.) and thus of a semantically framed network. Accordingly, social relations and the specific form they take are contingent upon a web of other relations. However, that means that network constellations and focal processes to a considerable extent shape individual interactions, as they do actors' perceptions of self and perceptions of self by others. In case of focal processes, relational and dynamic constellations can give rise to paths of interaction that can hardly be influenced by individual actors once the process is set in motion. Over time, interactions become tied in with perceptions and circumstances to an extent that departing from the path of interaction once taken is possible only at the expense of considerable effort.

---

[2]   For Luhmann, the notion of semantics has the edge on the term culture in several aspects: First, the notion of semantics does not run the risk of becoming a catch-all term, because the notion of semantics is strongly focused on the aspect of shared understanding. Second, the meanings used in certain situations can be analyzed separately in order to complete the interaction analyses, which otherwise are focused on social processes and structures. Third, the notion of semantics can be used to analyze the term "culture" itself, which was created in the seventeenth century in order to handle the increased cultural contingency.

[3]   As mentioned earlier, semantic analyses can be performed on a great variety of research objects. They can include role patterns as well as key concepts. Hence, the methods of analysis turn out to be no less heterogeneous, although areas involving language provide an especially fruitful terrain for hermeneutical procedures (cf. Hitzler and Honer 1997).

The network constellations involve, for instance, the prevailing relations of power, patterns of alliances and cooperation, influential configurations of (formal and informal) relationships, and also existing barriers and rivalries. The formation of (sub-)groups, intensification of contacts, creation of new positions, rearrangement, and elimination of actor positions are all manifestations of network dynamics. The commonly employed methods of formal network analysis, such as the blockmodel method, are suited for empirically capturing some of the structural and dynamic aspects (see Wasserman and Faust 1998:394 ff.). Such an analysis can be complemented by examining the emergence of an interaction or by a sociological figuration analysis (see, inter alia, Sofsky and Paris 1991).

(3) The level of interventions: The four-level concept draws a sharp distinction between interactions and interventions. Interventions arise from micropolitical calculus of individual actors and thus reflect attempts at influencing ongoing sequences of interaction. Interventions can unfold an unintended life of their own at the interaction level, as, for instance, unintentional arguments demonstrate.

For this reason, it is not only a process of assigning an identity and a position within a network, as described earlier in the second paragraph. A reduction of this kind would be the result of a purely relational constructivist perspective. Instead, actors actively individually appropriate a position, bring to bear their own motivations, and thus virtually give shape to the position in question. The motives may be geared toward consolidating or changing one's position in relation to other actors, accumulating means of power, or actively engaging in networking.[4] Once the "interpretive construct" (Lenk 1987) of "network actor" takes its position, the actor begins actively interpreting and reinterpreting the self and the environment to assess the potential scope for intervention. An adequate and sufficiently detailed interpretation of focal processes in networks, network constellations, and one's role therein is a prerequisite for being able to evaluate the chances of achieving the goals of an intervention.

Thus, successfully launching an intervention requires far more than sound motives. An intervention stands or falls on the translation of motives (mental level) into calculated interventions (social actor level) based on interpretations of the interaction network adequate to the situation. The considerations entering into such interventions must be based on an adequate conception of both the network and the focus of network interactions (second level).

Ego's subjective view of the web of relations of which ego is part is of course not identical to alter's external view of the same network.

---

[4] The concept of micropolitics (cf. Küpper and Ortmann 1992) or, in the world of employment, career politics, as proposed by Hitzler and Pfadenhauer (2003) allows observing how such motives translate into interventions.

Irrespective of the answer to the unproductive question as to which perception is more real, we maintain that actors are confined to their subjective views, which provide the only basis for actor decisions on interventions, the shape they might take, the aims pursued, and the means employed. From this, however, it follows that (empirically based) insight into an actor's subjective perception of a network, specifically, is crucial for an adequate understanding of interventions. And this precisely is the main contribution of qualitative methodology to network analysis.

To the extent that an intervention fails to achieve its objective, this may have a root in a discrepancy between the internal and external perceptions of the respective networks[5] since how the other network actors receive and respond to an actor's contribution plays a decisive role in goal attainment. Transforming an intervention into a contribution to interaction is for the most part the product of interpretations on the part of a "community of interpretation." In the process, the interpretation does not necessarily have to focus on the essence of what the initiator actually intended. For instance, there may be a deliberate misunderstanding. For this reason, it cannot suffice to limit an actor analysis to interventions and their underlying motives. Rather, the key to a relevant analysis of interaction is to also consider the modalities and appropriateness of alter's interpretations as well as the prevailing set of social relationships. Seen from this angle, producing and interpreting stories can be conceived of as a particular form of intervention.[6]

The success of an intervention is not in the hand of the intervening party alone. It also depends on the circumstances of a network, which can never be completely transparent to any individual actor. That means that, in principle, any actor's deliberate efforts can have unintended side effects no matter how straightforward the intention. Yet, actors have no other choice than to launch interventions to the best of their knowledge, time and again, in order to give their motives a form of expression to which others can potentially respond in the first place. It has already been mentioned that qualitative procedures

---

[5] This corresponds with the insight Berger and Luckmann (1966) adopted from Cooley, Dewey, and Mead according to which actors in constituting interaction are required to engage in a "reciprocity of perspectives."

[6] Because there does not exist any isolated actor position in a network, an intervention strategy can fail no matter how much care and determination go into planning. Other network actors may engage in counteracting strategies that are more influential, or network structures and dynamics may deflect an intervention in other directions. Such changes in direction thus result from actors providing stimuli that trigger a chain of interactions at the network level; the emerging paths of interaction lead to a change in direction or, rather, to an autonomous momentum that may run contrary to the initiator's intentions.

of collecting network data are the methods of choice for collecting empirical information about such interventions and interpreting them (e.g., observation methods, video analyses, interviews reflecting past interaction). Only qualitative methodology permits accessing the subjective perception of actor constellations and social relationships that is required to gain an adequate understanding of the concrete interventions observed. Nevertheless, quantitative methods should not be excluded at this level (e.g., to analyze the "community of interpretation" in an adequate way).

(4) The level of emotional expression: From the actor's strategic activities with regard to focal interactions, we must distinguish analytically the signals an actor sends in face-to-face situations. They express the degree of actor affiliation with the respective network of social interaction and the prevailing semantic context (e.g., a youth subculture with its own jargon, norms, and values).[7] Such affiliation is mainly expressed via ritualized action or non-verbal communication in everyday face-to-face interactions. Pongratz (2002), for instance, was thus able to show that controversy with superiors can occur at the workplace without threatening the formal social order if employees at the same time send signals of subordination at the non-verbal level. Such demonstrative expressions of acknowledging the prevailing social relations play a key role in maintaining and perpetuating an ongoing interaction. They are additional signs indicating the "proximity" or "distance" of two network actors that are accessible to (qualitative and quantitative) observation methods. In this sense, they can serve as a potential corrective to the subjective assessments of social relationships obtained through qualitative methods.[8] For a long time, interpretive approaches, conversation analyses, and analyses of interaction systems (cf. Garfinkel 1986; Suchman 1987; Goffman 1988 ; Sacks 1992; Luff et al. 2000) were by and large the only approaches in sociology to take expressions of this kind into consideration. In recent years, however, greater efforts have been made to find appropriate means of empirically capturing the meanings emanating from gestures, facial expressions, and body postures (for the state-of-the art of this line of research, see Pongratz 2003:172 ff.). Those subtle expressions that accompany any

---

[7] Strictly speaking, this also represents a level of intervention in its own right. Since these interventions are of a special kind, requiring their own specific methodology, it makes sense to introduce an analytical level of its own for such interventions.

[8] In this case, we are looking at a second possibility of qualitatively approaching network structures based on observation alone. The individual relations that make up the overall picture of the web of relationships gained from other data sources are determined more precisely by the systematic observation of the respective encounters. The key issue is how the mostly non-verbal representations and expressions of affiliation indicate "proximity" and "distance" to the respective counterpart.

activity also extend legitimation to the semantic framework.[9] They are to be recorded and analyzed in exemplary situations (such as the routine meetings of an administration) based on observation methods (video recording; cf. Häussling 2009).

Those four levels interlock in many ways: Non-verbal expressions of affiliation make use of semantics that allow conveying pleasure, approval, closeness, or other emotional states in a certain interaction setting through facial expression, gestures, body posture, or tone of voice. The same holds true for interventions. Interventions, too, rely on semantics that define a contribution, for instance, as an order, a question, or an act of assistance. Those semantics are of a collective nature, for actors employing such forms and patterns in making their contributions are aware of the fact that the other participants have internalized their meanings (via socialization and processes of learning) just the way they themselves have (see Berger and Luckmann 1966:129 ff.).

The network level assumes a key position in this multilevel model because the effects of micropolitical interventions on the formation of interactions can be observed at this level as can the ways in which the given semantic framework is appropriated and put to use. Since the community of interpretation translates interventions and non-verbal expressions of affiliation into contributions to interactions, those interventions and expressions take effect at the network level by influencing interaction processes also shaped by social structures (e.g., power structures) and the autonomous momentum that such processes unfold. Sometimes, a new semantics of interaction can also be established at this process level (e.g., a new greeting ritual as a sign of identification and belonging to a subculture) and then may enter into the semantic context of interaction. Operationalization of these theoretical considerations will be exemplified using the following case study.

A Case Study on the Implementation of Knowledge Management in a Company Department

This case study is a companion study of the implementation of knowledge management measures in the sales department of an auto manufacturer. The semantics of knowledge management is situated in a field

---

[9] However, this mode of anchoring macro-phenomena in a micro-context is also relevant for linking the micro- and macro-levels in that now societal aspects become visible in the expressions of individual actors. At the same time, those macro-phenomena are perpetuated and vested with legitimacy through action. Drawing on Giddens' notion of "duality of structure" (Giddens 1984: 25–28), we might speak of a *duality of semantics* in this context.

of tension rooted in developments within businesses throughout the Western world, which are widely debated in public discourse (societal semantics). Among these developments are the widespread introduction of information and communication technologies in business administrations and the intensification and interconnectedness of information flows that go along with it; reduced product life cycles in nearly saturated, hotly contested markets that have become global; the far lower cost of industrial production in so-called developing and newly industrializing countries; an increased customer orientation geared toward providing higher quality services; a sharp rise in the complexity of the work and decision-making process of businesses; staff fluctuation due to personnel cutbacks, relocation of production; and so on[10]; and the globalization of markets (for goods and services as well as labor markets) and competition requiring businesses to engage in networking with their environment (e.g., business networks [cf. Sydow and Windeler 2000], outsourcing, juridification, Europeanization, etc.).

Those ubiquitous developments at the same time indicate an increasing knowledge orientation of businesses, which has far-reaching consequences for interaction among employees (cf. Reinmann-Rothmeier and Mandl 2000). It is characterized by a sheer explosion of information and the elevation of knowledge transfer to become a key issue in the business process. As far as the transferred contents are concerned, they not only involve matters of greater complexity (due to the higher degree of interconnectedness) but typically also have a much shorter lifespan than in the past in terms of topicality and validity. Those transformations go hand in hand with dense informational interdependencies between organizations and their environments (increased market dependency, financial interdependencies, etc.), resulting in communication virtually overrunning company boundaries and thus rendering them less significant.

These and other features of an increasing knowledge orientation of businesses also entail a number of problematic consequences for everyday work life, which so far could not be contained even by the most sophisticated information management systems. One such consequence is the informational overload employees face, which becomes most conspicuously manifest in overflowing mailboxes. In connection with this, potential sources of knowledge may suffer from a loss of transparency. Simultaneously tackling the same problems in different departments in an uncoordinated fashion or even disregard of important information are possible consequences. At the same time, there is a danger of important information remaining unused.

---

[10] In many companies, that development in particular has led to the dissolution of informal structures that had evolved over lengthy periods of time and had ensured an effective knowledge transfer among colleagues.

Businesses employ the semantics of knowledge management to respond to these global developments. These semantics seek to establish new standards for knowledge transfer, communication, and information exchange within the company. The goal thus is for business processes to accord with those imposed semantics in the future. For this reason, I will first briefly introduce aspects of the knowledge management doctrine relevant to the case. Then I will turn to the concrete case under study. The following sections are divided up according to the four-level concept. While the first section introduces the level of semantic context with reference to the case under study, the second section is devoted to the level of concrete interaction. The level of interventions by department staff is addressed in the third section before finally the level of expressions of affiliation is discussed in the fourth section.

On the Semantics of the Knowledge Management Doctrine[11]

For more than a decade now, the management concepts of "the learning organization"[12] and "knowledge management" rate highly with business consultants and businesses, and even with non-profit organizations. Willke defines knowledge management as "the totality of organizational strategies for the creation of an 'intelligent' organization. With regard to persons, it involves the level of competence, training, and learning capacity of the membership throughout the whole organization; concerning the organization as a system, it is a matter of creating, utilizing, and developing collective intelligence and the 'collective mind'; and as regards technological infrastructure, knowledge management is primarily about how and how efficiently an organization puts to use a communication and information infrastructure matching its mode of operation" (Willke 2001:39 – author's translation from German). Consequently, knowledge management measures have to prove adequate in the following three dimensions:

(1) The social dimension: The social dimension paints a new picture of employees as valuable bearers and creators of knowledge; in terms of employees' everyday work experience, this demands coping with new knowledge-oriented tasks, responsibilities, and

---

[11] Management jargon is deliberately used throughout the entire chapter to capture linguistically the formative power of semantics as it transforms social relations. That which is posited almost as an absolute in pleasant-sounding terms has grave consequences for the employees, no matter whether they applaud or attempt to fend off the measures in question.

[12] For the concept of the "learning organization" see, e.g., Probst and Büchel (1998).

objectives. Social competence, in particular, plays a key role as a necessary prerequisite for openly dealing with knowledge.

(2) The organizational dimension: At the organizational level, knowledge management measures are expected to contribute to creating a knowledge-friendly organizational culture. Reducing the mechanisms of control, improving the transparency of decisions, employing a considerate and cooperative style of leadership, and establishing new generally binding standards for knowledge transfer are considered to be especially important means of achieving that objective. Such a call for self-organization and decentralization in conjunction with delegating decisions corresponds with the insight that processes of growing complexity and dynamism escape deliberate organizational planning and control.

(3) The technological dimension: This dimension of knowledge management is often referred to by the catchword "information management," which denotes the development of new and more "intelligent" databases and data networks (e.g., Lotus Notes).

There hardly exist any specially developed management measures for this purpose. Rather, knowledge management deliberately relies on a new mix of methods that have proven effective in the past decades (lean management, teamwork schemes, etc.) (see Wuppertaler, 2000:77–94). The novelty of knowledge management lies in the focus on improving the process of knowledge transfer as well as communication and information exchange within a company (also see Willke 2001:19 ff.). New standards of organizing the future workflow are to be imposed – or, cast in the terminology proposed in this chapter, work situations are framed by a semantics that becomes the key measure for individual and collective success.[13]

The Network Level of Interaction

In examining the network level of interaction, we may analytically distinguish two axes of interpretation as shown in the second section. One axis is supposed to represent the structural aspects of the social entity under study; in this case, it is the sales department and how it

---

[13] As is the case with many management measures, such a new semantics can of course also be used to lay the argumentative groundwork for changes already planned (such as reducing or rejuvenating staff). Nevertheless, the means cannot simply be chosen at will. The measures are adopted based on expectations that they will help a company cope with its most urgent problems.

is embedded in processes of knowledge transfer that extend beyond the individual departments. The other axis sheds light on the dynamic aspects of this department. Since both aspects are closely connected, they will be introduced accordingly in an interconnected fashion. The following section is organized according to the sequence of events: The first subsection is concerned with the actual state of the department and the appropriateness of change. The second subsection addresses the implementation phase and introduces the measures in detail. The third subsection describes the anticipated scenario of the department's future underlying those management measures: How is knowledge transfer to take place, and what structural framework needs to be created for this purpose?

The Department Status Quo and Expediency of Change. The sales department of an auto manufacturer at the center of the study[14] consists of 50 employees organized in five teams. Each team has a team leader, and a department manager is in charge of the department as a whole. The fact that the department was newly formed six months prior to the study by merging two previously (also spatially) separate departments poses a special challenge. Subdivision A might be described as the "old factory culture." It consists of two large teams, the members of which mostly entered the company as trainees and have worked there for decades in jobs with a strong technical focus. In contrast, subdivision B can be characterized as "business-minded." It is comprised of small dynamic teams who operate with a market focus. Most employees of subdivision B are university graduates and considerably younger than the subdivision A staff. The employee interviews show that at the outset there existed a rivalry between the two department cultures. Even four years after the merger, there were still few contacts extending across the old boundaries. In spite of measures designed to enhance networking across the newly defined areas of work and responsibility of the individual teams, the traditional reservations were further cultivated (both sides referred to one another as "those over there").[15] Thus the quantitative analysis performed on the catalogue of network analytical questions contained in the question-

---

[14] In this study, data weres collected in three waves in 2003, 2005, and 2007: All employees were interviewed and asked to complete a self-administered questionnaire, expert interviews were conducted with executives, documents were analyzed, and participant observation was carried out.

[15] Even a future workshop that in the course of an entire weekend gave department staff an opportunity to openly voice problems, fears, and concerns and get to know "those over there" failed to yield any lasting effects.

naire,[16] which all department staff were asked to complete, produced a telling, sobering account of the status quo. Although we observed that in individual cases regular channels of communication had been established between the previously separate subdivisions A and B, as far as informal contacts were concerned, department staff not only perpetuated the antiquated divide but also engaged in team-specific processes of closure.[17] Figure 4.1 shows the results of the analysis.[18]

Already before the merger, the department staff's daily tasks largely consisted of obtaining information for sales purposes and preparing it for various target groups, for instance, in the form of operating manuals.[19] Finding the information needed at any point in time is a contingent process in light of today's information explosion. Thus, the majority of staff members complained in the interview about spending most of their time looking for adequate information. At the same time, they are swamped with a mass of irrelevant information especially by email.

The department crucially depends on information supplied from outside of the department and in turn is required to provide knowledge to third parties as well. Among the external sources of information are other company departments (in-plant relationships), sales departments in other countries (in-company relationships), the network of appointed dealerships referred to as the field organization (external relationships$_1$), and (big) customers (external relationships$_2$). From a network theoretical point of view, sources outside the department represent peripheral nodes of the network that are grouped around the department as the network core, which displays a higher density of information exchange. The department is not only the hub for collecting, processing, and

---

[16] The response rate to the questionnaire was 70%. However, part of the respondents showed reservations in answering the network analytical questions, especially concerning informal contacts (even in the light of legally binding guarantees of anonymity).

[17] The leader of the team Technical Consulting (node 22), who headed a team of the other subdivision prior to the merger, is an exception in this respect.

[18] Note the following for a better understanding of the illustrations: As to the intensive formal relationships, four questions were asked requesting the respondent to name the three most important persons in each case. Figure 4.1a presents the aggregate results. Two questions were asked regarding the most prominent informal relationships (again responses were limited to naming three persons). The results are summarized in Figure 4.1b. The respondents could also name persons outside of the department to whom they entertained intensive formal or informal contacts (nodes 51–61). The members of the department were assigned numbers from 1 to 50 at random. Nodes representing individual team members are shown in shades of gray to distinguish the teams. Arrows indicate relationships that can involve various forms of formal or informal interaction. Department staff who did not answer network analytical questions and were not mentioned as significant others by other persons are displayed as isolated nodes on the right-hand margin of the illustration (this involves only staff of subdivision B).

[19] Almost all staff, in the interviews and again in responding to the questionnaires, referred to this type of knowledge work as the "day-to-day core activity."

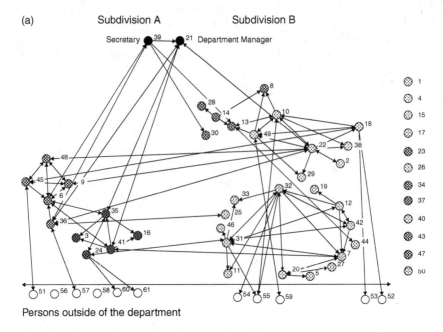

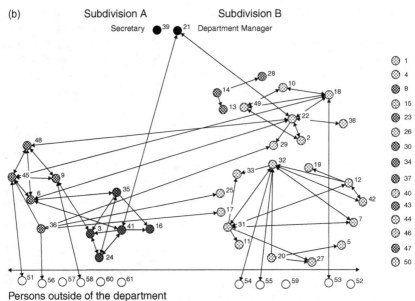

Figure 4.1. Intensive contacts: (a) formal and (b) informal

relaying heterogeneous information. It is also the place for complex data exchanges and cooperation in generating knowledge.

In the process of department restructuring, the department manager embraced the key idea of knowledge management to turn the department into a "community of practice"[20] organized around knowledge transfer as the main value creating activity.[21] If such a community is successfully established, that environment should guarantee an open exchange of information: Problems can be discussed openly without running the risk of getting caught up in micropolitical games – at least this is what this management doctrine leads us to expect (see Romhardt 2002:19 f.). Forms of cooperation based on mutual trust among department colleagues are expected to provide the basis for processes of knowledge transfer in accordance with the principles of solidarity. More intensive cooperation would also create channels for accessing "tacit knowledge" (Polanyi 1958)[22] – the generally hardly verbalized practical know-how – which is considered to be especially valuable. The measures adopted for achieving that objective are presented in the next section.

The Implementation Stage: Knowledge Management in Detail. The department has attempted to implement a whole bundle of measures geared toward establishing the envisioned "community of practice." The measures will be introduced in the following along the three dimensions of knowledge management (see the section "On the Semantics of the Knowledge Management Doctrine"). Improving the existing data platform to serve as an "intelligent" IT platform for knowledge transfer represents a technical measure.[23] The platform is to function

---

[20] Lave and Wenger (1991) first introduced the concept of a "community of practice."

[21] The minutes of a team leader workshop give an instructive account of this vision: "As Sales Support Center we want to take the lead by providing convincing services, installing best practice processes, and engaging in innovation. In our role as Competence Center for demand-oriented information and knowledge management, we want to be the benchmark [of our company] in terms of relevant product information and knowledge management and enthuse our customers. We want to produce added value based on innovative processes, high product quality, new services, and competent and motivated staff [...]" (internal department document).

[22] Nonaka and Takeuchi (1997) discuss the significance of "tacit knowledge" for knowledge management.

[23] However, in an expert interview the department manager mentioned that only when additional social and organizational knowledge management measures are implemented will this platform be able to perform this function effectively and comprehensively. By his own account, the point is for his department to "live" the ideas of knowledge management one day. In this context, virtually on a philosophical note, he spoke of "creating more space" and characterized that space in terms of a "space of thought," a "space of support," a "space of encounters," a "space of time," and a "space for the informal" (cf. interview transcript – translated from German). We will return to the space metaphor in more detail later on.

not only as an archive of knowledge, like a conventional database, but also as a dynamic realm for the exchange of thought and experience. For this purpose, discussion fora and a support function to allow retrieving information via a search engine will be set up. Partly automated filters serve as a first means of reducing potential information overload.

Considering the fact that two separate departments are to form one under the banner of a "community of practice," uniting them in one location becomes a crucial task with great symbolic impact. The department manager, as he explains in the interview, is well aware of the importance of the issue.[24] Much more is therefore involved than merely creating new office space. For this reason, a new office concept was developed as a social measure extending beyond mere building measures to give the idea of community a spatial expression. The concept was designed to promote the development of the envisioned network of knowledge exchange within the department. The new office concept draws on familiar concepts of desk sharing where staff members have no permanent workplace but choose a vacant desk as they arrive at work (see Neuhaus 2002:42 ff.). Employees keep files and their personal items in mobile containers waiting on them in the entrance area upon arrival at the office. This reduces office supplies, working utensils, and personal accessories to a minimum. In the end, the main tool required to go about one's work is the computer at each desk.

The office concept intends for workplaces to be arranged in a way that actively fosters communication between the members of the various teams. Thus, the workplaces are not supposed to be strictly arranged according to team membership, rank, or other criteria of similar kind. The desks are grouped in a cloverleaf fashion or set up in groups of two or three. In addition, there are individual workplaces for undisturbed working or ones that are equipped with special database connections or software. A deliberate effort is made to create spaces conducive to informal communication, such as a kitchen, and also a living room–type zone for relaxation as well as meeting rooms. Tellingly, an information center is located in a central position that will be open to members of other departments and certain visitors.[25] For legal reasons, Figure 4.2 is limited to giving an outline of the basic principles of the office concept.

[24] The department manager repeatedly emphasized that a "consensual" solution to the issue of office space was being sought. To arrive at such a solution, the final plan was developed iteratively in several rounds of discussions facilitated by two interior designers involving representatives of all teams so that individual wishes could be taken into account (cf. interview transcript).
[25] It is telling because this arrangement also symbolizes, in terms of how space is organized, the central importance of knowledge and information to the department.

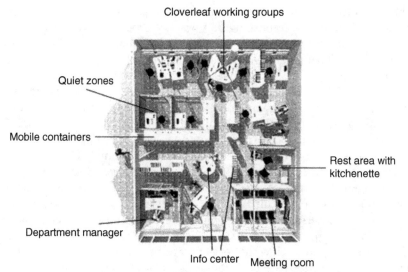

Figure 4.2. Diagram illustrating the new office concept

Furthermore, organizational measures are conceived to reduce organizational regulations, work guidelines, and mechanisms of supervision. This is due to the fact that, because of the complexity of knowledge transfer, forms of centralized control and supervision are obsolete. Instead, knowledge transfer must take place in self-directed ways. The more the transfer of knowledge becomes the decisive factor for success, the more important it is to provide the process with a stable, reliable, and transparent set of rules since the processes as such cannot be organized in a standardized fashion. The department manager consistently applies the doctrine of knowledge management in viewing the creation of a community spirit and peer pressure as a means of achieving the envisioned self-regulation. This consideration shall be elaborated in the following section.

The department scenario as anticipated by management: social considerations in dealing with knowledge

It has already been mentioned that by applying the idea of a "community of practice" to knowledge management the department is to become a community of competent, dedicated, and, above all, cooperative knowledge workers. To achieve this, the department has to be formed into a communication network in a way that enables greatly reducing the information load each individual must deal with. Joint efforts in searching information are perceived as a way of tapping synergies so that each person does not have to search all sources on their own. In this sense, the community functions as a catalyst and accelerator of ongoing communication and business processes. Role assignments in the community are expected to emerge on their own from the dynamics and network structures that mark the setting.[26] This leads to establishing best practice procedures that eventually turn into community standards, which all staff members are obliged to comply with depending on their role in the network.

In this respect, the individual employee can be conceived of as a "knowledge agent"[27]: The community assigns staff the task of carefully researching and filtering the great mass of information for knowledge relevant for sales purposes and passing it on to the respective person in charge. Staff members are not autonomous actors but rather actors in charge of certain tasks on behalf of the community. However, the sales support center staff are not the only ones expected to assume the role of agent; rather, designated contact persons from other departments are supposed to act in this function as well (for instance, said contact person of the research and development department [R&D department in the following]). By means of establishing rapport with such persons, they are motivated to view the core operations of their own departments from a sales perspective. And it does not end here! The sales support center also casts its customers into the role of agents. Developing a system for recording and analyzing complaints enables utilizing valuable user knowledge for improving products and customer services. Thus, ideas are not only produced, by definition, in the R&D department; they can also emerge from customer feedback.

Hence, the network structure and network dynamics themselves cast those involved in the process of knowledge creation into the role of agents. As explained in the section "The Conceptual Framework of Interpretation," we draw on White's network theoretical conception of identity to describe this process of allocating positions (cf. White 1992). According to White, a person is assigned an identity by the surrounding social networks.[28] In the case in question, following White, we may conclude that the actors of the communication network are assigned a functionally predefined agency for purposes of knowledge acquisition based on personal networks that already predispose certain individuals for the pursuit of certain kinds of information.

[26] In the case study, a staff member is on good terms with a member of the research and development department due to his previous job history. Other members of the sales support center receive only scanty information from that department. The employee entertaining the good contacts will act as an intermediary in charge of all future requests for information from the R&D department. The community was assigned this task because of the specific position this person occupies in the network.

[27] Although the proximity to principal-agent theory (cf., e.g., Richter and Furubotn 2003) indicated in using the notion of agent is intended, this does not mean to suggest agreement with all of its theoretical implications; in fact, I consider certain parts of the theory to be quite problematic.

[28] We may thus think of networks as (individually) preceding the individual actor. In other words, the network defines the individual.

The legitimacy of the organization then is reflected less in individual staff anticipatively developing technologies of the self, as governmentality studies postulate (cf. Bröckling et al. 2000), rather than in widely observed individual compliance with ubiquitous community demands,[29] which become manifest as pressure to conform and live up to expectations. The basic intention of knowledge management measures thus aims at systematically dismantling sanctuaries of the individual and replacing them with communalized spaces. The new department office concept sends the same message (see the subsection "The Implementation Stage"): The contents of mobile containers remain the only remnants of individuality. Everything else speaks a clear language: As a member of the department, the important issue is not where my space in the office is but rather my entry into the community. The community acts as a comprehensive support network as long as "we" comply with community demands. At the same time, the office concept actually cuts down on privacy. No matter where one is seated, one constantly faces different members of the community, emphasizing the interchangeability of the individual as a medium of the community. The person opposite to me is both observer and a potential source of sanctioning who speaks with the voice of the community. Only after taking its designated place and deferring to the community is the individual put in a position to successfully perform its work.

Interventionist Responses of Department Staff

But how do individual staff members respond to those new realities created at the semantic level via the doctrine of knowledge management and at the interaction network level by way of the structural measures discussed earlier? Do dynamics really take hold at the network level as management claims so that individual performance and career pathways have to conform to the new structural and semantic requirements? If this were the case, we would have to expect changes in an individual employee's perception of his or her network segment reflecting such tendencies. In particular, we could expect to observe the contacts desired by the department manager to "those over there," that is, to members of what was formerly the other department.

---

[29] This assessment follows from the seemingly utopian demands on the "community of practice" as a "group of people (...) who perceive themselves both as teachers and students, (...) who speak candidly about mistakes and failure, (...) who listen to one another, attempt to establish a mutual understanding, and seek to avoid using their knowledge to compete for economic advantages" (Romhardt 2002:19 f. – author's translation from German).

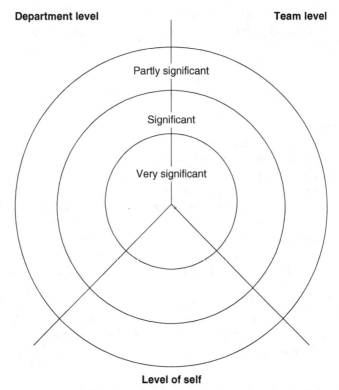

Department level   **Team level**

Partly significant

Significant

Very significant

Level of self

Figure 4.3. Network map used in the interviews for charting persons (members of the department or other persons relevant to the work setting), objects, and circumstances according to significance

To assess this, staff members were presented the network map shown in Figure 4.3 during the course of the interviews – it draws on the network map used by Kahn and Antonucci (1980:383–405), which differentiates actors (or objects and circumstances) according to significance along a system of concentric circles indicating gradations of importance. Buttons representing persons are placed in the respective circle according to the significance of the person in question.[30] For the staff interviews, the circle was subdivided into three subject areas. The first area referred to the key processes of value creation in the department and the role the teams and department management play in those processes. The second subject area concerned the main processes, structures, and actors (including persons not part of the team) at the team level, while the third area addressed the actor level, inquiring about the

---

[30] Straus (2002:196 ff.) provides an overview of the variety of network maps suitable for use in qualitative interviews.

interviewee's abilities and strengths (and weaknesses) as concerns his or her daily work.

Here we will only be able to discuss the findings at the department level in more detail. The staff members participating in the interviews were asked to characterize the department's core activities, place the individual teams onto the network map according to their importance for those core activities, and to explain their assessment of each team.

The differences in the way the department and its main structures and processes are perceived are striking. The respective narratives are in some cases diametrically opposed. The different perceptions of one and the same department also extend to the positioning of the teams within the department. The staff referred to as the "old factory culture" (subdivision A) nearly unanimously mentioned the provision of information and technical support as the department's core tasks – thus the tasks that their teams stand for. Those staff members at the same time complain about department management showing too little interest in those core tasks and also lacking sufficient knowledge. They see their performance not being adequately appreciated.

In contrast, the staff members of the business-minded teams (subdivision B) with few exceptions refer to product information and generating information, and thus their own area of work, when asked about the key tasks of the department. They present themselves as the teams performing the main integrative functions since they command both technical know-how and knowledge of modern marketing. They view themselves as a kind of task force that refines and processes raw technical data and facts, thus rendering them marketable in the first place. They emphasize the importance of team members' individuality and consider soft skills more important than expert knowledge.

Accordingly, all staff interviewed – with few exceptions – rated their own team as very important. Most notably, the assessments differed along the former department boundaries. The teams representing the other department culture were considered much less relevant – and mutually so. The interviews showed that the reasons for this lie in the incompatibility of the prevailing modes of action and interpretation in the respective teams. The members of the business-minded teams viewed the teams representing the "old factory culture" as antiquated since, according to the former, the latter perceive the merger of the two subdivisions as a "hostile takeover" and fail to understand the new situation defined by saturated markets and predatory competition where good products and advice based on facts is simply not enough. Staff members of the "old factory culture" view the business-minded teams with similar skepticism. According to the former, the latter are "storytellers" who lack a firm grounding and unwarrantedly enjoy staging themselves as important. Furthermore, the technical teams accuse the business teams of being favored by department management and trace this to their greater effectiveness in showcasing their performance and blinding department management. In reality, according to credible statements made in the course of the interviews with department management, the latter has a very critical relationship to one of the business-minded teams, to its team leader in particular.

Such misjudgments demonstrate the extent to which narratives emerging from specific positions and perspectives can take on a life of their own, lacking a real foundation that could provide the necessary basis for coming to terms with one another across team boundaries. With this lack of such a common basis, one team inevitably perceives the other's interventions in a biased manner. Moreover, the divide can hardly be overcome since there is little willingness to consider the needs of the other team and understand its perspective. According to White and Ardelt, this is a typical process of organizational closure that entails three consequences: "First, a general disparagement of the outgroup and/or an aggrandizement of the ingroup, second, an overemphasis on perceived differences between other attributes of the in- and outgroup, as well as, third, actions relatively favoring the ingroup" (see Witte and Ardelt 1989:463–83).

Participant observation of team and other meetings and on-site at the department confirmed the impression gained based on the network map. We were able to observe that attempts at approaching one another frequently led to misunderstandings – especially concerning the exchange of information. The business-minded teams perceived the interventions of staff representing the "old factory culture" as nitpicky, too much focused on facts and too little on people, inefficient, and obsessed with details. Staff members associated with the "old factory culture," on the other hand, interpreted the activities of the business-minded teams as superficial, out of touch with reality, and more concerned about putting on an impressive show. Barriers also exist with regard to different styles of working and strategies in dealing with problems. Whereas the teams representing the "old factory culture" in most cases go about their work according to a rigid order where problems are addressed one at a time in order of occurrence, the business-minded teams, due to their pronounced project orientation, tend toward new solutions or – if possible – toward strategies of working around the problem. On the one hand, these differences are manifestations of completely different role patterns for team members – experts in charge of certain tasks (even the team leader is first among equals) versus project managers – and, on the other, they are expressions of clearly contrasting sources of the appreciation of work – expertise versus making a convincing impression. Whenever those working methods, role patterns, and forms of appreciation cross paths, critical situations are bound to arise.[31]

The heterogeneous forms of intervention and the biased interpretations of the respective other have an adverse impact on mutual exchange. Members of the business-minded teams perceive the teams representing the "old factory culture" as simply being to slow and too little focused on essentials in responding to their requests. Conversely, staff members of the "old factory culture" get annoyed about the simplified and partly distorted presentation of technical information in glossy brochures, which, in their view, only cost a lot of money and contain mistakes that they then have to iron out in case of customer inquiries. According to their verdict, not just the brochures but also those staff members lack substance. In other words, both teams gain the impression that the others deliberately take a biased view of their own course of action in terms of its relevance and achievements while at the same time they are mostly unwilling to accept that they also represent the other team's approach in a distorted fashion as well. This issue is also reflected in the results of a standardized survey.

Those approaches and interpretations result in processes of closure within the individual teams, which, as mentioned previously, also become manifest in ostentatious displays of team spirit. It could nevertheless be observed, especially at the level of non-verbal representations and expressions of affiliation, how the own team was used to counter the department manager's vision of the future. This will be briefly outlined in the following final section.

Expressions of Affiliation on Part of Department Staff

According to our observations, the staff appears to come to terms with the changes demanded of them. In conducting their daily business, they resort to ritualistic patterns of behavior to express an attitude of conformity with the community. For instance, we repeatedly observed gestures indicating subordination of the self to the team (e.g., being available in case of unexpected problems). In such situations, staff frequently displayed signs of loyalty to colleagues (e.g., expressions of respect for the know-how of other team members) and engaged in expressions of solidarity, such as a repeatedly observed, expressly demonstrated chummy

---

[31] Particularly surprising in this respect is that staff members, having changed from one department culture to the other in the course of job rotation, have also quickly assimilated the modes of intervention and also the views of the new team, and now take a critical stance toward their previous team.

behavior (putting an arm around a colleague's shoulder, patting a colleague on the back, having a chat). In contrast, toward members of the other department culture, avoidance behavior and behavior indicating distance or lack of time (for instance by turning away from the other) was also observed repeatedly.

These and other signals expressing commitment to the community and subordination within the team can be viewed as an instrucitve maneuver on the part of the staff. On the one hand, they indicate to the department manager that they are willing to go along with his vision of the future of the department – in anticipation of this vision so to speak. The staff members in this way display a pronounced community spirit and readiness to defer to the community. Although this form of anticipating the changes the department manager hopes for appears to underscore his claim to leadership and decision-making authority (in spite of the cooperative style of leadership otherwise cultivated), the staff, on the other hand, seems to strategically employ such displays of conformity to delay or even obstruct the actual realization of the idea of community at the department level. For their expressions of solidarity in fact strengthen the team, establish a more favorable position for the team in terms of how it ranks within the department, and in this way clearly distances itself from the other teams. Corporate identity is thus reinforced at the team level only and tacitly played off against the department.[32] A formal network analysis of the intensive informal contacts additionally confirmed that team focus (see Figure 4.1b).

Those "micropolitical" strategies (cf. Küpper and Ortmann 1992) can be taken as signs for a struggle over a four-year period over the future semantics of interaction and the fact that the department manager has failed to successfully implement the envisioned changes in spite of his favorable position in the setting. The implemented measures can actually thwart the department manager's original intentions and, as the case study exemplifies, even lead to drawing sharper lines between the teams. At any rate, team interventions dealt a decisive blow to the envisioned model of a "community of practice."

Whatever the outcome of the struggles over the framing of the knowledge system in the department under study, communication centered on knowledge has gained significance in any event –in the perspective of both management and staff. The stalemate can be described as a micro-political

---

[32] The respective team leader acts as an important ally supporting his team in subverting such endeavors at forming a community since his strategic position is also threatened by that development. The observation of executive meetings revealed an accordingly tense relationship between the team leaders and the department manager.

struggle over leadership at the semantic versus the operational level. As management decides to give greater significance to communication centered on knowledge, there is also a shift in attention on the part of the staff: Since such communication processes have gained greater importance and have increasingly become an area where careers are decided, staff has no choice but to give them more attention. In that respect, at least the deeper semantics of knowledge management (irrespective of success in implementing individual measures) has prevailed in that the staff shows greater commitment to engaging in effective networking.

Conclusion

The object of research presented here represents a pronounced and thus particularly instructive case of a clash between the level of semantics (first level), the levels of intervention (third level), and the level of emotional expression (fourth level). By contrast, the interaction level (second level) as such forms the arena where the interventions take place, the new semantics (of knowledge management) take hold, and the resulting measures fully unfold their formative power. The fact that the different levels of interaction point in completely different directions underscores the need for analyzing concrete interaction arrangements from several levels.

If, in the case under study, the analysis were to be restricted to subjective perceptions on the part of staff or to semantics only, the discrepancies between expectations (of control) and staff behavior would remain invisible. The same is also bound to be true for the methodical approach. Here, too, the question of whether one should opt for qualitative or quantitative, hermeneutical or formal methods of interaction analysis is completely misleading. Rather, the question to be asked concerns the proper research design to enable a triangulation of methods. Precisely in this sense, I propose and put up for discussion the conception of interaction introduced here as a possible solution. This concept not only allows identifying and combining the perspectives and research questions related to those methods by means of distinguishing four levels; in focusing on interaction, it also emphasizes a subject area that the network subject matter is already headed for. The notion of network predisposes the sociological observer toward focusing on (webs of) relationships and processes. Qualitative network analysis, on the other hand, focuses on closely knit, significant, and time-intensive contacts of individual network actors due to its egocentric perspective. This suggests a choice of a theoretical framework based on a relational concept of interaction – even more so since, in focusing on cooperation centered on knowledge within the divisions of a company, our research concerns an area where relationship patterns evolve and are brought to life in face-to-face interactions.

Qualitative network analysis enables reconstructing the network of interactions from the perspective of the respondent. The same perspective underlies actor interventions.[33] For this reason, it is indispensable to reconstruct the actor's perspective of the network. Qualitative interviews – with the aid of network maps and other forms of visualization – additionally have the important advantage of permitting the systematic tracing of ego's significant social relationships, thus minimizing the risk of overlooking relevant persons.[34] By contrast, by employing quantitative or formal network analysis – which aims at generating responses to network-related questions from all relevant actors – we expect to produce a topographical image of the network.

Consequently, the majority of the methods in this line of analysis address issues of cluster or clique formation, "structural holes" (Burt 2001), power relations (triad research), role patterns, and systems of social positions (blockmodel analysis). They take into consideration that interactions exhibit a momentum of their own, form corridors of action, and involve elements of power and dependency that play a decisive role in determining the further course of focal processes. Knowledge of such parameters is necessary to be able to identify at all whether an actor assumes a central or peripheral position in a network, why certain groups of people stand apart and cannot make use or can only make limited use of certain connections, and what information background they have, which in turn affects the patterns of interpretation they rely on. Those "emergent" aspects – if you will – cannot be adequately accounted for based on qualitative network analysis alone, just as formal network analysis cannot provide a detailed explanation of the reasons why a network actor intervenes in a certain way, what motivates an actor to get in close touch with certain persons – and not with others – and the qualitative attributes of such contacts.

Both approaches – qualitative as well as quantitative – are warranted. And not just warranted at that! Both approaches are of equal importance for gaining a comprehensive understanding of courses and constellations of interaction and must be incorporated in the research design accordingly. Because of this, the ensemble of empirical methods itself increasingly takes the shape of a network, the interconnections of which must of course be conceptually configured in appropriate ways. It

---

[33] In this context, Betina Hollstein (2002:73 f.) also speaks of "ideas of relationships (perception and interpretation schemes) and normative orientations guiding action" (author's translation from German).

[34] Written questionnaires, which are generally the instrument of choice in formal network analysis, can never rule out chances of missing important others.

is precisely this aspect that network research will have to focus attention on in the years to come.

References

Berger, Peter L. and Thomas Luckmann. 1966. *The Social Construction of Reality. A Treatise in the Sociology of Knowledge.* New York et al.: Doubleday.

Bröckling, Ulrich, Susanne Krasmann, and Thomas Lemke, eds. 2000. *Gouvernementalität der Gegenwart. Studien zur Ökonomisierung des Sozialen.* Frankfurt/M.: Suhrkamp.

Burt, Ronald S. 2001. "Structural holes versus network closure as social capital." Pp. 31–56 in *Social Capital: Theory and Research*, edited by N. Lin, K. S. Cook, and R. S. Burt. Aldine: de Gruyter.

Drew, Paul and Anthony Wootton, eds. 1988. *Erving Goffman. Exploring the Interaction Order.* Cambridge: Polity Press.

Engel, Uwe. 1998. *Einführung in die Mehrebenenanalyse. Grundlagen, Auswertungsverfahren und praktische Beispiele.* Opladen, Wiesbaden: Westdeutscher Verlag.

Garfinkel, Harold. 1986. *Ethnomethodological Studies of Work.* London: Routledge & Kegan Paul.

Giddens, Anthony. 1984. *The Constitution of Society: Outline of the Theory of Structuration.* Berkeley, Los Angeles: University of California Press.

Goffman, Erving. 1977. *Frame Analysis. An Essay on the Organization of Experience.* Frankfurt/M.: Suhrkamp.

Haller, Max 1999. *Soziologische Theorie im systematisch-kritischen Vergleich.* Opladen: Leske + Budrich.

Häussling, Roger. 2005. "Netzwerke und Organisationen – konträre oder komplementäre gesellschaftliche Mechanismen?" Pp. 265–86 in *Organisationsgesellschaft. Facetten und Perspektiven*, edited by W. Jäger and U. Schimank. Wiesbaden: VS Verlag.

———. 2003. *Soziale Prozesse als Netzwerkspiele. Soziologische Essays zu Leitaspekten der Netzwerktheorie.* Moscow/Stuttgart [German/Russian]: Logosaltera.

———. 2009. "Video analyses with a four level interaction concept: A network-based concept of human-robot interaction." Pp. 107–31 in *Video Interaction Analysis. Methods and Methodology*, edited by U. T. Kissmann. Frankfurt/M.: Peter Lang Verlag.

Hillmann, Karl-Heinz, ed. 1994. *Wörterbuch der Soziologie.* 4th ed. Stuttgart: Kröner.

Hitzler, Ronald and Anne Honer, eds. 1997. *Sozialwissenschaftliche Hermeneutik. Eine Einführung.* Opladen: Leske + Budrich.

Hitzler, Ronald and Michaela Pfadenhauer, eds. 2003. *Karrierepolitik. Beiträge zur Rekonstruktion erfolgsorientierten Handelns.* Opladen: Leske & Budrich/VVA.

Hollstein, Betina. 2002. *Soziale Netzwerke nach der Verwitwung. Eine Rekonstruktion der Veränderungen informeller Beziehungen.* Opladen: Leske + Budrich

Kahn, Robert L. and Toni Claudette Antonucci. 1980. "Convoys over the life course: Attachment, roles, and social support." Pp. 253–68 in *Life-Span Development and Behavior*, vol. 3, edited by P. B. Baltes and O. B. Brim. New York: Academic Press.

Küpper, Willi and Günther Ortmann. 1992. *Mikropolitik. Rationalität, Macht und Spiele in Organisationen*. 2nd ed. Opladen: Westdeutscher Verlag.

Lave, Jean and Etienne Wenger. 1991. *Situated Learning*. Cambridge: Cambridge University Press.

Lenk, Hans. 1987. "Das Ich als Interpretationskonstrukt: Vom kognitiven Subjektivitätskonzept zum pragmatischen Handlungszusammenhang." Pp. 152–82 in *Zwischen Sozialpsychologie und Sozialphilosophie*, edited by Hans Lenk. Frankfurt/M.: Suhrkamp.

———. 1995. *Schemaspiele. Über Schemainterpretation und Interpretationskonstrukte*. Frankfurt/M.: Suhrkamp.

Luff, Paul, Jon Hindmarsh, and Christian Heath, eds. 2000. *Workplace Studies: Recovering Work Practice and Informing System Design*. Cambridge: Cambridge University Press.

Luhmann, Niklas 1997. Die Gesellschaft der Gesellschaft. 2 vols. Frankfurt/M.: Suhrkamp.

Neuhaus, Ralf. 2002. "Moderne Bürokonzepte – Wirtschaftlichkeit durch Telearbeit und Desk-Sharing, in Angewandte Arbeitswissenschaft." *Zeitschrift für die Unternehmenspraxis* 173:42–61.

Nonaka, Ihujiro and Hirotaka Takeuchi. 1997. *Die Organisation des Wissens – Wie japanische Unternehmen eine brachliegende Ressource nutzbar machen*. Frankfurt/M.: Campus.

Ortmann, Günther. 1995. *Formen der Produktion. Organisation und Rekursivität*. Opladen: Westdeutscher Verlag.

Polanyi, Michael. 1958. *Personal Knowledge*. Chicago: University of Chicago Press.

Pongratz, Hans. 2002. "Legitimitätsgeltung und Interaktionsstruktur. Die symbolische Repräsentation hierarchischer Verfügungsrechte in Führungsinteraktionen." *Zeitschrift für Soziologie* 31(4):255–74.

———. 2003. *Die Interaktionsordnung von Personalführung. Inszenierungsformen bürokratischer Herrschaft im Führungsalltag*. Wiesbaden: Westdeutscher Verlag.

Probst, Gilbert J. B. and Bettina S. T. Büchel. 1998. *Organisationales Lernen. Wettbewerbsvorteil der Zukunft*. 2nd ed. Wiesbaden: Gabler.

Reinmann-Rothmeier, Gabi and Heinz Mandl. 2000. *Individuelles Wissensmanagement. Strategien für den persönlichen Umgang mit Information und Wissen am Arbeitsplatz*. Bern: Huber Verlag.

Richter, Rudolf and Eirik G. Furubotn. 2003. *Neue Institutionenökonomik. Eine Einführung und kritische Würdigung*. 3rd ed. Tübingen: Mohr Siebeck.

Romhardt, Kai. 2002. *Wissensgemeinschaften – Orte lebendigen Wissensmanagements*. Zurich: Versus Verlag.

Sacks, Harvey. 1992. *Lectures on Conversation*. Edited by G. Jefferson. Oxford: Blackwell.

Sofsky, Wolfgang and Rainer Paris. 1991. *Figurationen sozialer Macht. Autorität – Stellvertretung – Koalition.* Opladen: Leske und Budrich.

Straus, Florian. 2002. *Netzwerkanalysen. Gemeindepsychologische Perspektiven für Forschung und Praxis.* Wiesbaden: Deutscher Universitäts-Verlag.

Suchman, Lucy. 1987. *Plans and Situated Actions.* Cambridge: Cambridge University Press.

Sydow, Jörg and Arnold Windeler, eds. 2000. *Steuerung von Netzwerken. Konzepte und Praktiken.* Opladen and Wiesbaden: Westdeutscher Verlag.

Wasserman, Stanley and Katherine Faust. 1998. *Social Network Analysis. Methods and Applications.* 4th ed. Cambridge: Cambridge University Press.

Weber, Max. 1978. *Economy and Society. An Outline of Interpretive Sociology.* Berkeley, Los Angeles: Univiversity of California Press.

White, Harrison C. 1992. *Identity and Control. A Structural Theory of Social Action.* Princeton, NJ: Princeton University Press.

Willke, Helmut. 2001. *Systemisches Wissensmanagement. Including Case Studies by Carsten Krück, Susanne Mingers, Konstanze Piel, Trosten Strulik and Oliver Vopel.* 2nd ed. Stuttgart: Lucius & Lucius.

Witte, Erich H. and Elisabeth Ardelt. 1989. "Gruppenarten, -strukturen, -prozesse." Pp. 463–83 in *Organisationspsychologie. Enzyklopädie der Psychologie D/III/3*, edited by E. Roth. Göttingen: Hogrefe.

Wuppertaler Kreis E.V., ed. 2000. *Wissensmanagement im mittelständigen. Untern.*

Part II

Mixed Methods Applications

5

Social Networks, Social Influence, and Fertility in Germany: Challenges and Benefits of Applying a Parallel Mixed Methods Design

Laura Bernardi, Sylvia Keim, and Andreas Klärner

Introduction – Social Networks and Fertility

In this chapter we present a parallel mixed method research design applied in the field of fertility research. Our project aims at generating a comprehensive understanding of the network effects on fertility intentions and behavior. These effects have attracted the interest of researchers in demography and family sociology over the last 20 years (Bongaarts and Watkins 1996; Kohler 2001; Kohler and Bühler 2001; Bernardi and Klärner 2014). The central question of our research is how intimate life-course decisions of individuals and couples about becoming parents are influenced by social interactions with parents, siblings, relatives, friends, but also with colleagues as well as more contingent encounters that constitute individuals' social networks.

Most research in this area has concentrated on providing evidence for social network effects measured at the macro-level, for example, for a significant relation between the geographical correlation of the diffusion of contraceptive knowledge and changes in fertility behavior. Researchers also have recorded social network effects on value change concerning gender roles, the role of women in society, the desired number of children, attitudes toward cohabitation, and so on (Kohler and Bühler 2001; Rindfuss et al. 2004). Central for this research are hypotheses involving the role of social learning and social norms (e.g., Montgomery and Casterline 1996; Casterline 2001; Kohler 2001) and social support (cf. Bühler 2007). Studies about network influence on fertility choices so

This chapter is part of the project "Social Influence on Family Formation and Fertility in Northern Germany." The project is funded by the Independent Research Group "The Culture of Reproduction" at the Max Planck Institute for Demographic Research in Rostock, Germany.

far have been conducted mainly in developing countries (e.g., Kohler et al. 2001; Madhavan et al. 2003) or in post-socialist transformation societies (e.g., Philipov et al. 2006; Bühler and Philipov 2007; Bühler and Fratczak 2007), giving support to the thesis that better access to social support increases the likelihood to become parents. It is argued that in these countries traditional values and family and tribal structures are pre-dominant and therefore social networks serve as substitutes for malfunctioning or non-existent welfare-state institutions. Also, individualization and post-modern orientations – often considered as forces against social cohesion and therefore against effective and powerful influences by persons from the social network – are not so far spread in these countries. Yet, little is known about how social networks affect fertility intentions and behavior in western European societies that are characterized by individualization processes that tend to diminish the importance of traditional family bonds. Nevertheless, various studies in other research areas, for example, on the relevance of social capital for dropping out of school in the United States (Coleman 1988), yield the assumption that personal relations are also relevant to individuals' behavior in western countries and can therefore also be applied to fertility research. A considerably large research field deals with intergenerational support (e.g., Aquilino 2005; Mandemakers and Dykstra 2008) and provides evidence for the existence and relevance of various forms of reciprocal support between parents and children in western countries. Research in the United States and other western countries on the intergenerational transfer of fertility patterns and the transmission of family values and ideals shows a positive correlation across generations and among siblings (Axinn et al. 1994; Murphy and Wang 2001; Steenhof and Liefbroer 2008). Besides relatives, other relations such as peers are important factors of secondary socialization affecting fertility, as research on teenage pregnancies has shown (Billy and Udry 1985; Arai 2007). There exists qualitative evidence that peers are also influential on the fertility choices of post-adolescent populations like that composed of adult couples (Bernardi 2003). Based on these grounds, we argue that processes of social influence are effective in western settings and analyzing these processes can add to our understanding of individuals' fertility behavior. In our research project we addressed the following empirical questions: (1) How is social influence transmitted, and which mechanisms are effective? (2) Which type of network relations are influential as far as fertility intentions and behavior of couples is concerned? and (3) How do different network structures affect these processes of social influence?

In the following we present our study on social networks and fertility in Germany using a parallel mixed methods design. We show how such a design is best suited to address our research questions, we present how it was applied, and we discuss the benefits and limitations of such a design.

Social Networks and Fertility in Eastern and Western Germany: An Empirical Case Study

Our study is located in two settings in Germany: an eastern German city and a western German city. We chose a comparative approach contrasting persons from eastern and western Germany, because evidence shows their fertility patterns differ and little is known about variation in the composition and structure of their personal relations.

Germany can be described as a country comprising two very different fertility patterns, which have been identified as two different fertility regimes (Kreyenfeld 2004): one in the eastern part (the former German Democratic Republic or GDR) and one in the western part (the former Federal Republic of Germany or FRG). The differences can be seen in the age of the mother at the birth of the first child, as well as in the level of childlessness. Women born in 1940 in East Germany gave birth to a first child on average at age 22, while their West German counterparts were older by 2.2 years. The difference increased to 4 years in the cohorts born in 1958. The FRG generation of 1958 had children later, if at all: The percentage of childlessness rose to 23 percent (compared to 12% in the generation of 1940), whereas in the GDR it dropped from 12 percent to 8 percent for the same generations (Kreyenfeld 2001). At present, parity progressions to first birth are faster, and to second births they are slower by age in eastern Germany (Konietzka and Kreyenfeld 2004). Moreover, being enrolled in education or being unemployed strongly lowers the risk of childbearing in western Germany but much less so in eastern Germany (Kreyenfeld 2001). The differences between eastern and western Germany date back to the time of the division of Germany after the Second World War. The political regimes had fundamentally different social and family policies: Social policies in the GDR were designed to favor women's labor-force participation. They were geared to minimize job interruptions after childbirth by supplying inexpensive childcare. It is not surprising, then, that women's labor-force participation in 1989 was 82 percent in the GDR – mostly full-time jobs – compared to 56 percent in the FRG (Hülser 1996:47). In the FRG, however, state support for parents was oriented toward an "employment–motherhood sequence," with mothers who had small children experiencing long interruptions and employed at the most part-time. The consequences of the different family policies survived the post-unification policy changes, possibly owing to the transmission of consolidated differences in values and perspectives from one generation to the next.

Few studies have compared systematically social networks in eastern and western Germany and do not converge in their results. While some find considerable differences in network composition, as, for example, a higher share of kin in eastern German networks (Uhlendorff 2004), others stress that the composition of the networks has changed considerably in both parts of Germany after the unification, and that one should not overstate the pre-unification differences (Nauck and Schwenk 2001). Given these premises, our research aims at:

1. Exploring the mechanisms of social influence on fertility intentions
2. Identifying the informal relationships salient in fertility decision-making
3. Analyzing how the mechanisms of influence and structural properties of the social networks are related.

On the one hand, in order to pursue these aims, our attention needs to turn to the interactions individuals are engaged in, to the flows of emotional and material exchanges taking place among network members. We need to understand the meaning attributed to relationships and exchanges by the individuals involved in them. On the other hand, we need to know about the structural properties of the networks, like their size density and composition.

The exploration of processes of social influence, the meanings and relevancies attributed to personal relations as well as to the process of family formation, is best achieved by qualitative research methods. Qualitative methods follow the guiding principles of openness to the subject, of considering the subjective perspectives of the persons involved and their multidimensionality and aim at "understanding" the "subjective meanings" individuals give to their action (Flick 2002:25). Research instruments that follow these principles allow to explore a topic and and give a "thick description" (Geertz 1973) – in our case – of the personal relations and processes of social influence involved in the process of thinking about family formation.

The need to understand meanings and processes in their structural context, however, calls for quantitative research methods. We want to compare network structures among respondents forming different subgroups. Therefore we need to collect an adequate amount of comparable network data.

Our perspective is therefore both actor-centered and structural; we collect data that are both explorative and standardized (cf. Hollstein, this volume). For this reason we apply a mixed methods research strategy combining open and standardized procedures of data collection and aim for a (for qualitative projects) rather large sample size, which will produce qualitative insights into individual perceptions and meanings as well as standardized measures.

Social Networks and Fertility: A Parallel Mixed Methods Research Design

The mixed methods approach has proven useful in a variety of empirical social research topics, such as the welfare of children and family (Burton 2004), the labor market behavior of ethnic minorities (Nee et al. 1994), as well as women's social capital (Hodgkin 2008). Yet, researchers interested in population processes and phenomena have rarely taken advantage of the experience of neighbor disciplines. There are still very few empirical studies based on mixed methods approaches and most of them deal with non-western populations (e.g., Short et al. 2002). Claire Bidart and Daniel Lavenu (2005) studied the impact of different life trajectories such as entry into the labor market, geographical mobility, and family formation on the size and composition of the personal networks of 66 young people in Normandy (France). But, to our best knowledge, none of those studies addressed the inverted effect of social network influences on family formation behavior.

Combining qualitative and quantitative approaches often results in difficulties due to the different epistemological positions and different research cultures they are based on; however, many authors argue that "there are more overlaps than differences" between both research approaches (Brannen 2005:175). They stress that it is not only possible but also helpful to integrate qualitative and quantitative research in one design, for one method can compensate for the weaknesses and blind spots of the other (Flick 2002).

The mixed methods design may involve different forms of sequencing and sampling patterns (cf. Hollstein, this volume): One way is to conduct a (representative) large quantitative survey first and then as a second step choose some of the survey's respondents for a qualitative interview (cf. Maya-Jariego and Dominguez, this volume); an alternative way is to first conduct qualitative interviews and then use the results to develop a survey instrument which is then in a second step used on a representative sample of the population. Both sequential designs are very resource and time intense. An alternative is a parallel design, applying qualitative and quantitative instruments simultaneously onto the same sample.

A combination of both methods can take place on the level of data collection, but it may also take place on the level of data analysis: Qualitative data, for example, interview passages, can be quantified by determining the frequency of categories and using statistical methods of data analysis.

We have opted for a parallel design, applying qualitative and quantitative instruments simultaneously onto the same set of respondents – mainly for two reasons: one methodological and one practical. From the methodological point of view, we had an interest in testing the impact of the structural features of the networks like their heterogeneity and their degree of density, with the narratives about fertility and family plans. More practically, a sequencing procedure with two different samples would have been more time consuming and costly, and we did not have the resources for it. This strategy allows us to produce complementary data and we try to benefit from the advantages each method holds while minimizing the disadvantages (Hollstein, this volume). At the level of data collection we decided to combine (a) a qualitative interview with (b) a standardized collection of network data and some relevant network partners' characteristics. At the level of data analysis, we conducted qualitative analysis using such methods as thematic coding, but we also quantified qualitative data so they could be included in the analysis of the quantitative network data and bring together insights from the qualitative and quantitative analyses on each case.

In the following we first introduce the sampling procedure and later the instruments of data collection and the reasons why they were chosen in detail.

Social Networks and Fertility: A Parallel Mixed Methods Sampling Strategy

Deciding for a mixed methods strategy that applies qualitative and quantitative instruments of data collection onto the same respondents asks for a special sampling strategy. Thereby tensions arising from the epistemological different positions need to be solved. Qualitative research aims at a maximal variation in experiences. In the tradition of Grounded Theory this asks for a theoretical sample that samples along the way of analyzing the data and adds new cases until a certain level of saturation in the analysis is reached. A more predictable and less time-consuming alternative would be a quota sample that specifies the characteristics for which maximal variation is searched for. Qualitative samples usually comprise a rather small number of cases because data collection and analysis of each case is very time intense. Quantitative research, in contrast, aims at measuring the effects of selected variables in a population. The sample therefore is clearcut and representative of the population.

Samples in studies using quantitative research instruments are usually rather large in order to calculate significant statistical results.

We found a feasible compromise in using a quota sample. We set a minimum number of respondents that should have certain characteristics (residence in eastern or western Germany, level of education, gender) that should provide an adequate basis for statistical analyses in order to measure some of the effects of social networks on this particular population. Additionally, we restricted our sample to respondents with medium or higher education, excluding respondents from lower social strata. We focused on persons with medium and higher education who were prone to extend their educational periods because it is known that longer terms of education can lead to postponement of childbearing.

Respondents were collected based on a purposive sampling of individuals. We collected a primary sample, or ego sample (with all egos being the individuals selected through the quota sampling procedure). The criteria defining the quota for the ego sample are the city where the individual spent his or her secondary school years and the type of school and school class attended. We selected two highly comparable German cities situated in the north of the country at the shore of the Baltic Sea: Rostock (eastern Germany) and Lübeck (western Germany). They are comparable in the size of their resident population (around 200,000 inhabitants) and, for example, their relatively high unemployment rate (13.8% in Lübeck as compared to 7.6% in western Germany, and 18.2% in Rostock as compared to 17.7% in East Germany in the year 2002). They shared the same religious, historic, and economic background until the Second World War. After the post-war period Rostock and Lübeck were subjected to different political, economic, and social systems, the German Democratic Republic (East Germany) and the Federal Republic of Germany (West Germany), which affected all areas of individual and social life, and therefore also different family and fertility regimes emerged. The type of school attended is either a *Gymnasium* (equivalent to the American high school or the British grammar school) or a *Realschule* (an intermediate secondary school), providing a medium or higher level of education. Egos graduated from school between 1991 and 1994 and were thus aged between 27 and 31 at the time of the interview. We chose this cohort because family formation is likely to be a salient issue for individuals of this age group and because the social network of these individuals may have experienced parenthood. We aimed at collecting interviews for the ego sample with 8 men and 8 women of each type of school for both cities, which adds up to 32 ego interviews in each setting. Respondents were identified via school classes. We contacted all

Table 5.1. *Composition of the ego and alter sample by sex and education*

	Lübeck		Rostock		Total
	Women	Men	Women	Men	
Higher Education	12 egos, 13 alters	6 egos 3 alters	13 egos 13 alters	7 egos 8 alters	38 egos 37 alters
Medium Education	8 egos 5 alters	9 egos 4 alters	6 egos 4 alters	6 egos 1 alter	29 egos 14 alters
Total	20 egos 18 alters	15 egos 7 alters	19 egos 17 alters	13 egos 9 alters	67 egos 51 alters

schools with an official letter to the school director asking for a contact person of the respective graduation years. Additionally, we contacted individuals of these schools via a social network site based on school classes. After we had some initial respondents we conducted a snowball sampling by asking these respondents to name further individuals with whom they spent their school years.

In addition to the ego sample, we collected a subsample composed of three relevant members of egos' social network (alters' sample). Each main respondent was asked if his three most important network partners (alters) would agree to be interviewed. The interviewed alters were then mostly one of ego's parents, the current partner, and a close friend. Table 5.1 presents the composition of the ego and alter sample.

Contrasting ego and alter interviews promises several advantages: First, we learn from each respondent directly how they think about family formation and how they think about their network partner's situation and do not need to rely on only ego's information on alter's characteristics, behaviors, and attitudes – which may not be valid (e.g., Pappi and Wolf 1984). Second, ego and alter both describe their relationship and interactions, so that the analysis can draw on information from and the perspectives of both persons involved. Third, we can receive information from alter on ego that ego could not give, did not want to give, or forgot. This can be the case with such potentially difficult and painful topics as disease, abortion, or artificial reproduction. Collecting ego and alter interviews and analyzing dyadic relations allows deep insights into the exchanges between network partners, into the meanings they give to certain issues, and allows one to study the various mechanisms of social influences and preconditions for the effectiveness of social influence.

Our sample now is adequate for answering our research questions on the relations between networks structures and composition and, for example, the attitudes toward childbearing. However, it does not allow generalizing the results of the quantitative data to the German population, because the respondents were not selected randomly.

Social Networks and Fertility: Mixing Methods at the Level of Data Collection Instruments

One step in mixing methods in research is to apply a combination of qualitative and quantitative research instruments. In this study a combination of four research instruments has been applied, which shall be presented in detail in this section: a semi-structured interview, a network chart, a network grid, and a socio-demographic questionnaire.

The Semi-Structured Interview

The research questions demand an instrument of data collection that allows being open but also allows having a focus on the research topic. This combination is found in semi-structured interviews as the problem-centered interviews (Witzel and Reiter 2012). The problem-centered interview stands in the traditions of Grounded Theory (Glaser and Strauss 1999) and many authors describe it as adequate method for combining deductive (i.e., theoretically pre-structured) and inductive (i.e., open) elements (e.g., Mey 1999:145). It aims at the respondents' subjective perspectives by using narrative incentives. The respondents are asked to report in detail about a certain issue. The resulting longer narrations allow deep insights into the respondents' experiences, perceptions, and the meanings they designate to certain issues. In our case these narrative incentives allowed a detailed exploration of the respondents' ideas and desires concerning having children as well as on their personal relations and on the processes of social influence. Additionally, narrative incentives help to avoid social desirability and short answers on a superficial level (Schütze 1977).

Problem-centered elements, however, ensure that the respondents do not stray too far from the main research issue when talking about their experiences and views (Witzel and Reiter 2012). Certain topics are asked for, independent of what the respondents are talking about and how they set relevance in their lives and the meanings they attach to certain issues. For example, in our guideline we have questions on the desire for children that are also asked of persons who do not come to speak about the issue by themselves when presenting their past experiences and future plans. But that the questions were designed specifically to learn more about processes of social influence.

The interview guideline covered the following topics:

1. life course since leaving school;
2. job career, professional development, and future plans;

3. partnership history;
4. family formation and having children;
5. personal relations, social influences, and the social network;
6. general values and life goals, attitudes towards staying childless.

The order of these parts as well as the order of the questions within each part are not predetermined, and the interviewer adapts them to the way the respondents present their views and experiences during the interview.

The general guideline was adapted according to different character-istics of the respondents: (1) For childless respondents (ego and alter), we added questions on intentions of having the first child or staying childless; (2) for respondents with children (ego and alter), we added questions on their experiences with having the first child and their inten-tion to have an additional child; and (3) for respondents from the older generation, who already have adult children (mostly egos' parents), we added questions on their past experiences with family formation and how they view their children's situation today and what they would advise them. This part of the interview provides us with rich information on biographic events after graduation, ranging from school, partner-ship history, the current partner, orientations, meanings, and expecta-tions concerning childbearing, interaction with the partner on the topic, the characteristics of informal social relations, and interaction related to family formation, life-course goals, and expectations. The qualitative component of our study relies partially on the systematic analysis of this part of the interview through theoretical and thematic coding (Strauss and Corbin 1998; Flick 2002).

The Network Chart

To assess and evaluate the influence of social networks on fertility choices, we use an adapted version of the hierarchical mapping procedure employed successfully in social psychology (Antonucci 1986; Straus 2002).

We asked respondents to use a diagram of six graded concentric cir-cles, with the smallest circle in the center containing a word representing ego as displayed in Figure 5.1.

Each of the circles represents different levels of the perceived relevance of the network partner, and we rated them numerically from the outside of the chart, labeled 1 (a little important), to the inside of the chart, labeled 6 (very important). The space outside the chart is labeled not important at all, and the lower right corner was reserved for persons perceived as problematic. The network chart was done for each respondent separately, but we were able to link the data of ego and its alters for further analysis.

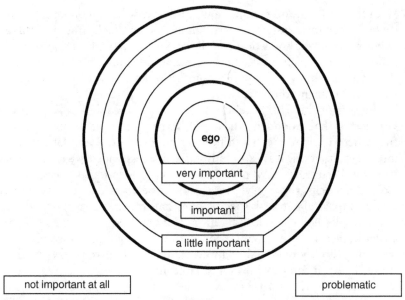

Figure 5.1. The network chart

The chart was introduced by a name-generating question, which was read to each respondent:

> The mid-point of the circles represents you. In the circles around, you can place persons you know. You can also indicate how important they are to you at the moment. The two closest circles are for very important persons, the next two circles are for persons who are important, and the two outer circles are for persons who are at least a little important. Outside of the circles you can place persons who are not at all important to you or rather problematic.

Then the respondents were asked to indicate the first name of their network partners on colored and sticking markers and to place them onto the network chart. Since a major challenge in network research is how to define the boundaries of networks (Hollstein 2006) and how to efficiently collect relevant network partners, we decided to use this rather vague stimulus of "importance" and give the respondents freedom to explain to us what this means to them. We used the open stimulus as a first step to explore the variety of dimensions of relevance and to assess the kinds of relationships relevant to fertility decision-making. While the respondents filled in the chart, we asked them to explain their choices in their own words, for instance, the reason behind including a specific person and the meaning of placing them in a given circle.

With this think-aloud technique we also asked the respondents to specify how they interpreted the term "importance" each time. For further exploration several questions on the network partners' age, profession, residence, frequency of contact, duration and quality of the relationship, partnership status, parity, and attitudes toward having children were asked during the interview.

The network chart is beneficial for respondents as well as for the interviewer. For the respondent, the use of the network chart brings cognitive ease when trying to recall and to describe their personal relations in the interview situation. It is especially easier for respondents with large networks to keep track of who they have already mentioned. Also, the network chart helps the interviewer to collect network data in a systematic way and to be able to ask specific questions on each person mentioned, for example, how they feel about having children. The systematic and structured form of data collection with a network chart promises better comparability of social relations than a qualitative interview alone. Additionally, it can provide quantifiable measures on the network structure. However, this form of data collection also has to be taken with a critical eye concerning the validity of the instrument (Hollstein 2001). Individuals may have different understandings of what the generator question means to them; therefore it is difficult to compare the networks across individuals. A second concern is when conducting an explorative network study you may want to be as open as possible with the network generator. A generator that collects a broad variety of relations allows analyzing which of the collected relations are relevant network partners. In all this, the qualitative part plays a major role, because it allows exploring what (a) the network generator means to the respondents and (b) the relations that are relevant for the attitudes and behavior under study. We therefore embedded the network chart into the qualitative interview, and while it was being filled out various questions on the relationships inserted were as well as on the respondents' definition of the network generator. This procedure leads to a very extensive, precise, and subtle view on the respondents' social networks.

The network chart allows measuring the strength of the relationship between ego and her/his alters and the network size. Using this chart provides us with, on the one hand, comparable network data, due to its structured and standardized approach, but also the meanings of certain relationships and the composition and structure of the network as a whole can be evaluated more deeply within the interview.

The network we generate with the network chart shows the relationships between our respondents (ego) and their network partners (alter); this is called the first order star. The relations among these network partners (the first order zone) are not included. Therefore, we have added as a third instrument of data collection a network grid.

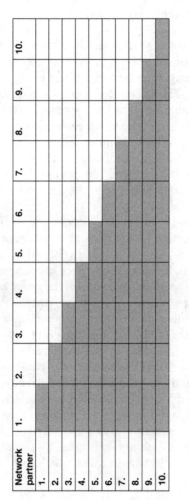

Figure 5.2. The network grid

The Network Grid

The network grid allows collecting in a standardized way to what extent the network partners are in contact with each other. Given that it is very time intense to collect the ties among all network partners, especially in large networks, we use a network grid that focuses only on the ten most important network partners, as indicated in the chart. The ten most highly rated persons from the chart were therefore entered into a classic network grid (see Figure 5.2).

The respondents were asked to indicate the extent to which each person mentioned was acquainted or befriended with any other in the grid, ranked on a five-grade scale ranging from 0 (don't know each other) to 4 (have close contact). This scale allows collecting the frequency of contact and the closeness. It becomes problematic for persons who are close but do not meet often or for persons who know each other well but currently are in conflict and therefore have stopped seeing each other. Here the data collection profited from being embedded in a qualitative interview where doubts could be easily expressed and discussed. The network grid allows measuring the tie strength between the ten most important alters as well as the network density.

Network charts and grids are central tools in the interview. We use them as a mixed data collection tool in itself as they are conceived to gain in-depth information to be analyzed qualitatively and quantitatively. On the one hand, it provides rich descriptions of the ongoing social influence within the network; on the other hand, it records the structural characteristics of the ego-centered networks (density, size, closeness, and tie strength). We deliberately chose to collect data from the same cases in the qualitative and quantitative parts of the study. The main reason for this is a theoretical one: Working with separate samples in the study of social influence on family formation would artificially create an analytical barrier between two processes that are tightly linked to each other. To have valid data on the social interaction embedded in the social network structure, we need to collect complete and complex information, including subjective meanings and norms, narratives on interaction, and information on the structure of the network. The network grid allows collecting in a standardized way to what extent the network partners are in contact with each other.

The Socio-Demographic Questionnaire

At the end of the interview a short socio-demographic questionnaire collected systematic data on:

- Ego's socio-demographic characteristics: Age, place of living, educational status, occupation, income, working hours per week, number and age of children, religion

- The socio-demographic characteristics of ego's current partner: Age, educational status, occupation, working hours per week, number and age of children, religion
- Important characteristics of the partnership: duration of the relationship, duration of cohabitation, division of tasks in the partnership
- Socio-demographic characteristics on ego's parents, siblings, and four closest friends: age, place of living, duration of friendship, educational status, marital status, number and age of their children.

The quantitative data from the network chart network grid and socio-demographic questionnaire were inserted into the statistical software STATA, which calculated network measures (e.g., size, density), and the data were analyzed with the help of the software EGOnet and Visualyzer.

Social Networks and Fertility – Analyzing Strategies and Empirical Findings

Our analyses have so far focused on analyzing the qualitative and quantitative material separately, as well as on mixing qualitative and quantitative analyses. The purely qualitative analyses led us to identify at least four different mechanisms of social network influence regarding fertility intentions and behavior:

a) Social support: Through social interactions individuals can gain access to specific resources or abilities owned by other persons. These resources are also termed the social capital of an individual and can give instrumental, emotional, or informational support (Bourdieu 1986; Lin 2001a, 2001b).

b) Social learning: The experiences and observations individuals make in their social networks shape their attitudes, intentions, and behavior. Social interaction provides the ground for social comparison and role modeling (Bandura 1962; Merton 1968; Dahrendorf 1977).

c) Social pressure: Social networks are the space where personal orientations and moral values are learned, discussed, enforced, or questioned; where deviance may be sanctioned and compliance rewarded. Moral values and norms can be reproduced and strengthened in social interactions, but those interactions can also contribute to value change.

d) Social or emotional contagion: Additionally, individuals can spontaneously pick up emotional states and behaviors of groups or other individuals they come in contact with (e.g., Lippitt et al. 1952; Hatfield et al. 1994). This change in emotional state, initiated through contact with network members, can alter individuals' behavior.

Additionally, the qualitative analyses revealed considerable differences between our eastern and western German respondents concerning the perceptions and experiences dealing with economic uncertainty and its effects on family formation as well as concerning ideas on how to organize family life and paid work within the couple and the degree to which family formation is considered as something that needs to be planned carefully. Whereas our western German respondents favored a very rigid sequential model of family formation, where job security and career perspectives of the male partner had to be established before having a child would be considered, our eastern German respondents followed a parallel approach where job security and family formation are only loosely interconnected and a balance between employment burdens and family life is desired (Bernardi and Keim 2007; Bernardi et al. 2008). We are also able to show that intergenerational support concerning child care is much more important for our western German respondents, and that this subjective dependency gives the older generation sanctioning power to enforce adherence to a more traditional model of gendered division of household and family tasks (Klärner and Keim 2011).

The analyses combining qualitative and quantitative data have focused on friendship dyads (Bernardi et al. 2007) aimed at identifying network partners that influence ego in his attitudes and behavior regarding family formation (Keim et al. 2013) and have looked at the ideational models of the family and the perception of life goals alternative to having children (Keim 2011a) and certain related structural characteristics to fertility intentions (Keim et al. 2009).

In the following paragraphs we present selected results of these analyses that highlight the potential of a parallel mixed methods design.

Which Ties Are Influential When Individuals Think about Family Formation?

One major concern in network research is the correct identification of relationships that are relevant for the research question (Hollstein 2006). To identify relevant others, that is, persons or group of persons who influence ego's framing of fertility intentions and family formation planning, we used a descriptive statistical analysis of the quantitative data collected with the network chart. Using this analysis we could determine network members' importance by type of relationship (see Figure 5.3).

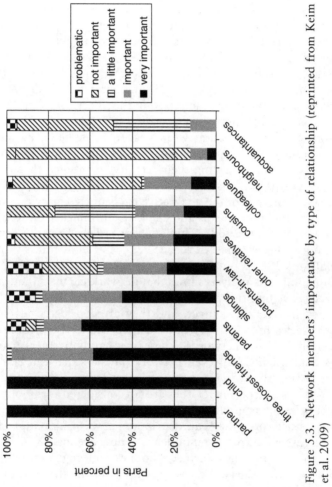

Figure 5.3. Network members' importance by type of relationship (reprinted from Keim et al. 2009)

Descriptive statistics show that our respondents rate persons such as partners, close friends, parents, and siblings mostly in the range of (very) important. Persons (or groups of persons) such as colleagues, neighbors, and acquaintances are mostly placed in the outer circles of the network chart and labeled as little important or not important. The descriptive analysis tells us about the subjective importance of different types of relationships and the qualitative analysis helps us to understand what the category "importance" means to the respondent. Looking at the description of the quality of the relationship, (very) important persons are characterized as engaged in frequent contact with ego, emotionally close, and give and receive help on a regular basis. In network terminology these persons can be regarded as strong ties (Friedkin 1982; Burt 1987; Marsden and Friedkin 1993). In contrast, little or not important network partners are characterized in the interview as emotionally distant from ego, and mutual reciprocity is not expected from them. Those persons can be regarded as weak ties. Against the background of our research interest, the question arises if strong ties are those who influence egos most in forming their fertility intentions, that is, if strong ties are in this case also the relevant ties. Thus, in a second step, we applied an analysis of the qualitative parts of the interviews in order to determine the mechanisms and channels of influence on fertility intentions (Keim et al. 2008). This analysis is based on the principles of Grounded Theory (Glaser 1965, 1992; Glaser and Strauss 1999; Corbin and Strauss 2008).

Our combined analysis shows that network partners that can be considered as strong ties (they are rated as "(very) important," they are engaged in frequent contact, and they are considered as emotionally close) exert a broad variety of influences and have sanctioning power, especially in dense networks. These are mainly partners, parents, siblings, and friends. However, network partners that can be considered as weak ties (they are rated as "little important," they are mostly not engaged in frequent contact, they are not considered as emotionally close) can be relevant as providers of certain pieces of information; especially in sparse networks they can distribute "new" information, for example, on fathers taking parental leave. These are mainly acquaintances, colleagues, team mates, former school or college mates, and so on. To know how these network partners are influential, we cannot simply infer conformity in behavior among relevant networks partners. Their influence may go in opposite directions (parents asking for grandchildren while friends postpone childbearing), and the qualitative insights show that the meanings attached vary: Children in the network can be perceived positively and motivate own childbearing intentions, and they can also be perceived negatively and prevent egos from having children (yet). Our data also showed that many respondents have certain

"groups of reference," which can be very large: "my social environment" or "my group of friends and acquaintances," or very special, as
"the people I went to school with" or "the people I went to university
with." They serve as comparative standards: Do they already have children? How many? Based on this, the respondents judge if they would
be early or late if they had a child now, which is – as our qualitative
analyses have shown – an important factor in building a feeling of readiness for engaging into parenthood. These groups of reference cannot be
inferred from the network structure; they strongly depend on the individual's subjective perceptions and evaluations: Who do they perceive
as being in a comparable situation and who do they evaluate as worthy
to compare to?

Social Networks and Ideational Models of the Family

To determine the relation between mechanisms of influence and structural properties of the social networks a second analysis focused on
how young adults conceptualize their own family and if children belong
to their ideational model of the family (Keim 2011a, 2011b). We have
analyzed how ideational models of the family and connected values are
transmitted, negotiated, and challenged in social networks for the subsample of respondents from the western German city. Comparing the
quantitative network measures with the qualitative coding, we were able
to distinguish three main kinds of networks, ideational models, and connected fertility intentions (a more differentiated discussion of six network types can be found in Keim 2011a).

The family-centered network is dense and includes a high share of
kin and local ties (see Figure 5.4). It corresponds with the ideational
model of the family as a couple with children, and mostly having children is considered a self-evident step in the life course. Respondents with
this type of network either already have children or intend to have a
child soon. In these networks a coherent system of values is transmitted
and reproduced, and in the dense network structure influence mechanisms that involve social pressure make it difficult to challenge them.
The information on having children that is available in these networks
is mostly positive; it fosters and motivates respondents to have a child of
their own. Additionally, having children is eased in these networks by
having access to substantial support.

The heterogeneous network is sparse and contains many friends and
acquaintances and only a low share of kin and local ties (see Figure 5.5).
Respondents embedded in this type of network also conceptualize family as a couple with children, but although they indicate that they would
prefer to have children in their life at some point, they are presently
childless and mostly are postponing childbirth and discuss at length the

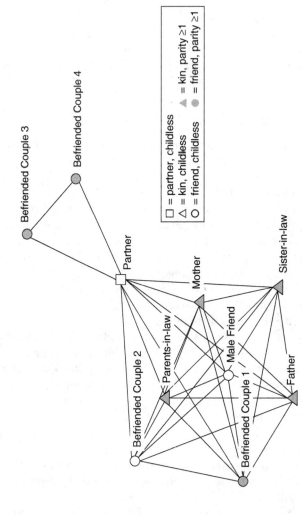

Befriended Couple 3

Befriended Couple 4

Befriended Couple 2

Parents-in-law

Mother

Male Friend

Partner

Befriended Couple 1

Father

Sister-in-law

□ = partner, childless   ▲ = kin, parity ≥1
△ = kin, childless   ● = friend, parity ≥1
○ = friend, childless

Figure 5.4. Family-centered network (reprinted from Keim 2011a:206. With kind permission from Springer Science + Business Media B.V.)

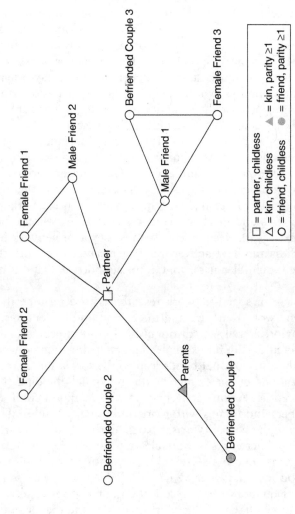

Figure 5.5. Heterogeneous network (reprinted from Keim 2011a:213. With kind permission from Springer Science + Business Media B.V.)

difficulties involved with taking this decision (e.g., on combining family and work, choosing the right time, finding the right partner, etc.). Due to the heterogeneity in network partners, the information and values transmitted in these networks are not consistent. Information on the positive aspects of having children by some network partners is contrasted with information on the negative aspects of parenthood by others. The respondents do not see a clear-cut sequencing of events as those embedded in family-centered networks; they rather have to find their own way of when and how to form a family. This often involves uncertainty on how to act and leads to fertility postponement. This uncertainty is also fostered by the fact that respondents in heterogeneous networks cannot expect to rely on as much support as persons in family-oriented networks, because important network partners may live too far away for regular practical help or the respondents are simply not sure if and to what extend they could ask them for help in case they had a child.

The childfree-by-choice network is sparse and includes a low share of kin, many persons that share similar interests (in job or hobby), and no or only a few children (see Figure 5.6). The respondents report that their networks have changed considerably in the last years and that they have decreased contacts to persons who have children because they lacked common interests and increased contacts to persons who do not want to have children (yet). Respondents with this type of network intend to remain childless and have actively built themselves a network that provides a niche for childlessness, containing supportive relations fitting to their needs.

One problem in social network research is to determine the causal relations of network structure and the formation of intentions, respectivelym behavior, as well as to distinguish selection effects from influence (cf. Steglich et al. 2010); for example, does embedment in networks consisting mainly of traditional bonds lead to the formation of traditional conceptualizations of the family or do individuals holding these traditional conceptualizations actively choose to maintain connections to family members and friends with more traditional attitudes? The problem of determining causality arises particularly when structural information on social networks is available only from one point in time as it is usually the case in cross-sectional survey data. One advantage of our mixed methods design is that we have available not only cross-sectional data from our quantitative data collection but also retrospective, qualitative data about changes in network structure and the meaning of the networks for our respondents from the narrative part of the interview. Thus, we are better able to separate the selection of network partners based on individual attitudes, intentions, and behavior from the influence the network partners exert. Our combined analysis shows that – not surprisingly – both processes are prominent. On the one hand, individuals

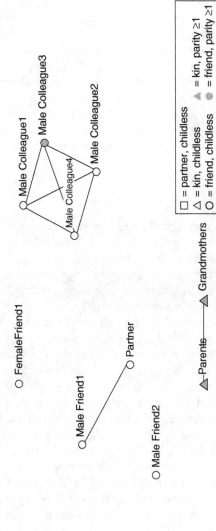

Figure 5.6. Childfree-by-choice network (reprinted from Keim 2011a:215. With kind permission from Springer Science + Business Media B.V.)

are influenced by their network partners to hold similar attitudes and behave similarly; on the other hand, they select network partners who conform to their own attitudes and behavior. "Therefore, the opportunity for choosing new network partners as well as the ways social influences are exerted (and their effectiveness) strongly depend on the type of network the respondents are embedded in. For example, some family-centred networks are reported to be very stable over time. In these dense networks it is difficult to exclude single persons as well because it is difficult for new persons to enter the circle of friends. The heterogeneous and childfree-by-choice networks in contrast show much more dynamics and include contacts of shorter duration. Regarding processes of social influence, in family-centred networks, influence mechanisms such as as social learning, social pressure, contagion, and support motivate and foster individuals to have children, while in heterogeneous networks the influences are often less pronounced, less effective, and may go in different directions, also fostering the postponement of having children (see also Keim 2011b).

Outlook

Our project has been designed as a cross-sectional study. To learn more about network effects and the duality of social influence and the selection of network partners, a longitudinal design would be necessary. To this aim, we are currently re-contacting our respondents in order to explore if they have had a child in the meantime and how their life as well as their social relations have changed.

To capture and to measure the different dimensions of social networks' influence on individual fertility intentions and behavior we developed a survey questionnaire based on the insights from this mixed methods project. Up until now, most survey instruments in this field of family research have focused either on the effect of communication networks on the spreading and acceptance of birth control techniques and the emergence of new values and ideational models (Kohler et al. 2001; Rindfuss et al. 2004) or on the impact of support networks on individuals' fertility intentions (Bühler and Fratczak 2007). Our research shows that (1) these components cannot be isolated and have to be considered as interlinked and interrelated aspects of social network influence, and (2) at least two important aspects of social networks' influence remain unconsidered: social pressure and social contagion.

To measure social network influences our questionnaire contains several instruments to collect data on the following domains: (1) fertility-relevant social support, (2) information about emotionally close persons (strong ties) as well as weak ties relevant in the fertility context, (3) structural information about ego's network (size, density, etc.), (4) information about ego's perception of reference groups, (5) measurements of social pressure and contagion, and (6) information about the selection of network partners.

The questionnaire has been pre-tested and at the moment is in the field.[1] We will have a representative sample of N = 500. The sample will have a quota of 50 percent women and 50 percent men. Since the questionnaire has only been tested with highly educated people, we will have a quota of 20 percent of the respondents with a lower level of education. Respondents are sampled for being childless and in partnership. The age range will be 20 to 30. These criteria were chosen to include respondents who are in their fertility decision-making process.

Discussion: Mixing Methods – Challenges and Benefits

In this chapter we have presented the design and some results of a parallel mixed methods research design in the area of social networks and fertility research. In the discussion we now focus on the challenges we encountered when realizing our research approach and discuss its strengths and limitations.

Challenges in Realizing the Parallel Mixed Methods Approach

In our concluding discussion we turn our attention to four main problems we encountered.

1) Epistemological orientations in the research team: When designing a mixed methods study researchers must be aware of the standard procedures as well as the quality criteria in both qualitative and quantitative methods. Since there are still remainders of the ideological divide between "positivist" quantitative and "story-telling" qualitative methods and methodological training in universities still tends to focus on either one or the other strand, students and researchers often lack knowledge and experience for using the potential of mixing and combining only seemingly exclusive methods. In the process of designing the study many choices have to be made on how to mix both methods, balancing the costs and benefits as well as the requirements of each. The researchers involved may have different interests in the project – some focusing more on the qualitative data, others more on the quantitative. The process

[1] An internal report with an overview of the questionnaire modules can be requested from the authors.

of negotiating these interests to find a good solution for designing the mixed methods study should not be underestimated.

2) Representativity and sampling procedure: When collecting structured network data as well as qualitative data on the same set of respondents simultaneously, a first compromise must be made concerning the sampling: While qualitative sampling aims at being representative or "typical" for a phenomenon, quantitative sampling aims at being representative for a population. While the former usually comprises a smaller sample size and a circular process of collecting and analyzing data, the latter usually demands a larger sample size and a linear process of first collecting and then analyzing all data. We found a feasible compromise for combining the different sampling logics in setting a minimum number of respondents who should have certain characteristics (residence in eastern or western Germany, level of education, gender). Thus, the sample is large enough to provide an adequate basis for statistical analyses distinguishing subgroups but small enough so we could conduct extensive qualitative interviews with each respondent. Additionally, we limited the population under study, by restricting our sample to respondents with medium or higher education and excluding respondents from lower social strata. Our sampling procedure is adequate for answering our research questions on the relations between network structures and composition and, for example, the attitudes toward childbearing, but it does not allow generalizing the results of the quantitative data, because the respondents were not selected randomly.

3) Data management: Since mixed methods research deals with two different kinds of data, researchers employing a parallel mixed methods design onto the same sample also have to work with two different data sets: a corpus of transcribed interviews in text format (.doc or .rtf) and a data file usable with statistical software packages such as SPSS or STATA. Problems arise because these data sets cannot be viewed as totally independent but they are interlinked and non-exclusive. The same information may be contained in both data sets, yet in a different format. Modifications in one data set, for example, the correction of a typo in the interview or the subsequent clarification of an incomprehensible interview extract, can affect the other data set. The interview data can also be used to supplement information in the data file, for example, when missing socio-demographic details about alters in the data file can be derived from the interview transcripts. Data management in this case demands researchers who are familiar with the peculiarities of each data set. Researchers must be able to navigate huge amounts of written text as well as a complex data file with – in our case – hundreds of variables. Since modifications in one data set, for example, the creation of a new set of variables, may make it necessary to consult the other data set,

a routine of data storage and strict documentation of data modification has to be implemented. Other problems that are not peculiar for
mixed methods research nevertheless arise. Coding of interview data
with a software   package for qualitative data analysis (Nvivo, Atlas.ti,
MaxQDA) in a team of researchers is challenging. Often these packages
are not suited for collaborative work and merging of codes may lead to
confusion.

4) Underexploitation of data: Connected to the compromises that have
to be made in the sampling strategy, which results in a rather large sample
for a qualitative study, is the problem of balancing data collection and data
analysis. The parallel mixed methods design of the study leads to a very
time-intense phase of data collection, which produces a large amount of rich
qualitative as well as quantitative data. Concerning the qualitative material we – so far – have only focused on three specific topics. Nevertheless,
the data would allow processing many more research questions. Mixing
methods we have looked, for example, at friendship dyads, but not yet at
partnership dyads and parent–child dyads; we have analyzed mechanisms
of influence and identified fertility-relevant network partners, but we have
not explored the composition and relevance of certain cliques.

Benefits of Mixing Methods in a Parallel Design

Despite being a demanding undertaking, mixed methods research
designs have unique strengths. One major advantage lies in the potential
to adopt simultaneously an actor and a structural perspective.

In our comparative study on social networks and fertility, the qualitative insights (actor perspective) are crucial to apprehend what family
formation and parenthood mean to young adults and in which way they
perceive their childbearing intentions being affected by the social and
relational environment in which they are embedded. Only with this in-
depth work can we identify the reasons why certain network members
are influential and under which conditions: Respondents mention families they know and qualify them for being positive or negative examples, they estimate the support and availability they can expect from
their network members, they described closeness to friends rather than
relatives being built on shared values and interests, and they identify
themselves as mothers and fathers with reference to relationships with
their own mother and father. We realized that not only the network
characteristics and positions are of relevance, but also how certain relations are evaluated as well as the meanings conveyed in social interactions (Keim et al. 2013).

The quantitative insights (structural perspective) are best suited to
collect comparable information on network structure and composition,
which enabled us to build a typology of social networks (Keim 2011a).

As soon as we have finished building the quantitative data set, we will be able to use the quantitative data to their full potential and, for example, correlate them with fertility intentions.

Another strength of a mixed methods approach is that it fosters the development of innovative research methods and therefore leads to advances in methodological discussions. For example, our research contributes to the methodological discussion about appropriate tools for network data collection. The network chart proved to be an ideal tool for combining qualitative and quantitative research interests. The tool is handy and easily understandable for interviewers and respondents and visualizes the network composition within the process of data collection.

Our research contributes to knowledge of demography and family sociology. The impact of social networks on individuals' fertility intentions and behavior and on family and partnership relations has been acknowledged since Elizabeth Bott's (1957) pioneering study on "Family and Social Networks." Despite recent research in this area focusing mainly on non-western countries with the explorative qualitative part of our research we were able to demonstrate the relevance of social networks in a western country such as Germany. Further, with the combination of qualitative and quantitative research methods we were able to show relevant mechanisms of influence and their dependence on structural network characteristics.

References

Antonucci, Tony C. 1986. "Measuring social support networks: Hierarchical mapping technique." *Generations* 10(4):10–12.

Aquilino, William S. 2005. "Impact of family structure on parental attitudes toward the economic support of adult children over the transition to adulthood." *Journal of Family Issues* 26(2):143–67.

Arai, Lisa. 2007. "Peer and neighbourhood influences on teenage pregnancy and fertility: Qualitative findings from research in English communities." *Health & Place* 13(1):87–98.

Axinn, William G., Marin E. Clarkberg, and Arland Thornton. 1994. "Family influences on family size preferences." *Demography* 31(1):65–79.

Bandura, Albert. 1962. "Social learning through imitation." Pp. 211–69 in *Nebraska Symposium on Motivation*, edited by Marshall R. Jones. Lincoln: University of Nebraska Press.

Bernardi, Laura. 2003. "Channels of social influence on reproduction." *Population Research and Policy Review* 22(5–6):527–55.

Bernardi, Laura and Sylvia Keim. 2007. "Anfang dreißig und noch kinderlos? Lebenswege und Familienmodelle berufstätiger Frauen aus Ost- und Westdeutschland." Pp. 317–34 in *Ein Leben ohne Kinder. Kinderlosigkeit in Deutschland*, edited by Dirk Konietzka and Michaela Kreyenfeld. Wiesbaden: VS Verlag.

Bernardi, Laura and Andreas Klärner. 2014. "Social networks and fertility." *Demographic Research* 30(23):675–704.

Bernardi, Laura, Sylvia Keim, and Holger von der Lippe. 2007. "Social influences on fertility: A comparative mixed methods study in eastern and western Germany." *Journal of Mixed Methods Research* 1(1):23–47.

Bernardi, Laura, Andreas Klärner, and Holger von der Lippe. 2008. "Job insecurity and the timing of parenthood: A comparison between eastern and western Germany." *European Journal of Population* 24(3):287–313.

Bidart, Claire and Daniel Lavenu. 2005. "Evolutions of personal networks and life events." *Social Networks* 27(4):359–76.

Billy, John O. G. and Richard J. Udry. 1985. "Patterns of adolescent friendship and effects on sexual behavior." *Social Psychology Quarterly* 48(1):27–41.

Bongaarts, John and Susan C. Watkins. 1996. "Social interactions and contemporary fertility transitions." *Population and Development Review* 22(4):639–82.

Bott, Elizabeth. 1957. *Family and Social Network. Roles, Norms, and External Relationships in Ordinary Urban Families.* New York: The Free Press.

Bourdieu, Pierre. 1986. "The forms of capital." Pp. 241–58 in *The Handbook of Theory: Research for the Sociology of Education*, edited by John G. Richardson. New York: Greenwood Press.

Brannen, Julia. 2005. "Mixing methods: The entry of qualitative and quantitative approaches into the research process." *International Journal of Social Research Methodology* 8(3):173–84.

Bühler, Christoph. 2007. "Soziales Kapital und Fertilität." *Kölner Zeitschrift für Soziologie und Sozialpsychologie*, Sonderheft 47:397–419.

Bühler, Christoph and Ewa Fratczak. 2007. "Learning from others and receiving support: The impact of personal networks on fertility intentions in Poland." *European Societies* 9(3):359–82.

Bühler, Christoph and Dimiter Philipov. 2007. "Social capital related to fertility: Theoretical foundations and empirical evidence from Bulgaria." Pp. 53–81 in *Vienna Yearbook of Population Research 2005*, edited by Gustav Feichtinger and Wolfgang Lutz. Vienna: Verlag der Österreichischen Akademie der Wissenschaften.

Burt, Ronald S. 1987. "Social contagion and innovation: Cohesion versus structural equivalence." *American Journal of Sociology* 92(6):1287–1335.

Burton, Linda M. 2004. "Ethnographic protocol for welfare, children and families: A three city study." Pp. 59–69 in *Workshop on Scientific Foundations of Qualitative Research*, edited by Charles C. Ragin, Joane Nagel, and Patricia White. National Science Foundation. (http://www.nsf.gov/pubs/2004/nsf04219/nsf04219.pdf.)

Casterline, John B., ed. 2001. *Diffusion Processes and Fertility Transition.* Washington, DC: National Academy Press.

Coleman, James S. 1988. "Social capital in the creation of human capital." *American Journal of Sociology* 94 (Supplement): S95–S120.

Corbin, Juliet M. and Anselm L. Strauss. 2008. *Basics of Qualitative Research: Techniques and Procedures for Developing Grounded Theory.* 3rd ed. Los Angeles: Sage.

Dahrendorf, Ralf. 1977. *Homo sociologicus.* Opladen: Westdeutscher Verlag.

Flick, Uwe. 2002. *An Introduction to Qualitative Research.* London: Sage.

Friedkin, Noah E. 1982. "Information flow through strong and weak ties in intraoganizational social networks." *Social Networks* 3(4):273–85.

Geertz, Clifford. 1973. *The Interpretation of Cultures.* New York: Basic Books.

Glaser, Barney G. 1965. "The constant comparative method of qualitative analysis." *Social Problems* 12(4):436–45.

———. 1992. *Basics of Grounded Theory Analysis.* Mill Valley, CA: Sociology Press.

Glaser, Barney G. and Anselm L. Strauss. 1999. *The Discovery of Grounded Theory: Strategies for Qualitative Research.* Hawthorne, NY: Aldine De Gruyter.

Granovetter, Mark S. 1973. "The strength of weak ties." *American Journal of Sociology* 78(6):1360–80.

Hatfield, Elaine, John T. Cacioppo, and Richard L. Rapson. 1994. *Emotional Contagion.* Cambridge: Cambridge University Press.

Hodgkin, Suzanne. 2008. "Telling it all: A story of women's social capital using a mixed methods approach." *Journal of Mixed Methods Research* 2(4):296–316.

Hollstein, Betina. 2001. *Grenzen sozialer Integration. Zur Konzeption informeller Beziehungen und Netzwerke.* Opladen: Leske + Budrich.

———. 2006. "Qualitative Methoden und Netzwerkanalyse – ein Widerspruch?" Pp. 11–35 in *Qualitative Netzwerkanalyse. Konzepte, Methoden, Anwendungen,* edited by Betina Hollstein and Florian Straus. Wiesbaden: VS Verlag.

Hülser, Oliver. 1996. *Frauenerwerbstätigkeit im Transformationsprozeß der deutschen Vereinigung.* Nuremberg: IAB.

Keim, Sylvia. 2011a. *Social Networks and Family Formation Processes: Young Adults' Decision Making about Parenthood.* Wiesbaden: VS Verlag.

———. 2011b. "Social networks and family formation." Pp. 112–28 in *Families and Kinship in Contemporary Europe,* edited by Riitta Jallinoja and Eric Widmer. Houndmills: Palgrave Macmillan.

Keim, Sylvia, Andreas Klärner, and Laura Bernardi. 2009. "Qualifying social influence on fertility intentions: Composition, structure and meaning of fertility-relevant social networks in western Germany." *Current Sociology* 57(6):888–907.

———. 2013. "Tie strength and family formation: Which personal relationships are influential?" *Personal Relationships* 20(3):462–478.

Klärner, Andreas and Sylvia Keim. 2011. "(Re-)Traditionalisierung und Flexibilität. Intergenerationale Unterstützungsleistungen und die Reproduktion von Geschlechterungleichheiten in West- und Ostdeutschland." Pp. 121–44 in *Reproduktion von Ungleichheit durch Arbeit und Familie,* edited by Peter A. Berger, Karsten Hank, and Angelika Tölke. Wiesbaden: VS Verlag.

Kohler, Hans-Peter. 2001. *Fertility and Social Interaction: An Economic Perspective.* Oxford: Oxford University Press.

Kohler, Hans-Peter and Christoph Bühler. 2001. "Social networks and fertility." Pp. 14380–88 in *International Encyclopedia of the Social and Behavioral*

Sciences, edited by Neill J. Smelser and Paul B. Baltes. Oxford: Pergamon/ Elsevier.

Kohler, Hans-Peter, Jere R. Behrman, and Susan C. Watkins. 2001. "The density of social networks and fertility decisions: Evidence from South Nyanza District, Kenya." *Demography* 38(1):43–58.

Konietzka, Dirk and Michaela Kreyenfeld. 2004. "Angleichung oder Verfestigung von Differenzen? Geburtenentwicklung und Familienformen in Ost- und Westdeutschland." *Berliner Debatte Initial* 15(4):26–41.

Kreyenfeld, Michaela. 2001. *Employment and Fertility: East Germany in the 1990s*. PhD Dissertation, University of Rostock, Rostock, Germany.

———. 2004. "Fertility decisions in the FRG and GDR: An analysis with data from the German Fertility and Family Survey." *Demographic Research, Special Collection* 3(11):276–318.

Lin, Nan. 2001a. *Social Capital: A Theory of Social Structure and Action*. Cambridge: Cambridge University Press.

———. 2001b. "Building a network theory of social capital." Pp. 3–30 in *Social Capital*, edited by Nan Lin, Karen S. Cook, and Ronals S. Burt. New York: Aldine De Gruyter.

Lippitt, Ronald, Norman Polansky, and Sidney Rosen. 1952. "The dynamics of power: A field study of social influence." *Human Relations* 5:37–64.

Madhavan, Sangeetha, Alayne Adams, and Dominique Simon 2003. "Women's networks and the social world of fertility behavior." *International Family Planning Perspectives* 29(2):58–68.

Mandemakers, Jornt J. and Pearl A. Dykstra. 2008. "Discrepancies in parent's and adult child's reports of support and contact." *Journal of Marriage and Family* 70(2):495–506.

Marsden, Peter V. and Noah E. Friedkin. 1993. "Network studies of social influence." *Sociological Methods & Research* 22(1):127–51.

Merton, Robert K. 1968. *Social Theory and Social Structure*. New York: The Free Press.

Mey, Günter. 1999. *Adoleszenz, Identität, Erzählung. Theoretische, methodische und empirische Erkundungen*. Berlin: Köster.

Montgomery, Mark R. and John B. Casterline 1996. "Social learning, social influence and new models of fertility." *Population and Development Review* 22(1):151–75.

Murphy, Michael and Duolao Wang. 2001. "Family-level continuities in childbearing in low-fertility societies." *European Journal of Population* 17(1):75–96.

Nauck, Bernhard and Otto G. Schwenk. 2001. "Did societal transformation destroy the social networks of families in East Germany?" *American Behavioral Scientist* 44(11):1864–78.

Nee, Victor, Jimy M. Sanders, and Scott Sernau. 1994. "Job transitions in an immigrant metropolis: Ethnic boundaries and the mixed economy." *American Sociological Review* 59(6):849–72.

Pappi, Franz U. and Gunter Wolf. 1984. "Wahrnehmung und Realität sozialer Netzwerke. Zuverlässigkeit und Gültigkeit der Angaben über beste Freunde." Pp. 281–300 in *Soziale Realität im Interview*, edited by Heiner Meulemann and Karl-Heinz Reuband. Frankfurt am Main: Campus.

Philipov, Dimiter, Zsolt Spéder, and Francesco C. Billari. 2006. "Soon, later, or ever? The impact of anomie and social capital on fertility intentions in Bulgaria (2002) and Hungary (2001)." *Population Studies* 60(3):289–308.

Rindfuss, Ronald R., Minja K. Choe, Larry L. Bumpass, and Noriko O. Tsuya. 2004. "Social networks and family change in Japan." *American Sociological Review* 69(6):838–61.

Schütze, Fritz. 1977. "Die Technik des narrative Interviews in Interaktionsfeldstudien, dargestellt an einem Projekt zur Erforschung von kommunalen Machtstukturen." Bielefeld: o.V.

Short, Susan E., Feinian Chen, Barbara Entwisle, and Zhai Fengying. 2002. "Maternal work and child care in China: A multi-method analysis." *Population and Development Review* 28(1):31–57.

Steenhof, Liesbeth and Aart C. Liefbroer. 2008. "Intergenerational transmission of age at first birth in the Netherlands for birth cohorts born between 1935 and 1984: Evidence from municipal registers." *Population Studies* 62(1):69–84.

Steglich, Christian, Tom A. B. Snijders, and Michael Pearson. 2010. "Dynamic networks and behavior: Separating selection from influence." *Sociological Methodology* 40(1):S.329–93.

Straus, Florian. 2002. *Netzwerkanalysen: gemeindepsychologische Perspektiven für Forschung und Praxis*. Wiesbaden: Deutscher Universitätsverlag.

Strauss, Anselm L. and Juliet M. Corbin. 1998. *Basics of Qualitative Research: Techniques and Procedures for Developing Grounded Theory*. London: Sage.

Uhlendorff, Harald. 2004. "After the wall: Parental educational attitudes in East- and West-Germany." *International Journal of Behavioral Development* 28(1):71–82.

Witzel, Andreas and Herwig Reiter. 2012. *The Problem-Centred Interview. Principles and Practice*. London: Sage.

6

Two Sides of the Same Coin: The Integration of Personal Network Analysis with Ethnographic and Psychometric Strategies in the Study of Acculturation

Isidro Maya-Jariego and Silvia Domínguez

In this chapter we propose and describe a mixed method approach to assess the process of acculturation of host individuals, based on previous ethnographic and psychometric research of Latina immigrants in Boston (US) and Latin American immigrants in Andalucía (Spain) (Domínguez and Maya-Jariego 2008). Personal network analysis and visualization are combined with interviews, participant observation, and psychometric scales in a two-way iterative process of research, based on the assumption of a contingent relationship between the kind of acculturation experience and the type of personal network. This procedure is particularly useful to understand the complexities of the process of acculturation, taking into account both the topology on the intergroup situation and the interactive nature of the intercultural contact.

This chapter illustrates the application of a sequential explanatory design for the study of acculturation. It mainly uses the description of personal networks (Hollstein 2011) in combination with ethnography, observation, and the application of psychometric scales. The contributions to investigating social networks consist of the incorporation of network perceptions and interpretations by participants, examining how individuals position themselves in the social environment.

Introduction

In this chapter we propose a mixed methods approach to study acculturation processes. While both cross-cultural psychology and the sociological literature on assimilation have contributed to a more complex understanding of the process of acculturation, the grand majority of studies have concentrated on apprehending the integration experiences of immigrants. In this chapter we offer a look at the "other side" of acculturation, that is, at the experiences of the host population, or of members of the dominant group who come into contact with immigrants, through a mixed methods approach combining ethnographic and psychometric strategies using personal networks, which is particularly well adapted to this focus of research. Thus, our methodology integrates personal network analysis with other research strategies and combines an examination of both immigrants and host individuals. First we introduce both sides of the concept of acculturation and then we review the contribution of network analysis to the study of acculturation. The third section will expose our previous mixed method research and the characteristics of this approach, and we finish with a discussion of the advantages and limitations of our approach.

The Process of Acculturation

The process of acculturation "comprehends those phenomena which result when groups of individuals having different cultures come into continuous first-hand contact, with subsequent changes in the original culture patterns of either or both groups" (Redfield, Linton, and Herkovits 1936:149). There is a long tradition of ethnographic and psychometric studies that examines the transformation of values, attitudes, and behaviors at both the individual and the collective levels. Over the last three decades there has been a massive increase in the number of studies on acculturation, examining the experience of immigrants, expatriate managers, and students studying abroad, together with other trends associated with globalization.

Although without explicitly using the term, early studies of acculturation were carried out by anthropologists and sociologists in the 1920s and the 1930s. In the "Memorandum for the Study of Acculturation," published in the *American Anthropologist*, a seminal paper that aimed at defining a research agenda and at systematizing the studies in this area, Redfield, Linton and Herkovits (1936) developed a definition and some recommendations for the study of acculturation. They also anticipated that assimilation might not be the only outcome resulting from intercultural contacts, as documented by diverse ethnographic works (see, e.g., Redfield and Villa-Rojas 1943; Thurnwald 1932).

More recently, John W. Berry's (1980) cross-cultural model of acculturation has contributed greatly to the expansion of the research in this area. It is a two-dimensional model based on the principles of (a) cultural maintenance orientation and (b) extent of contact and participation with the external group. According to Berry, intercultural contact may result in assimilation, segregation, integration, or marginalization. These four ideal types describe the situations in which individuals separate themselves from the dominant culture (separation), adopt the characteristics of the new culture and neglecting the former one (assimilation), combine both cultural backgrounds (integration), or just experience problems managing conflictive circumstances (marginalization). This framework has been applied extensively to research in immigrants' psychological adaptation and acculturative stress and accounted notably for the recent focus on minorities in developed countries (compare to the diversity of contexts of the original research on acculturation).

This approach has lately been an object of criticism. From an interpretative standpoint, Berry's framework is seen as a mechanistic linear model that does not capture the complexity of the process of acculturation. In the same vein, based on constructivist assumptions, some authors argue that this model presents a lack of attention to culture and to the dynamics of intercultural contact, whereas the concept of "strategies of acculturation" presumes intentionality and consciousness in the experiences and reactions of the individuals (Bhatia and Ram 2009; Chirkov 2009a, 2009b, 2009c; Cresswell 2009; Tardif-Williams and Fisher 2009; Waldram 2009; Weinreich 2009).

However, Berry (2009) convincingly addresses these critics. Culture is conceptualized as a pre-existing phenomenon that is also created during social interaction. In his counter-argumentation, he argues for the joint examination of psychological and cultural acculturation and defends the combination of both *emic* (involving analysis of cultural phenomena from the perspective of one who participates in the culture being studied) and *etic* (involving analysis of cultural phenomena from the perspective of one who does not participate in the culture being studied) approaches as "necessary and complementary" (Berry 2009:368). Even with certain conceptual or methodological limitations, the assessment of acculturation strategies is nowadays a core feature of cross-cultural research.

A similar and parallel evolution has been observed in macro-social studies. The literature on assimilation in sociology in the United States has changed from a straight linear model of assimilation toward a segmented assimilation model (Gans 1992; Portes and Zhou 1993). The straight assimilation model was based on European American immigrants who were culturally similar to the earlier settlers in the United States and who arrived in conjunction with the beginning of industrialization, which eventually created high-wage jobs with little education necessary. This context allowed immigrants to assimilate in a straight-line fashion. The segmented assimilation model emerged as immigrants from Latin America, Africa, and Asia arrived with distinctive cultures and identifiers in terms of skin color and language spoken, and many settled in areas where marginalized minorities already lived. The immigration wave started by the 1965 law occurred in conjunction with the establishment of a two-tier labor market that favored a high level of education for a few while having an abundance of low-wage service jobs for those with little education. This context provides divergent assimilation paths for new immigrants, including the conventional upward, or "straight-line," assimilation and downward assimilation in conjunction with marginalized minorities, as well as selective acculturation or the choosing of an amalgamation of both cultures and biculturalism (Portes and Rumbaut 2001).

The Other Side of Acculturation

From its inception, acculturation has been seen in both psychology and sociology as a bidirectional process of mutual adaptation. There is also strong evidence showing that acculturation entails two-way processes of change. However, as explained earlier, research has mostly been focused on the cultural adjustments and changes experienced by immigrants and minority groups. It is only in the last couple of years that the acculturative experiences of majority individuals and communities (or "host" individuals when we refer to countries receiving international migration) has attracted some new attention (Dinh and Bond 2008), suggesting that it is a neglected and promising area for research. Nevertheless, to date, very few studies on the acculturation of the native population by their exposure to immigrants have been published.

As in the case of minority individuals, intercultural contact experiences contribute significantly to the variance in the attitudes of the majority individuals toward other ethnic groups, as well as in the awareness of discrimination and racial issues (Dinh et al. 2008). However, it is not simply a reversible process insofar as differential social status may greatly condition the intercultural contact situation (Hsiao and Witting 2008). Among other factors, socioeconomic climate, political will, social norms and values, community dynamics, historical background, and the structure of the organizations involved in resettlement moderate successful inclusion of immigrants and refugees into a host community (Prilleltensky 2008; Sakamoto and Truong 2008; Silka 2008; Smith 2008; Tseng and Yoshikawa 2008).

Minority and majority members (or immigrants and host individuals) are not in a reverse equivalent position. In part the acculturation of each collective is a parallel process, because at the individual level for both – minority and majority members – the changes in values, attitudes, and behaviors depend, for example, on the content, quality, frequency, and intensity of the intercultural contact experiences. However, they differ at the meso-level: The context behind majority–minority relations provides a different context for each side of the coin. Mainstream society has more power to define the conditions and norms of interaction, whereas the minority has more opportunities for contact and/or to be influenced by the exo group. In this sense, acculturation seems to be a reciprocal but asymmetric process. We will turn to this point later; now, we evaluate the contribution of personal network analysis to acculturation studies.

Personal Networks and Acculturation

Acculturation frequently occurs as part of an ecological transition (Bronfenbrenner 1979), for example, migration, relocation, or international exchange programs. Recurrently, researchers document the changes in social support networks in order to describe psychological adaptation and social integration. Among other strategies, the building of a typology of social support networks serves to predict adjustment, well-being, depression, labor insertion, social assimilation, and acculturation (Maya-Jariego and De la Vega 2004). Most of these studies make use of size and composition measures. Geographical relocation generally contributes to a more heterogeneous composition and also compels the rebuilding of social support networks in terms of size and structure.

The ethnic composition of the personal network reflects in part the position of the immigrant in the contact situation between minority and majority communities. At the aggregated level, the distribution of ethnic composition in personal networks reflects the topology of the intergroup contact and gives an idea about the absorption of the minority into the majority. In both cases, following the tradition of personal network studies, composition is described through attribute-based analyses that summarize the relationships of the respondent to network members (McCarty 2002).

However, the structural properties of personal networks may also be a proxy to the process of acculturation (Lubbers et al. 2007, 2009; McCarty et al. 2007; Molina et al. 2007, 2008). For instance, the average centrality measures of host individuals in the personal networks of immigrants indirectly inform the intercultural experiences of respondents (Domínguez and Maya-Jariego 2008), and the same may be expected from other contexts of interaction between majority and minority members. On average, host individuals play a secondary role (compared to co-ethnics) in the personal networks of immigrants. On the other hand, host individuals tend to gain in centrality over time, contributing to a gradual process of socialization in the new country for foreigners.

Furthermore, the structure of the personal network itself shows the process of acculturation. For instance, in previous studies, we have observed an inverse relationship between the level of metropolitan mobility and the density of personal networks of university students. The participation in two different social spaces is expressed in less structural cohesion, and it seems that personal networks gain in average betweenness in the active phases of ecological transition (Maya-Jariego and Holgado 2009). We can also expect a positive relationship between acculturation experiences and betweenness centralization of the personal network during personal transitions.[1]

After this review of the state of studies of acculturation, in the next sections we propose a mixed methods approach for such studies. This methodology integrates personal network analysis with other research strategies and combines an examination of both immigrants and host individuals. First we describe the research design we used in the two studies, one in Spain and the other in the United States; next we present a concrete case study of this methodology; and finally, our findings will usher conclusions on the advantages and the limitations of such a mixed methods approach.

Integration of Personal Network Analysis with Ethnographic and Psychometric Strategies: A Comparative Mixed Methods Research Design in the United States and Spain

In a former paper, we mixed methodologies to carry out a comparative study of two different minority–majority contexts (in the United States and Spain). The research was innovative both in its topic and its methods: We used mixed methods approaches to research the acculturation of host individuals. While we used two different methods, both utilized personal network analysis to examine the acculturation of host individuals in Spain and United States (Domínguez and Maya-Jariego 2008).

In the first study we obtained a sample of personal networks of Latin American and European residents in Spain: They were Argentinean, Ecuadorian, German, and Italian living in Cádiz and Seville. This procedure allowed us to identify the Spanish individuals that were experiencing direct interactions with foreigners, and therefore some level of acculturation. We compared the centrality measures obtained through interviews of host individuals and co-ethnics in the personal networks

---

[1] *Betweenness* is the number of shortest paths between all alters that a node lies upon (it is a characteristic of an actor's position in a network). *Average betweenness* is an aggregated indicator for the personal network, calculated as the mean of betweenness centrality of all the nodes of the network. Finally, *betweenness centralization* is an indicator of the whole graph and then a characteristic of the network.

of immigrant respondents, examining the socio-metric role of the former. We found that Spaniards tend to have a lower centrality measure than co-ethnics for the personal networks of the four groups that we analyzed. Personal network analysis was then combined with other strategies: First, cluster analysis served to build a typology of personal networks. This classification demonstrated that the socio-metric role of host individuals indirectly informed the stage of acculturation of immigrants. Next, we used psychometric scales to check differences between the clusters. For instance, applying the Sense of Community Index (McMillan and Chavis 1986) we observed that the feeling of belonging to the group of co-ethnics immigrated to Spain was clearly related to the type of personal network. Finally, in a second interview, personal network visualizations were presented to respondents to obtain a subjective description and interpretation of the position of Spaniards in their networks. The second study was an ethnographic study of Latin American immigrant women living in Boston (US), which served to identify host individuals playing a key role in these women's social integration. We focused on human service providers who served Latin American immigrants to see how that exposure acculturated them to Latin American cultures. For this study, we developed a typology of intercultural contact and changes involved in attitudes, perceptions, and ideas, and we analyzed the personal networks of host individuals which were representative of each category. Specifically, we distinguished between host individuals embedded in groups of immigrants ("residents") and host individuals with few contacts with foreigners and, comparatively, soft experiences of acculturation ("travelers"). In the middle, "frontier brokers" acted as integrative bridges for immigrants. The ethnographic typology was then combined with personal network analysis. For this, network information was collected from respondents previously classified in the three categories mentioned earlier. The graphic representations of the personal networks were presented to the interviewees, which provided an interpretation of their relationships with foreigners and their experiences of acculturation. In the immigrants' case, it seemed that a more intense experience of acculturation was tied to less cohesion in the personal networks of host individuals.

In some way, both studies followed an inverse strategy for analyzing acculturation. In Spain, the building of a typology of personal networks was the starting point to find individual differences in psychometric scales. In the United States, the construction of an ethnographic typology was the first step before examining the personal networks of respondents. In Spain, we observed the role of host individuals in the personal networks of immigrants, whereas in the United States we examined the experience

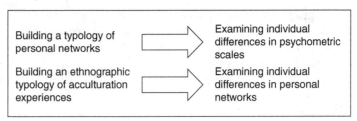

Figure 6.1. Two strategies in the study of acculturation

of human service providers that served Latin American migrants, who in turn were present in the North Americans' personal networks.

The first study shows an exploratory use of personal network analysis to describe individual differences in acculturation. In the second case, personal network analysis is used to validate the ethnography of acculturation (see Figure 6.1) (Tashakkori and Teddlie 2003). Both may be described as concurrent qualitative–quantitative approaches, with equal status (Creswell 2003; Johnson and Onwuegbuzie 2004; Ivankova et al. 2006), although quantitative methods were more significant for the research in Spain and qualitative methods were more significant for the study of Boston's personal networks. This combination of strategies enables the investigation of the structure, the content, and the processes of personal networks at the same time, as well as a kind of simultaneous exploration from an "outsider's" and an "insider's" view (Edwards 2010).

On the other hand, both studies coincide in the use of visualizations of personal networks to obtain a qualitative interpretation from respondents (for a description of this methodology and mixed methods implications, see Molina, Maya-Jariego, and McCarty, this volume).

In sum, although they functioned independently, these studies showed complementary approaches to researching the "other side" of acculturation. Building on this former paper, we now propose and describe a mixed methods approach to assess the process of acculturation of host individuals. The procedure is inspired by previous research, although it has not been empirically validated. It provides a generic framework to the study of acculturation, mixing the two strategies summarized in Figure 6.1. To present this interactive mixed methods procedure, as well as the integration of personal network analysis with other methodologies, is the main focus of this chapter. The methodology as well as the contributions and limitations of the approach are discussed in the following.

An Interactive Examination of Intercultural Contact

We propose a three-step procedure to examine the process of acculturation associated with international migration.

(1) *Screening host individuals through the personal networks of immigrants.* International migration entails different opportunities for intercultural contact between newcomers and host individuals. The members of the minority usually have a high average probability of intercultural experiences. However, host individuals fluctuate between intense direct intercultural contact and no interaction with immigrants at all, passing through indirect and vicarious experiences of acculturation. The topology of the interaction between both groups defines the distribution of individual acculturation experiences.

Examining the personal networks of immigrants is a way to locate host individuals and then to analyze the patterns of interaction they maintain with the members of the minority. For example, through personal network analysis we can obtain the centrality measures of host individuals that usually interact with the immigrant respondents. We can also examine the multiplicity of the relationship and the participation of host individuals in the cliques and clusters of the immigrants' networks, as well as other structural properties.

The screening phase allows, first, to list host individuals who potentially experience acculturation and, second, to describe the positions and the roles they play in the personal networks of immigrants.

(2) *Ethnographic study and personal network analysis of host individuals.* The second step consists in examining the intercultural contact and experiences of the host individuals listed in the screening phase. Observations and interviews are combined along with fieldwork to describe the changes in attitudes, values, and behavior related to intercultural contact. Personal network analysis and visualization are also applied to detect immigrants, to describe the pattern of interactions with them, and to interpret – in collaboration with the respondents – the intercultural experiences and changes that take place after continuous contact.

Examining the personal networks of host individuals is a way to describe the types of interactions they maintain with immigrants and then to analyze the acculturation experiences they live. In a similar way to the first phase, but taking the inverse point of view, social desirability is minimized to the extent that the description of acculturation is based on the analytical information about social interaction previously obtained. Personal network visualizations are used to produce a self-report on intercultural contact and acculturation experiences.

This second phase is conceptualized in order to describe the way host individuals process their contacts with immigrants. In this case, structural analysis is used to describe the positions and the roles the immigrants play in the personal networks of host individuals.

(3) *Interactive analysis of intercultural contact.* Finally, the information obtained from immigrants (phase 1) and host individuals (phase

Table 6.1. *A three-step procedure for the interactive study of acculturation*

1. *Screening host individuals through personal networks of immigrants*	• List of host individuals through analysis of the personal networks of immigrants. • Description of the socio-metric positions of host individuals in personal networks of immigrants.
2. *Ethnographic study and personal networks analysis of host individuals*	• Assessment of strategies and discourses of host individuals about intergroup relationships and changes brought on through that relationship. • Description of socio-metric position of immigrants in personal networks of host individuals.
3. *Interactive analysis of intercultural contact*	• Theoretically driven interactive analysis of acculturation.

2) is compared, integrated, and contextualized. Through personal network analysis we can take micro-observations of the structure of intercultural contact between groups or communities. The combination of both approaches makes possible an interactive assessment of acculturation. The experience of intercultural contact depends on the background, values, and characteristics of the people in a situation. For instance, immigrants whose behavior and attitudes correspond to an assimilation scheme represent a different acculturation potential for host individuals than those who are more inclined to favor segregation.

Even with some limitations that we will review later, the combination of personal network analysis of immigrants and host individuals may serve as a proxy to the process of acculturation. Structural analysis of acculturation is particularly sensitive when mixed with ethnographic strategies and when personal network visualizations are used to obtain a self-report by host individuals. In this part, theory, processes, and models of acculturation orient the analysis.

The last phase is a comparison of the personal networks of immigrants and host individuals who participated in the study. Two sides of the same coin are examined in order to make an interactive analysis of acculturation.

In the next section we offer an example of this mixed methods procedure summarized in Table 6.1, with the illustration of the case of a recent migrant in Spain. The respondent was surveyed as part of the first study, but a follow-up interview was carried out to provide a full representation of the methodology.

Exploring the Other Side of the Coin: First Links of an Ecuadorian Woman with Host Individuals in Spain

María Fernanda is an Ecuadorian woman who lives in Spain, serving as a domestic worker for a monthly salary of 600 Euros. She arrived after her husband and has been residing in Seville for 2 years. At the time of the interview she was 33 years old and planned to return to Ecuador in a few years.

Her personal network is divided in three main components connected by her husband Fabian, who is the actor with the highest degree, closeness, and betweenness centrality scores. The relatives residing in Ecuador constitute a strong and dense group, representing half of the members of the personal network. María Fernanda, still a newcomer, keeps regular and very frequent contact with family members by phone. There is a significant exchange of informative and emotional support with them (see Figure 6.2, represented with Netdraw; Borgatti 2002).

The second half of her personal network is composed of people living in Spain. María Fernanda works in domestic service for her boss, Marina, and her two daughters. Although they are very often in contact, the boss and the employee maintain a very formal relationship. Five Ecuadorian immigrants and one Spaniard therefore make up María's main source of social support in the host country: It is very common to socialize with other compatriots who are in the same situation following an international relocation. Usually they face the (same) problems as recent immigrants, with whom they share resources and coping strategies. Yet, as we see, María has also developed a relationship with a Spaniard, Marina.

María Fernanda's personal network in Spain is very dependable on the contacts previously deployed by her husband Fabian. She was absorbed after her migration by Fabian's small group of friends, composed mainly of Ecuadorian immigrants. The only Spaniard in this group is Encarna, whose boyfriend is Ecuadorian and who started to socialize with immigrants as she was serving as a volunteer in a migrant support organization.

Twenty percent of the alters mentioned by the respondent are Spaniards. Host individuals have on average a lower measure of centrality than co-ethnics. Ecuadorians have on average 2.83 times more degree, 1.37 more closeness, and 8.52 more eigenvector centrality than the Spaniards mentioned by ego.[2]

---

[2] *Centrality* is a measure of how connected the node is to other nodes within the network. *Degree* is the number of direct ties for each node. A single alter is highly close if it is connected by short paths to many other alters (*closeness*). Degree and closeness measures tend to be strongly correlated. *Betweenness* is the number of shortest paths between all alters that a node lies upon. See Faust and Wasserman (1999) and Carrington, this volume.

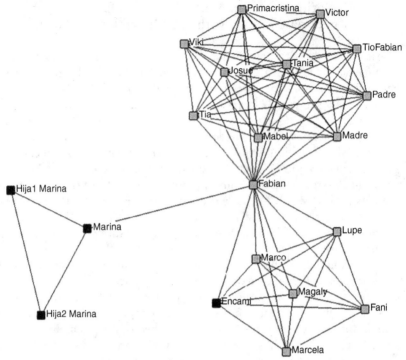

Figure 6.2. Example of the personal network of an Ecuadorian immigrant in Spain

The case of María Fernanda is representative of recent migrants' personal networks (Maya-Jariego 2006). Most of her contacts are from the same ethnic group; half of the alteri reside in the sending country and new ties are fairly contingent with the context of opportunities. In the short term, interpersonal relations in Spain seem to be related to family regrouping, imposed by the labor context or just coming from other relationships.

In this example, two types of context are relevant for the formation of inter-ethnic relationships: the workplace and non-profit organizations. The labor context provides a space for contact between immigrants and host individuals, as illustrated by the case of María Fernanda and her boss Marina's family. On the other hand, Encarna (a Spanish woman) started to socialize with Ecuadorians while volunteering for a non-governmental organization that provides services for immigrants. In the process, she was absorbed by a group of Ecuadorian friends. As part of Fabian's network, she established a relationship with María Fernanda afterwards.

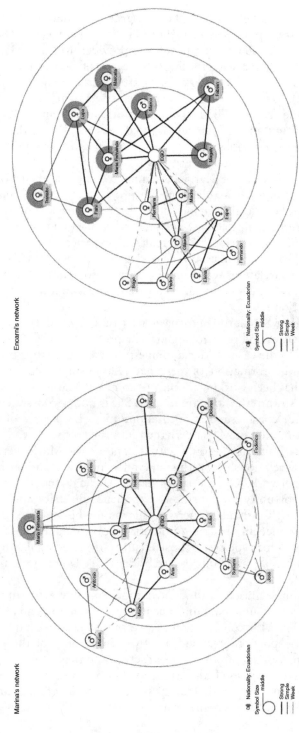

Figure 6.3. Ecuadorian immigrants in the personal networks of host individuals

The personal networks of both María (Ecuadorian) and Encarna (Spanish) are represented in Figure 6.3, using VennMaker (Schönhuth 2007). Although not a relevant support provider, Marina (María's boss) is the second actor with the highest degree of betweenness in María Fernanda's personal network (only after her husband, as shown in Figure 6.2). Marina has a homogeneous network, mainly constituted of relatives and friends. The Ecuadorian working at home is the only element of cultural diversity in her personal network. Due to the power differential between boss and employee, the impact for the host individual in terms of acculturation is very small.

On the contrary, Encarna is immersed in the Ecuadorian culture. Participating as a volunteer in a program for immigrants and her Ecuadorian boyfriend have introduced her to a new way of life. She has experienced both a prolonged intercultural contact and an active process of acculturation. Curiously, intercultural experiences and interactions with exo groups are mutually dependent processes. As a consequence, interpersonal relations with more potential for cultural conflicts and acculturation are also associated to individuals with lower opportunities for interaction.

Although a Spaniard, Encarna is part of an Ecuadorian group, and her experiences and resources tend to be pretty similar to that of María Fernanda. In the case of María, domestic service is a labor context that facilitates the formation of personal relationships. However, María Fernanda has been working for only 6 months at Marina's home. Marina is a bridge toward the host community. She is both a contact with a high potential for conflict and acculturation, and a key source of resources for the integration of María Fernanda into the host society.

Marina's home is the only actual context for María Fernanda to deploy new relationships with some independence from her husband's personal network. On the other hand, María Fernanda is the only actual opportunity for Marina to experience diversity and acculturation. Although difficult to persist, this is an employee-based relationship with noticeably bridging potential. For a detailed description of the ethnographic typology of host acculturation distinguishing "travellers," "residents," and "integrative bridges" see Domínguez and Maya-Jariego (2008).

This example illustrates the contribution of an interactive mixed methods procedure to understanding acculturation. It follows an explanatory sequence. First, the combination of quantitative network indicators with qualitative reports by respondents gives an account of the pattern of interaction, looking into both the structure and the content or processes of the networks. Second, the crossed views between the standpoints of immigrants and host individuals provide a more complex analysis of the interaction. The concurrent use of personal networks of minority and majority members allows for a deeper understanding of the topology of intergroup contact (as in the contrast between Figures 6.2 and 6.3). Finally, we have documented the interactive nature of the analysis, emphasizing the dependence of the acculturative potential of intercultural encounters on the individuals who interrelate, as well as on the networks in which they are embedded. For instance, we have shown that María Fernanda will obtain plainly different resources when interacting with her friend Encarna or with her boss Marina.

As we have shown with this example, the three-step procedure integrates personal network analysis with psychometric and ethnographic studies, playing respectively an exploratory and validating role. To conclude, we now assess the contribution of network methods in the traditions of psychometric and ethnographic research on acculturation. The contributions of the mixed methods approach are contextualized in the psychological and anthropological literature on acculturation. We now present our findings before finishing with some reflections on the challenges and benefits of using the mixed methods strategy for the research on intercultural contexts.

Personal Network Analysis and Psychometric Studies

The study of acculturation generally includes the application of psychometric scales for the particular language groups and geographic contexts concerned. They are frequently bidimensional scales highlighting the explicit discourse of respondents about their values and attitudes toward the two cultures in contact, and examining the personal strategies to manage this intercultural experience. However, some efforts have been made to build more complex scales, with an orthogonal structure or a more flexible approach. Even when two groups or cultures are the main reference for the intergroup contact, the assessment of multiple senses of communities may be more appropriate and realistic (see, e.g., Maya-Jariego 2004; Maya-Jariego and Armitage 2007).

Personal network analysis is an indirect approach to the study of acculturation. It consists of a systematic evaluation of the patterns of interaction of the respondent (whether with members of the endo group or of the exo group). Unlike psychometric scales, the informant is not providing an explicit conscious declaration of his/her strategies to manage the intercultural contact. In fact, emergent structural properties are surprising even for the respondents themselves. Moreover, this procedure is less influenced by social desirability. Obtaining information on personal networks is less transparent for the respondents, whereas they can consciously define themselves according to the image of their acculturation strategies that they would like to transmit. Actually, respondents answer differentially to acculturation questions depending on the interviewers: Individuals emphasize the original cultural characteristics when they are examined by co-ethnics and accentuate the changes in behaviour, values, and attitudes when interviewed by host individuals (Maya-Jariego 2001).

The combination of an explicit assessment and network information may be fruitful to describe the different outcomes associated with intercultural contact. It is a more comprehensive approach that takes into account both social interaction and personal identification processes. In some way, it is comparable to the simultaneous use of observation and interviews in ethnographic studies. Psychometric scales provide efficient measures of acculturation (or sense of community) and function as good empirical predictors for a wide array of subjective and objective adjustment outcomes. It has been documented that acculturation varies through different types of personal networks (Lerner and Brandes 2007; Maya-Jariego and De la Vega 2004; Molina et al. 2007). Nevertheless, as we have suggested earlier, the ethnographic approach is an alternative way to complement network information.

Finally, personal network analysis offers a description of the individual context while acculturation is focused on the direct perception of the subject. Therefore, it is a way to combine personal and contextual information, those related respectively to the processes of identification and the matrix of interpersonal interaction.

Personal Network Analysis and Ethnographic Studies

Ethnography is the study of human societies and culture through the utilization of participant observation, interviews, and/or questionnaires. A particular ethnographic design is to observe individuals as they come into contact with each other, and over time, begin to demonstrate new patterns of behaviors, ideas, and attitudes. Through observation social relationships are uncovered, and through interviews an ethnographer can begin to determine the nature of social links and attributes of the social ties involved. Once the ties have been identified and classified, one can describe the dynamics in terms of ethnography-revealed networks. Given that culture is transmitted through social relationships, ethnography can help to illuminate ideas, values, and attitudes as individuals under observation interact with each other. As such, ethnographic research is a well-suited method to understand the acculturation of individuals.

Social network analysis provides ethnographers with the opportunity to systematically collect necessary information on the relationships and their characteristics. Through semi-structured interviews focused on social relationships, ethnographers can focus on pertinent questions as well as allow the respondents to elaborate in an open manner on particular related subjects. This type of ethnographic inquiry has been coined "structured discovery:" The in-depth interviews and observations are focused on specific topics but allow flexibility in order to capture unexpected findings and relationships (Burton et al. 2001; Winston et al. 1999). Through structured discovery, the ethnographer can use interview guides specifically focused on the attributes of interpersonal ties in terms of support or leverage, strength or weakness, and emphasize how reciprocity may be maintained or not. Through the use of inventories, ethnographers interested in collecting information on social relationships in which respondents are embedded can do so in a systematic and organized manner. In this sense, social network analysis has contributed to ethnography by providing a structured system for their discovery and definition.

Now, ethnography has also contributed greatly to the study of social networks and of their attributes. A consequent number of important works have used social networks to study immigrants and their structural assimilation and acculturation. Among these are Olwig's (2007) ethnography of family networks and cultural identity of West Indian families spanning 60 years throughout several continents. Olwig found that being "West Indian" is not necessarily rooted in ongoing visits to their countries of origin, or in ethnic communities in the receiving countries, but rather in family narratives and the maintenance of family networks. Menjívar's (2000) ethnography of Salvadorian immigrants in San Francisco demonstrates how reciprocity under economic scarcity cannot not be maintained, and disrupts family networks. Bashi (2007) focused on West Indian immigrants in London and New York to examine, through a network-driven dynamic, the migration of successful immigrants and to research how their social mobility, secured via anchors, that is, through an ever-expanding network based on reciprocity, assured their success. Lastly, Domínguez (2011) led a comparative ethnography of Latin American immigrant women living in low-income concentration areas to see how networks supported migrants in their process of integration. The reasons behind the termination of relationships, the maintenance of reciprocity, and the fluidity behind relationships were uncovered only after more than two years of ethnography. In addition, Domínguez demonstrated the workings of bridges (individuals who connect dissimilar groups to each other) by showing the latter's motivations for bridging and the consequences that bridging had for the immigrant women in terms of integration.

These ethnographic accounts of social networks demonstrate this mixed methods methodology's capacity to accurately display social relationships as they come and go, thus demonstrating their dynamism and fluidity. Ethnography made possible the revealing of the motivations behind the action of forging ties, the consequences of those actions, and the reasons for starting and ending relationships. Ethnography allows the identification of the attributes of the social links and thus characterizes the nature of the networks as support, leverage, or both. In a certain way, it is due to ethnography that we can characterize ties. As such, ethnography permits the revealing, the unveiling, and the classifying of networks. In this sense, ethnography vividly emphasizes how relationships are intricately involved in the acculturation process, acting as social models that influence attitudes and value alterations (see also Avenarius and Johnson, this volume).

This three-step procedure has shown the potential for researching creatively integrating ethnography and network analysis. Due to the extended contact time between researchers and respondents developed during ethnography, the discovery of information is greatly facilitated. It is thanks to this relationship that more comprehensive information can be gained about the ties involved in the respondent's social network. This also makes possible a quantitative analysis, whereby the strength of the observed ties may be assigned a number that then can be placed into a diagram using software for visualization. In sum, through the relationship between the ethnographer and the respondents, social ties gathered ethnographically can be quantified and integrated into a mixed methods dynamic.

While quotes and observations can provide a good illustration of the qualities of ties in terms of ethnicity, gender, and strength behind each relationship, the rich nature of ethnographic inquiry comes alive when one can visualize the network composition in a diagram fashion. The focus of the ethnographic component of this social network analysis was to evaluate how members of the dominant culture (or "hosts") had incorporated immigrants into their personal networks as a measure of acculturation. Consequently, seeing the distribution of host culture as differentiated by immigrants in the network diagram was primordial (see Figure 6.3). It was in this fashion that one "resident" showed almost all immigrants besides her family members in her network (e.g., the case of Encarna in the study reported earlier). This visualization depicts the full significance of high levels of acculturation manifested in the centrality played by immigrants in personal networks of host individuals. Additionally, using a diagram made it possible to see when only a couple of immigrants were situated in the periphery of the social network of the host culture member and thus integrated into the network of "travelers" (Domínguez and Maya-Jariego 2008). In sum, the utilization of social network analysis and visualization clearly represents the composition of networks whose information was gathered ethnographically in a rich and complex fashion.

Conclusion and Discussion: Mixing Methods – Challenges and Benefits

Even with its ethnographic origin, the application of psychometric bidimensional scales has been the most common approach to current studies of acculturation. In this chapter we have proposed a mixed methods procedure to examine intercultural contact, partially based in personal network analysis (and derived from Domínguez and Maya-Jariego 2008).

Acculturation is understood as the mutual changes resulting from a situation of prolonged intercultural contact. Mixed methods may contribute to the topological and interactive analyses of the processes and outcomes associated with intercultural contact. Our proposal consists of several steps: listing host individuals through analysis of the personal networks of immigrants; describing the socio-metric position of host individuals in those networks; examining personal strategies and discourses of host individuals about the contact situation; describing the socio-metric position of immigrants in the personal networks of host individuals; and, finally, deploying a theory-driven interactive analysis of acculturation. As we see, along this process, network analysis and acculturation assessment are mixed and sequenced.

With this procedure, ethnographic, psychometric, and network analysis strategies are used in conjunction. However, it is not only a combination of qualitative and quantitative approaches but also an assessment of structure and activity, micro and macro processes and individual and contextual variables. The integration of strategies shows the complementarity of these methods, which in turn shapes subsequent steps in the research process, covering especially – among others – development functions (Greene et al. 1989).

Personal network analysis permits a topological examination of the space of intergroup contact. It may be used to assess the insertion of the minority into the host society structure and represent the boundaries between both groups. On the other hand, two different points of view are combined: the position of host individuals in the personal networks of immigrants and, reversely, the position of immigrants in host individuals' personal networks. This entails a combination of contacts that may result in different probabilities for the establishment of new relationships (with also a diverse potential of acculturation).

The procedure is particularly well suited to the examination of individual experiences. However, it has limitations when it comes to capturing the collective dimension of acculturation, which would need a whole network approach. The blending of personal networks, however, could be used at the aggregated level to describe communities. Furthermore, the interactive mixed approach proposed here could be replicated at the meso- or macro-levels.

Acculturation is both a natural and cultural phenomenon (Berry 2009). There are relevant basic psychological processes underlying the intercultural individual experience. On the other hand, each context provides a particular situation of contact, which introduces variation and diversity. Both approaches can be combined so as to discover commonalities, compare individuals in different intercultural contexts, and describe the unique inter-subjective experiences of single cultures. Mixed methods contribute to the merging of nomothetic and idiographic strategies. Complex methodological approaches are required to address interactive and mutual changes of prolonged intercultural contact.

References

Bashi, Vilna. 2007. *Survival of the Knitted: Immigrant Social Networks in a Stratified World.* Palo Alto, CA: Stanford University Press.

Berry, John W. 1980. "Social and cultural change." Pp. 211–79 in *Handbook of Cross-Cultural Psychology: Social Psychology,* vol. 5, edited by II. C. Triandis and R. W. Brislin. Boston: Allyn and Bacon.

———. 1997. "Immigrants, acculturation, and adaptation." *Applied Psychology: An International Review* 48:5–33.

———. 2003. "Conceptual approaches to acculturation." Pp. 17–37 in *Acculturation: Advances in Theory, Measurement and Applied Research,* edited by K. M. Chun, P. B. Organista, and G. Marín. Washington, DC: American Psychological Association.

———. 2009. "A critique of critical acculturation." *International Journal of Intercultural Relations* 33:361–71.

Berry, John W., Uichol Kim, Thomas Minde, and Doris Mok. 1987. "Comparative studies of acculturative stress." *International Migration Review* 21: 491–511.

Bhatia, Sunil and Anjali Ram. 2009. "Theorizing identity in transnational and Diaspora cultures: A critical approach to acculturation." *International Journal of Intercultural Relations* 33:140–49.

Borgatti, Stephen P. 2002. *Netdraw: Network Visualization Software.* Lexington: Analytic Technologies.

Bourhis, Richard Y., Léna C. Moïse, Stephan Perreault, and Sacha Senécal. 1997. "Towards an interactive acculturation model: A social psychological approach." *International Journal of Psychology* 32:369–86.

Bronfenbrenner, Urie. 1979. *The Ecology of Human Development: Experiments by Nature and Design.* Cambridge, MA: Harvard University Press.

Burton, Linda M., Robin Jarrett, Laura Lein, Stephen Matthews, James Quane, and Debra Skinner. 2001. *Structured Discovery: Ethnography, Welfare Reform, and the Assessment of Neighborhoods, Families, and Children.* Paper presented at the Society for Research and Development of Children, St. Louis, MO, April 2001.

Chirkov, Valery. 2009a. "Introduction to the special issue on Critical Acculturation Psychology." *International Journal of Intercultural Relations* 3:87–93.

———. 2009b. "Critical psychology of acculturation: What do we study and how do we study it, when we investigate acculturation?" *International Journal of Intercultural Relations* 33:94–105.

———. 2009c. "Summary of the criticism and of the potential ways to improve acculturation psychology." *International Journal of Intercultural Relations* 33:177–80.

Cresswell, James. 2009. "Towards a post-critical praxis: Intentional states and recommendations for change in acculturation psychology." *International Journal of Intercultural Relations* 33:162–72.

Creswell, John W. 2003. *Research Design. Qualitative, Quantitative and Mixed Methods Approaches.* 2nd ed. London: Sage.

Dinh, Khanh T. and Meg A. Bond. 2008. "The other side of acculturation: Changes among host individuals and communities in their adaptation to immigrant populations." *American Journal of Community Psychology* 42(3–4):283–85.

Dinh, Khanh T., Traci L. Weinstein, Melissa Nemon, and Sara Rondeau. 2008. "The influence of Asian Americans on white American college students: Acculturation, awareness of racial discrimination, and psychological adjustment." *American Journal of Community Psychology* 42(3–4):298–308.

Dominguez, Silvia. 2011. *Getting Ahead: Social Mobility, Public Housing, Immigrant Networks.* New York: New York University Press.

Domínguez, Silvia and Isidro Maya-Jariego. 2008. Acculturation of host individuals: Immigrants and personal networks. *American Journal of Community Psychology* 42:309–27.

Edwards, G. 2010. "Mixed-methods approaches to social network analysis." ESRC National Centre for Research Methods Review paper.

Faust, Katherine and Stanley Wasserman. 1999. *Social Network Analysis: Methods and Applications.* Cambridge: Cambridge University Press.

Gans, Herbert J. 1992. "Second-generation decline: Scenarios for the economic and ethnic futures of the post-1965 American immigrants." *Ethnic and Racial Studies* 15:173–92.

Greene, Jennifer C., Valerie J. Caracelli, and Wendy F. Graham. 1989. "Toward a conceptual framework for mixed-methods evaluation designs." *Educational Evaluation and Policy Analysis* 11(3):255–74.

Hollstein, Betina. 2011. "Qualitative approaches." In *The Sage Handbook of Social Network Analysis,* edited by J. Scott and P. J. Carrington. London: Sage.

Hsiao, James and Michele Witting. 2008. "Acculturation among three racial/ethnic groups of host and immigrant adolescents." *American Journal of Community Psychology* 42(3–4):286–97.

Ivankova, Nataliya V., John W. Creswell, and Sheldon L. Stick. 2006. "Using mixed-methods sequential explanatory design: From theory to practice." *Field Methods* 18:3–20.

Johnson, R. Burke and Anthony J. Onwuegbuzie. 2004. "Mixed methods research: A research paradigm whose time has come." *Educational Researcher* 33:14–26.

Lerner, Juergen and Ulrik Brandes. 2007. "Comparing networks by their group structure with an application to acculturation networks," XXVII Sunbelt International Conference on Social network Analysis. Corfu, Greece, May 1–6 [www.egoredes.net].

Lubbers, Miranda, José Luis Molina, and Christopher McCarty. 2007. "Personal networks and ethnic identifications: The case of migrants in Spain." *International Sociology* 22(6):720–40.

Lubbers, Miranda J., José Luis Molina, Jurgen Lerner, Ulrik Brandes, Christopher McCarty, and Jorge Ávila. 2009. "Longitudinal analysis of personal networks. The case of Argentinean migrants in Spain." *Social Networks* 31(5).

Maya-Jariego, Isidro. 2001. "Sesgos de medida y problemas de muestreo en las encuestas de poblaciones inmigrantes." *Metodología de Encuestas* 3(2):197–213.

———. 2004. "Sentido de comunidad y potenciación comunitaria." *Apuntes de Psicología*, 22(2):187–211.

———. 2006. "Mallas de paisanaje: el entramado de relaciones de los inmigrantes." Pp. 257–76 in *Geografías del desorden. Migración, alteridad y nueva esfera social*, edited by J. L. Pérez Pont. Valencia: Universidad de Valencia.

Maya-Jariego, Isidro and Neill Armitage. 2007. "Multiple senses of community in migration and commuting: The interplay between time, space and relations." *International Sociology* 22(6):743–66.

Maya-Jariego, Isidro and Lia de la Vega. 2004. "Levels of multiplexity and types of support providers: Personal networks of Indian immigrants in Argentina." XXIV International Sunbelt Social Network Conference. Portorož (Eslovenia), May 12–16, 2004.

Maya-Jariego, Isidro and Daniel Holgado. 2009. "Geographical mobility and personal transitions: Covariation of personal networks and social networks data." European Research Collaborative Project Meeting on Dynamic Analysis of Networks and Behaviours. Oxford, June 30, 2009.

McCarty, Chris. 2002. "Structure in personal networks." *Journal of Social Structure* 3 [www.cmu.edu/joss/].

McCarty, Christopher, Miranda J. Lubbers, and José Luis Molina. 2007. "Using the E-I index with personal network structural data as a measure of acculturation." Presented at XXVII Sunbelt International Network for Social Network Analysis, May 1–6, Corfu, Greece.

McMillan, David B. and David M. Chavis. 1986. "Sense of community: A definition and theory." *Journal of Community Psychology* 14:6–23.

Menjívar, Cecilia. 2000. *Fragmented Ties: Salvadoran Immigrant Networks in America*. Berkeley: University of California Press.

Molina, José Luis, Jurgen Lerner, and Silvia Gómez. 2008. "Patrones de cambio de las redes personales de inmigrantes en Cataluña." *REDES-Revista hispana para el análisis de redes sociales* 15(4):36–60.

Molina, José Luis, Miranda J. Lubbers, and Christopher McCarty. 2007. "Using personal network composition and structure to explain ethnic identity." Presented at XXVII Sunbelt International Network for Social Network Analysis, May 1–6, Corfu, Greece.

Navas, Marisol, María S. García, and Antonio J. Rojas. 2006. "Acculturation strategies and attitudes of African immigrants in the South of Spain: Between reality and hope." *Cross Cultural Research* 40(4):331–51.

Navas, Marisol, Antonio J. Rojas, María García, and Pablo Pumares. 2007. "Acculturation strategies and attitudes according to the Relative Acculturation Extended Model (RAEM): The perspectives of natives versus immigrants." *International Journal of Intercultural Relations* 31:67–86.

Olwig, Karen F. 2007. *Caribbean Journeys: An Ethnography of Migration and Home in Three Family Networks*. Durham, NC: Duke University Press.

Portes, Alejandro and Rubén G. Rumbaut. 2001. *Legacies: The Story of the Immigrant Second Generation*. Berkeley: University of California Press.

Portes, Alejandro and Min Zhou. 1993. "The new second generation: Segmented assimilation and its variants." *Annals of the American Academy of Political and Social Science* 530:74–96.

Prilleltensky, Isaac. 2008. "Migrant well-being is a multilevel, dynamic, value dependent phenomenon." *American Journal of Community Psychology* 42(3–4):359–64.

Redfield Robert, B. Linton, and M. J. Herskovits. 1936. "Memorandum for the study of acculturation." *American Anthropologist* 38(1):149–52.

Redfield, Robert and Alfonso Villa-Rojas. 1943. *Chan Kom, a Maya Village*. Chicago: University of Chicago Press.

Sakamoto, Izumi, Y. Yi Wei, and Lele Truong. 2008. "How do organizations and social policies 'acculturate'to immigrants? Accommodating skilled immigrants in Canada." *American Journal of Community Psychology* 42(3–4):343–54.

Schönhuth, Michael. 2007. "VennMaker 1.0 und andere Gewächse aus dem Garten des Exzellenzclusters. Selektive Betrachtungen." Unveröff. Vortrag auf der Beiratstagung des Exzellenzclusters am 22./23. Februar 2007 in Mainz/Waldhausen.

Silka, Linda. 2008."Finding community in studies of host community acculturation." *American Journal of Community Psychology* 42(3):365–67.

Smith, R. S. 2008."The case of a city where 1 in 6 residents is a refugee: Ecological factors and host community adaptation in successful resettlement." *American Journal of Community Psychology* 42(3):328–42.

Tardif-Williams, Christine and Lianne Fisher. 2009. "Clarifying the link between acculturation experiences and parent–child relationships among families in cultural transition: The promise of contemporary critiques of acculturation psychology." *International Journal of Intercultural Relations* 33:150–61.

Tashakkori, Abbas and Charles Teddlie. 2003. *Handbook of Mixed Methods in Social & Behavioral Research*. London: Sage.

Thurnwald, Richard. 1932. "The psychology of acculturation." *American Anthropologist* 34:557–69.

Tseng, Vivian and Hirokazu Yoshikawa. 2008. "Reconceptualizing acculturation: Ecological processes, historical contexts, and power inequities." *American Journal of Community Psychology* 42(3):355–58.

Waldram, James B. 2009. "Is there a future for 'Culture' in acculturation research? An anthropologist's perspective." *International Journal of Intercultural Relations* 33:173–76.

Weinreich, Peter. 2009. "'Enculturation', not 'acculturation': Conceptualising and assessing identity processes in migrant communities." *International Journal of Intercultural Relations* 33:124–39.

Winston, P., Ronald J. Angel, Linda M. Burton, P. Lindsay Chase-Lansdale, Andrew J. Cherlin, Robert A. Moffitt, and William J. Wilson. 1999. *Welfare, Children, and Families: A Three-City Study, Overview and Design.* Retrieved May 19, 2003 (web.jhu.edu/threecitystudy/images/..../Wave_1_User_Guide.doc).

7

Adaptation to New Legal Procedures in Rural China: Integrating Survey and Ethnographic Data

Christine B. Avenarius and Jeffrey C. Johnson

Introduction

This chapter portrays the implementation of a fully integrated mixed methods research design aimed to capture the ongoing process of social change in mainland China. We approach the study of social change by combining the investigation of existing social structures in China with an exploration of Chinese peoples' perceptions about the function and role of social relationships in the process of adapting to new social practices. Our specific focus for the study of social change is the recent establishment of the rule of law in China, which is perhaps one of the most sweeping social reforms in the history of the country. To capture the mutual impact of structure and cognition on the agency of a rural Chinese citizen, we used a research design that integrates not only our multitude of questions and influencing concepts, but also different types of data and a range of data collection and analysis techniques. As discussed in the introduction of this volume, we identify this fully integrated mixed methods research design in reference to a typology developed by Teddlie and Tashakkori (2006:15).

A focus on the implications of legal reforms for social change in rural China allows us to thoroughly explore network effects in local communities. The Chinese legal system was one of the social institutions that received a major overhaul by the Chinese government as part of its economic reform package initiated in the late 1970s. In 1992, the National People's Congress formally recognized that a sound market economy must be based on the rule of law and expected civil courts to

Support for this research was provided by NSF BCS 0525023. Special thanks to Liu Lu, He Lili, Tian Fei, Yang Sijia, Han Fei, He Congzhi, Li Suoshuang, Li Jingming, and the villagers of Li village for their kindness and cooperation.

provide legal services to all citizens alongside criminal courts (Potter 2001; Wang 2000). This decision has provided Chinese people with the option of settling civil disputes through formal adjudication by a judge at court in addition to the traditional practice of mediation based on the principles of reciprocity assisted by a local authority.

How do Chinese citizens navigate these new opportunities for social behavior? Since norms and laws are important components of culture, our research wants to understand the significance of offering conflict resolution at court as an agent for social change and economic development. We are interested to learn how Chinese people experience this social change. In particular, we want to know how changes in the procedures of the Chinese justice system influence individual choices to engage in this alternative mode for solving conflicts. Hence, the guiding question for our research went beyond the exploration of who uses adjudication at court and why. Taking the implications of the changed rules of conduct into account and linking them to existing cultural practices, we ask: What explains the likelihood of taking a case to court?

Experiences during previous research projects conducted in mainland China and extensive literature review familiarized us with the specific characteristics of the Chinese social order. As the next section of this chapter introduces in detail, the traditional Chinese social system, rooted in the teachings of Confucius, is not individual-based or society-based, but relationship-based (Fei [1939] 1992). Hence we want to pay special attention to the function of social relationships in the process of finding conflict resolutions. Studying the characteristics of both whole networks and personal networks will provide us with insights to evaluate how social relationships influence social behavior at the group level and individual level. Additional data on peoples' opinions about the role of relationships will allow us to understand the changes that the traditional Chinese social order has experienced in recent history. We also hypothesize that the structure of social relationships and the perceptions about social relationships and legal procedures influence each other and play a role in the adoption of new forms of conflict resolution.

This chapter features a description of the individual components of our mixed methods research design, including meta-inferences on the ongoing changes in rural China gained from the integration of methodological and analytical approaches. First, however, we review the background information that constitutes the context for our fully integrated mixed methods research design. This includes a theoretical reflection of the interrelation between the study of social network structures and social cognition, a cultural background that describes the specific cultural meaning of social relationships in China, a legal background depicting the current range of conflict resolutions, and the ethnographic background of this case study, Li Village in Hebei province. The chapter concludes with a discussion of benefits and challenges of this specific research design.

Social Networks and Cognition: Studying Social Change in China

Theoretical Background: Combining Social Network Analysis and Consensus Analysis

One of the major theoretical contributions of social network analysis is its ability to demonstrate the interrelatedness of a range of cultural practices or rather the embeddedness of human behavior and decision making processes within networks of social relationships (Granovetter 1985; Schweizer 1997). This theory of social embeddedness has assisted social scientists to overcome the constraints of rational choice theory in explaining decision-making processes and adapting to social change.[1] Rational choice theory has been criticized for its narrow focus on self-interest, and the neglect of altruism and origins of choices and preferences (March and Olsen 1984; Williamson 1985; North 1990; Ensminger 1992; Brinton and Nee 1998; Scott 2001). Analysis of network characteristics such as structural holes or bridging ties (Burt 1992) allows the understanding of how informal norms, including trust, are reinforced and how information travels and influences decisions (Passy and Giugni 2001; Barr et al. 2009).

However, the theory of social embeddedness does not explain which cultural values motivate actors to interact, trust, or make decisions to adopt new practices. The personal attitudes and perceptions of individual cultural actors influence their interaction with others (Emirbayer and Goodwin 1994). In turn, perceptions and decisions, for example, the decision to participate in social movements (Rosenthal et al. 1985; Passy and Giugni 2001), can at times be influenced by positions in the network structure. Hence, a combination of social embeddedness theory and social cognition is needed to understand why some people embrace new cultural practices such as taking a dispute to court and others refrain from such activities. As we describe in the following, our research design combines the tools of social network analysis and cultural consensus

---

[1] The social movement literature that represents social change and the literature on adaptations of innovations have not been included in this discussion due to their extensiveness and very little overlap with the topic at hand.

analysis to accomplish this (Holland and Quinn 1987; Wasserman and Faust 1994; Weller 2007).

Social network structures reveal the dynamic processes that bring cultural actors together or drive them away. In this volume, the study of network dynamics is highlighted in the chapters by Wald, Gluesing et al., and Rogers and Menjivar. This chapter focuses predominately on network effects that are a result of internal dynamics. One area that reveals these effects is network homophily, the degree of similarity among members. Together with the notion of network density, homophily serves as an indicator of relationships that foster the development of trust, social coherence, and adherence to existing norms (Lin 2001). Cultural consensus analysis elicits the nature and distribution of cognition in terms of what cultural values and motivations exist within a cultural group (Romney et al. 1986). This type of analysis also reveals how values and motivations are structured in the minds of actors and how they are related to decisions initiating social interactions and adopting new cultural practices, for example, the pursuit of justice at a regional court in rural China.

Cultural Background: The Traditional Chinese Social Order

Throughout Chinese history, the embeddedness in webs of kinship relations has been considered responsible for economic and political inequalities between families and their individual members. Those who belonged to particular powerful lineages had more influence than others (Ruf 1998). In the early 1950s, the Chinese Communist Party started a land reform and the collectivization of all forms of production. Party officials also abolished the existing social classes with a call for an ongoing "class struggle" against former landlords and other "bad elements," for example, business owners (Chan et al. 1984). However, in the late 1970s and early 1980s, the Chinese government reversed its previous policies and initiated economic reforms that enabled both private business initiatives and the return of economic responsibilities to the household level. These reforms have made it possible for household members to expand their social relationships beyond kinship obligations and to engage in various business activities in addition to agricultural production (McKinley 1996; Oi 1999).

In the context of rural Chinese society, relatives and neighbors continue to be important confidantes. Former classmates also fulfill important functions. However, many of these social roles overlap, for example, a neighbor is both a cousin and a former classmate. In addition, in the Chinese world view relationships are based on obligations and responsibilities (Jacobs 1982; Kipnis 1997). Fei Xiaotong (1939), the first widely known anthropologist in China, explains that a member of Chinese culture sees him- or herself as an individual embedded in concentric circles of society. In the core of all circles is the person, surrounded by his or her family members, followed by lineage members, the special interest groups or association he or she is a member of, and lastly the larger society. In reference to Confucian teachings, the traditional Chinese social system defines each member of society as a social and interactive being, not as an isolated, separate entity.[2] As a result, a Chinese person sees the world as a reflection of his or her relations to others and the particular circumstances that unite them. The indigenous Chinese term for such a particularistic tie is *guanxi*.[3] The notion of "having a *guanxi*" expresses the fact that two individuals are engaged in social exchange with each other (Jacobs 1982). The building of *guanxi* always entails the recognition of a hierarchical relationship, either in the very subtle sense of "older and younger brother" or the person "seeking" the *guanxi* relation and the person "granting" the *guanxi* relation. Following the principles of Confucius, *guanxi* arises from the obligation of subordinates to fulfill obligations to those of supposedly greater power and influence (Yang 1957; King 1994; Kipnis 1997).

To understand social and cultural change in China, we need to investigate the current practices and beliefs regarding particularistic relationships (Yan 1992; Yang 1994; Bian 1997; Wank 2002). For our specific interest in the adoption of new conflict resolution strategies among rural Chinese citizens, the study of their social relationships needs to include an assessment of their ability to reach people outside their primary groups of local kin group members. Social relationships to people in political and economic positions at the county or provincial level might serve as a social resource that in turn influences the diversity of the local social networks (Van der Gaag and Snijders 2005). In other words, the classic approach to the analysis of personal networks with the help of name generators (McCallister and Fischer 1983) should be extended to include the collection of data using Lin's (2001) position generator to understand social mobility. The people who can be reached by knowing somebody who knows someone in a particular position, that is, the equivalent of a guanxi, provide a person with influence and the means to obtain their goals. These kinds of connections might also widen rural people's horizons and expose them

---

[2] The social philosophy of relationships is founded on the Confucian principles of *lun*, which means "differentiated order," and *li*, the "rules of proper conduct." The concept of lun stresses differentiation between people, specifically fathers and sons, husbands and wives, seniors and juniors, superiors and subordinates, and so forth (King 1994). It is a system of complimentary social roles with distinct status differences.

[3] An etymological analysis of the Chinese term reveals that the word consists of the meaning for "gate, passage through a gate" and "thread."

to a different set of values. Knowing the range of people a person has access to through the resources of his or her network ties informs us about their potential willingness to choose newly established methods of conflict resolution.

Legal Background: Different Forms of Conflict Resolution Available in Rural China

In rural China disputes have traditionally been resolved through mediation by a third party rather than adjudication, as is common in most western legal systems. According to Chinese legal tradition, law was related to criminal law and mainly associated with the concept of punishment (Wang 2000; Gallagher 2006; Michelson 2007). Civil rights, supervision of government, or ideas of justice were not considered to be an extension of the law. Even though the Chinese government has made the rule of law and adjudication at court available to all citizens as part of its economic reforms program, it also made the recommendation that both informal and formal mediation at the village level and formal mediation at court at the county level should be exhausted before resorting to adjudication (Tanner 1999; Potter 2001). Dispute resolution by mediation is oriented fundamentally on the principles of reciprocity with the goal to reestablish harmony and peace in the social order (Zhao 2003). Any mediation at the village level is both the product of social relationships and the instrument that manages these relationships.

Informal mediation refers to the personal selection of a family member, friend, or neighbor by one or both disputing parties to serve as a moderator. Formal mediation takes place when two people in disagreement have reached no resolution with the help of a trusted individual and turn to the official village mediator installed by the village-level committee of the Communist Party. Procedures and outcomes are then documented. If no agreement can be reached, the official mediator recommends taking the dispute to the local court at the township level. If mediation at the local court fails to come to a resolution, the disputants may take the case and present it to a judge at the county level court, who then carries out adjudication. It follows that taking a dispute to court is only the last step in a series of reconciliation efforts in which mediation continues to play a prominent role.

Typical incidents that upset the balance in relationships between family members, neighbors, fellow villagers, or business partners include disagreements about family division after a son's marriage, distribution of inheritance, the repayment of borrowed money, or land use rights such as the inattention to borders between land plots for planting or housing construction, and the compensation for land that has been rented from a fellow villager and converted to industrial use.

Ethnographic Background: The Case of Li Village

Geographically, Li village is located within the administrative boundaries of a township in Zhao County, part of Shijiazhuang prefecture in the northern Chinese province Hebei.[4] The distance from the center of the city of Shijiazhuang is approximately 120 kilometers. The village has about 4,830 inhabitants living in 900 separate households and is widely known for its pear production. Pear production was started in the seventeenth century and brought the village a modest level of wealth that was sustained during the era of collectivization between the early 1950s and late 1970s (Zhao 2003). After decollectivization in 1983 farmers converted all agricultural space to pear cultivation.

In addition, many farmers started sideline businesses. Among the farmers interviewed for this research, only 21 percent of all households were not involved in any sideline activity. The majority of households had some stakeholder interest or ownership in a freezer facility. Others engage in long-distance trade of pears, organizing the transportation of fruits and their direct marketing in cities throughout mainland China. Additional sideline businesses in the service sector include ownership of convenience stores or market stands, repair services, and restaurants. Several households own or are co-owners of factories that produce goods needed for pear production and distribution, such as paper mills, paper carton factories, fruit net factories, and soft drink factories. Finally, a few households have members who work in these factories as wage labors or earn a salary by teaching in the local school or working on construction sites.

Administratively, Li village is presently treated as a single entity that together with other neighboring villages belongs to a nearby township which in turn is part of a county and its administrative services. During collectivization the village used to be organized into eight separate production teams. At that time the village itself constituted a brigade that belonged to a commune (Guldin 2001). The latter was equivalent to the present-day township. Although the village is now considered a single administrative unit, the division into eight production teams continues to be recognized by villagers. For example, informants specified the addresses of friends and family members as located in a particular production unit rather than a particular alley or street. In addition, due to

---

[4] Li village is a pseudonym. Our collaborator, Dr. Zhao Xudong, gave the village this label when he wrote about the insights from his dissertation fieldwork, and we have continued the practice (Zhao 2003).

the relatively consistent outcome of the pear harvest each year, which ensures high economic stability, the village has a considerably high rate of village endogamy. Two-thirds of all women between the ages of 25 and 40 have remained in the village after marriage rather than marrying into a neighboring village community. Out-migration has been rather low. However, this is gradually changing due to the increasing rate of young villagers who obtain a higher education and seek jobs in the county seat, provincial capital, or other cities throughout China.

A Fully Integrated Mixed Methods Research Design to Understand Adaptation to New Legal Procedures in Rural China

The goal of this research was to investigate the direction and magnitude of interdependence between actual social structures, beliefs about the role of social structures, and perceptions about legal processes and establish what explains the likelihood of taking a dispute to a judge at court in rural China. We describe our approach based on Teddlie and Tashakkori's (2006) typology of mixed methods research designs as featured in the introduction of this volume. Hollstein (this volume) delineates four design stages: the conceptualizing stage, the methodological experiential stage, the analytical experiential stage, and the inferential stage. Our research design involved an integration of quantitative and qualitative approaches at all four stages, in respect to research questions, data collection methods, data analysis methods, and interpretation of the findings.

Conceptualizing Stage

The objective to understand the interrelatedness of social structure and social cognition for the case of adaptations to new legal procedures in rural China is essentially based on the integration of two research concepts. Similarly, we developed the guiding question, What explains the likelihood of taking a case to court?, after the exploration of a combination of qualitatively and quantitatively oriented questions. The qualitative question, "Who is taking a dispute to the court at the county level?", informed the quantitative question, "How many villagers are taking a case to court?" This led to the qualitative question, "Why is a villager taking a case to court instead of local village mediation?", which triggered the quantitative questions, "What structural position in the village network facilitates taking a case to court?" and "What wealth level is facilitating taking a case to court?" Yet we also realized that we needed to add further qualitative questions, namely, "What do villagers perceive to be a fair procedure at court that makes it preferable to local mediation?" and "What do rural Chinese citizens perceive to be the best preparation, including economic and social characteristics, to win a case at court?"

It follows that we had to design data collection methods and analysis techniques capable of finding insights toward all of these questions. From the beginning we planned to collect data on several areas of information: on the structure of informants' social relationships at both the personal level and the whole village network level; on the preferences of informants for conflict resolution strategies; on their beliefs regarding the fairness and justice of the newly established rule of law at regional courts; on the perceived role of social relationships, *guanxi*, in dispute resolutions; and on the actual role of social relationships in influencing informants' preferences and beliefs regarding legal processes in China. We conceptualized that we needed several phases of data collection, each followed by data analysis that informed the design of the next data collection instrument. An exploratory phase of data collection and analysis should be followed by an explanatory phase testing the distribution and reliability of findings (Johnson 1998).

However, we did not decide on the design of all data collection instruments, sampling strategies, and sample sizes at the start of our inquiries in 2004. We anticipated two to three seasons of fieldwork and agreed to ground our data collection efforts in the ethnographic tradition of participant observation. We also wanted to start our first season of data collection with the establishment of a baseline of the social world of rural villagers, collecting extensive network data, similar to the idea of establishing a census at the beginning of a village study. The combined analysis of participant observation data and network data from a representative sample of villagers in the first year of data collection made it clear that we should indeed include data on social cognition. At that point we conceptualized another two seasons of data collection and analysis, designing and integrating qualitative and quantitative methods to deepen our understanding of adaptations to new legal procedures in rural China. The first-year analysis results also assisted our efforts to solicit outside funding from the U.S. National Science Foundation.

Experiential Stage: Methodological and Analytical Tools

Since the data collection and data analysis periods of our research design were intertwined during each season in the field, we are unable to uncouple the methodological and analytical experiential stages from each other. Following Teddlie and Tashakkori's (2006) suggestion, we present the two phases folded into one section. As cultural anthropologists we conduct both data collection and data analysis firmly embedded in the framework of participant observation (Schensul et al. 1999; Johnson and Weller 2002; Bernard 2006). Participant observation constitutes the core of ethnographic fieldwork with the goal of finding explanations of human behavior from a holistic research perspective (Agar 1980). It represents an overall strategy for collecting data rather than a single method and requires the researcher to engage in a mixture of data collection and data analysis throughout his or her period of co-habitation with members of the culture they study. This was also the case during our research on adaptations to new legal procedures in rural China. During each data collection season the lead author, who is fluent in standard Chinese language, lived with local villagers and participated in informal discussions and village activities.

Within the framework of participating in the cultural practices of a different culture and observing daily activities, conversations, and interactions, the ethnographer engages in systematic data collection (Bernard 2006). Data collection is systematic in the sense that throughout the time period spent with members of another culture, ideally a whole calendar year, the researcher repeats her or his own activities, observes similar activities among different people, and asks similar questions from a range of more or less representative informants. In addition to a range of observations at different locations and different time points that call for the meticulous recording of field notes, anthropologists distinguish between four basic types of interview strategies: informal, unstructured, semi-structured, and structured (Bernard 2006). They differ in the level of comparability of the information they obtain from individual informants. Informal interviews resemble chats with a range of either conveniently recruited or purposefully approached informants. Unstructured interviews are devoted to a specific topic and allow informants to present as much of their insights as they are willing to reveal. Semi-structured interviews are carefully prepared lists of questions that stimulate each informant in a comparable way. Structured interviews, often called surveys or questionnaires, produce the highest level of comparable data across informants. They consist primarily of closed questions that allow informants to answer with yes or no or pick their answer from a range of prepared choices. In addition, anthropologists use a range of elicitation techniques to increase the reliability of recall among informants they interview with either unstructured or semi-structured interviews using props to jog the informant's memories or present them with completion tasks, and so on (de Munck and Soto 1998; Johnson and Weller 2002).

Table 7.1 depicts a list of all data collection instruments and sampling strategies ordered by data collection instrument, year of conduct, sampling strategy, number of observations or informants, type of data

Table 7.1. *The five data collection instruments and their methods of analysis*

Data collection instruments	Year	Sampling strategy	Number of observations	Type of data	Level of data comparability	Method of data analysis
Participant observation of local meetings and discussions	1 2 3	Convenience Sample	42 64 55	• Qualitative	Low	• Qualitative: Text analysis of field notes • Quantification of reoccurring themes in field notes
Informal interviews about disputes with community leaders and mediators	1 2	Convenience Sample	30 20	• Qualitative	Low	• Qualitative: Text analysis of field notes • Quantification of reoccurring themes
Semi-structured interviews on social networks and economic activities	1	Snowball sample based on random walks	183	• Qualitative • Quantitative	Medium to high	• Quantitative: Statistical analysis of network data • Quantification of observations and reoccurring text to compute wealth indicator • Qualitative: Text analysis of responses • Qualitative: Visualization of network structures
Unstructured interviews on perceptions of fairness in conflict resolutions	2	Purposive Sample	46	• Qualitative	Low	• Quantitative: Statistical analysis of responses • Quantitative: Statistical analysis of demographic information • Quantification of reoccurring themes in the interview transcript • Qualitative compilation of suitable sentence for consensus analysis
Interviews with a structured and a semi-structured part on cultural consensus of perceptions, preferences for conflict resolutions, and network resources	3	Stratified Random Sample	158	• Qualitative • Quantitative	High	• Qualitative: Consensus analysis • Qualitative analysis: Identifying related themes in the text • Quantitative analysis of position generator data in networks measuring numbers of lawyers and judges known in a network • Quantitative: Logistic regressions of correlations between attitudes and the access to certain network positions

produced with the instrument, level of comparability of data, and the method of data analysis. For the categories that depict the type of data and the method of data analysis we clearly specify its qualitative or quantitative nature.

This overview also reflects the fact that observations and informal interviews occurred during all three sessions of data collection and informed the design of the unstructured, semi-structured, and structured interview instruments that collected systematic data in years 1, 2, and 3. With the exception of the interview instrument for the final and third season of data collection, all data collection instruments were designed while in the field based on data analysis of field note texts, a common practice among ethnographers (Emerson et al. 1995). This approach to data collection and analysis increases the validity and reliability of data (Bernard 2006).

Year 1

Informed by both qualitative and quantitative analyses of the field notes from observations and informal interviews with villagers in general, village leaders, administrators, and lawyers in the township and at the county level, we developed an instrument for semi-structured interviews eliciting social network data and observations of visible wealth. We then assembled a team of six student researchers from the Sociology Department at China Agricultural University (CAU) that we trained for two weeks in data collection techniques and interview practices (Johnson and Weller 2002; Bernard 2006). Our sampling strategy called for two types of informants: a larger group of randomly selected villagers and a smaller group of purposively selected villagers as a control group. The second group consisted of 30 informants, who were selected because they all had been involved in a dispute in the last five years as identified by Zhao (2003) in his original fieldwork on conflict resolutions in Li village. For the first group, expected to capture a representative cross section of villagers, we used a snowball sampling strategy based on random seeds (Klovdahl 1989). The rationale for this approach was to acquire information about the properties of the whole village network without interviewing all households in the village (Klovdahl 1989).

This sampling strategy benefitted from the fact that Li village still recognizes the administrative division of eight production teams created during the era of collectivization between 1950 and 1983. Each household is registered in the household registration book by the number of its respective production team. We randomly selected five households in each production team as seeds for the interviews on network data, which amounted to a total of 40 informants in 8 teams serving as seeds. From the network contacts that each head of household mentioned we randomly selected the next informant. For each seed we completed a three-step four-node random walk, meaning each seed introduced us to three additional informants in the chain (Klovdahl 1989). Hence, the plan was to collect a total of 160 interviews from random walks and 30 purposively selected informants from the second groups. However, due to data collection errors and unfinished interviews we have only 183 completed interviews instead of 190.

In terms of interview content, we made a special effort to interview heads of households since network questions were designed to elicit data on a range of social and material resources obtained through the combined ties of all household members. These heads of households were asked about their social relationships with relatives; non-kin group members including neighbors, friends and fictive kin, and partners in business activities; and anyone else they are likely to talk to about important matters. In reference to Lin's (2001) position generator approach we then elicited information about the villagers' ability to reach people in certain positions such as government officials (i.e., cadres) outside the village, judges, lawyers, and so on. The informants were also interviewed about occurrences of past or ongoing disputes over land use or borrowed money. In addition, we recorded information about the size and age of their house, including the number of stories and the presence or absence of beds in the main living room,[5] and ownership of utility and consumer goods, including the size of TV sets, motor bikes, cars, refrigerators, and so on. This allowed us to compute an indicator of visible wealth.[6]

Using the software programs SPSS and UCInet (Borgatti et al. 1999) the analysis of this comparatively large data set provided us with quantitative information about the characteristics of social relationships in rural China. SPSS processed the number of ties in each of the 183 personal networks, the number of ties that reached outside the production team an informant belonged to, and the number of ties to alters outside the village, for example, individuals living in the county seat or provincial capital. In addition, we used SPSS to compute the wealth indicator for each informant as a rank in reference to the total number of 183. The software program UCInet aided the processing of quantitative data that provided information on the level of density of each personal network as evident from several network indicators calculated in reference to the

---

[5] Traditionally, the main room of any rural Chinese house prominently featured a large heated bed (*kang*) that served all household members (Yan 2003). The absence of a bed in the main room of the house indicates modernization efforts.

[6] This method is admittedly coarse and flawed. We have since engaged in an additional research project that investigated emic evaluations of affluence (Liu and Avenarius 2008, unpublished manuscript). Analysis of these data is ongoing and has not been incorporated into the present chapter.

whole village network, namely, the informants' ranks of degree centrality, closeness centrality, betweenness centrality, and eigenvector centrality (Freeman 1978; Wasserman and Faust 1994).

A qualitative display of the quantitative data computed by UCInet was produced with the software program Pajek (Batagelj and Mrvar 2002). The network visualizations of both the whole village network and the embedded structures of personal networks emphasized qualitatively what the numeric parameters had revealed already. The picture of the whole village network showed that the community was densely connected, particularly within small geographic regions of the village, the former administrative unit of production teams. Network images of personal networks exemplified the limited geographic range of ties further once we color coded nodes based on the location of settlement that corresponded with each node. In addition, we analyzed the interview texts qualitatively, looking for co-occurring themes in stories about business developments and disagreements with others over money lending and borrowing. We recorded the topics and compared them to content that was mentioned in the same interview, looking for patterns across informants. This allowed us to develop hypotheses about preferences and beliefs regarding different conflict resolution strategies.

When the analysis of network properties including centrality scores in reference to the whole village network was completed, we compared these data to the informants' scores of visible wealth and the presence or absence of disputes they had taken to court. We realized that informants with either high or low ranks of either degree centrality, betweenness centrality, or closeness centrality scores within the village network had not reported any incident of taking a case to court.

Year 2

As anticipated, the data analysis of the first season of data collection efforts produced as many questions as insights. Hence, we designed a two-part strategy that would add information on the other much needed dimension of our project: the social cognition of villagers about the function of social relationships and the fairness of the different conflict resolution strategies. This concept included a first phase of collecting qualitative data in year 2 and a second phase of testing the distribution of the findings during a third season of data collection activities. This plan called for the accumulation of data that would allow a cultural consensus analysis as the conclusion to all three research seasons in the field (Weller 2007:339). As in the previous fieldwork periods, we continued to conduct participant observation in addition to informal interviews with community leaders, mediators, and lawyers and elicited data on personal network activities.

We initiated data collection in year 2 by conducting unstructured interviews with a purposive sample of informants in Li village.[7] The decision for unstructured instead of semi-structured interview instruments was based on the need to collect a wide range of opinions and stories about fairness and justice and the role of relationships rather than responses to specific trigger questions. While each interview started with the same general question, respondents could take their answer in different directions in terms of content and length of elaboration (Spradley 1979; Agar 1980). These interviews covered a range of topics from the fairness of the education system to disputes that had occurred within people's circles of family and friends to evaluations of the dispute solution process and the current state of the legal system. Each unstructured interview lasted an average length of 90 minutes. All interviews were taped, transcribed, and translated.[8]

The sampling design for the unstructured interviews called for a six-cell purposive sampling strategy in an age-by-gender format based on three different age groups among both male and female informants, with approximately six informants per cell being interviewed. Our aim was to interview at least 36 informants. The three age groups were created in response to political events since the establishment of the People's Republic of China in 1949 that have shaped the life experiences of informants. Our assumption was that older informants who came of age before the Chinese Cultural Revolution, which took place between 1966 and 1976, would display different opinions than informants who grew up during the Cultural Revolution and younger informants who experienced decollectivization during their school years. The sample was further controlled for dispute experience, including at least one or two people with disputes in each sampling cell. Experience with disputes was determined on the basis of a snowball sampling technique in which informants were asked to help identify individuals who had been through one or more disputes (Johnson 1990). After five months of fieldwork we had collected complete sets of interviews with 46 rural informants that fulfilled the requirements of our purposive sampling strategy.

---

[7] This NSF-funded portion of the project (over the course of two years) also had an urban component. Both the exploratory and explanatory phases of this project included a roughly equal number of informants in the provincial capital of Shijiazhuang, which accounts for the length of time spent in China by the lead author.

[8] In 2006, Christine Avenarius conducted the unstructured interviews in the urban areas alone and in the rural areas with an assistant (He Lili), who helped out with the local dialect, the *fangyan*, that occasionally caused difficulties in mutual understanding. The tapes were transcribed by research assistants He Lili, Tian Fei, He Congzhi, and Han Fei at China Agricultural University and translated by Liu Lu and Yang Sijia, graduate students at East Carolina University.

The transcribed and translated narratives of these interviews constitute a rich body of data that we analyzed both qualitatively and quantitatively. The qualitative analysis included the search for themes in the text and linguistic overlaps to related themes. The quantitative analysis produced a list of word frequencies and a quantification of reoccurring themes both within the text of a single interview transcript and across all interview transcripts. To this day, we continue to use the text material for new queries, for example, about attitudes regarding the fairness of the education system to allow advancement of rural people in Chinese society. However, in late 2006, our explicit goal for the analysis of these narrative texts was the preparation of an interview instrument to be administered in the summer of 2007 that produced data that both showed the distribution of attitudes and perceptions among Chinese people and tested a set of explanations emerging from the exploratory data. Specifically, the third-year interview instruments should serve to produce a cultural consensus model among rural Chinese citizens (Weller 2007; Romney et al. 1979, 1986).

To accomplish this, we analyzed the content of the interview narratives for common statements and created collections of quotations that were meaningful for the understanding of Chinese people's views of dispute solution processes and legal procedures and the role of social relationships (LeCompte and Schensul 1999:187). A team of four researchers, the two authors and two graduate students, independently reviewed the transcribed interviews and identified sentences that dealt with ideas about the Chinese justice system, the role of gift giving, corruption, the role of social relationships in conflict resolution procedures, and the perceived morality of these actions. We ranked statements by frequency and importance of content (Johnson and Weller 2002). Finally, we chose 64 statements to be featured in the data collection instrument of the second project phase, constituting the core of the data instrument for year 3. After editing some of the statements for clarity we worded half of the statements positive, for example, "The Chinese legal system is complete and mature," and half of them negative, for example, "China is not yet ruled by law since the legal system is incomplete." This was meant to balance the statements to avoid possible response set bias patterns in the following data collection period.

In addition, we checked the translated interview transcripts for reoccurring stories of disputes that had been experienced by either an informant him- or herself, or a relative, neighbor, or friend. A selection of five cases served as a tool for the elicitation of preferred conflict resolution on the interview instrument designed for the third year of data collection. Each case was presented with a choice of four different conflict resolution strategies, ranging from "neglecting the matter," to "local mediation," to "taking a case to court" and a combined strategy of mediation followed by a court attendance. A good example of the systematic understanding of preferences by asking informants to link contexts with their preferred strategy can be found in Romney et al. (1979) in their study of concepts of success and failure and Weller et al. (1987) in their study of beliefs about corporal punishment.

Year 3

The final data collection instrument for year 3 included a large section with structured interview questions as described earlier and a smaller section with semi-structured questions.[9] The latter part elicited information on relationships that could serve an informant with social, economic, and political resources, for example, links to people who held positions of army members, political leaders at various administrative levels, physicians, bank managers, lawyers, and judges. The semi-structured part also asked to list characteristics of a moral person, evaluations of the moral climate in present-day China, and the esteemed monetary level of morally acceptable bribes.

This interview instrument with multiple parts was administered to a stratified random sample of informants over the course of one month. We used the village map that displayed all households as our sampling frame from which we randomly selected 120 household locations, equally distributed over the eight production teams. From this list of households we then purposively selected individuals in each household that fit the age by gender distribution established in the previous year. We had trained a new group of six sociology students from CAU to conduct the interviews under the supervision of the lead author. Every morning during data collection we assigned each student an informant profile for the day, for example, "Find a young woman (born after 1972)" in the assigned household or "Find a man born before 1953" in another assigned household. The total number of completed structured interviews was 158 rural residents. The additional interviews were necessary to establish an equal distribution of interviews by age and gender that had not been accomplished after the initial 120 household were interviewed.

We analyzed the quantitative data produced by the structured part of the interviews with statistical tests available in SPSS and used Anthropac software to compute the cultural consensus model devised by Romney et al. (1986) to establish the level of agreement within the sample population.[10] The qualitative data of the semi-structured

---

[9] At the core of each structured interview was the elicitation of agreement or disagreement regarding the above-mentioned 64 statements. Informants were asked to state if they thought a sentence read to them was true or false, and to take a guess if they were uncertain about an item (Johnson and Weller 2002).

[10] The interpretation of data analysis results also benefitted a comparison of this rural consensus model with the consensus model derived from those in the urban sample who had been presented with the exact same interview instrument.

sections of the interview instrument were treated to a comparison of themes. The free listed items regarding moral characteristics, however, were quantified using Anthropac software (Borgatti 1996). We also calculated their salience scores, capturing the order in which descriptors were mentioned. This set of interviews yielded a few important findings. While we can conclude that a coherent cultural model exists for the rural sample regarding their interpretation of the fairness of the current legal system, we also detected a few noteworthy outliers. We found a correlation between the number of social and economic resources in the informants' network and their preferred conflict resolution strategy.[11]

Summary of Experiential Phase

The detailed description of our multi-step and multi-stage research design has two noteworthy aspects: It evolved over time, and it integrated qualitative and quantitative methods of data collection and analysis for all five data-collection instruments. As Table 7.1 has shown, we used five different instruments to collect data ranging from participant observation to structured interviews. Each step of data collection produced a range of data, some only qualitative, some both qualitative and quantitative. The level of comparability of data obtained from one informant to the other differed, as did the range of information obtained. The more structured a data collection instrument, the more comparable the information from one informant to the other, but with less range of new information. The data from each data collection effort were analyzed both qualitatively and quantitatively. The findings from each methodological procedure informed the design of the next data collection instrument. It follows that the combination of a variety of data collection instruments and data analysis methods is what allows us to make comprehensive inferences.

Inferential Stage

Full integration of qualitative and quantitative data collection and data analysis methods resulted in crossover analysis in which the interpretation of results for each data set informed the design of the next data collection instrument. The combination of all inferences, an integration of findings, then allowed us to understand the context of an individual's decision to take a dispute to court.[12] We have been able to draw

---

[11] It is important to keep in mind that preferred conflict resolution strategy is not necessarily linked to any experiences with disputes that were settled in public.
[12] According to our data, only 10% of all known dispute cases in the village were brought to adjudication at court.

several major conclusions. In this section we reflect on a few incidents that exemplify how the combination of different types of data leads to a more comprehensive understanding than the analysis of a single type of data.

From the participant observation of informal village meetings and discussions we learned how ideas about new legal procedures are formed and what degree of openness villagers reach in their thought exchanges, and we were able to identify the range of opinions about the usefulness of taking a dispute to court. Informal interviews with village leaders, mediators, and lawyers provided us with background information about the script of specific dispute occurrences. By the end of the first year of the project the analysis of the semi-structured interviews on social relationships had revealed that a surprising large number of ties elicited from informants linked to villagers of Li village (an average of 78 percent) and more than half of the number of ties were located within the same production team. Among informants who had one or two ties to non-relatives outside the village, we found a range of social, political, and economic resource positions, including lawyers, county-level party secretaries, and province-level government officials. We also had computed centrality measures and wealth indicators. However, neither network composition, network position, nor wealth indicators correlated with taking a case to court. For example, informants with high betweenness centrality scores did not express any interest in taking a case to court or support other people's decision of taking a case to court.

However, data from the first and second years of interviews on ideas about justice and fairness also introduced us to villagers who had taken a dispute to court or were willing to embark on such an endeavor. Although this group of people was a minority among villagers, we were interested to learn if they had anything in common that explained their propensity to take a case to court. The network analysis had identified them as being neither in very prominent network positions nor having extreme levels of poverty or affluence. Their networks did not feature a lack of ties or an abundance of ties. However, the qualitative analysis of opinions from interviews conducted in year 2 showed us that their opinions and ideas set them slightly apart from the majority of villagers. When comparing the statements from year 2 with statements incorporated into the consensus model data of year 3 we were able to confirm the divergence. This was further corroborated when we specifically reviewed data for the 20 informants who were part of all three data sets with larger amounts of comparable data (in years 1, 2, and 3).

To illustrate this approach, here is a quote by an informant from the unstructured interviews of year 2, about the nature and fairness of the current Chinese legal system. The quote is representative of statements shared by the majority of informants who believe that social relationships and the presentation of gifts to establish or emphasize the request to consider the influence of social relationships are more important than evidence to get a successful outcome at court. Rural residents continue to trust that relationships are the best tools to navigate the new legal system: "If you are just a common person who has no relationship, the judges at court will take more money from you, because common people have no relationships, no (in) doors and no (in) roads. Even if you take somebody in court, it's not easy. Such kind of common people like us have no chance in court but to be bullied."

None of the small number of informants who either had taken a case to court or were considering taking a case to court made statements with related content. This sentiment was incorporated in the data collection instrument of the third year as one of the 64 statements that informants were asked to agree or disagree about. "If both sides give presents to the judge, whoever gives the most will win the law suit." The majority of rural informants agreed and affirmed the power of money in the case of conflict resolution at court. When we revisited the data and compared answers for the small minority of people who felt positive about taking a case to court, we noticed that most of them had rejected that statement. Learning about these different viewpoints regarding the impact of social relationships initiated another second look, this time at the data on social resources. We reviewed the data on knowing people outside the village, reaching a government official, lawyer, judge or high-level army member which we had collected in year 1 and year 3. Independent of taking a case to court or not, we found a correlation between informants who had rejected the saliency of social relationships, or *guanxi*, as the only operating mechanism at court and informants who listed a lawyer as a member of their social network. Many of these lawyers were former classmates or members of the extended family who live outside the village. Their presence in villagers' personal networks represents access to information, but not necessarily the occurrence of a law suit in that household (Avenarius 2009).

After integrating our findings we have come to the following meta-inferences regarding the interrelatedness of social structure and cognition (Teddlie and Tashakkori 2006:24). Taking a dispute to court is not dependent on the availability of money to bribe officials or the most central influential position in a network. Rather, the few ties that villagers maintain to outsiders fulfill important functions. It is not the size of networks that matters but the content, the reach of particular ties to specific gatekeepers of information. In addition, within the village certain structural positions alleviate individuals of their obligation to settle their disputes exclusively within the framework of mediation. In this respect, the significance of the betweenness centrality score in explaining the likelihood of dispute occurrences provides insights into specific Chinese cultural practices. The effect of betweenness centrality in reference to dispute occurrences is negative, informing us that people with bridge positions in the village network are highly unlikely to get involved in publicly known disputes. Only the less connected and less influential rural residents will dare to start the process of mediation that might or might not lead to more formal mediation and eventually adjudication. In contrast, the most affluent villagers said they would refrain from going to court since they have other means to settle a dispute, such as influencing other people through intermediaries within their social network or paying large sums of money to appease others. Informants with the highest ranks of centrality scores expressed the opinions that their web of relationships is the best remedy for any problem or conflict in life.

While rural residents certainly benefit from what Granovetter (1973) called the "strength of weak ties" in the sense that those with outside ties are more knowledgeable about the legal system which eventually compels some of them to try different types of conflict resolutions at the expense of established relationships, a majority of villagers are not ready to forgo their beliefs in the power of relationships. Many informants suggested using money to compensate for their lack of access to "resource-generating" relationships, despite moral condemnation of gift giving and bribery. They see opportunities to achieve personal goals or change the economic situation of their household based on the cultural assumption that relationship building is the key to personal advancement. The persistence of beliefs about the usefulness of particularistic ties, *guanxi*, also shows that to date the rule of law has neither been fully practiced nor been fully accepted and understood in rural China. The rule of relationships continues to serve as an important mechanism of social control.

Discussion: Benefits and Challenges of Our Fully Integrated Mixed Method Research Design

The fully integrated mixed methods research design allowed us to understand both the potential and the limitations of network positions in rural China and provided us with inferences about the agency of individuals in the process of responding to cultural change (Emirbayer and Goodwin 1994). The research design evolved over the course of three years of data collection and analysis. Each step of adjustment in the data collection instrument created a deeper understanding of the interrelatedness between social structure and cognition. In particular, the fully integrated design enabled us to evaluate both the quantitative and qualitative properties of rural Chinese social networks, including the viewpoints of rural citizens themselves. The resulting findings describe what specific social structures mean to the people who create and maintain them.

However, the evolving nature of our research design, while beneficial to capture the interrelatedness of structure and perception, also posed its own challenges. Our interest in collecting a diverse range of information, including relationships, opinions, and perceptions, made us treat each data collection instrument as its own knowledge generating entity. We designed sampling strategies that corresponded with the needs of a specific instrument and brought us in contact with a maximum range of different informants. However, in hindsight it would have also been advantageous to have the same information for the same set of households, using the same sample of informants for all data collection instruments. While we had purposively built some overlap into the samples from years 1, 2, and 3 due to our interest in disputes, the total number of intersecting informants for all three years was merely 20 heads of households.

Nevertheless, in all five data collection phases we obtained data on social relationship structures and ideas about social relationships and the legal system. The resulting knowledge of what exactly rural residents believe and assume has assisted our interpretation of the structural differences in a meaningful way. We were able to identify that rural residents continue to be firmly bound in their social circles of family members and relatives. The limited range of network diversity influences the likelihood of rural people's access to information about economic opportunities and legal procedures.

Combining the analysis of social structures with the analysis of social cognition enabled us to understand the meaning of social relationships in the context of rural Chinese culture. Variations in perceptions about the rule of law and the mechanism of adjudication are driven by structural differences. Beliefs regarding the opportunities and limitations of the new legal systems are influenced by "who you know" or the presence of ties to village outsiders (i.e., knowing a lawyer). The execution of such beliefs further depends on a specific level of connectivity within the whole village network. A social actor who actually takes a case to court is neither isolated nor in a position of high centrality between fellow villagers. We would not have been able to pinpoint these interrelations without the combination of analyzing both structure and cognition and without the use of both qualitative and quantitative approaches of data collection and analysis.

References

Agar, Michael H. 1980. *The Professional Stranger. An Informal Introduction to Ethnography.* New York: Academic Press.

Avenarius, Christine B. 2009. "Social networks, wealth accumulation, and dispute resolution in rural China." Pp. 17–35 in *Networks, Resources and*

Economic Action, edited by C. Greiner and K. Waltraud. Berlin: Dietrich Reimer Verlag.

Avenarius, Christine B., Duran Bell, Zhao Xudong, and Liang Yongjia. 2005. "Social networks, wealth accumulation, and dispute resolution in rural China." Paper presented at the 25th International Sunbelt Social Network Conference, Redondo Beach, CA.

Barr, Abigail, Jean Ensminger, and Jeffrey C. Johnson. 2009. "Social networks and trust in cross-cultural economic experiments." Pp. 65–90 in *Whom Can We Trust? How Groups, Networks, and Institutions Make Trust Possible*, edited by K. Cook, R. Hardin, and M. Levi. New York: Russell Sage Foundation.

Batagelj, Vladimir and Andrej Mrvar. 2002. *Pajek* (Version 0.82). Ljubljana: University of Ljubljana.

Bernard, H. Russell. 2006. *Research Methods in Anthropology: Qualitative and Quantitative Approaches*. 4th ed. Walnut Creek, CA: Altamira Press.

Bian, Yanjie. 1997. "Bringing strong ties back in: Indirect connection, bridges, and job search in China." *American Sociological Review* 62(3):355–85.

Borgatti, Stephen P. 1996. *ANTHROPAC 4.96*. Natick, MA: Analytic Technologies.

Borgatti, Stephen P., Martin G. Everett, and Linton C. Freeman. 1999. *UCINET* (Version V). Columbia, SC: Analytic Technologies.

Brinton, Mary C. and Victor Nee, eds. 1998. *The New Institutionalism in Sociology*. New York: Russell Sage Foundation.

Burt, Ronald S. 1992. *Structural Holes: The Social Structure of Competition*. Cambridge, MA: Harvard University Press.

Chan, Anita, Richard Madsen, and Jonathan Unger. 1984. *Chen Village under Mao and Deng*. Berkeley: University of California Press.

Emerson, Robert M., Rachel I. Fretz, and Linda L. Shaw. 1995. *Writing Ethnographic Fieldnotes*. Chicago: University of Chicago Press.

Emirbayer, Mustafa and Jeff Goodwin. 1994. "Network analysis, culture and the problem of agency." *American Journal of Sociology* 99(6):1411–54.

Ensminger, Jean. 1992. *Making a Market: The Institutional Transformation of an African Society*. New York: Cambridge University Press.

Espinoza, Vincente. 1999. "Social networks among the urban poor: Inequality and integration in a Latin American city." Pp. 147–84 in *Networks in the Global Village. Life in Contemporary Communities*, edited by B. Wellman. Boulder, CO: Westview Press.

Fei, Xiaotong. [1939] 1992. *From the Soil, the Foundations of Chinese Society: A Translation of Fei Xiaotong's Xiangtu Zhongguo, with an Introduction and Epilogue by Gary G. Hamilton and Wang Zheng*. Berkeley: University of California Press.

Freeman, Linton C. 1978. "Centrality in social networks. Conceptual clarification." *Social Networks* 1:215–39.

Gallagher, Mary E. 2006. "Mobilizing the law in China: 'Informed disenchantment' and the development of legal consciousness." *Law and Society Review* 40 (4):783–816.

Gargiulo, Martin and Mario Benassi. 1999. "The dark side of social capital." Pp. 298–322 in *Social Capital and Liability*, edited by S. Gabbay and R. Leenders. Norwell, MA: Kluwer.

Gold, Thomas, Doug Guthrie, and David Wank. 2002. "Introduction to the study of Guanxi." Pp. 3–20 in *Social Connections in China: Institutions, Culture, and the Changing Nature of Guanxi*, edited by T. Gold, D. Guthrie, and D. Wank. Cambridge: Cambridge University Press.

Granovetter, Mark S. 1973. "The strength of weak ties." *American Journal of Sociology* 78(6):1360–80.

———. 1985. "Economic action and social structure: The problem of embeddedness." *American Journal of Sociology* 91(3):481–510.

Guldin, Gregory Eliyu. 2001. *What's a Peasant to Do?: Village Becoming Town in Southern China*. Boulder, CO: Westview Press.

Holland, Dorothy and Naomi Quinn. 1987. *Cultural Models in Language and Thought*. Cambridge: Cambridge University Press.

Jacobs, Bruce. 1982. "The concept of guanxi and local politics in a rural Chinese cultural setting." Pp. 209–36 in *Social Interaction in Chinese Society*, edited by S. L. Greenblatt, R. W. Wilson, and A. Auerback Wilson. Westport, CT: Praeger.

Johnson, Jeffrey C. 1990. *Selecting Ethnographic Informants*. Newbury Park, CA: Sage Publishers.

Johnson, Jeffrey C. 1998. "Research design and research strategies." Pp. 131–71 in *Handbook of Methods in Cultural Anthropology*, edited by H. Russell Bernard. Walnut Creek, CA: Altamira Press.

Johnson, Jeffrey C. and Susan C. Weller. 2002. "Elicitation techniques for interviewing." In *Handbook of Interview Research: Context and Method*, edited by J. F. Gubrium and J. A. Holstein. Thousand Oaks, CA: Sage.

King, Ambrose Y. C. 1994. "Kuan-hsi and network building: A sociological interpretation." Pp. 109–26 in *The Living Tree. The Changing Meaning of Being Chinese Today*, edited by W. Tu. Stanford, CA: Stanford University Pres.

Kipnis, Andrew B. 1997. *Producing Guanxi. Sentiment, Self, and Subculture in a North China Village*. Durham, NC: Duke University Press.

Klovdahl, Alden S. 1989. "Urban social networks: Some methodological problems and possibilities." Pp. 176–210 in *The Small World*, edited by Manfred Kochen. Norwood: Ablex.

LeCompte, Margaret D. and Jean J. Schensul. 1999. *Analyzing and Interpreting Ethnographic Data*. Walnut Creek, CA: Altamira Press.

Lin, Nan. 2001. *Social Capital. A Theory of Social Structure and Action*. Cambridge: Cambridge University Press.

March, James G. and Johan P. Olsen. 1984. "The new institutionalism: Organizational factors in political life." *American Political Science Review* 78:734–49.

McCallister, Lynne and Claude S. Fischer. 1983. "A procedure for surveying personal networks." Pp. 75–88 in *Applied Network Analysis. A Methodological Introduction*, edited by R. S. Burt and M. J. Minor. Beverly Hills, CA: Sage.

McKinley, Terry. 1996. *The Distribution of Wealth in Rural China*. Armonk, NY: M. E. Sharpe.

Michelson, Ethan. 2007. "Climbing the dispute pagoda: Grievances and appeals to the official justice system in rural China." *American Sociological Review* 72(2):459–85.

De Munck, Victor C. and Elisa J. Sobo. 1998. *Using Methods in the Field: A Practical Introduction and Casebook*. Walnut Creek, CA: Altamira Press.

North, Douglass C. 1990. *Institutions, Institutional Change, and Economic Performance*. Cambridge: Cambridge University Press.

Oi, Jean C. 1999. *Rural China Takes Off: Institutional Foundations of Economic Reform*. Berkeley: University of California Press.

Oi, Jean C. and Andre G. Walder. 1999. *Property Rights and Economic Reform in China*. Stanford, CA: Stanford University Press.

Passy, Florence and Marco Giugni. 2001. "Social networks and individual perceptions: Explaining differential participation in social movements." *Sociological Forum* 16(1):123–53.

Potter, Pitman B. 2001. *The Chinese Legal System. Globalization and Local Legal Culture*. London and New York: Routledge.

———. 2002. "Guanxi and the PRC legal system: From contradiction to complementarity." Pp. 179–95 in *Social Connections in China: Institutions, Culture, and the Changing Nature of Guanxi*, edited by T. Gold, D. Guthrie, and D. Wank. Cambridge: Cambridge University Press.

Romney, A. Kimball, Tom Smith, Howard E. Freeman, Jerome Kagan, and Robert E. Klein. 1979. "Concepts of success and failure." *Social Science Research* 8:306–26.

Romney, A. Kimball, Susan C. Weller, and William Batchelder. 1986. "Culture as consensus: A theory of cultural and informant accuracy." *American Anthropologist* 88(2):313–38.

Rosenthal, Naomi, Meryl Fingrudt, Michelle Ethier, Roberta Kant, and David McDonald. 1985. "Social movements and network analysis: A case study of nineteenth-century women's reform in New York State." *American Journal of Sociology* 90(5):1022–54.

Ruf, Gregory A. 1998. *Cadres and Kin: Making a Socialist Village in West China, 1921–1991*. Stanford, CA: Stanford University Press.

Schensul, Stephen L., Jean J. Schensul, and Margaret D. LeCompte. 1999. *Essential Ethnographic Methods: Observations, Interviews, and Questionnaires*. Walnut Creek, CA: Altamira Press.

Schweizer, Thomas. 1996. *Muster sozialer Ordnung. Netzwerkanalyse als Fundament der Sozialethnologie*. Berlin: Dietrich Reimer Verlag.

———. 1997. "Embeddedness of ethnographic cases: A social networks perspective." *Current Anthropology* 38(5):739–60.

Schweizer, Thomas and Douglas R. White. 1998. "Revitalizing the study of kinship and exchange with network approaches." Pp. 1–10 in *Kinship, Networks and Exchange*, edited by T. Schweizer and D. R. White. Cambridge: Cambridge University Press.

Scott, Richard W. 2001. *Institutions and Organizations*. 2nd ed. Thousand Oaks, CA: Sage.

Spradley, James P. 1970. *You Owe Yourself a Drunk. An Ethnography of Urban Nomads*. Boston: Little, Brown.

Spradley, James P. 1979. *The Ethnographic Interview*. New York: Holt, Rinehart and Winston.

Tanner, Murray S. 1999. *The Politics of Lawmaking in Post-Mao China. Institutions, Processes and Democratic Prospects*. Oxford: Clarendon Press.

Teddlie, Charles and Abbas Tashakkori. 2006. "A general typology of research designs featuring mixed methods." *Research in the Schools* 13(1):12–28.

Teddlie, Charles and Abbas Tashakkori. 2009. "Integrating qualitative and quantitative approaches to research." Pp. 283–317 in *The Sage Handbook of Applied Research Methods*, edited by L. Bickman and D. J. Rog. Thousand Oaks, CA: Sage.

Van der Gaag, Martin and Tom A. B. Snijders. 2005. "The resource generator: Social capital quantification with concrete items." *Social Networks* 27:1–29.

Vermeer, Eduard B., Frank Pieke, and Woei Lien Chong, eds. 1998. *Cooperative and Collective in China's Rural Development: Between State and Private Interests*. Armonk, NY: M. E.Sharpe.

Wang, Zhenmin. 2000. "The developing rule of law in China." *Harvard Asia Quarterly* 4(4).

Wank, David. 2002. "Business-state clientelism in China." Pp. 97–115 in *Social Connections in China: Institutions, Culture, and the Changing Nature of Guanxi*, edited by Thomas Gold, Doug Guthrie, and David Wank. Cambridge: Cambridge University Press.

Wasserman, Stanley and Katie Faust. 1994. *Social Network Analysis*. New York: Cambridge University Press.

Weller, Susan C. 2007. "Cultural consensus theory: Applications and frequently asked questions." *Field Methods* 19:339–68.

Weller, Susan C., A. Kimball Romney, and Donald P. Orr. 1987. "The myth of a subculture of corporal punishment." *Human Organization* 46:39–47.

Williamson, Oliver E. 1985. *The Economic Institutions of Capitalism*. New York: Free Press.

Yan, Yunxiang. 1992. "The impact of rural reform on economic and social stratification in a Chinese village." *Australian Journal of Chinese Affairs* 27:1–23.

Yan, Yunxiang. 2003. *Private Life under Socialism: Love, Intimacy, and Family Change in a Chinese Village, 1949–1999*. Stanford, CA: Stanford University Press.

Yang, Lien-sheng. 1957. "The concept of 'pao' in Chinese social relations." Pp. 291–309 in *Chinese Thought and Institutions*, edited by John K. Fairbank. Chicago: University of Chicago Press.

Yang, Mayfair Meihui. 1994. *Gifts, Favors and Banquets: The Art of Social Relationships in China*. Ithaca, NY: Cornell University Press.

Zhao, Xudong. 2003. *Power and Justice. Dispute Resolution, Authority and Plurality in Rural China* (in Chinese). Tianjin: Tianjin Ancient Books Publisher (Tianjin Guji Chubanshe).

8

Mixing Ethnography and Information Technology Data Mining to Visualize Innovation Networks in Global Networked Organizations

Julia C. Gluesing, Kenneth R. Riopelle, and James A. Danowski

Introduction

This chapter presents an example of an embedded research design drawing on a case example of empirical research that mixed ethnography and automated data mining to analyze communication networks in global organizations. The goal of the research was to dynamically visualize network structure and content across geographic, organizational, and cultural boundaries. We conducted the study described in this chapter as part of a United States National Science Foundation funded research study to examine how innovations are diffused in global networked organizations. The theory, methods, and tools that helped us conduct our investigation are varied and many, and it will not be possible to do them all justice in this chapter. However, it is our intent to illustrate the value of combining approaches from quantitative, automated data collection and analysis with a grounded ethnographic approach. The quantitative network analysis was given greater weight in the overall study design. However, the ethnographic data were gathered in parallel with automated quantitative data collection and with special emphasis on the triangulation of data that served to both validate and corroborate results. The approach demonstrates how ethnographic methods provide both relevant content and context that can be incorporated into IT-based techniques for data mining and network analysis.

We will demonstrate how the ethnography both validated and grounded the results we found through our analysis of electronic data as well as how the ethnography provided insights that gave our interpretation of the results depth and face validity with the organizational

Research for this chapter was supported by an award from the Human and Social Dynamics Division of the National Science Foundation, Award #SES-0527487, September 2005 to August 2010.

members we studied. We have organized this chapter to provide the reader first with some context for our study by briefly stating the problem and the research question and reviewing the theory and research related to networks, information technology, and diffusion in organizations. Next we discuss the appropriateness of using mixed methods in our study of networks in a global organization. Third, we describe the study procedures and both the quantitative and qualitative methods and results. Finally, we conclude with a discussion of the implications for researchers of innovation networks and practitioners in global networked organizations who manage them and work in these networks.

Statement of the Problem: Diffusion of Innovations in a Global Networked Enterprise

Managing the diffusion of innovations across the global enterprise requires knowledge of both the content and the structure of complex communication networks. Existing research does not address directly a central problem faced by today's management: how best to diffuse new ideas, processes, and technologies across the global enterprise given its dynamic, emergent, and elusive character (Cross et al. 2002). Because of the dynamic and rapidly changing structure of organizational communication and innovation networks, many researchers in information systems in particular have begun to recognize the importance of better alignment between information technology infrastructure and business systems and have turned to adapting popular social network technologies for business use. IT professionals are also recognizing the utility of diffusion of innovation theory to study implementation problems (Al-Gahtani 2001; Mustonen-Ollila and Lyytinen 2003; Weitzel et al. 2003).

However, despite the ubiquity and sophistication of information technology, organizations have not taken advantage of the capabilities inherent in the information system itself as a method to manage implementation (Zack 2000). Social network theorists (Borgatti and Foster 2003), however, have reviewed the burgeoning field of social network research in organizational contexts and pull to the foreground the theoretical linkages of academic network research with managerial considerations of organizational networks. Cross and Parker (2004) emphasize the explosion in computing technologies that have the potential to link network theory with practice and advance data collection and representation. It has become widely recognized in this decade that the network perspective reflects the fundamental structure of social processes. Borgatti and Foster (2003) show the exponential growth curve for studies on social networks in *Sociological Abstracts*, reviewing nearly 200 studies of social networks and organizations at both the inter- and intraorganizational levels. Organizational and communication scholars have addressed the emergence of knowledge networks in global organizations and their relationships with information-technology–driven organizations (Contractor and Eisenberg 1990). Researchers have been developing sophisticated computational simulation models for testing hypotheses about networks and information diffusion, changes in individuals' and group knowledge and interaction networks, the dynamics of cultural influence networks, and how shared beliefs evolve, focusing on their co-evolution with information technology (Carley and Krackhardt 1996; Carley 1996; Contractor et al. 1998; Harrison and Carroll 2002). *The New York Times* (Eakin 2003) is even publishing articles about the popularity of network theory, and there are best-selling books on the topic (Gladwell 2000; Barabasi 2002; Buchanan 2002; Johnson 2001; Watts 1999, 2003; Strogatz 2003). Physicists have conducted numerous studies of networks and various social practices, modeling them in high-order mathematical network terms (Newman 2002).

Network Theory

Network theory, as it has been applied to the study of human behavior and relationships, is comprised of multiple theoretical approaches. Monge and Contractor (2001, 2003) state that there are 10 families of theories that have been used to explain the emergence, maintenance, and dissolution of communication networks in organizations. With a long tradition in sociology, organizational theory, and anthropology, network analysis is a form of structural analysis with both theory and methods intimately linked (Rogers and Kincaid 1981; Bernard and Ryan 1998; Monge and Contractor 2001; Borgatti and Foster 2003). The analysis technique is most often used to uncover the pattern of interpersonal communication in a social system by determining who talks to whom, and by investigating both structural and relationship properties of networks (Valente 1995, 1996; Cross et al. 2002). Monitoring emerging networks identifies where greater leverage can be gained for channeling diffusion resources (Cotrill 1998; Carley 1995). Our current research is not directly focused on interorganizational networks; however, there is a stream of studies that investigates interorganizational network predictors of organizational adoption of innovations (Davis1991; Haunschild 1993; Palmer et al. 1993; Powell et al. 1996; Gulati and Westphal 1999; Geletkanycz et al. 2001).

Of particular relevance to our research are studies of the social construction of innovation networks. Poole and DeSanctis (1990) have examined how actors and structures in a social system influence each other in a recursive relationship. In a longitudinal study conducted at a U.S. public works department, the duality of this relationship was empirically validated using the output from simulation techniques in comparison with actual network evolution (Contractor et al. 2000). Harrisson and LaBerge (2002) explored the process of diffusion of a socio-technical innovation among workers of a large microelectronics firm. Network analysis revealed how innovation is constituted and the communicative form it takes by tracing the chain of arguments and responses. Burkhardt and Brass (1990) demonstrated in their study how the diffusion of an innovation altered the network structure based on the knowledge and information individuals possessed about the innovation. Investigating resistance to the introduction of ISO quality standards in a transport company, Torenvlied and Velner (1998) discovered that contagion of resistance in an informal trust network is a significant barrier to diffusing innovations.

Diffusion of Innovations

Research on the diffusion of innovations spans almost seven decades and includes more than 5,000 studies. No other field in the behavioral and social sciences represents more effort by more scholars in more nations (Rogers 2003). Diffusion is "the process by which an innovation is communicated through certain channels over time among members of a social system" (Rogers 1983:5). An innovation is an idea, practice, or object that is perceived as new by an individual or another unit of adoption. An innovation can refer to new knowledge; to new technologies such as information technologies, product improvements, or manufacturing technologies; or to a new process for doing work in organizations. While there is a large body of extant research about innovation based on product or process life cycle (Utterback 1996; Fine 2001), the study we describe in this chapter is grounded in the theoretical and methodological traditions in communication and social network research.

Our focus on measuring diffusion using data gathered from an organization's IT infrastructure does not suggest that face-to-face interaction is unimportant to diffusion. To the contrary, our ethnographic examples will illustrate how we have mapped such networks in alignment with the digital data. Moreover, we assume that IT-based networks are correlated with face-to-face network structures, following the findings of Haythornthwaite and Wellman (1998). They reported that social network data on media use among members of a co-located research group showed that pairs with closer ties used more media to communicate.

Diffusion Networks

Networks are important to the diffusion of innovation (Debresson and Amesse 1991) because they posit that the ties between individuals influence the spread of an innovation. Most diffusion models are contagion/epidemic/cohesion/relational models where information about innovation is passed from one person to another through direct contact. Valente (1995, 2005) identified only six studies that exist in the public domain that utilized network models of the diffusion of innovation with both network data and time of adoption data. He reanalyzed data from three of the studies to demonstrate how relational network models, structural network models, threshold models, and critical mass models aid our understanding about how ideas, products, and opinions "take off" and spread with varying speed through a social system. Valente (1995) conceptualized a network threshold model that is both relational and structural and provides a more accurate measure of a person's innovativeness. He calls out the need for more network and diffusion research that measures adoption over time while collecting network data so that estimations of various network effects can be better performed (Valente 2005). To address this need we developed and tested diffusion theories by collecting data using a new "digital diffusion dashboard" methodology that utilizes companies' information technology infrastructure to create unobtrusive and continuous monitoring of their communication exchanges about an innovation to trace diffusion and also communication networks as they co-evolved. The "digital diffusion dashboard" involved tapping into the electronic data available through a company's IT infrastructure and then using off-the-shelf software[1] for display and ease of implementation. Using the analogy of the automobile dashboard, we created the diffusion dashboard and the specific gauges in collaboration with our industry partner. To validate and calibrate the dashboard and provide deeper contextual explanations for the diffusion and network patterns we observed in the dashboard, we executed an ethnographic study among organizational members working on the

---

[1] To display data as gauges, for example, we propose to use off-the-shelf modeling software such as that being developed by Bass Economics, founded by the developer of the highly cited Bass Model of diffusion (Bass 1969), which is near release of a beta version of Excel and SAS templates for modeling diffusion curves on the desktop (see www.basseconomics.com).

innovation. The next section in this chapter explains more about why we chose to combine the IT-based diffusion dashboard with ethnography and how we conducted the study mixing these quantitative and qualitative methods.

The Appropriateness of an Embedded Mixed Methods Approach to Studying Organizational Diffusion Networks

Quantitative approaches generally assume that predefined variables have similar meanings across multiple settings, ignoring the influence of context. Qualitative approaches, on the other hand, help us to understand local perceptions and differing meanings for phenomena, explicating "the ways people in a particular setting come to understand, account for, take action, and otherwise manage their day-to-day situations" Miles and Huberman (1994:7). Bartunek and Seo (2002), in their commentary on how qualitative research can add new meanings to quantitative research, also suggest that it is important to explore how organizational members understand and make sense of constructs that are important to academic researchers, such as innovation, in order to validate their definition in local contexts. For example, studies of global teams as relatively new organizational phenomena revealed how context interacts with task and technology as well as how global team members negotiate a working culture across contexts (Gluesing 1998; Gluesing et al. 2003; Riopelle et al. 2003; Baba et al. 2004). Researchers choose methodological approaches that affect how they understand the phenomena they study. Qualitative research can be helpful, and is often necessary, to both validate and to explore organizational constructs, phenomena and local meanings, and, most importantly, the interactions that create the meanings. The combination of qualitative and quantitative methods to explore organizational networks, particularly in distributed networks and mobile work that span geographies and cultural contexts, stimulates the development of new understandings about the variety and extent of organizational members' experiences with important phenomena across global networked organizations (Meerwarth et al. 2008).

Mixed methods exemplified by the embedded design in this study also accomplish what Stephen Barley and Gideon Kunda have called "bringing work back in" (2001:76). They argue that in order to understand post-bureaucratic organizing, especially in this era of global organizations and with structures that must adapt to flows of information, resources, and technologies that are continually in flux, the methods we employ as researchers should aid us in developing concepts and theories that are congruent with the complexities of today's organizations and organizing processes. Social and communication networks have always been a part of organizing. Barley and Kunda (2001) believe that network theory and network analysis are important and relevant especially in today's global economy because they can help us to visualize the changing nature of work relations if we can gather longitudinal data on structures and the concrete activities that constitute them. They state that longitudinal network data that can capture the dynamics of networks complemented with a grounded approach to gather data on post-industrial work are critical to move organization studies forward and make them relevant for scholars and practitioners alike. Combining the quantitative approach of gathering network data through automated means and analyzing these data can be supplemented to great advantage by ethnographic data obtained through observation and interviews. Ethnography provides descriptive data about the patterns of work, the language people use to describe their work as well as the meaning it has for them, and contextually sensitive information about work relations. In addition, ethnographic data have the potential to generate analytic constructs that can enable foundational work in developing new theories and concepts and produce better images of post-bureaucratic organizing. White and Johansen (2005) also advance the proposition that linking ethnographic fieldwork with network analysis and theory can go a long way in explaining emergence and dynamics in complex interactions, like those that constitute post-bureaucratic organizing.

The next section describes the methods and tools we employed to conduct a study at a large global manufacturing enterprise using dynamic network analysis and participant observation supplemented by interviewing, combining quantitative methods and grounded qualitative fieldwork to understand the structure, work practices, and situated meanings of work on an innovation project as it evolved over more than a year.

Study Methods and Tools

This study of an innovation, which we will call Advanced Technology Innovation (ATI), spanned geographies and cultures in a global enterprise and hence required the collaboration of many people, including a team internal to the organization who could access and work with the IT infrastructure and facilitate the ethnographic research. We worked together over the period of one year to gather data and conduct ongoing analysis using many tools and data sets. We present here an example that is illustrative of the automated e-mail data-collection process and the ethnographic fieldwork to both validate the e-mail networks that

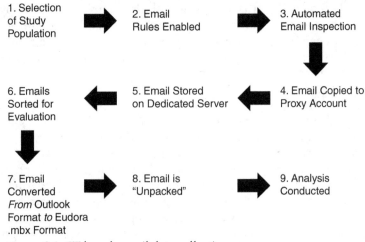

Figure 8.1, IT-based e-mail data collection process

emerged in the analysis of the e-mail data and to better understand the interactions of the actors in the network and their "native" views of the innovation. We used the results of this analysis to help us construct our "digital diffusion dashboard."

Automated Data Collection Process

After achieving approval from the legal staff in the company and from our university institutional review boards to conduct the research, the first step in gathering data was to determine the automated data-collection process, depicted in Figure 8.1 with a brief description of the basic steps as follows:

1. The project team of 298 people served as the population for the innovation diffusion study.
2. Thirty-eight people who agreed to participate in the study enabled e-mail rules.
3. Automated inspection of e-mail using the e-mail rules took place on inbound/outbound e-mails.
4. E-mails were sent to a proxy e-mail account.
5. Incoming e-mails were stored on a dedicated secure server.
6. E-mails were sorted for evaluation.
7. E-mail was converted to a Eudora .mbx file for analysis.
8. E-mail was "unpacked," removing forwarding headers and added nested e-mails to the database of stored e-mails for analysis.
9. Analysis of e-mail data was conducted.

E-mails from January 2005 through November 2007 were gathered from among the top 25 percent of the population of individuals formally participating in the project. An initial solicitation for participation was sent to the population of 298 project team members. From this group, 38 people consented to be active participants in the study, allowing us to gather and monitor their e-mails about the project. We did not gather all the participants' e-mails, only those filtered according to a list of key words related to various aspects of the innovation project. The network of 38 participants resulted in roughly 45,000 e-mails and links among more than 2,000 people across the enterprise communicating about the project over time.

Digital Diffusion Dashboard

One of the primary goals of our research was to develop a prototype of an IT-based "digital diffusion dashboard" to help managers in a change agent role accomplish three objectives: visualize the innovation networks over time, measure the performance of the innovation network, and manage the performance of the network to accelerate innovation and increase the likelihood of adoption. While we will not discuss the dashboard in detail in this chapter, it is important to describe the metrics that are part of the dashboard and the various software tools we used to obtain different network measure that would tie into the dashboard metrics. The dashboard metrics were designed to answer seven important evaluative questions that a manager might want to know about an innovation:

1) Who Is Talking?
   - Who is talking about the innovation?
   - What groups of the company do they represent?
   - What levels of the company are talking about the innovation?

2) Who Are the Champions?
   - Who is central in the network?

3) How Is the Team Collaborating?
   - Who is involved in the network?
   - Are the right people talking?
   - Is anyone missing?

4) What Is the "Buzz" about the Innovation?
   - What are people saying about the innovation?

5) What Is the Emotion of the Team?
   - Are people talking positively or negatively about the innovation?

6) What Is the Rate of Adoption?
   - Is the innovation diffusing fast enough?
   - Is it spreading throughout the organization as it should?

7) What Is the Value Proposition?
   - What is the value of the innovation to the organization?

Note: The seventh metric, "What Is the Value Proposition?", is not obtained through any IT data collection but represents the business case created by management.

The dynamic social network analysis software tools[2] helped to define the majority of the innovation metrics. Condor is the central tool that helped define the majority of the innovation metrics, providing the data used to answer the questions about who is talking to whom, who the champions are, what people are saying about the innovation, and what the rate of adoption is. Condor creates dynamic views and network statistics, which provide the macro view of change. Navicat, a graphical user interface for the MySQL database underlying Condor, is used to extract user networks and text from the Condor database for more in-depth analysis, such as comparing different groups or different times to see how network structures and content vary. Triad census software, TRIADS, is a part of the Multinet software program and provides data about how the team is collaborating. Negopy, also a part of Multinet, provides additional information about the subgroups in the team and their collaboration. MultiNet, Negopy, Triad Census, UCINET, and NetDraw are all used to determine groups and roles and to analyze text in an iterative fashion. WordLink further defines what is being said

---

[2] *Condor* was created by Peter Gloor (and Cooper 2007) at MIT and is a network visualization program; contact: Peter A. Gloor (pgloor@mit.edu). *Negopy* was created by Bill Richards (deceased) at Simon Frasier University and is now part of *Multinet*, created by Andrew Seary at Simon Frasier University; contact: Andrew Seary (seary@sfu.ca). *UCINET* was created by Steve Borgatti, M. G. Everett and L. C. Freeman. *Pajek* was developed by Valdimir Batagelj and Andrej Mrvar at University of Ljubljana, Slovenia. *Triads* is a modification of the triad census FORTRAN software program created by Walker and Wasserman. The modification was done by Danowski and Riopelle, co-authors of this chapter; contact: James A. Danowski (jdanowski@gmail.com) and Ken Riopelle (kenriopelle@wayne.edu). *Family Tree* Maker (http://www.familytreemaker.com) is a genealogy program that makes excellent organizational charts. *Linguistic Inquiry and Word Count (LIWC)* reads text files and is used to compute a Positivity Index. It was developed by Fredrickson and Losada (2005). *WordLink* was created by Jim Danowski (1982, 1993a, 1993b, 1993c), a chapter co-author, and is a program that counts the frequency of all uniquely occurring words and word pairs in a body of text for content analysis and to assess change over time in word usage; contact: James A. Danowski (jdanowski@gmail.com).

about the innovation, and the software program Linguistic Information and Word Count (LIWC) provides the data metric about the emotion on the team. WordLink and LIWC access a single file or group of files and perform sequential analyses of each file to evaluate the positive or negative valence of the text.

Ethnographic Data Collection

The purpose of the ethnographic research was to validate the measures we gathered to construct the dashboard and to understand more deeply the perspectives of a cross section of people about the ATI product and project. We designed the ethnography to supplement the IT-based communication network analysis by providing people's perspectives on their communication relationships related to ATI, including their e-mail communication. The results of the ethnography provided a comparison of what people believed about ATI and their project-related communication with the same type of data gathered from examining actual e-mail communications.

Through ethnography we also sought to understand the meaning of the innovation to the people involved in the project and to learn what they considered to be the best things about both the project and the process as well as to gather their suggestions about how to remove some of the barriers to progress. In addition to gathering information via ethnographic interviews about people's communication networks, we also were interested in assessing qualitatively the emotion of the team to compare it with the results of the quantitative, IT-based analysis results.

The ethnographic sample included a global cross section of people involved in the ATI project to obtain a broad set of perspectives about the innovation product and innovation project process. The respondents reflected a mix of participants involved in the global project team including people from the following areas in the company:

- Office of the General Counsel
- Product Management
- Design and Ergonomics
- Project Management
- Finance
- Core Project Staff

For the example we present in this chapter, we conducted 12 semi-structured interviews and shadowed the daily activities of two people central to the project. The interview protocol can be found in Appendix A. The interview protocol included:

- Fourteen open-ended questions
- A set of communication network questions to solicit names of people with whom respondents communicated by any means about ATI and how often they communicated
- Questions about the top three people in the respondents' networks and estimates of the frequency of communication among them
- Questions about the top three people with whom the respondents exchanged e-mail about ATI and estimates of the frequency of e-mail communication among them

The shadowing was conducted by two different ethnographers over several days and included the observation and notation of the following:

1 Topic of conversation
2 Type of communication exchange (face-to-face, phone, meeting, audio or video conference, etc.)
3 Duration of the communication event
4 General communication climate or tone (e.g., positive to negative on a scale of 1 to 10)
5 Dynamics of the interaction.

The ethnographic data about the ATI innovation product and project team enabled us to build confidence in the data and results produced by our automated data-collection and analysis process. In the following section, we highlight some of the comparative study results to illustrate the power of mixing these methods.

Comparison of Automated and Ethnographic Network Analysis Results

The findings we present in this section illustrate the study results comparing two metrics on our "digital diffusion dashboard" – Emotion and Team Collaboration – as an example of both the mixed methods approach we used in the ATI study and also the value that this quantitative and qualitative approach provided to our research.

The Emotion

Figure 8.2 shows the positivity to negativity ratio over time for the ATI project. We used the Linguistic Inquiry and Word Count (LIWC) software program to evaluate the context of words used in the e-mail data. The program takes text data and determines the count and the percentage at which the participants use positive or negative emotions, words,

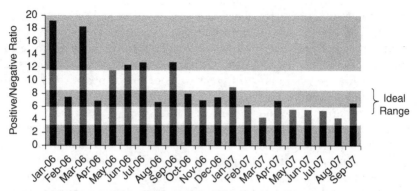

Figure 8.2. The Emotion Score Plot for ATI (the Losada Line is at 2.9, the threshold point at which teams flourish or flounder)

self references, or words that refer to specific topics and other characteristics of the e-mail talk. From this tool it is possible to compute a positivity index or the ratio of the positive to negative talk of a team over time. Fredrickson and Losada (2005) developed predictors of human flourishing that they characterized as thresholds defined by a ratio of positive to negative words and defining a positivity to negativity ratio of 2.9 to 1 as the lower threshold at which people are able to perform well in a team. This threshold point of 2.9 is referred to as the "Losada Line." Teams who "flourish" have a ratio of positivity to negativity within a zone of 2.9:1 to 11.6:1. High-performing teams were found to have a ratio of 5.6:1. Above a ratio of 11.6:1, there can be so much positive affect that it may begin to lose its benefit in helping teams to flourish, instead creating a "halo" effect which can cause team members to lose sight of important barriers or obstacles that must be overcome. The Losada Zone (Fredrickson and Losada 2005) characterizes an environment that allows behavioral flexibility, innovation, and creativity. In the chart depicted in Figure 8.2, it is evident that the ATI project team was flourishing in the Losada Zone and was engaging in positive talk, or Buzz, about the innovation.

The analysis of the ethnographic data validated the results of the LIWC positivity index. We analyzed the responses across the interviews and coded them for positive and negative words. There was a predominance of positive talk, but also some negative comments as well. Overall, the people we interviewed considered the product to be innovative and a "thoughtful application of existing technologies to better meet the needs of the customers." "It is absolutely the right thing to do," and "It is very exciting." People think the product is important because it will drive people to the stores and lead them to buy the company's products. People are realistic about the constraints inside the company and about the competitive pressures. They also see the need to keep pushing the innovation envelope and to fight against a mentality of negativity. People stated that the product is taking the company to the next step of technology improvements, but also that it's a "lot of work … it's complex" because it crosses so many different parts of the company. It is a challenge of global coordination.

According to those interviewed, a "best thing" about the product is not the product itself, but the set of design principles that govern the product, "the things that should govern the products that we release, and those principles like motherhood and apple pie, be attentive to your customers' needs, be connected – allow customers to connect to other parts of their lifestyle; be approachable – trigger the customer's curiosity and encourage exploration, and be clear – provide information that they want and need within the context is right, and use a language that they're familiar with."

The execution of the product requires integration in process as well, which people see as another "best thing." One respondent said, "People were coming together, design, engineering, human factors, marketing, executives, etc. … we're all coming together and collaborating early on and openly about what this system should be, and to me this is a different way we do things at the company." This process is producing a product that is truly a "human machine interface change" that is "based upon real customer feedback" and a "holistic experience."

When the interview respondents talked about the ATI project itself, they most often mentioned the learning involved in the radical innovation, both product and process, that the project has required. They stated that the new ways of working in a global, cross-functional collaborative project helped break down traditional barriers, both cultural and organizational. They also mentioned as top-of-mind the involvement of the right kind of people to bring energy to the project and to do the kind of problem-solving required to work in new ways on a breakthrough product. The egalitarian aspect of the teamwork is also a factor that the interviewees saw as contributing to the project's progress and expected success. The openness to perspectives was considered critical to the new ways of working and to inventing new solutions to problems. Some of the first thoughts that people mentioned also concerned the emerging partnership with Europe to create a Global ATI product. They talked about "roadblocks from overseas … a little bit of friction with North America and Europe being connected … so now what they already have on the road we are now trying to force fit into what ATI was and so that's now defining what ATI is, is what Europe already has. That goes right back to the first thought, the ideal versus the reality." However, the project has not "strayed that much away from the original idea."

It is clear from these example results that ethnographic interviews are consistent with an elaborate nature of the talk that is characterized by the positivity index depicted in Figure 8.2. The talk also reflects the views of those interviewed about the nature of their team processes and collaboration. They were positive about the collaborative way they worked and about their connections across corporate and geographic boundaries. The same type of result was evident in the network analysis that we conducted on both the automated and the ethnographic network data we gathered.

Team Collaboration

To illustrate how we analyzed the collaborative communication network in the ATI project using both IT-based, automated data-collection methods and ethnographic data, we have chosen two examples that depict the communication network by organizational level and the reciprocity in communication among the team members. We begin with a discussion of the IT-based e-mail collaboration network and then describe the characteristics of the collaboration network that emerged from the ethnographic interviews.

IT-Based E-Mail Collaboration Network. The automated process for analyzing the communication network for the ATI project involved a longitudinal analysis of e-mail. The example we include here shows how we created a "picture" of the overall collaboration across time by using Multinet and a triad census to characterize the network communication patterns across levels of the organization. The e-mail data were rich enough to allow for coding of individuals by organizational level as well as according to the linkages and reciprocity in their e-mail communication. A collaborative communication network will have communication links across levels and between people in the same level and a high proportion of fully reciprocated triads. The triad census profile is based on 16 unique triad communication types where a triad is the interaction among three nodes. Each type is a three-digit comparison of links among three individuals where the first digit represents the number of reciprocal links among people in the triad, the second digit represents the number of one-way links, and the third digit represents instances of no communication. A triad in which there is no communication among the three people will have a three-digit descriptor of 003. A fully reciprocated triad will have a description of 300.

Figure 8.3 displays the triads across levels within the ATI e-mail communication network. The even distribution of 300 triads throughout the

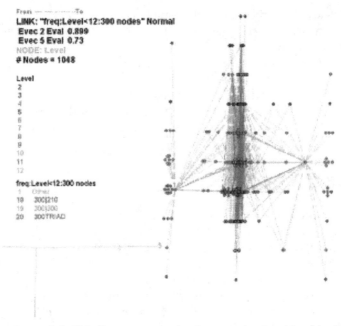

Figure 8.3. Triadic communication by organizational level in ATI

many levels of the organization and network indicates that there is a strong linkage across the network and active collaboration among the team members.

The Ethnographic ATI Collaboration Network. In the interviews, the respondents were asked to describe their communication networks. Specifically, they were asked whom they communicate with about ATI through any means and to estimate how often they communicate with these people. Next the respondents were asked to name the top three people they communicate with among those they had named. They were also asked to name the top three people with whom they exchange e-mail about ATI. These questions were intended to determine the structure of the overall ATI communication network for the 12 interview respondents and to provide some insight about the similarities and differences between their overall communication network and their e-mail network.

The findings of the ethnographic network analysis are presented in the next section and include a description of the overall network and of the top three communication and e-mail relationships followed by a comparison of them.

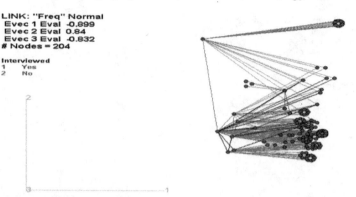

LINK: "Freq" Normal
  Evec 1 Eval -0.899
  Evec 2 Eval 0.84
  Evec 3 Eval -0.832
Nodes = 204

Interviewed
1 Yes
2 No

Figure 8.4. Twelve interview respondents and their communication network relationships

The Overall Communication Network. The 12 interview respondents named a total of 328 people with whom they communicated. The number of relationships that respondents named ranged from 2 to 134, with an average of 27 names. Figure 8.4 is a map showing the network relationships of all 12 respondents with their named relationships. The map shows a similar pattern of communication across hierarchical levels in the organization to that revealed by the data collected through the automated e-mail process.

The single dots toward the left of the graph represent the 12 interview respondents and the clustered dots on the right indicate the people respondents say they communicate with about ATI. The network is quite extensive given that it represents the communication network of only 12 people who were interviewed.

The Top Three Communication Relationship Network. The interview respondents were asked to name the top three people with whom they communicate about ATI, illustrated in Figure 8.5. One respondent was only able to name two people; therefore there are a total of 35 people in this "top three" communication network.

The highest concentration of people in the center of the network represents those who have the highest amount of interconnection in the network, those centrally involved in the delivery of the ATI product.

The group structure was confirmed using the software program Negopy. The Negopy analysis revealed that there is only one group in the top three communication relationship network. Figure 8.6 shows this single group uncovered by the Negopy analysis.

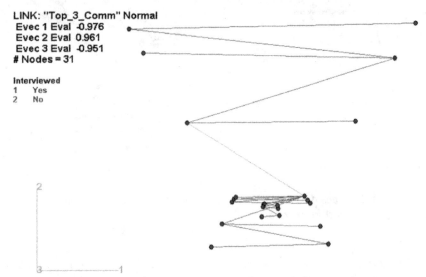

Figure 8.5. Twelve interview respondents and their top three communication relationship networks

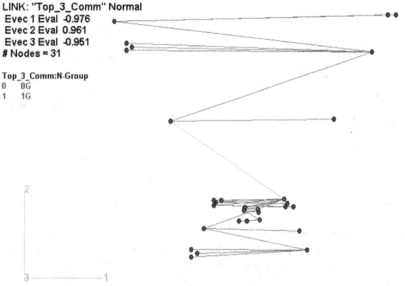

Figure 8.6. Single group in the top three communication relationship
networks

In Figure 8.6, the dots clustered in the middle indicate the single subgroup in the network. The outer dots represent people who are more

LINK: "W_Top_3_Email" Normal
Evec 1 Eval -1.0
Evec 2 Eval 0.868
Evec 3 Eval -0.864
Nodes = 30

Interviewed
1   Yes
2   No

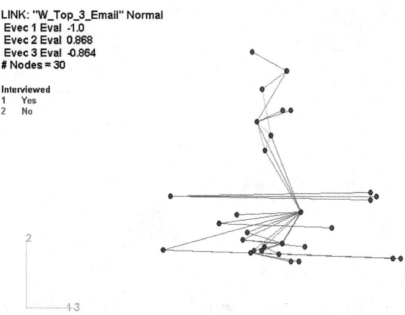

Figure 8.7. Twelve interview respondents and their top three e-mail relationship networks

loosely connected but still part of the same group. On average, the 12 respondents say they communicate with the 35 people in the top three communication relationship network several times per week.

The Top Three E-Mail Relationship Network. The 12 interview respondents were asked to name the top three people with whom they e-mail about ATI. Figure 8.7 shows a network map of the 35 people in the top three e-mail network.

In Figure 8.7, there appear to be two distinct subgroups that make up the e-mail network. This group structure was confirmed using the software program Negopy. The Negopy analysis revealed that there are two groups in the top three e-mail relationship network. Figure 8.8 shows the two groups uncovered by the Negopy analysis.

In Figure 8.8, the dots at the top of the graph represent one subgroup in the network, a core group of central staff intimately involved in the execution of the ATI project. The small, light gray cluster of dots at the bottom center of the graph represents a second subgroup comprised of program representatives and those involved in functional support groups outside the core engineering staff.

On average, the 12 respondents say they communicate via e-mail with the 35 people in the top three e-mail relationship network somewhere

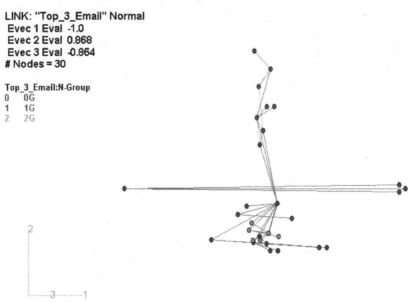

LINK: "Top_3_Email" Normal
Evec 1 Eval -1.0
Evec 2 Eval 0.868
Evec 3 Eval -0.864
Nodes = 30

Top_3_Email:N-Group
0   0G
1   1G
2   2G

Figure 8.8. Two sub-groups in the top three e-mail relationship network

between several times a week and weekly, slightly less often than they say they communicate in the top three communication network relationship overall.

Comparison of the Top Three Communication Relationship Network and Top Three E-Mail Relationship Network. To understand how the top three communication relationship network compares with the top three e-mail communication network we computed the overlap between the two networks. Table 8.1 presents the results of this analysis. Approximately 66 percent or 23 of the 35 people named in these top three networks were the same. Thirty-four percent or 12 people were different between the two networks. There is significant overlap in the two top three networks.

Five of the 12 people who were interviewed named the same people as part of both their communication relationship network and their e-mail relationship network. Four people named two out of the top three people as part of both networks. One person said that one out of the three people in the communication network was also part of the e-mail network. Two people said there was no overlap at all between the people in the communication network and the e-mail network. Further examination of the data revealed that the people with the

Table 8.1. *Comparison of top three
communication relationships and top three
e-mail relationship networks*

Network Top 3 Nominations (Communication vs E-Mail)		
Nominations	Count	Percent
Same	23	66%
Different	12	34%
Total	35	100%

most overlap in their communication and e-mail networks are those who are part of the central core team on the project who work most closely with one another. Those who report the least overlap tend to be people in managerial positions who serve as liaisons across groups. Figure 8.9 represents a network map of the combined top three communication and e-mail networks.

Negopy analysis revealed that there is only one group in the combined top three network. The few links in light gray at the center of the graph indicate those relationships that are the same across the two networks. The dark gray links represent the top three e-mail-only links that are not part of the top three communication network. E-mail is clearly an important communication tool in the ATI team. It complements and extends the communication relationships, especially in linking cross-functional groups, and is a good representation of the overall communication network in the ATI team.

Shadowing and Collaboration Patterns. The shadowing of the daily activities of two people in the team on several different occasions supplemented the data gathered through the interviews. Shadowing revealed that communication across boundaries takes place through many different means on a continuing basis: in meetings, brief hallway conversations, and in phone calls as well as through e-mail. The e-mail activity was minimally observed in the shadowing, confirming that the face-to-face communication activity is a strong network component among the core people in the ATI project. The meetings provided face-to-face communication links across functional boundaries and levels in the company. E-mail provided these same communication links but was less collaborative and more focused on documentation and the general giving of direction to team members. The shadowing confirmed the results of the network analysis groupings and how e-mail is used.

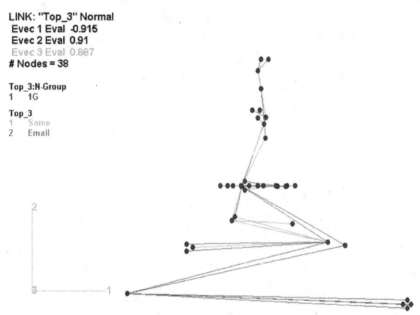

LINK: "Top_3" Normal
Evec 1 Eval -0.915
Evec 2 Eval 0.91
Evec 3 Eval 0.887
Nodes = 38

Top_3:N-Group
1   1G

Top_3
1   Same
2   Email

Figure 8.9. Combined top three communication and e-mail networks

The ethnographic study provides evidence that there is significant overlap between the overall communication network for ATI and the e-mail network. Where the e-mail network is different, it is used to link people across distance and functional boundaries and makes an important contribution to the integration of the ATI team. E-mail appears to be an accurate representation of the ATI communication network as a whole, and we could be confident that the "digital diffusion dashboard" tool that we were prototyping would be useful for innovation managers in monitoring the emotion and the collaboration in the team.

Conclusion

In this chapter we have demonstrated how a quantitative, automated approach and a qualitative, ethnographic approach were used to investigate collaboration and innovation in a global networked organization. Taken together, they can enhance both understanding and explanation of network patterns, particularly when the development and diffusion of innovation are facilitated by information technology yet are influenced by local contexts and meanings. The example we presented of a global innovation team in a large manufacturing organization involved thousands of people who were spread across the organization and were in different countries. We were able to harness information that already flows through the company's IT communication infrastructure. In this case we relied on e-mail to look into the company's innovation processes. Detailed analyses of the data we collected using automated means make it possible to create an IT-based "digital diffusion dashboard" to monitor metrics in near real time about a collaborative innovation network that is extensive and spans geography, an analysis task that would be practically impossible using the usual network surveys that would have required extensive time, effort, and travel. The examples provided in this chapter illustrate how both emotion and collaboration can be analyzed using e-mail data and several software tools. Calculating a positivity index provides a measure of positive to negative talk in e-mails and a metric to assess the emotional state among non-collocated team members. Our analysis also showed how collaboration took place across levels of the organization and the extent of the collaboration as measured by the number of triads we found within and across levels.

New combinations of methods for who-to-whom network analysis of e-mail, positivity indexing, and hierarchical modeling of networks are particularly useful in the new world of intensive and extensive information exchange through technology use in organizations. We can gain increased understanding of the diffusion of technological innovations in IT-based environments and global networked organizations where innovations are appearing in greater numbers at a faster pace and diffusing more rapidly, often facilitated by global teams. Automated means of data collection, coupled with powerful software tools for analyzing both text and networks, hold great promise for mapping the contours of global networked organizations and the organizing processes themselves in near real time and over time.

Yet an understanding of micro-organizational processes and contextual variation in both meanings and behaviors is necessary if we are to avoid a simplified, overly undifferentiated or homogenized view of postbureaucratic organizing. The IT-based analytics can tell us much about how networks are structured and how they evolve as well as about the central messages that flow through the communication networks. However, ethnography can help us uncover new patterns of work, emergent roles, and different meanings for an innovation within global networks. For example, in our shadowing of team members we observed that almost everyone was constantly on the move from meeting to meeting and location to location, spending little time at their desks. People were sending and receiving e-mails on their phones and using them for other important business functions as well. This pattern would not have been evident in an analysis of the automated data. It was very important for us to learn about how e-mail exchange takes place so that we could design a dashboard for managers that would work on smart phones and not just on the desktop.

Network analysis of the data we gathered through our interviews was very closely matched to the patterns we found in the analysis of our e-mail data. We learned that face-to-face networks differed from e-mail networks primarily because e-mail was generally the only option for communicating across distance. However, our interviews also revealed that there were different patterns of e-mail use in Europe and in the United States. In the primary European location, managers did not engage in e-mail exchange with those whose offices were nearby; interpersonal communication was the norm. Our analysis of the e-mail networks alone did not reveal this practice.

It is our belief that to understand global organizing, especially in the postindustrial or postbureaucratic organizations that are enabled by information technology, mixing research methods is a good way to accomplish both depth and breadth of understanding and to keep pace with emerging patterns and meanings. This type of research will be facilitated by ever more sophisticated information technologies and analytical tools but will also need to be grounded in context and conducted by a team of researchers who can observe and talk to people as they engage in their day-to-day work activities. Quantitative and qualitative methods, automated IT-based data collection, and in-depth ethnography are complementary and should be a necessary part of research design for organization studies going forward. Researchers also need to have an understanding of both quantitative and qualitative methods and their strengths and weaknesses, to know best when and how to use these complementary methods. We advocate a position of "both–and" and not "either–or," favoring an embedded design, mixing methods to design and execute organizational network studies that will be both comprehensive and explanatory. We have tried to show in this chapter that it is possible to design research that takes full advantage of information technologies to gather large amounts of data for data mining and network analysis, but also to embed qualitative methods in parallel and in a measured, targeted way to maximize the richness of results while minimizing the costs usually involved in long-term, labor-intensive ethnographic studies.

Appendix A. Interview Protocol

Start Time: (e.g., 10:05 a.m.)
End Time: (e.g., 11:00 a.m.)
   Part I

   1.   First, when you think of the ATI product, what thoughts first come to mind? [3 Probes: What else? Other thoughts? Anything else?]
   2.   What are the best things about the ATI product? [3 Probes]

3. Now, when you think of the ATI project itself, what thoughts first come to mind? [3 Probes: What else? Other thoughts? Anything else?]
4. What would you say are the best things about the ATI project? [3 Probes]
5. What aspects of the ATI project might need improvement? [3 Probes]

Part II

6. Who are the people you communicate with about ATI? Tell me their names. [Multiple Probes until they can think of no others]

Communication table

Name				Frequency of Communication				
1 Multiple times per day	2 Daily	3 Several times per week	4 Weekly	5 Several times per month	6 Monthly	7 Quarterly	8 Less than quarterly	9 Rarely
1.								
2.								
3.								
4.								
5.								
6.								
7.								
8.								
9.								
10.								
11.								
12.								
13.								
14.								
15.								

[Continue listing names until respondent has no further names to offer.]

7. How often do you communicate with _____? [Repeat, asking about each name given. Provide the interviewee with the list of frequency responses.]

8. Of the people you named, remind me which three you communicate with most often about ATI, through any means? Tell me their names.
   A =
   B =
   C =

9. How often do think that A and B communicate about ATI with one another (give your best estimate)? [If says "don't know," say: "Then give your best estimate, please."]
___ Multiple times per day
___ Daily
___ Several times per week
___ Weekly
___ Several times per month
___ Monthly
___ Quarterly
___ Less than quarterly
___ Rarely
___ Never

10. How often do you think B and C communicate? [If says "don't know," say: "Then give your best estimate, please."]
___ Multiple times per day
___ Daily
___ Several times per week
___ Weekly
___ Several times per month
___ Monthly
___ Quarterly
___ Less than quarterly
___ Rarely
___ Never

11. How often do think that A and C communicate? [If says "don't know," say: "Then give your best estimate, please."]
___ Multiple times per day
___ Daily
___ Several times per week
___ Weekly
___ Several times per month
___ Monthly
___ Quarterly
___ Less than quarterly
___ Rarely
___ Never

12. Who are the three people that you e-mail most frequently about ATI? These three people can be entirely different ones from the previous questions or some or all can be the same. Tell me their names.
Name A (e-mail):
Name B (e-mail):
Name C (e-mail):

13. How often do you e-mail with A about ATI?
    ___ Multiple times per day
    ___ Daily
    ___ Several times per week
    ___ Weekly
    ___ Several times per month
    ___ Monthly
    ___ Quarterly
    ___ Less than quarterly
    ___ Rarely
    ___ Never

14. How often do you e-mail with B about ATI?
    ___ Multiple times per day
    ___ Daily
    ___ Several times per week
    ___ Weekly
    ___ Several times per month
    ___ Monthly
    ___ Quarterly
    ___ Less than quarterly
    ___ Rarely
    ___ Never

15. How often do you e-mail with C about ATI?
    ___ Multiple times per day
    ___ Daily
    ___ Several times per week
    ___ Weekly
    ___ Several times per month
    ___ Monthly
    ___ Quarterly
    ___ Less than quarterly
    ___ Rarely
    ___ Never

16. How often do you estimate that A and B e-mail about ATI with one another?
    ___ Multiple times per day
    ___ Daily
    ___ Several times per week
    ___ Weekly
    ___ Several times per month
    ___ Monthly
    ___ Quarterly
    ___ Less than quarterly

___ Rarely
___ Never

17. How often do you estimate that B and C e-mail about ATI?
    ___ Multiple times per day
    ___ Daily
    ___ Several times per week
    ___ Weekly
    ___ Several times per month
    ___ Monthly
    ___ Quarterly
    ___ Less than quarterly
    ___ Rarely
    ___ Never

18. How often do you estimate that A and C e-mail about ATI?
    ___ Multiple times per day
    ___ Daily
    ___ Several times per week
    ___ Weekly
    ___ Several times per month
    ___ Monthly
    ___ Quarterly
    ___ Less than quarterly
    ___ Rarely
    ___ Never

Part III

19. How does ATI fit into the company business strategy [3 Probes]
20. What do you think the outcomes of ATI will be?
22. Is there anyone that you want to talk with about ATI, but that you haven't been able to reach? What are their names and what would you like to say?
23. How do you personally feel about ATI?
24. What is helping to move the ATI innovation forward? [3 Probes]
25. What are the barriers to the ATI innovation? [3 Probes]
26. What ideas do you have on how to remove these barriers? [3 Probes]
27. What is your role on the ATI project? [3 Probes]
28. Finally, in general terms, what is the meaning of innovation?

References

Al-Gahtani, S. 2001. "The applicability of TAM outside North America: An empirical test in the United Kingdom." *Information Resources Management Journal*, 14(3):37–46.

Baba, M., J. Gluesing, H. Ratner, and K. Wagner. 2004. "The contexts of knowing: Natural history of a globally distributed team." *Journal of Organizational Behavior* 25:547–87.

Barabasi, A. L. 2002. *Linked: The New Science of Networks*. New York: Perseus.

Barley, S. R. and G. Kunda. 2001. "Bringing work back in." *Organization Science* 12(1):76–95.

Bartunek, J. M. and M. Seo. 2002. "Qualitative research can add new meanings to quantitative research." *Journal of Organizational Behavior* 23:237–42.

Bass, F. M. 1969. "A new product growth model for consumer durables." *Management Science* 15(5):215–27.

Bernard, H. R., ed. *Handbook of Methods in Cultural Anthropology*. Walnut Creek, CA: Altamira.

Bernard, H. R. and G. W. Ryan 1998. "Text analysis: Qualitative and quantitative methods." Pp. 595–646 in *Handbook of Methods in Cultural Anthropology*, edited by H. R. Bernard. Walnut Creek, CA: Altamira.

Borgatti, S. P. and P. C. Foster. 2003. "The network paradigm in organizational research: A review and typology." *Journal of Management* 29(6):991–1013.

Bostrom, ed. 1982. *Communication Yearbook, 6*. New Brunswick, NJ: Transaction Books.

Buchanan, M. 2002. *Nexus: Small Worlds and the Groundbreaking Science of Networks*. New York: W. W. Norton.

Burkhardt, M. E. and D. J. Brass. 1990. "Changing patterns or patterns of change: The effects of a change in technology on social network structures and power." *Administrative Science Quarterly* 35:104–27.

Carley, K. M. 1995. "Communication technologies and their effect on cultural homogeneity, consensus, and the diffusion of new ideas." *Sociological Perspectives* 38(4):547–71.

———. 1996. "Communicating new ideas. The potential impact of information and telecommunication technology." *Technology in Society* 18:219–30.

Carley, K. M. and D. Krackhardt. 1996. "Cognitive inconsistencies and non-symmetric friendship." *Social Networks* 18:1–27.

Contractor, N. S. and E. M. Eisenberg. 1990. "Communication networks and new media in organizations." Pp. 143–172 in *Organizations and Communication Technology*, edited by J. Fulk and E. Steinfield. Newbury Park, CA: Sage.

Contractor, N., D. Zink, and M. Chan. 1998. "IKNOW: A tool to assist and study the creation, maintenance, and dissolution of knowledge networks." Pp. 201–217 in *Community Computing and Support Systems (Lecture Notes in Computer Science, 1519)*, edited by T. Ishida. Berlin: Springer-Verlag.

Contractor, N., R. Whitbred, F. Fonti, A. Hyatt, B. O'Keefe, and P. Jones. 2000. "Structuration theory and the evolution of networks." Presented at the 2000 Winter Organizational Science Conference, Keystone, CO.

Cotrill, K. 1998. "Networking for innovation." *Chemical Week* 160(7):39–41.

Cross, R. and A. Parker. 2004. *The Hidden Power of Social Networks*. Boston: Harvard Business School Press

Cross, R., S. P. Borgatti, and A. Parker. 2002. "Making invisible work visible: Using social network analysis to support strategic collaboration." *California Management Review* 44(2):25–46.

Danowski, J. 1982. "A network-based content analysis methodology for computer-mediated communication: An illustration with a computer bulletin board." Pp. 904–25 in *Communication Yearbook*, vol 6, edited by F. Bostrom. New Brunswick, NJ: Transaction Books.

———. 1993a. "Automatic narrative generation via statistical content analysis of large-scale textual collections." Presented at Conference on Computing for the Social Sciences, National Center for Supercomputing Applications, May 18–21, University of Illinois at Urbana-Campaign.

———. 1993b. "Network analysis of message content." Pp. 197–221 in *Progress in Communication Science, XII*, edited by W. D. Richards and G. A. Barnett. Norwood, NJ: Ablex.

———. 1993c. "WORDij: A word pair approach to information retrieval." Pp. 131–36 in *Proceedings of the DARPA/NIST TREC Conference*. Washington, DC: National Institute of Standards and Technology.

Davis, G. F. 1991. "Agents without principles? The spread of the poison pill through the inter-corporate network." *Administrative Science Quarterly* 36:583–613.

Debresson, C. and F. Amesse. 1991. "Networks of innovations." *Research Policy* 20:363–80.

Eakin, E. 2003. "Connect, they say, only connect." *New York Times*, January 25.

Fine, C. H. 2001. "Innovation and economic performance in the automobile industry over the long twentieth century." Pp. 1–26 *Innovation and Economic Performance*, edited by R. B. Nelson, B. Steil, and D. Victor. Princeton, NJ: Princeton University Press.

Fredrickson, B. and M. Losada. 2005. "Positive affect and the complex dynamics of human flourishing." *American Psychological Association* 60(7):678–86.

Fulk, J. and E. Steinfield, eds. 1990. *Organizations and Communication Technology*. Newbury Park, CA: Sage.

Geletkanycz, M. A., B. K. Boyd, and S. Finkelstein. 2001. "The strategic value of CEO external directorate networks: Implications for CEO compensation." *Strategic Management Journal* 22(9):889–98.

Gladwell, M. 2000. *The Tipping Point*. New York: Little Brown.

Gloor, P. 2006. *Swarm Creativity: Competitive Advantage through Collaborative Innovation Networks*. New York: Oxford University Press.

Gloor, P. and S. Cooper. 2007. *Cool Hunting: Chasing Down the Next Big Thing*. New York: AMACON.

Gluesing, J. C. 1998. "Building connections and balancing power in global teams: Toward a reconceptualization of culture as composite." *Anthropology of Work Review* 18(2):18–30.

Gluesing, J. C., T. Alcordo, M. L. Baba, D. Britt, K. Harris, W. McKether, L. Monplaisir, H. Ratner, and K. Riopelle. 2003. "The development of global virtual teams." Pp. 353–80 in *Virtual Teams That Work: Creating Conditions for Virtual Team Effectiveness*, edited by C. Gibson and S. G. Cohen. San Francisco: Jossey-Bass.

Gulati, R. and J. D. Westphal. 1999. "Cooperative or controlling? The effects of CEO-board relations and the content of interlocks on the formation of joint ventures." *Administrative Science Quarterly* 44(3):473–506.

Harrisson, D. and M. LaBerge. 2002. "Innovation, identities and resistance: The social construction of an innovation network." *Journal of Management Studies* 39(4):497–521.

Harrison, J. R. and G. R. Carroll. 2002. "The dynamics of cultural influence networks." *Computation & Mathematical Organization Theory* 8:5–30.

Haunschild, P. R. 1993. "Interorganizational imitation: The impact of interlocks on corporate acquisition activity." *Administrative Science Quarterly* 38(4):564–92.

Haythornthwaite, C. and B. Wellman. 1998. "Work, friendship and media use for information exchange in a networked organization." *Journal of the American Society for Information Science* 46(12):1101–14.

Ishida, T., ed. 1998. *Community Computing and Support Systems (Lecture Notes in Computer Science*, 1519). Berlin: Springer-Verlag.

Johnson, S. 2001. *Emergence*. New York: Simon & Schuster.

Meerwarth, T., J. Gluesing, and B. Jordan, eds. 2008. *Mobile Work, Mobile Lives – Cultural Accounts of Lived Experiences*. NAPA Bulletin, 30.

Miles, M. B and A. M. Huberman. 1994. *Qualitative Data Analysis*. 2nd ed. Thousand Oaks, CA: Sage.

Monge, P. R. and N. S. Contractor. 2001. "Emergence of communication networks." Pp. 440–502 in *The New Handbook of Organizational Communication: Advances in Theory, Research, and Methods*, edited by F. M. Jablin and L. L. Putman. Thousand Oaks, CA: Sage.

———. 2003. *Theories of Communication Networks*. Oxford: Oxford University Press.

Mustonen-Ollila, E. and Lyytinen, K. 2003. "Why organizations adopt information system process innovations: A longitudinal study using Diffusion of Innovation theory." *Information Systems Journal* 13(3):275–97.

Newman, M. E. J. 2002. "The structure and function of networks." *Computer Physics Communications* 147:40–45.

Palmer, D. A., P. D. Jennings, and X. Zhou. 1993. "Late adoption of the multidivisional form by large U.S. corporations: Institutional, political, and economic accounts." *Administrative Science Quarterly* 38(1):100–31.

Poole, M. S. and G. DeSanctis. 1990. "Understanding the use of group decision support systems: The theory of adaptive structuration." Pp. 175–95 in *Organizations and Communication Technology*, edited by J. Fulk and E. Steinfield. Newbury Park, CA: Sage.

Powell, W. W., K. W. Koput, and L. Smith-Doerr. 1996. "Interorganizational collaboration and the locus of innovation: Networks of learning in biotechnology." *Administrative Science Quarterly* 41(1):116–45.

Riopelle, K.R., J. G. Gluesing, T. Alcordo, M. L. Baba, D. Britt, W. McKether, L. Monplaisir, H. Ratner, and K. Wagner. 2003. "Context, task, and the evolution of technology use in global virtual teams." Pp. 239–64 in *Virtual Teams That Work: Creating Conditions for Virtual Team Effectiveness*, edited by E. Gibson and S. G. Cohen. San Francisco: Jossey-Bass.

Rogers, E. M. 1983. *Diffusion of Innovations*, 3rd ed. New York: Free Press.

———. 2003. *Diffusion of Innovations*, 5th ed. New York: Free Press.

Rogers, E. M. and D. L. Kincaid. 1981. *Communication Networks: Toward a New Paradigm for Research*. New York: Free Press.

Strogatz, S. 2003. *Sync*. New York: Hyperion.

Torenvlied, R. and G. Velner. 1998. "Informal networks and resistance to organizational change: The introduction of quality standards in a transport company." *Computational & Mathematical Organization Theory* 4(2):165–89.

Utterback, J. M. 1996. *Mastering the Dynamics of Innovation*. Boston: Harvard Business School Press.

Valente, T. W. 1995. *Network Models of the Diffusion of Innovations*. Cresskill, NJ: Hampton.

———. 1996. "Social network thresholds in the diffusion of innovations." *Social Networks* 18:69–89.

———. 2005. "Network models and methods for studying the diffusion of innovations." Pp. 98–116 in *Recent Advances in Network Analysis*, edited by P. J. Carrington, S. Wasserman, and J. Scott. Cambridge: Cambridge University Press.

Watts, D. 1999. *Small Worlds: The Dynamics of Networks between Order and Randomness*. Princeton, NJ: Princeton University Press.

———. 2003. *Six Degrees: The Science of a Connected Age*. New York: W. W. Norton.

Weitzel, T., Wendt, O., Westarp, F., and Koenig, W. 2003. "Network effects and diffusion theory: Network analysis in economics." *International Journal of IT Standards and Standardization Research* 1:1–21

White, D.R. and U.C. Johansen. 2005. *Network Analysis and Ethnographic Problems*. Lanham, MD: Rowman & Littlefield.

Zack, M. H. 2000. "Researching organizational systems using social network analysis." Proceedings of the 33rd Hawaii International Conference on System Sciences, Maui, Hawaii (http://web.cba.neu.edu/~mzack/articles/socnet/socnet.htm).

Part III

*New Methodological Approaches
Used in Mixed Methods Designs*

9

Fuzzy-Set Analysis of Network Data as Mixed Method: Personal Networks and the Transition from School to Work

Betina Hollstein and Claudius Wagemann

Introduction

Entering the labor market marks a decisive juncture in setting the course for a young adult's career and future life. In the face of increasing youth unemployment and rapidly shifting labor markets, the question of the determinants of successful or unsuccessful transitions into gainful employment deserves particular attention. In this chapter, we analyze the conditions that affect these school-to-work transitions. To do so, we focus on the particularly vulnerable group of youth with less education, who face higher risks in this phase of life. We ask under which conditions do these youth, after a failed search for an apprenticeship, actually succeed in finding work? We investigate both individual characteristics (such search behaviors) and the network aspects – functional aspects (cognitive, instrumental, and emotional support of network members), structural aspects (like network size and composition), and attributes of network members, such as occupational status of parents.

The database consists of qualitative longitudinal data collected by the Collaborative Research Center (CRC) 333 "Perspectives on the Development of Work" based at the Ludwig Maximilians University of Munich. We conducted a secondary analysis of these data using fuzzy set analysis, a particular form of Qualitative Comparative Analysis (QCA; Ragin 2000, 2008). In this chapter, we demonstrate how and under what conditions fuzzy set QCA can be employed to conduct research into social networks. We consider QCA a mixed method as it integrates thick descriptions, a common feature of qualitative methods, with data reduction, which is characteristic of quantitative methods. It is especially suited for the analysis of medium-sized samples as it specifically allows us to model both complex solutions and equivalent terms of solutions for combinations of factors. As we will demonstrate, the application

237

of fuzzy set analysis facilitates systematic case comparisons and supports the construction of typologies that strongly build on the individual cases. Methodologically, our study is considered a "conversion design" (Tashakkori and Teddlie 2009), in which qualitative data are transformed into numeric data. The various network aspects are described as individual characteristics and then used to explain individual behavior.

The chapter consists of five parts. After providing a brief overview of the conditions affecting the transition from school to work, we will present the research project "How Networks Matter. Network Resources of Young Adults and Their Transition to the Labor Market": the study's objectives, its specific perspective on social networks, the database, and sample. In the third section, we focus on the analytical method applied – fuzzy set QCA (Ragin 2000, 2008). We then explain how exactly QCA integrates qualitative and quantitative analyses and illustrate in the fourth section the analytic steps taken. Finally, in the fifth section we discuss the benefits of this mixed methods strategy as well as the potential and the current challenges it holds for research into egocentric networks.

Entering the Labor Market: Conditions of Successful or Failed Transition to Working Life

The first entry into the labor market is significant for further employment and for the life course more generally. Factors such as educational achievements and qualifications are important individual-level determinants of career entry (Shavit and Müller 1998). Young adults with low or no educational certificates face especially challenging transitions to work (Solga 2005). Young less-educated women are a particularly disadvantaged group. In Germany, being a woman affects the labor market trajectories even more than does the school form or certificate achieved because of structural conditions, such as limited choice of occupation, and individual characteristics, like lack of self-efficacy (Lex 1997). Career orientations (Heinz et al. 1998), as well as aspects of personality, such as the self-perceived potential for achievement or the willingness to learn (Fend 1991), have been shown to be crucial. In the context of developmental psychology and concepts on the development of identity, an individual's career exploration behavior (Flum and Blustein 2000; Kracke and Schmitt-Rodermund 2001; Kracke 2002) is deemed to be the single most important prerequisite for reaching a fit between one's own aptitudes and those required for the aspired career (Super 1990; Marcia 1993).

Since Mark Granovetter's ([1995] 1974) groundbreaking study "Getting a Job," research has emphasized the significance of social relationships for both job searching and employment practices. When employees are asked how they found their job, typically between one- and two-thirds of the respondents report that they heard about it through personal contacts (Lin and Ao 2008). In general, that proportion is higher among entrants than at later stages of career development (Lin et al. 1981a, 1981b). In case of first-time applicants aspiring for higher positions, the contact person's socio-economic status is even more significant than the candidate's own level of education (Lin et al. 1981a).

Yet, social relationships can smoothen the transition to the workforce in more ways than by supplying information and social contacts that facilitate awareness of and access to available jobs. This may range from financial support to practical advice on writing applications (Steiner 2004). Often, family members provide assistance, information, and orientation regarding career choices (Mortimer et al. 2002; Steiner 2004) or represent important role models (Coleman and Hendry 1990; Hoose and Vorholt 1996). Socialization research indicates that family processes influence the formation of educational and occupational aspirations (Schnabel et al. 2002). The same holds true for the development of related values, such as work motivation (Mortimer and Kumka 1982; Kohn and Schooler 1983) and work attitudes like self-discipline or the willingness to comply with codes of conduct (Fend 1998). Furthermore, trustful relationships can act as a buffer against stress by supporting coping at both the emotional and cognitive levels as well as in terms of bolstering one's self-image (Pfaff 1989).

On the other hand, personal relationships can also be an impediment, as difficult family situations, like parental unemployment, separation, or addiction problems, are frequently found among young adults experiencing problems in securing their first job (cf. Kraheck 2004; Solga 2005). These situations can put considerable strain on the children, thereby adversely affecting their motivation and performance. Missing or negative role models are a further negative factor (Wilson 1997). Insufficient information on the system of vocational education and training or a general lack of orientation regarding possible fields of occupation also seems to be a common problem among young people who fail to gain a foothold in the labor market (Kraheck 2004).

Another question hardly addressed is how relationships with family, friends, and acquaintances work together at the point of career entry. What role does the social network of family, friends, and acquaintances play for the transition from school to work? In this respect, we have to state that most studies investigate individual relationships (e.g., among family members or peers) instead of the network as a whole. Or attention is directed to the network's specific contributions, like providing job-relevant information or assistance in making career choices. In focusing on the totality of an individual's relationships, the present chapter adopts a broader perspective on networks. We thus explore social networks in terms of their significance for a successful start into the world of work. This perspective enables us to determine which network members matter and what kinds of network support matters. Furthermore, the explanatory value of structural network features, such as size, heterogeneity, or the stability of membership composition, can be examined. In particular, we shed light on the relationship between network aspects and individual-level determinants (like a person's exploratory behavior).

We investigate these issues in the case of young adults with low levels of educational attainment who initially failed to secure an apprenticeship. Bearing this particularly unfortunate combination in mind, we ask for the conditions under which successful integration into the labor market might still be achieved. What combinations of network aspects and individual characteristics lead to success against the odds?

Mixed Methods Data Collection and Sampling

The analyses reported were carried out in the research project "How Networks Matter. Network Resources of Young Adults and Their Transition to the Labor Market."[1] The project provides rate longitudinal tracking of social networks and their effects during the transition to working life and seeks to analyze the conditions under which these networks are effective. We conducted a secondary analysis of data initially collected within the Munich Collaborative Research Center (CRC)[2] "Perspectives on the Development of Work." In the CRC's project module A6, "Young Adults' Career Trajectories, Social Networks, and Identity Development" (Keupp et al. 2008), a total of 88 teenagers and young adults from southern Germany (45 men and 43 women) participated in three rounds of data collection: interviews about their career entry experiences and their social networks. The respondents were between

---

[1]　The research project "How Networks Matter. Network Resources of Young Adults and Their Transition to the Labor Market" has been funded by the German Research Foundation (DFG; project code HO 2120/4–1; funding period 2007–2010; principal investigator: Betina Hollstein). The study has four objectives: (a) to take stock of network effect at the time of career entry; (b) to identify the explanatory contribution of formal network structures (e.g., network size and composition, stability of alteri) for understanding network effects; (c) to investigate the young adults' own contributions in terms of activating network resources and making use of available network potentials; and (d) to identify influences and interdependencies, compensatory effects, or cumulative processes based on the prospective longitudinal data.

[2]　Collaborative Research Centers (Sonderforschungsbereiche – SFB) are research programs funded by the German Research Foundation (DFG) for up to 12 years with the purpose of creating core research areas at universities by establishing long-term research collaborations.

17 and 19 years old at the time of the initial interview scheduled at the very beginning of their vocational education and training.[3] The second wave was conducted at the end of the training period and a final wave took place two years later.

Sample

The study's sample included two groups that are similar in that both have rather low levels of formal qualification yet differ in terms of their respective employment histories and prospects. While one group underwent a smooth transition to the system of vocational education (selection criterion: apprenticeship in local government) and has fairly good chances of gaining standard employment, the young adults in the other group experienced relatively bad starts. Our analysis will focus on the second group, whose attempts to gain a foothold in the world of work failed. At the time of the initial interview, they were registered as unemployed and took part in special youth employment assistance programs (and were contacted via these programs to participate in this study). Due to their problematic previous employment career, these young adults constitute a typical "at-risk" group for discontinuous employment histories (Keupp et al. 2008).

Data

In a multistage data-collection process, the aforementioned research group A6 combined qualitative biographical interviews with more standardized instruments:

(1) Guided, open-ended interviews. The interview schedule revolved around the topics "work/employment history" (crucial stages of schooling, the search for a training opportunity, the current employment situation, and plans for the future), "leisure time/ friends" (leisure activities, significance of friends and acquaintances), and "family" (current residential situation and detachment from the parental home). Further questions regarding the respondents' network and social resources as well as their self-image and plans for the future were included. The network

---

[3] Germany's dual apprenticeship system, a significant sector providing vocational education and training, is unusual in combining both schooling in vocational schools and work in firms, which provides standardized and comprehensive vocational competence that often provides smooth transitions to employment often in the firm that provided the apprenticeship. This contrasts with the emphasis on general education and on-the-job training characteristic of the United States and the school-based vocational education offered in France.

chart (see 3a in this list) was presented whenever issues were raised concerning network-related aspects of their lives.

(2) Sociographic questionnaire. This questionnaire was used to gather sociographic details comprising personal data, such as the respondents' age, marital status, and the number of siblings, as well as basic career-related information, like work history and current employment, school education and qualifications, and the parents' occupations. During the second and third rounds of data collection, the respondents were also asked about changes compared to the respective previous round.

(3) Network generators. Furthermore, four different types of network generators were included (Keupp et al. 2008):

(a) Network chart: Extensive network data were captured during all three rounds of data collection. The Munich research group designed the network chart EGONET.QF especially for that purpose (Straus 1994, 2004; Keupp et al. 2008).[4] When employing this instrument, the respondents are shown a chart depicting six concentric circles and asked to mark sectors that they view as relevant to their lives (e.g., family, friends, and work). The significance of individual sectors in relation to one another is indicated by their size, similar to a pie chart. Whenever a particular area of life is touched upon during the interview, the interviewer will also ask for initials of persons important to the interviewee and insert them into the chart of concentric circles. First of all, the chart provides an instrument for the systematic inquiry about network members, but it also acts as a kind of stimulus to generate further narrations. Moreover, the visual representation[5] will help both the interviewer and the interviewee in referring to the various relationships and ensures that the former can "keep an eye" on all network relationships when asking about particular instances of social support.

(b) Characteristics of the alteri (network members): Additional data were collected with regard to the individual network members, for instance, on the duration of the respective relationships. Information on the employment and occupational status of parents, friends, or peers was also collected.

---

[4] The *network chart* EGONET.QF (developed by Straus 1995) is not to be confused with the *network data processing software* Egonet.QF (developed by Pfeffer/Straus/Hollstein 2008).

[5] For a comparative review of different types of network charts and diagrams, see Hollstein and Pfeffer (2010). Cf. also Molina et al. (this volume) on the use of visualizations in network studies.

(c) During all interviews, the respondents were repeatedly asked about the social support they had received from members of their network (e.g., "You just told me how it was when you quit vocational training. Back then, who was important to you, who supported you? Please indicate those persons (on the network chart) and tell me in what ways they supported you"). The interviewers explicitly wanted to know about the network resources as perceived by the respondents themselves and what their help-seeking behavior had looked like. Both issues were addressed with respect to three selected problems in a Life Event Questionnaire (a practical problem of life, a psychosocial problem, and one associated with unemployment or job search).[6]

(d) Changes in the network: During the second and third waves, the current network chart was compared with the former network(s). Particularly interesting were changes regarding the existence and relevance of individual relationships: What happened to the relationships that are no longer mentioned? Why and how did some persons become more (or less) important, and how did new relationships emerge? What are the underlying reasons for changes in the proximity or distance to ego?

Data Processing

The data gathered by the Munich research group were made available to the current GRF-project "How Networks Matter." Altogether, this material comprised approximately 12,500 pages of text (interview transcripts, LEQs, and field notes) and a total of 264 network charts.

In order to process, analyze, and file the network charts, we developed a tailor-made software, Egonet.QF (Pfeffer, Straus, and Hollstein 2008). The software enables a quick, systematic overview of attributes of the alteri and it significantly simplifies the description and analysis of network structures, like network size, its composition in terms of role relationships, eventual changes in network composition, as well as the stability of the alteri across the three waves of data collection. Moreover, it can be applied in combination with other commonly used software in the field of social network analysis (e.g., Pajek, UCINET).

---

[6] The Life Event Questionnaires listed a number of possible life events from different areas, such as work, friends and leisure time, health, residential, and economic situation. Based on this list, the respondents were asked if those events had occurred – and mattered – in their lives. Some of the items particularly referred to network relationships (e.g., "I quarreled a lot with my fellow workers"; "I found a new friend"; "I often felt lonely"; "There was no one to help me").

In order to handle the interview data, we identified a preliminary set of categories based on our own research questions and a coding scheme developed for the current project. For coding the data, we then used the software package Atlas/ti. The coding enabled us to scan the extensive body of text for individual aspects (e.g., all network members mentioned or different instances of support) while facilitating the organization and administration of the data. Coding is an essential step, as comprehensive interview and case memos are created during this process. These memos capture key details, such as biographical data, important aspects of the relationships to members of the network, and the support provided by network members (in general and with respect to career entry). Further items are individual action orientations and patterns of action that are reflected in the general conduct of life. The researchers' preliminary interpretations were also documented. Together with the coded interviews and the network charts, the memos provide the basis for our further analysis with fuzzy-set QCA.

Methodical Contribution of QCA

Why QCA?

Methodically, we have opted for Qualitative Comparative Analysis (QCA). This method has been well known since the 1980s, when the American social scientist Charles C. Ragin (1987) presented a systematic mode of comparative analysis building on the use of truth tables and Boolean algebra – instruments that had, implicitly or explicitly, been used in previous comparative research (Caramani 2008). The core aim of QCA is to detect what conditions or combinations thereof can count as necessary or sufficient for given outcomes. Over the years, these causal relationships have been removed from the context of Boolean algebra in which they were initially embedded and have been re-interpreted in set-theoretic terms. In this view, causal relationships of necessity and sufficiency are now interpreted as relationships between sets.

Many hypotheses formulated in the social sciences can be considered as set-theoretic in this particular sense. In an empirical survey, Gary Goertz explicitly lists 150 hypotheses about necessary conditions in the field of international relations alone (Goertz 2003); hypotheses about sufficient conditions are similarly widespread in the social sciences (Ragin 2000). Put simply, set-theoretic hypotheses work with "if–then" hypotheses that can be distinguished from the "the more, the more" version of standard statistical analyses. This leads to some interesting differences. Let us assume that having been convicted for a crime is a sufficient condition for subsequent problems in entering the labor market. This would mean that – in order to verify our hypothesis – we should not be able to find a single person convicted of a crime who did not face difficulties in entering the labor market. However, this hypothesis does not make any assumptions about persons who have never been convicted: They may or may not have problems in entering the labor market. In contrast, a standard statistical approach would assume that if persons with a criminal backgrounds have difficulties in finding employment, those without such a background will not. Persons without a criminal background who nevertheless have problems finding a job falsify the statistical hypothesis but not the set-theoretic one since the latter only makes assumptions with respect to the presence of a criminal career but not with regard to its absence.

This particular characteristic of set-theoretic hypotheses is called "asymmetric causation" (as opposed to "symmetric causation" in standard quantitative analysis). Other specific features of causation in set-theoretic methods, such as QCA, are equifinal and conjunctural causation. Equifinal causation says that conditions are sometimes alternatives to one another. For instance, one can imagine that there is more than one way of entering the labor market so that it is possible to compensate for factors that promise some success. This approach is different from most (though not all) quantitative techniques, such as OLS regression, where effects are added (unifinal causation). Conjunctural causation refers to the fact that, sometimes, causes exert effects not in an isolated manner but in concert with other causes.

Summing this up, QCA's specific features relate to the fact that the specific causality it employs can be used for detecting asymmetric, equifinal, and conjunctural causal processes. Its focus is on sufficient and necessary conditions. Based on the algorithm used, it is also possible to determine so-called INUS and SUIN conditions, which can easily count as very sophisticated forms of causation. INUS stands for a condition that is an "insufficient but necessary part of a condition which is itself unnecessary but sufficient for the result" (Mackie 1974:62). For instance, in the formula $A * B + C * D \rightarrow Y,$[7] all four conditions A, B, C, and D are INUS conditions. Neither of them is a sufficient condition, but all of them are parts of (composed) conditions that are themselves not necessary but sufficient conditions for Y. By contrast, SUIN stands for a "sufficient but unnecessary part of a factor that is insufficient but necessary for the result" (Mahoney, Kimball, and Koivu 2009). The formula $(A + B) * (C + D) \leftarrow Y$[8] depicts such SUIN conditions. The Boolean

---

[7] This formula has to be read in the following way: the asterisk (*) indicates a Boolean multiplication and stands for a logical AND. The plus sign (+) indicates a Boolean addition and stands for a logical OR. The arrow ($\rightarrow$) denotes a sufficient condition. Thus, the formula says that there are two alternative paths (A * B and C * D) that logically imply Y, both of which are composed of two conditions (A and B in the case of the first alternative, C and D in the case of the second one).

[8] The arrow in the inverse direction ($\leftarrow$) indicates a necessity relation.

multiplication indicates that both factors (the factor A + B and the factor C + D) are necessary for Y – but both of these factors offer alternatives. Neither A nor B is necessary, but it is necessary that at least one of the two is present. SUIN conditions can be best called mutually alternative necessary conditions.

It goes without saying that the treatment of sufficient, necessary, INUS, and SUIN conditions is nothing new for comparative social science. However, QCA's merits include that it renders them explicit, standardizes them, and offers a powerful analytical instrument that can be applied to more than just a few cases.

QCA has often also been referred to as an appropriate technique to deal with so-called "mid-sized n," that is to say, data sets that do not reach the number of cases needed for statistical analysis yet still go beyond the often performed comparative analyses based on two, four, or, more rarely, eight cases. It is, of course, true that QCA can theoretically be applied to all data situations – although the results might be less interesting if only a small number of cases is analyzed. Nevertheless, QCA indeed works best with a medium-sized sample. However, this should not be the reason for preferring QCA to any other method in a given analysis; rather, the decision in favor of QCA should be motivated by a set-theoretic orientation; an emphasis on asymmetric, equifinal, and conjunctural causation; and an interest in necessary, sufficient, INUS, and SUIN conditions. Having said this, it is a positive side effect that mid-sized data sets can easily be analyzed with QCA. This is of special interest for comparative social research.

Since its first introduction, QCA has been continuously refined. A major step was taken by overcoming the need to formulate conditions and outcome as dichotomies (that is, a condition or outcome can only be present or absent) when so-called fuzzy sets were introduced (Ragin 2000). Since then, analysts differentiate between crisp-set QCA (csQCA), where the conditions and the outcome are dichotomous, and fuzzy-set QCA (fsQCA), where the conditions and the outcome can be graded in order to indicate the degree to which a condition or an outcome is present. Thus, we can go beyond solely defining either successful or unsuccessful career entries, but rather are now also able to consider partial successes and partial failures. Further developments include the introduction of parameters of fit and a standardized algorithm for the analysis of necessary and sufficient conditions (Ragin 2008). It can be said that, by now, QCA belongs to the standard repertoire of social science techniques.[9]

---

[9] Apart from Ragin's own seminal contributions (Ragin 1987, 2000, 2008, for many others), textbooks exist in which the technique is explained, e.g., Schneider and Wagemann (2012).

QCA as a Mixed Method

QCA is considered both a research design and an analytical method (Wagemann and Schneider 2010:378). The latter refers to the algorithm that has continuously been improved and integrated over the years. However, QCA is also a research design that extends beyond the "analytic moment" as such: The choice in favor of QCA determines both the preparation and the interpretation of the analytic moment.

In the Introduction to this volume, QCA has been presented as an advanced method for integrating quantitative and qualitative thinking. It can count as a mixed method in itself. Since the acronym stands for Qualitative Comparative Analysis, calling QCA a mixed method may seem counterintuitive. However, the reality is more complex. First of all, clearly defining "qualitative" and "quantitative" is no easy task. The definition employed in this volume (see the Introduction by Hollstein, this volume) is our own understanding of these terms. Definitions vary between disciplines and national research contexts, even among university departments. Ironically, the subtitle of the book in which Ragin (1987) initially launched QCA was "Moving Beyond Qualitative and Quantitative Strategies." This rather suggests that neither alternative would fit in the case of QCA; QCA would be a "third way."

The perspectives on QCA have changed over the years. Today, QCA is understood as a qualitative method, although not all advocates of more interpretive qualitative methods will readily agree. The introduction of (non-dichotomous) fuzzy sets and, later on, parameters of fit, such as consistency and coverage, not only creates a terminological proximity to standard statistical techniques but has also made the standardized mathematical algorithm so complex that it raises some doubts as to the clear identification of QCA as a qualitative method. However, it is only fair to admit that neither the name nor the label "QCA" were specifically mentioned in Ragin's 1987 book. Both emerged only after the initial publication. Ragin himself now seems to prefer the term "case-oriented" (Ragin 2000:23),[10] although he also explicitly states in the same volume that QCA belongs to the methodological tradition of qualitative research (Ragin 2000:13). The term "diversity-oriented" is also used (Ragin 2000:19).

To emphasize QCA's integrative nature with regard to qualitative and quantitative approaches, we now give some examples to provide some insight into how QCA works.

---

[10] With this, Ragin refers to the terminology of variable-oriented versus case-oriented approaches, which is often seen as an alternative dichotomy to the usual distinction between quantitative and qualitative approaches (Ragin and Zaret 1983; Ragin 2004; Della Porta 2008; for a critique see Bartolini 1993:173, fn. 9).

Looking at QCA results would suggest that QCA is in fact a quantitative method. First of all, QCA results usually comprise a vast amount of numbers, logical operators, and solution formulas. The graphical forms of representation are also very similar to what is known from statistical analysis (Schneider and Grofman 2006). This correspondence is not surprising since QCA is a highly systematic and standardized approach in which numbers, graphs, and logical operators typically serve to reduce complexity and thereby contribute to a better understanding of the patterns under analysis. Second, the QCA algorithm is highly standardized. Once the values of the conditions and the outcome are determined and important parameters are set, the process automatically follows the logic of set-theoretic analysis. The final results of QCA analyses can also be subsumed in comparatively short overviews, pointing to a quite rigid frame of sufficient, necessary, INUS, and SUIN conditions. Third, current evaluation parameters for QCA results bear much similarity to the proceedings in quantitative analysis. Coverage and consistency calculations (Schneider and Wagemann 2007; Ragin 2008) have become ever more crucial for QCA. Finally, the sheer need to transform concepts into values of 0 and 1 (as in csQCA) or into values between 0 and 1 (as in fsQCA) is a similarity between QCA and standard statistical approaches.

Yet, there are as many good arguments for underlining the qualitative aspects of QCA: First, single cases play an important role in QCA as the conditions to be analyzed are derived from a careful preliminary case-by-case examination. It is obvious that this inductive step of analysis is largely based on interpretive methods like Grounded Theory (Glaser and Strauss 1967). Like many qualitative approaches, QCA takes a holistic perspective on cases. The cases are then broken down according to their properties and subsumed under configurations of properties. In fsQCA, this leads to an analysis of ideal types where only marginally different cases are analytically grouped together with other cases belonging to the same ideal type. The single-case perspective also plays a role after the "analytic moment," that is, when the equifinal solution paths have to be linked back to single cases (Schneider and Wagemann 2010:410f.). Second, although there are some semi-automatic features in assigning fuzzy values to single cases, there cannot be any doubt that the theory-guided and case-oriented mode of calibration will always remain dominant. "In the hands of a social scientist [...], a fuzzy set can be seen as a fine-grained, continuous measure that has been carefully calibrated using substantive and theoretical knowledge" (Ragin 2000:7). In-depth case knowledge is an essential prerequisite for any meaningful fuzzy-set analysis (Hall 2003:389) – which holds true for qualitative analysis in general (Mahoney 2000:398). Furthermore, not all variations of a quantitative variable are necessarily considered meaningful for fsQCA analysis. Ragin calls this the difference between relevant and irrelevant variation (Ragin 2008: 83). Third, although QCA involves "algebra," Boolean algebra is not the kind of algebra where objects are counted or weighed. Rather than adding up and multiplying figures, Boolean algebra limits itself to the observation of whether a phenomenon exists or not. In other words, Boolean algebra places a greater emphasis on the *qualis* (Latin for "how is it?") of a phenomenon than on its *quantum* (Latin for "how much is it?"). Furthermore, QCA invites the researcher to continuously move back and forth between ideas and evidence (Ragin 1994:76; Ragin 2004:126). This means, "[using] theory to make sense of evidence and [...] evidence to sharpen and refine theory" (Ragin 1991:225). It should be pointed out that this does not have anything to do with data manipulation. Quite the contrary, it is a process of acknowledging evidence and using this evidence to reformulate the previous hypotheses, which could be referred to as "learning" in the most positive sense. Such a procedure – although recommended for all types of research – is more typical for qualitative than for quantitative research since the design of quantitative research projects (i.e., the data-collection phase) often does not allow a later review of the data from a different angle. And last but not least, the predominantly qualitative character of QCA is underlined by its very specific perspective on causality in considering equifinal, conjunctural, and asymmetric causation, in other terms on principles that can be seen as characteristics of qualitatively oriented case studies. On a continuum between qualitative case precision and quantitative simplification for generalization purposes, QCA can certainly be located somewhere between the extremes – but probably closer to the qualitative interest in adequately modeling complex causal processes.

In short, QCA can be considered a "mixed method" itself. In contrast to other mixed methods designs, it not only combines several methodological approaches but also borrows principles from various methods in order to arrange them into a new methodological strategy. As such, QCA is an integrated mixed method. Nevertheless, quantitative and qualitative features can still be traced. The quantitative features are, above all, related to the systematic way in which QCA operates whereas the qualitative features mainly consist of explicit case orientation and dealing with causal complexity. Although QCA definitely is a mixed method, the "qualitative side" is obviously dominant.

How Networks Matter. Applying Fuzzy-Set Analyses

Based on our research project on the significance of personal networks for young adults' career entry, we now illustrate the core steps in constructing the fuzzy values and conducting the fuzzy-set analyses. Quantitative and qualitative aspects are strongly linked at these stages of the research process.

Selecting the Conditions and Constructing the Fuzzy Values

As mentioned earlier, the calibration of fuzzy values requires in-depth knowledge of both the cases and the concepts to be used in the analysis. However, case knowledge is already important in determining what to analyze: Conditions can only be derived from a clear qualitative analysis of given cases, coupled with insight from the existing scholarly literature. In our project, the theoretical perspective was geared toward including (structural and functional) network aspects as well as the individuals' characteristics (orientations and behavioral aspects).

In investigating what a successful career entry depends upon, we distinguish two sets of conditions (cf. Table 9.1):

(i)   In terms of individual-level conditions, particular aspects of behavior and orientations of the respondents are taken into account. We consider career exploration behavior and distinct occupational aspirations, and ask whether or not a physical or mental impairment is given. The incidence of such impairments is an example of a condition the significance of which became apparent only in the course of the single-case analyses.

(ii) The network conditions refer to network-based resources or restrictions. On the level of functional network aspects, we differentiate between instrumental support (e.g., career-related advice, information, or contacts), cognitive support (e.g., motivation, appreciation, and acknowledgement related to career entry), and emotional support (cf. Diewald 1991; Hollstein 2001), and the opposite phenomenon of active obstruction. We furthermore consider measures of network structure, like size, composition, and stability, as well as the existence of particular network members, such as one's own children. Finally, we include characteristics of specific network members and sectors, like the parents' occupational status as well as potentially problematic situations in the family of origin (e.g., poverty, addiction problems, violence, abuse, etc.).

The selection criteria for the sample serve as control criteria in the analyses: whether the respondent was in vocational training at the time of the initial interview (yes/no); sex (male/female); geographical region (rural/urban background); and a low level of educational attainment. The next steps comprise the specification of the conditions and the construction and calibration of the fuzzy values. Both are based on in-depth knowledge of the single cases. The first steps of quantitative analysis will then typically lead to a redefinition of the conditions and the calibration of the fuzzy values. To give an example, in our initial calculations in which

Table 9.1. *Conditions – Overview*

I. Network resources and restrictions	II. Individual action/orientation
a. Network: Functional aspects – Cognitive/instrumental support provided by the network, directly related to the school-to-work transition (-t3) – Emotional support provided by the network (different network sectors; -t3) – Active obstruction (regarding the school-to-work-transition; -t3) *b. Network: Structural aspects* – Network size, heterogenity, stability (t1, t2, t3; Δt1-t3) – Children yes/no (-t3) *c. Characteristics of specific network members/ sectors* – Parents' occupational status (-t1) – Mother's employment status (-t1) – Family of origin: problematic constellation (-t1)	Exploratory behavior (t1-t3) Occupational aspiration (-t3) Impairment (physical, mental) (-t3)

all 88 respondents were still included, we investigated the outcome "successful transition to employment" (i.e., the successful completion of in-company vocational training and qualification-related employment at the time of the third wave of data collection). It became obvious, however, that only very few of the young adults who had initially failed to secure a training place or apprenticeship actually met both criteria: of having completed in-company training and holding a primary labor market job at the time of the third wave. Apparently, the two groups are so different ("two worlds") that different sets of conditions apply. We therefore split the analyses and will from now on focus those 35 young people who had not succeeded in finding an apprenticeship soon after graduating from upper secondary education. For this particular subsample, we now investigate a modified outcome: It is considered as "success" if a job on the primary labor market has been found within four years after the initial interview (irrespective of having completed vocational training[11]).

The construction and calibration of the conditions require the utmost effort and are part of the analysis. As we will illustrate in the case of the different network conditions, both specifying the conditions and constructing the fuzzy values can happen in a more "qualitative" or a more "quantitative" manner. The former applies, for instance, to dealing with functional network aspects (social support) whereas the handling of structural network parameters (like network size) is an example of the latter.

[11] This applies to 17 out of 35 respondents.

Functional Network Aspects. One of the conditions we use to describe functional aspects of the social network is the "perceived cognitive and instrumental support directly related to the school-to-work transition." Cases perfectly match this condition and are thus assigned the fuzzy value 1 if the following criteria are fully met: In situations perceived as playing a crucial role for career entry (e.g., finding or keeping a job), the respondents report to have received cognitive and instrumental support from more than one network sector (e.g., not only from family members but also from friends or colleagues). Fuzzy value 0.7 is assigned to cases in which the respondents are supported in situations of similarly key significance, but the support is partial in that it comes from one network sector only or is only of an instrumental type. For cases in which network support is only provided in situations less crucial to career entry or only in a sporadic or occasional manner, we assign fuzzy value 0.3, whereas the value 0 remains for cases with no employment-related support being volunteered by the social network so that the only assistance received is of the mandatory kind provided by public agencies.

A case perfectly exemplifying fuzzy value 1 is Pit, a young man from Munich. Pit expresses the feeling of being able to fully rely on his network whenever he needs it. He refers to the example of his mother who had "permanently" been there for him during his successful drug rehabilitation. His mother as well as his brother always stood by him and "believed in him." He also mentions a former colleague from his first (aborted) apprenticeship who helped him by arranging for vocational re-training in a kindergarten. There, everybody was very supportive and approving of him. Pit explains that the received support from colleagues, parents, and children was the main reason for him to complete vocational training this time. In this respect, he also mentions his friends, some social workers, and in particular his superior at the kindergarten who not only made his favorable opinion of Pit explicit but went so far as to accompany him on visits to public agencies in order to apply for the re-training, which was granted.

We are thus dealing with a complex, multidimensional condition. The attribution of fuzzy values is not automatic, as they are assigned in a qualitative manner by considering the case as a whole. In our example, we would have to identify whether or not the concept of "perceived instrumental and cognitive support directly related to the school-to-work transition" applies to a specific case – and to which extent the parameters are met. If new aspects arise from the single-case analysis, the conditions might be readjusted, followed by either a new calibration of the fuzzy values or a regrouping of the cases. Thus, for functional network aspects, a so-called "quantitizing strategy" (Teddlie and Tashakkori 2006; Tashakkori and Teddlie 2009) was applied, in which qualitative data (interview data) are transformed into numerical data (fuzzy values) in a conversion design (Teddlie and Tashakkori 2006; Tashakkori and Teddlie 2009).

Structural Network Aspects. In contrast, the fuzzy values for the condition network size – as a structural network feature – were constructed in a rather "mechanical" way. We only differentiated between large and small networks. With respect to the condition "large network," fuzzy value 1 was assigned to all cases that lie at least half a standard deviation above the mean network size (with the reference value being determined based on the subsample of 35 cases) whereas 0 was assigned to all remaining cases, representing the "absence of a large network." The same strategy was pursued for the condition "small network" as well as for the conditions "network heterogeneity" (with the reference value being the number of network sectors) and "stability of network members."

Characteristics of Specific Network Members/Sectors. In the third group of network conditions, a variety of strategies were applied. For example, mother's employment status was dichotomously differentiated in "mother employed at t1"or "not employed." But in terms of "Family of origin: problematic constellation," the fuzzy values are, as with the functional network aspects, the result of an in-depth qualitative reconstruction of individual cases.

In this design, functional and structural network aspects are transformed into fuzzy values. Thus, network aspects are converted into individual characteristics and can then be integrated into the QCA analysis to explain individual behavior, such as the successful or failed transition to work.

Different Analyses of "Outcome" and "No Outcome"

In this section, we demonstrate the application of the "analytic moment" in QCA, that is, the phase in which the fuzzy-set data are analyzed.[12] As mentioned earlier, QCA is usually understood as both a research design and an analytical technique (Wagemann and Schneider 2010:378). QCA has so far mainly been presented as a research design whereas we now focus on it as a technique. Following standard

---

[12] These examples primarily serve to demonstrate the application of QCA. For a comprehensive and detailed presentation of the analyses and a discussion of the results, see Hollstein and Töpfer (2013).

Table 9.2. *Employment in the labor market:*
Analysis of necessary conditions (men)

Condition	Consistency	Coverage (Triviality)
~impairment	0.95	0.82
~nw_size	0.91	0.75
nw_support	0.89	0.84

procedures (Schneider and Wagemann 2007:112ff., Schneider and Wagemann 2010:404f.), we will carry out different analyses for necessary and sufficient conditions.

To begin with the necessary conditions, based on theory and evidence from the first qualitative analysis, we assume that the men and women in our sample follow different causal logics. The decision is, therefore, to carry out two separate analyses for men and women. An alternative would have been to include sex as a formal condition. However, this would have entailed the disadvantage of being forced to use the same set of conditions for both sexes. Instead, the separate analyses for men and women enable us to analyze different sets of conditions for either sex.

We now present the result of the analysis of necessary conditions for the men's group (cf. Table 9.2). We only report those conditions showing acceptably high consistency[13] values (for the benchmarks, see Schneider and Wagemann 2010:406). If we consider 0.9 to be a good consistency level in the analysis of necessary conditions, we can conclude that the absence of physical or mental impairment is a necessary condition to gain a foothold in the primary labor market (consistency of 0.95). We could assume that impairments are not really a problem for the group under analysis; in that case, the "absence of impairment" would be a trivially necessary condition. However, the coverage value[14] shows an acceptably

[13] In brief, consistency values evaluate to what extent the conclusion as to whether a given condition (or combination thereof) is necessary or sufficient is really based on empirical data. It varies between 0 and 1. If it is 1, then the conclusion about the necessity or sufficiency of the condition under analysis is deterministic: No single item of the data set will partially or fully disconfirm the finding.

[14] Coverage varies, as consistency, between 0 and 1 and entails slightly different interpretations in the analysis of necessary and sufficient conditions: When dealing with sufficient conditions, the coverage value shows what share of the outcome can be explained and therefore corresponds best to the explained variance in quantitative designs. In case of necessary conditions, it indicates whether the necessary condition is trivial. A trivially necessary condition would, for instance, be that one needs to be born in order to find a job. While this is certainly true, it is also most trivial since to be born is a necessary condition for experiencing any social phenomenon, not only for finding a job. The word "coverage" is chosen, since the set of the condition exceeds that of the outcome by far.

high value, so that the absence of impairment is a truly necessary condition for the young men's access to the primary labor market. Similarly good values can be achieved for the condition "absence of a large network." While the consistency value is excellent, caution is recommended regarding the question of triviality. Although 0.75 is still acceptable, the absence of a large network seems to be rather widespread among our sample.

With a consistency level ranging slightly below 0.9, the aforementioned career-related support provided by the network only narrowly fails to satisfy the criterion for qualifying as a necessary condition. In spite of this minor deviation, one might still consider calling it a necessary condition, cautiously. [15]

For determining the sufficient conditions, we opted for a model including the conditions of impairment and career-related exploratory behavior, plus two conditions derived from our core research interest in the functions and characteristics of networks: the network's support in career entry and the maternal employment status (employed/unemployed) (cf. Table 9.3). We did not include "network size" in our model since further analyses indicated that its effect on successfully entering the labor market seems to be rather indirect in the sense that the network's size is a condition for support being provided.[16]

Two explanatory paths emerge that include both the absence of impairment and the existence of a career-supportive network. This is not surprising since these two conditions also qualified as "necessary" (or close to necessary) in the previous analysis of necessary conditions. However, a third condition has to be added to these two necessary conditions: This can either be a pronounced career exploration behavior or maternal employment status.[17] Indeed, when testing whether these two conditions can count as "functional equivalents,"[18] the result is positive: The consistency value of the necessary condition (exploratory behavior + mother_status) is

[15] Although no source gives a definite figure, it is generally understood that 0.9 and higher values are acceptable consistency levels for necessary conditions. Since too much rigor in applying these parameters is not helpful, consistency levels of 0.89 should not be discarded too easily.

[16] For a detailed explanation and description of this model, the calibration of the related fuzzy values, and a complete analysis, see Hollstein and Töpfer (2013).

[17] Interestingly, neither one of these two conditions qualifies as a necessary condition (even less as a sufficient condition), yet they satisfy the criteria for being both an INUS and a SUIN condition. This means that, although being neither necessary nor sufficient, these two conditions have important functions in the solution.

[18] This is a rather unknown module of QCA. "Functional equivalents" are those conditions that can be substituted for one another as necessary conditions for an outcome. In other words, it is necessary that one of them is present irrespective of the others (Schneider and Wagemann 2007:59f.). However, if too many conditions are considered functionally equivalent to one another, this tool loses its power, as it is obvious that at least one of the conditions has to be present if the particular outcome is observed.

Table 9.3. *Employment in the labor market: Analysis of sufficient conditions (men)*[19]

Model: impairment, exploratory behavior (expl), network_support, employment status_mother

	Raw cov	Unique cov	Consist
~impairment * nw_support * exploratory behavior	0.68	0.32	0.91
~impairment * nw_support * mother_status	0.52	0.15	0.97
Coverage: 0.84			
Consistency: 0.91			

Remainders: Conservative Solution, also Intermediate Solution.

0.96. Its coverage – the indication of whether this is a trivially necessary condition – is a bit lower (0.77).[20]

The parameters of fit for both the single paths and the total solution are more than satisfying. We can explain a major part of the outcome (coverage of 0.84), and our result is highly consistent with the empirical data (consistency of 0.91). The values of both parameters indicate an analysis well done (Schneider and Wagemann 2010:406, 414). In addition, the consistency values of the two paths are very high (both > 0.9), and the values for the raw and unique coverages reveal some overlap between the two paths, which is not surprising since they both comprise no less than two necessary conditions. Nevertheless, unique coverages of 0.32 and 0.15 show that both paths still explain parts of the outcome that cannot be explained otherwise.

We thus conclude that receiving instrumental as well as cognitive support from one's personal network is both a necessary condition and part of a sufficient set of conditions for successful career entry. Furthermore, the absence of pronounced career exploration behavior can evidently be compensated by another network feature, namely, the presence of a "working mom." For those three cases represented by this constellation, qualitative case reconstruction shows that the employed mothers exhibit very strong orientation to work. Even though the mother–son relationships in our sample are not universally har-

---

[19] The raw coverage indicates how much of the outcome the single path explains. Unique coverage indicates how much of the outcome is explained by that path, *which is not yet explained by the other paths.*

[20] The coverage value of functional equivalents is usually not too high since the statement about necessity becomes ever more trivial if many conditions are considered functionally equivalent to one another. Therefore, this lower coverage value does not raise any concern.

Table 9.4. *Truth table for men*

~ impairment	network_ support	exploratory behavior	mother_ employ- ment_ status	N	consistency
1	1	1	1	5	1.0
1	1	0	1	3	0.92
1	1	1	0	4	0.83
1	0	0	1	1	0.51
0	1	0	0	1	0.44
0	0	0	1	1	0.20
0	0	0	0	2	0.19

monious, the mothers still support, motivate, and monitor their sons (Hollstein and Töpfer 2013).

QCA experts may know that different formulas can result for the analysis of sufficient conditions depending on how the researcher chose to deal with the so-called logical remainders – those combinations of conditions that are not covered by empirically observable cases. A short look at the truth table of our analysis of sufficient conditions for the subsample of young men illustrates this (cf. Table 9.4).

If four conditions are used in an analysis, set-theoretic logic offers us $16 \ (= 2^4)$ combinations of conditions. However, we see that the young men under analysis can be grouped into only seven types. The theoretically possible nine other types simply do not exist. This goes back to the fact that the design is not experimental. The sample simply does not include any of the other theoretically possible constellations.[21] There are, for instance, no men in our data set who satisfy all of the following conditions at once: not being impaired (~impairment = 1), not receiving any career-relevant network support (network_support = 0), not showing any form of exploratory behavior (exploratory behavior = 0), and having a mother who does not work (mother_ status = 0). This combination is a logical remainder, and the researcher should not be tempted to manipulate calibration in such a way that all combinations are covered with cases. This so-called limited diversity is the rule rather than the exception. Depending on how these logical remainders are dealt with, different formulas result. A frequently applied but very risky procedure is to simulate all possible outcomes for the logical remainders and to choose the most parsimonious solution. This cannot be recommended

---

[21] This can occur if such combinations are not plausible, such as the famous "pregnant man"; if such combinations are plausible but have not come manifest due to the contingencies in the social world (such as the "female American President"); or if the sample is of a kind that not all combinations are covered by it.

Table 9.5. *Employment in the labor market: Analysis of necessary conditions (women)*[22]

Condition	Consistency	Coverage (Triviality)
~impairment	0.82	0.49
network_support	0.59	0.49
~network_obstruction	0.87	0.43
~child	0.91	0.44

since there are no theoretically sound reasons for preferring that particular solution over the others. The most parsimonious solution does not contradict the empirical evidence provided by the data, but can be based on implausible assumptions (such as on pregnant men). The conservative solution is also based on empirical evidence, but this solution is only based on the available information and no assumptions are made with regard to the logical remainders. In other words, the conservative solution gives us a minimal account of the causal situation that we can definitely be sure about. By means of a recently introduced software module, a compromise solution is now offered in which directional expectations are given for some (or all) conditions: The researcher has to specify ex ante if (s)he has strong reasons to believe that a given condition would entail a rather positive or negative effect on the outcome.[23] Following a logic of counterfactual analysis, assumptions on only those remainders are permitted that are in line with these theoretical expectations (for more details, see Ragin 2008:160ff.; Schneider and Wagemann 2012). In our example, the conservative and the intermediate solutions converge completely so that the solution is not only exclusively based on the empirically available information but is also not altered if we insert some theoretical expectations.

If we now repeat the analysis with the women in our sample, we get surprising results. First, the analysis of necessary conditions does not confirm the three conditions determined as necessary in the male subsample (cf. Table 9.5). The data set from the women's group instead suggested to include and test the necessity of the condition of not being a

---

[22] This table includes the only condition that, in case of the women, exceeds the 0.9 hurdle of a consistency value required for a necessary condition.

[23] Of course, this strategy entails a threefold problem: First, theoretical expectations that still need to be proven are used in order to prove them. Second, this opens the door for data manipulation: If there are too many of these theoretical expectations, it is obvious that a solution will be preferred that corresponds best to our own expectations. And finally, it is contradictory to the configurational logic of QCA to isolate single conditions and make assumptions about them separate from the other conditions.

Table 9.6. *Employment in the labor market: Analysis of sufficient conditions (women)*
Model: impairment, exploratory behavior, network_support, mother_employment status

	Raw cov	Unique cov	Consist
~impairment * mother_status * exploratory	0.38	0.12	0.81
~impairment * network_support * mother_status	0.32	0.06	0.85
Coverage: 0.44			
Consistency: 0.77			

Remainders: Conservative Solution

parent oneself – this time rather in terms of a potentially negative effect on young women's chances of entering the labor force.

As we can see, the consistency values of two conditions identified as necessary for the young men's career entry (absence of impairment and presence of network support) are significantly lower when the data set from the women is considered. In marked contrast, we find a fairly high consistency value for the condition of not being a parent (~child) so that it might count as a necessary condition. The consistency value for the condition "no obstruction of the transition to work by the network" (~network_obstruction) is very close to 0.9, another condition that played no role in the analysis of the male subsample. However, the real problem in this case is that the coverage values for all four conditions are rather low – that is to say, these conditions are mainly trivial.

Therefore, the analysis of necessary conditions for the subgroup of young women was slightly disappointing. The problem here is not only that the previously determined conditions do not work well but, moreover, the only identifiable necessary condition (~child) seems to be quite trivial. Nevertheless, a first insight gained from this result is that other conditions should be used to analyze the female group. This suggestion is supported by the findings from our following analysis of sufficient conditions (cf. Table 9.6). Once again, we use the four-condition model identified as appropriate for the male group and insert the women's data.

While the substantial result does not change much, compared to the men (for men and women we find two paths, both include ~impairment; for men and women there is one path with exploratory behavior and one path where this lack of exploratory behavior is compensated by network aspects), the evaluation parameters are fundamentally different and, above all, much worse. The consistency value of the total solution is tolerable, although far from being good (Ragin 2008:118; Schneider and Wagemann 2010:406), but the coverage value is, of course, completely unacceptable. This is also reflected by the raw and unique coverages of the two paths. Therefore, we have to accept (or, as it is often put in QCA, to learn from the evidence) that the analysis of women's and men's career entry experiences are substantially different. Remember that the condition of "not being a parent," which performed reasonably well in the analysis of necessary conditions, was not even included in our model. It is widely understood that having a child is usually more of an obstacle for women than for men as they transition into the labor market.

It is therefore expedient to develop another model that is more appropriate to capture the particular situation of young women, possibly even applying a completely different set of conditions. This is a further demonstration of the case sensitivity of QCA. It goes without saying that the strategy should not and cannot be based on just playing around with all the conditions until one arrives at a mathematically acceptable model. Instead, the new set of conditions for analyzing the women's sample have to be carefully specified and substantiated on the basis of theoretical assumptions and knowledge of the individual cases. Only then can the results be expected to be substantially relevant. After several attempts to establish new conditions and learn from the data, we were finally convinced that to analyze the situation of women the new model should not define the successful transition to the labor market as an outcome but rather its opposite, that is, the "non-occurrence of employment." A closer examination of the data set as a whole (including descriptive statistics) and of the single cases taught us that failure is more widespread among women than among men. As mentioned, QCA is an asymmetric method by which the result for the opposite of an outcome cannot automatically be derived from the analysis of that outcome.[24] This is an advantage insofar as the separate analysis of the absence of an outcome might reveal patterns that cannot be detected with standard statistical methods. A new analysis of the women's sample, this time using the outcome "non-occurrence of employment," produced the following results (cf. Table 9.7): First, the analysis does not reveal any necessary condition. For the analysis of sufficient conditions, only three conditions are inserted into the model: being a parent, not showing any career-related exploratory behavior, and having a problematic family background.

If we reformulate the career-related exploratory behavior in its negative version (~expl), we can see that any combination of any two of the

---

[24] An exception to this rule is if there are no logical remainders (Schneider and Wagemann 2010:408f.).

Table 9.7. *Non-occurrence of employment: Analysis of sufficient conditions (women)*
Model: child, exploratory behavior, family_problematic constellation

	Raw cov	Unique cov	Consist
child * ~exploratory	0.17	0.06	0.90
~exploratory * family_probl	0.46	0.36	0.75
child * family_probl	0.21	0.10	0.85
Coverage: 0.63			
Consistency: 0.79			

Remainders: Conservative Solution, also Intermediate Solution

three conditions used in the model counts as a sufficient condition. In other words, any of the three conditions can be missing if the other two are present – they are then sufficient conditions for the outcome "non-occurrence" of a young woman's successful career entry. The parameters of fit are admittedly better than in the previous analysis, but the low coverage value still indicates that our model cannot account completely for the outcome.

Conclusion

Based on a longitudinal study of the significance of personal networks for the transition from school to work among less-educated young adults, we demonstrated for the first time how fuzzy-set QCA can be usefully applied in investigating social networks.[25] Using QCA facilitates a more precise description of the conditions (network resources and restrictions as well as individual action orientations) under which a successful labor market integration may still be possible in spite of initial failure to gain access to vocational training. The same holds true for understanding those cases and constellations in which neither vocational training was completed nor a job found within four to five years after leaving secondary schooling.

We demonstrated how quantitative and qualitative steps are interlocked in data analysis. We argue that QCA can be understood as a mixed method: QCA integrates qualitative "thick" descriptions with the kind of data reduction that is typical of quantitative methods. As shown earlier, such an analysis can incorporate qualitative as well as quantitative network data. The integration of qualitative and quantitative steps

[25] For an application of crisp set QCA see Smilde (2005) study on the influence of networks on the conversion to evangelical groups in Venezuela.

is an essential part of QCA analysis: This was demonstrated for the selection of conditions and outcomes, the construction and calibration of the fuzzy values, and for the representation by means of evaluation parameters. Based on our data, we also explained why a separate analysis was required for the male and the female samples and illustrated the aspect of asymmetric causality by analyzing outcome versus no outcome in the women's group.

With respect to the young men, the (cognitive and instrumental) support provided by the personal network turned out to be a necessary condition for entering the primary labor market within a maximum period of five years, apart from factors like the "absence of a large network" and "not having a physical or mental impairment." Together with the presence of a supportive network, the latter factor is also part of a set of sufficient conditions for this particular group's successful transition to working life. On the other hand, career exploration behavior seems to be of only secondary importance: As the analysis shows, individual exploratory behavior can be compensated for by the presence of a network aspect – a "working mom" with her corresponding aspirations and orientations. In other words, having a working mom can act as a functional equivalent. However, further analyses reveal that these conditions evidently do not apply to the young women in our sample. In their case, network factors that impede career entry seem to be of greater significance, as the analysis of both the necessary conditions and the adjusted outcome "no successful transition to employment" indicates. Here, single-case analyses, a new calibration of the fuzzy values, and further comparative studies are needed to provide further insights.

Current challenges for QCA include the integration of temporal aspects (cf. DeMeur et al. 2009) and the development of further guidelines for calibration procedures. In our present analysis, we preferred mainly qualitative calibration methods with a strong focus on the individual cases. QCA requires a highly accurate procedure and compliance with many rules of "good conduct" in order to achieve its full potential. Paying the necessary attention to quality will also contribute to QCA's greater recognition in the scientific community.

In this contribution, we demonstrated how fuzzy-set QCA can be meaningfully applied to research into social networks. QCA seems to be especially well-suited to investigate network effects. Given the significant effort involved in the collection of network data, network studies are frequently faced with the problem of being restricted to relatively small sample sizes. In such cases, many statistical methods are not applicable – for instance, if the effects of or impacts on networks are under examination. Since QCA is applicable in analyzing medium-sized samples, it is of particular interest for network research. With regard to network effects, QCA allows the modeling of both complex solutions and functionally equivalent terms of solutions for combined conditions. It facilitates systematic case comparisons and supports the construction of typologies that strongly build on the individual cases, thus enhancing the explanatory power and generalizability of study results.

References

Adams, Gerald R. and Michael D. Berzonsky, eds. 2003. *Blackwell Handbook of Adolescence*. Malden, MA: Blackwell.

Adams, Gerald R., Thomas P. Gullotta, and Raymond Montemayor, eds. 1992. *Adolescent Identity Formation*. Newbury Park, CA: Sage.

Adler, Rolf H. et al., eds. 1996. *Psychosomatische Medizin*. Munich, Vienna, Baltimore: Urban und Schwarzenberg.

Bartolini, Stefano. 1993. "On time and comparative research." *Journal of Theoretical Politics* 5(2):131–67.

Bott, Elizabeth. 1957. *Family and Social Network*. London: Tavistock.

Boxman, Edward A., Paul M. de Graaf, and Hendrik D. Flap. 1991. "The impact of social and human capital on the income attainment of Dutch managers." *Social Networks* 13:51–73.

Brady, Henry E. and David Collier, eds. 2004. *Rethinking Social Inquiry: Diverse Tools, Shared Standards*. Lanham, MD: Rowman & Littlefield.

Brown, Duane and Linda Brooks, eds. 1990. *Career Choice and Development: Applying Contemporary Theories to Practice*. 2nd ed. San Francisco: Jossey-Bass.

Caramani, Danièle. 2008. *Introduction to the Comparative Method with Boolean Algebra*. London: Sage.

Coleman, James S., ed. 1990a. *Foundations of Social Theory*. Cambridge, MA: Belknap Press of Harvard University Press.

Coleman, James S. 1990b. "Social capital." Pp. 300–21 in *Foundations of Social Theory*, edited by J. S. Coleman. Cambridge, MA: Belknap Press of Harvard University Press.

Coleman, John C. and Leo B Hendry. 1990. *The Nature of Adolescence*. London and New York: Routledge.

Della Porta, Donatella. 2008. "Comparative analysis: Case-oriented versus variable-oriented research." Pp. 198–222 in *Approaches and Methodologies in the Social Sciences*, edited by D. Della Porta and M. Keating. Cambridge: Cambridge University Press.

Della Porta and M. Keating and Michael Keating, eds. 2008. *Approaches and Methodologies in the Social Sciences*. Cambridge: Cambridge University Press.

DeMeur, Gisèle, Benoit Rihoux, and Sakura Yamasaki. 2009. "Addressing the critiques of QCA." Pp. 147–67 in *Configurational Comparative Methods: Qualitative Comparative Analysis (QCA) and Related Techniques*, edited by B. Rihoux and C. C. Ragin. Thousand Oaks, CA: Sage.

Diewald, Martin. 1991. *Soziale Beziehungen: Verlust oder Liberalisierung?: Soziale Unterstützung in informellen Netzwerken*. Berlin: Ed. Sigma.

Fend, Helmut. 1991. *Identitätsentwicklung in der Adoleszenz: Lebensentwürfe, Selbstfindung und Weltaneignung in beruflichen, familiären und politisch-weltanschaulichen Bereichen.* Bern: Huber.

———. 1998. *Eltern und Freunde: Soziale Entwicklung im Jugendalter.* Bern: Huber.

Filipp, Sigrun-Heide and Peter Aymanns. 1996. "Bewältigungsstrategien (Coping)." Pp. 277–90 in *Psychosomatische Medizin*, edited by R. H. Adler, J. M. Herrmann, O. W. Schoenecke, T. Von Uexküll, and W. Wesiak. Munich, Vienna, Baltimore: Urban und Schwarzenberg.

Finch, Michael D. and Jeylin T. Mortimer. 1996. "Future directions for research on adolescents, work, and family." Pp. 221–37 in *Adolescents, Work, and Family: An Intergenerational Developmental Analysis*, edited by J. T. Mortimer and M. D. Finch. Thousand Oaks, CA: Sage.

Flum, Hanoch and David L. Blustein. 2000. "Reinvigorating the study of vocational exploration: A framework for research." *Journal of Vocational Behavior* 56(3):380–404.

Glaser, Barney G. and Anselm L. Strauss. 1967. *The Discovery of Grounded Theory. Strategies for Qualitative Research.* Chicago: Aldine.

Goertz, Gary. 2003. "The substantive importance of necessary condition hypotheses." Pp. 65–94 in *Necessary Conditions: Theory, Methodology, and Applications*, edited by G. Goertz and H. Starr. Lanham, MD: Rowman & Littlefield.

Goertz, Garyand Harvey Starr, eds. 2003. *Necessary Conditions: Theory, Methodology, and Applications.* Lanham, MD: Rowman & Littlefield.

Granovetter, Mark S. [1995] 1974. *Getting A Job: A Study of Contacts and Careers.* Cambridge, MA: Harvard University Press.

Hall, Peter A. 2003. "Aligning ontology and methodology in comparative politics." Pp. 373–404 in *Comparative Historical Analysis in the Social Sciences*, edited by J. Mahoney and D. Rueschemeyer. Cambridge: Cambridge University Press.

Harris, Judith R. 1998. *The Nurture Assumption: Why Children Turn Out the Way They Do.* New York: The Free Press.

Heinz, Walter R. et al. 1998. "Vocational training and career development in germany: Results from a longitudinal study." *International Journal of Behavioral Development* 22(1):77–101.

Hollstein, Betina. 2001. *Grenzen sozialer Integration: Zur Konzeption informeller Beziehungen und Netzwerke.* Leverkusen: Leske + Budrich.

Hollstein, Betina and Jürgen Pfeffer. 2010. "Netzwerkkarten als Instrument zur Erhebung egozentrierter Netzwerke." In *Unsichere Zeiten: Verhandlungen des 34. Kongress der Deutschen Gesellschaft für Soziologie*, edited by H. G. Soeffner. Frankfurt/M.: Campus.

Hollstein, Betina and Tom Töpfer. 2013. " Netzwerke als Ressource oder Restriktion? Arbeitsmarkteinstieg sozial benachteiligter junger Erwachsener – Eine Fuzzy-Set-Analyse von Netzwerkeffekten." Working paper. Hamburg: Universität Hamburg.

Hoose, Daniela and Dagmar Vorholt. 1996. *Sicher sind wir wichtig, irgendwie!? Der Einfluss der Eltern auf das Berufswahlverhalten von Frauen:*

Eine Untersuchung im Auftrag des Senatsamtes für die Gleichstellung. Hamburg.

Keupp, Heiner et al. 2008. *Identitätskonstruktionen: Das Patchwork der Identitäten in der Spätmoderne.* Reinbek bei Hamburg: Rowohlt.

Kohn, Melvin L. and Carmi Schooler. 1983. *Work and Personality: An Inquiry into the Impact of Social Stratification.* Norwood, NJ: Ablex.

Kracke, Bärbel. 2002. "The role of personality, parents and peers in adolescents career exploration." *Journal of Adolescence* 25(1):19–30.

Kracke, Bärbel and Eva Schmitt-Rodermund. 2001. "Adolescents' career exploration in the context of educational and occupational transitions." Pp. 141–68 in *Navigating through Adolescence: European Perspectives*, edited by J. E. Nurmi. New York: Routledge.

Kraheck, Nicole. 2004. *Karrieren jenseits normaler Erwerbsarbeit: Lebenslagen, Lebensentwürfe und Bewältigungsstrategien von Jugendlichen und jungen Erwachsenen in Stadtteilen mit besonderem Erneuerungsbedarf.* München; Halle.

Lex, Tilly. 1997. *Berufswege Jugendlicher zwischen Integration und Ausgrenzung.* München.

Lin, Nan and Dan Ao. 2008. "The invisible hand of social capital." Pp. 107–132 in *Social Capital: An International Research Program*, edited by N. Lin and B. Erickson. Oxford: Oxford University Press.

Lin, Nan, Walter M. Ensel, and John C. Vaughn. 1981a. "Social resources and strength of ties: Structural factors in occupational status attainment." *American Sociological Review* 46(4):393–405.

———. 1981b. "Full access social resources and occupational status attainment." *Social Forces* 59(4):1163–81.

Mackie, John L. 1974. *The Cement of the Universe.* Oxford: Clarendon.

Mahoney, James. 2000. "Strategies of causal inference in small-N analysis." *Sociological Methods & Research* 28(4):387–424.

———. 2003. "Strategies of causal assessment in comparative historical analysis." Pp. 337–72 in *Comparative Historical Analysis in the Social Sciences*, edited by J. Mahoney and D. Rueschemeyer. Cambridge: Cambridge University Press.

Mahoney, James and Dietrich Rueschemeyer, eds. 2003. *Comparative Historical Analysis in the Social Sciences.* Cambridge: Cambridge University Press.

Mahoney, James, Erin Kimball, and Kendra L. Koivu. 2009. "The logic of historical explanation in the social sciences." *Comparative Political Studies* 42(1):114–46.

Marcia, James E. 1993. "The status of the statuses: Research review." Pp. 22–41 in *Ego Identity: A Handbook for Psychosocial Research*, edited by J. E. Marcia, A. S. Waterman, D. R. Matteson, S. L. Archer, and J. L.Orlofsky. New York: Springer.

Marcia, James E. et al., eds. 1993. *Ego Identity: A Handbook for Psychosocial Research.* New York: Springer.

Mortimer, Jeyland T. and Donald Kumka. 1982. "A further examination of the 'Occupational Linkage Hypothesis'." *Sociological Quarterly* 23(1):3–16.

Mortimer, Jeylin T. and Michael D. Finch, eds. 1996. *Adolescents, Work, and Family: An Intergenerational Developmental Analysis*. Thousand Oaks, CA: Sage.

Mortimer, Jeylan T. et al. 2002. "The process of occupational decision making: Patterns during the transition to adulthood." *Journal of Vocational Behavior* 61(3):439–65.

Munck, Gerardo L. 2001. "The regime question: Theory building in democracy studies." *World Politics* 54(1):119–44.

Nurmi, Jari-Erik, ed. 2001. *Navigating through Adolescence: European Perspectives*. New York: Routledge.

Pfaff, Holger. 1989. *Stressbewältigung und soziale Unterstützung: Zur sozialen Regulierung individuellen Wohlbefindens*. Weinheim: Deutscher Studien Verlag.

Pfeffer, Jürgen, Florian Straus, and Betina Hollstein. 2008. *EgoNet.QF. Software for Data Collecting Processing and Analyzing Ego-Centric Networks. User's Manual for EgoNet.QF, Version 2.12*. Vienna, Munich, Berlin. Ms.

Ragin, Charles C. 1987. *The Comparative Method: Moving Beyond Qualitiative and Quantitative Strategies*. Berkeley: University of California Press.

———. 1991. "Introduction: Cases of 'What is a case?'" Pp. 1–17 in *What Is a Case?: Exploring the Foundations Of Social Inquiry*, edited by C. C. Ragin and H. S. Becker. Cambridge and New York: Cambridge University Press.

———. 1994. *Constructing Social Research. The Unity and Diversity of Method*. Thousand Oaks, CA: Pine Forge Press.

———. 2000. *Fuzzy-Set Social Science*. Chicago: University of Chicago Press.

———. 2004. "Turning the tables: How case-oriented research challenges variable-oriented research." Pp. 123–38 in *Rethinking Social Inquiry: Diverse Tools, Shared Standards*, edited by H. E. Brady and D. Collier. Lanham, MD: Rowman & Littlefield.

———. 2008. *Redesigning Social Inquiry: Fuzzy Sets and Beyond*. Chicago: University of Chicago Press.

Ragin, Charles C. and Howard S. Becker, eds. 1991. *What is a case? Exploring the Foundations of Social Inquiry*. Cambridge: Cambridge University Press.

Ragin, Charles C. and David Zaret. 1983. "Theory and method in comparative research: Two strategies." *Social Forces* 61(3):731–54.

Rihoux, Benoît and Charles C. Ragin. eds. 2009. *Configurational Comparative Methods: Qualitative Comparative Analysis (QCA) and Related Techniques*. Thousand Oaks, CA: Sage.

Šavît, Yôsî and Walter Müller, eds. 1998. *From School to Work: A Comparative Study of Educational Qualifications and Occupational Destinations*. Oxford: Clarendon Press.

Schmitter, Philippe C. 2002. "Seven disputable theses." *European Political Science* 1(2):23–40.

Schnabel, Kai U., et al. 2002. "Parental influence on students' educational choices in the United States and Germany: Different ramifications – Same effect?" *Journal of Vocational Behavior* 60(2):178–98.

Schneider, Carsten Q. and Bernard Grofman. 2006. "It might look like a regression ... But it's not! An intuitive approach to the presentation of QCA and fs/QCA results." Tokyo.

Schneider, Carsten Q. and Claudius Wagemann, eds. 2007. *Qualitative Comparative Analysis (QCA) und Fuzzy Sets: Ein Lehrbuch für Anwender und jene, die es werden wollen.* Opladen: Barbara Budrich.

Schneider, Carsten Q. and Claudius Wagemann. 2010. "Standards of good practice in Qualitative Comparative Analysis (QCA) and fuzzy-sets." *Comparative Sociology* 9(3):397–418.

Schneider, Carsten Q. and Claudius Wagemann, eds. 2012. *Set-Theoretic Methods in the Social Sciences: A User's Guide for Qualitative Comparative Analysis and Fuzzy-Sets.* Cambridge: Cambridge University Press.

Seawright, Jason and David Collier. 2004. "Glossary of selected terms." Pp. 273–313 in *Rethinking Social Inquiry: Diverse Tools, Shared Standards,* edited by H. E. Brady and D. Collier. Lanham, MD: Rowman & Littlefield.

Smilde, David. 2005. "A qualitative comparative analysis of conversion to Venezuelan evangelicalism: How networks matter." *American Journal of Sociology* 111(3):757–96.

Soeffner, Hans-Georg. 2010. *Unsichere Zeiten: Verhandlungen des 34. Kongress der Deutschen Gesellschaft für Soziologie.* Frankfurt/M.: Campus.

Solga, Heike. 2005. *Ohne Abschluss in die Bildungsgesellschaft: Die Erwerbschancen gering qualifizierter Personen aus soziologischer und ökonomischer Perspektive.* Opladen: B. Budrich.

Steiner, Christine. 2004. "Guter Rat ist teuer. Nutzung von Unterstützungs- und Beratungsleistungen durch Jugendliche bei der Suche nach Ausbildungsmöglichkeiten." Pp. 25–51 in *Jugend – Ausbildung – Arbeit. Bildung und Beschäftigung in Ostdeutschland,* Vol. 2, edited by B. Lutz, H. Grünert, and C. Steiner. Berlin.

Straus, Florian. 1994. *Netzwerkanalyse – Egozentrierte Netzwerkkarten als Instrument zur Erhebung von sozialen Beziehungen in qualitativen Interviews: Materialien (48) des Teilprojekts A6.* München.

———. 2004. *EGONET QF: Ein Manual zur egozentrierten Netzwerkanalyse für die qualitative Forschung.* München: Manuscript.

Super, Donald E. 1990. "A life-span, life-space approach to career development." Pp. 197–261 in *Career Choice and Development: Applying Contemporary Theories to Practice,* 2nd ed., edited by D. Brown and L. Brooks. San Francisco: Jossey-Bass.

Tashakkori, Abbas and Charles Teddlie. 2009. "Integrating qualitative and quantitative approaches to research." Pp. 283–317 in *The Sage Handbook of Applied Social Research Methods,* 2nd ed., edited by L. Bickmand and D. J. Rog. Los Angeles: Sage.

Teddlie, Charles and Abbas Tashakkori. 2006. "A general typology of research designs featuring mixed methods." *Research in the Schools* 13(1):12–28.

Vondracek, Fred W. and Erik J. Porfeli. 2003. "The world of work and careers." Pp. 109–29 in *Blackwell Handbook of Adolescence,* edited by G. R. Adams and M. D. Berzonsky. Malden, MA: Blackwell.

Wagemann, Claudius and Carsten Q. Schneider. 2010. "Qualitative Comparative Analysis (QCA) and fuzzy sets: The agenda for a research approach and a data analysis technique." *Comparative Sociology* 9(3):376–96.

Wegener, Bernd. 1991. "Job mobility and social ties: social resources, prior job, and status attainment." *American Sociological Review* 56(1):60–71.

Wilson, William J. 1997. *When Work Disappears: The World of the New Urban Poor.* New York: Knopf.

Youniss, James. 1980. *Parents and Peers in Social Development.* Chicago: University of Chicago Press.

10

Reconstructing Social Networks through Text Analysis: From Text Networks to Narrative Actor Networks

Joan Miquel Verd and Carlos Lozares

Introduction

The combined use of quantitative and qualitative methods is almost as old as sociological research, but this combination has only recently come to the forefront of the methodological debate. This is shown by the large number of reference works advocating a high level of methodological integration (Tashakkori and Teddlie 1998, 2003; Creswell 2003; Brewer and Hunter 2006; Creswell and Plano Clark 2007; Bergman 2008) that have been published since the late 1990s. However, works of this type have often limited their focus to the stage of gathering data. The methodological literature is fairly lacking in presenting and discussing strategies of analysis in which the data analysis is neither strictly quantitative (mathematical) nor strictly qualitative (interpretive). This chapter presents and discusses one example of this kind of analysis as applied to narrative interviews.

More precisely, this chapter presents an analysis procedure in which, from information obtained through qualitative techniques (narrative-biographical interviews) matrices of relations between actors are drawn up and analyzed using standard (quantitative) procedures of social network analysis. It is important to note that this transformation of narrative information from the interviews into a matrix of quantified data is preceded by a preliminary stage in which an interpretively generated code takes into account the syntactic and semantic nature of the text of the interviews. This strategy prevents loss of information about the content of the texts and respects the articulation of the textual units. The second stage, of transforming the already interpreted qualitative data to matrix form and submitting them to the corresponding algebra, can be

We would like to thank Silvia Domínguez, Betina Hollstein, Jan Fuhse, Julia Gluesing, and Sophie Mützel for their useful comments to earlier versions of this chapter.

described, in mixed methods terminology, as a "quantitizing strategy" (Tashakkori and Teddlie 1998:126; Onwuegbuzie and Teddlie 2003:355) or a "quantitative translation" (Boyatzis 1998:129). The particularity of our analysis lies in the fact that the quantitative data obtained are of a relational rather than a purely statistical-attributive nature.

According to the classification and typology of mixed methods designs presented in the Introduction (Hollstein, this volume) our analysis follows a conversion design, although with the above pointed particularity – in relation to the standard "quantitizing strategy" – of performing a first phase where an interpretive analysis and formalization of qualitative data is carried on. This procedure is applied in order to identify the social ambits (represented by different types of actors appearing in the narrations) that have a greater presence and influence in the training and employment pathways of a set of respondents. Specifically, from the identification of four main social ambits in the interviews (family, employment, friends, and training), we analyze the interactions and links between actors, relating the specific characteristics of these links to the type of trajectory followed by the respondent.

It is important to note that this network of actors is obtained in the same way as any network would be constructed from a biographical narrative: by transforming the analytically relevant codes of the narration into nodes in a network. The next step is to choose only the relations between the actors in this text network. This procedure is in line with previous methodological approaches that have held that a text can be analyzed as a network of meanings, so we devote a large part of the chapter to making a systematic review of these approaches. The procedure we follow is based particularly on the third type of approach that we review (network text analysis). However, we believe that leaving other, similar approaches outside the review would not do justice to some text analysis proposals that are methodologically innovative and largely unknown.

A Mixed Method for Analyzing Texts

Although the social network perspective has traditionally been oriented toward analyzing relationships between social actors, it can easily be applied to analyzing the relationships between the concepts or words in a text. In fact, this is a highly attractive application, insofar as the idea of a structure or "network of meanings" seems almost inseparable from the understanding of a text. In the framework of this application, some of the weaknesses attributed to the social network perspective – such as the difficulty of delimiting the set of units of which a network is composed and the fundamentally static nature of the most common analyses – are less problematic. Though all texts are the product of a dynamic process (van Dijk 1998:78–89), as a finished product of this process they are stable and static and their units can easily be delimited.

Bazeley (2003:410) includes among the mixed methods of data management and analysis those based on "mapping." In this category she identifies three different strategies that are very close to the use of a network perspective in the analysis: the use of standard social network analysis, the use of mapping semantic networks, and the use of cognitive mapping. What Bazeley calls "mapping semantic networks" is in fact an application of social network analysis (which she considers in its habitual definition, as analysis of contacts among actors in a network) to data of a textual type. This is the type of analysis that we deal with in this chapter. We will review the approaches to text analysis that are based on the transformation of qualitative data (mainly, but not exclusively, textual) into relational data, which may be analyzed both by using the habitual strategies of social network analysis and in a more holistic and interpretative way, considering the global structure of relationships between the nodes.

Merely applying the idea of relationship to text analysis[1] is not the same as applying the tools of social network analysis to text analysis. The main outcome of the transformation of the text into a network is a graph and its associated matrix that can be analyzed using either structural or relational strategies (Wasserman and Faust 1994).

Mohr (1998:358–59) distinguishes two main ways of approaching the analysis of cultural meaning structures using tools from social network analysis: by focusing on the connectivity of the nodes and by focusing on structural equivalence. Mohr's classification is based on the type of tools used in the data processing procedure. The classification criterion that we will use in this chapter is slightly different. It is based on the type of text decomposition that is used and the way in which the text is recomposed and reconstructed in the form of a network. In our case, we group the analysis procedures into three main clusters: (a) those that analyze associations between words by means of word graphs or word-by-word matrices, in which the codification is automated or semi-automated; (b) those that analyze word-by-word matrices in which the associations between words are the result of an interpretative coding, which involves a far more theoretically oriented reduction of the text by the analyst; and (c) those in which through the coding the analyst transforms the text into a set of connected terms or concepts and also identifies (of course interpretatively) the type of semantic relationships that exist among them. The three types of procedures involve different – and increasing, if we follow the order of presentation – degrees of involvement of the analyst

---

[1] A review of this kind of analyses can be found in Lozares et al. (2003). This article also shows precisely the points of contact and differences between the relational and network approaches.

in the process of interpreting and coding (or "translating") the text into a set of relations between terms or concepts.

In the following sections we will describe the general approaches into which the procedures can be divided but not enter into the specificities of each analysis procedure. Obviously, the particular use of certain strategies in the data processing will vary according to each research question and according to the specific procedure used for building the network. However, broadly speaking, one can identify some coincidences in the procedures. The first group of approaches analyze mode 1 matrices of words or their corresponding graphic representations. The second group uses mode 2 matrices (affiliation matrices), either word-by-word or word-by-actor. Finally, in the third group the use of matrices is far slighter due to the impossibility of representing different types of relationships in a single matrix. In this case, the network indicators are sometimes calculated directly from the graphs or obtained from multiple matrices that are used simultaneously.

To end this section, we would like to refer to the nature of the texts that can be analyzed using the procedures that we will present. They can be texts produced directly as such (written texts), texts resulting from the transcription of a verbal interaction (i.e., interviews or focus groups), or written notes taken from observation. These are texts that Ryan and Bernard (2000:770–71) have qualified as "free-flowing texts," which may provide raw text as an input for analysis or be previously coded. As discussed in the following, we are in favor of the latter. We think that converting a text into a network of meanings requires the interpretive involvement of the analyst, if possible, until the end of the analysis.[2] We believe that this is one way to get a real mixed analysis, combining a rigorous and transparent approach with the open and comprehensive nature of qualitative analysis.

The Social Network Perspective Applied to Texts

In this section we review approaches that analyze texts by considering them as networks of relationships. Although semantic networks[3] may be

---

[2] This is not self-evident in quantitizing strategies, which rely mainly on automated coding.

[3] This term is highly polysemic. We use it in a slightly more restrictive sense than that commonly used by other authors (e.g., Ryan and Bernard 2000). We define a semantic network as a graphic representation in the form of interconnected nodes and arcs (i.e., a graph) whose aim is to represent a given set of knowledge. Devices of this kind, in which graphs are used to (re)present the knowledge of a person, institution, or group, have been common since ancient times. Semantic networks display just ideas, subjects, or concepts (whether or not they come from a text analysis) without using social network analysis tools. See a review in Verd (2005) and the terminological debate developed by Doerfel (1998).

considered as initial steps or advances in the application of the network perspective to text analysis, we will not deal with them in this review, as they cannot be considered strictly as an application of the social network perspective to text analysis.

The type of application of the network perspective we consider is based on the possibility of coding a text, as in content analysis procedures, in order to reconstruct it as a system of relationships. Thus, the words, concepts, subjects, and so on, become nodes of a linguistic network by which they are related. The network structure (sometimes called a "map") resulting from the aggregation of relationships among words represents the whole text surface analyzed, and the words (nodes) are contextualized by their position in the structure. Through this procedure it is possible to exploit the heuristic strength of network representation and analysis. As indicated above, within this type of analysis one can distinguish three different tendencies: co-word analysis, structural equivalence analysis, and network text analysis.

Co-Word Analysis

This type of procedure is a relatively basic first level in the use of networks to represent and analyze texts. In the English language literature it is known as co-word analysis or word-network analysis (Popping 2000) and in the French language literature it is known as associated word network analysis (Jenny 1997). It consists basically in representing in a single network the co-occurrences of the main terms[4] in a given set of texts or documents (Danowski 1988, 1993; Freeman and Barnett 1994; Jang and Barnett 1994; Schnegg 1997; Leydesdorff 2004; Leydesdorff and Hellsten 2005; van Meter 2006; van Meter and de Saint Léger 2008; Danowski and Park 2009; Escobar 2009). There are several ways to determine the co-occurrences, ranging from their simultaneous presence in a sliding window of text of a given width to their simultaneous presence in a given paragraph or even text (in cases in which sets of texts are analyzed). Figure 10.1 shows an adaptation of the networks developed by Danowski (1993) based on the analysis of the words used in the descriptions of listeners' favorite radio stations.

It should be noted that in this type of analysis the relationship obtained is always the co-occurrence or simultaneous presence of words or terms in a given framework of communication, which does not necessarily involve starting from document analysis. In fact, the coincidence of terms can be obtained by directly taking persons as the "unit." However, in the cases in which the persons are the units, interpretive coding of the

---

[4] As in classical (quantitative) content analysis these can be the most frequent terms (*empirical approach*) or a list of previously selected terms (*dictionary approach*).

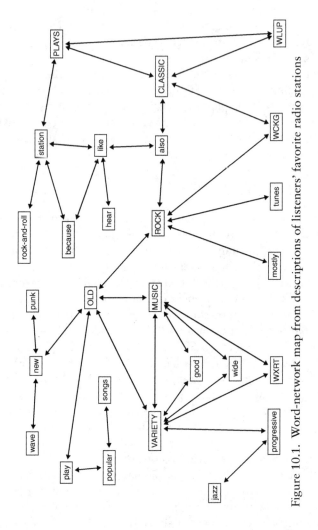

Figure 10.1. Word-network map from descriptions of listeners' favorite radio stations

text (typically, transcribed interviews) is habitual, as is a more structural processing of the data (such as including in the analysis information on the emitters and the linguistic terms used). These characteristics would place this type of analysis in the second group of approaches that we review later.

In analyses in which only the coincidences of terms are taken into account, the interpretative nature is very limited or null. This absence of interpretation is shown particularly if one uses computerized coding. In this case the analysis tends to commit the same errors as automated content analysis, and it has been severely criticized for this (Carley 1993; Popping 2000). Some type of human interpretation is therefore recommended in establishing the simultaneous presence of terms, whether by using terms of the same level of abstraction – as suggested by van Meter (1999:78) – or by previously processing the text – as in the work carried out by Corman et al. (2002) and Brandes and Corman (2003). In general, this type of analysis lacks an in-depth application of all the possibilities offered by social network analysis. The type of relationship that is coded is simply "coinciding/being near" in the text. The networks are used mainly as an instrument of graphic representation that offers versatility in matrix calculation. Little use is therefore made of the possibility of characterizing (in terms of intensity, sign, direction, or meaning) the relationships between the nodes of the resulting textual network. This is why Popping (2000:122) does not consider word-network analysis to be a true application of the social network perspective to text analysis, arguing that it has a thematic nature based exclusively on the co-occurrence of terms. The trade-off for these limitations is the great volume of information that can be analyzed and the speed of data processing.

Structural Equivalence Analysis

The studies that we have placed under this heading differ from the previous group in the desire to go beyond the simple analysis of words or terms that co-occur or are close to each other in a text. This objective is pursued through two simultaneous strategies: making a great effort of codification or selection of the terms or concepts[5] to be used in the analysis, and seeking in the data processing the common patterns of relationship among terms in the text.

---

[5] In this context we prefer to speak of terms or concepts to denote the effort of selection and sometimes abstraction performed by the analyst in this type of analysis. The terms that make up the networks and/or matrices used are not the words of the textual surface but summary words or simply codes assigned by the analyst by means of an explicit process of interpretation and connection with the theoretical framework and objectives of the research.

The research questions that these approaches try to answer can be summarized as follows: Is there a connection between the terms and concepts used (usually in a text) and the positions, profiles, or characteristics of the actors that use them? The main idea of the procedure is to study the roles played in the structure of relationships by the concepts analyzed and to link these roles with the social characteristics of the emitters or subjects to which the concepts are attributed. Thus, as in the case of word network analysis, what is analyzed is the relationship of co-presence, understood in this case as the coincidence of certain words or concepts in a given individual. The possibility of assigning a substantive content to the relationships between concepts is only used exceptionally.

The studies by Mohr (1994) and Martin (2000) perfectly illustrate this type of analysis. Mohr (1994) analyzes the New York Charity Directory of 1907 to determine how the social categories are grouped according to the characteristics of the relief that is provided to them. Martin (2000) analyzes the trades performed by the animals represented in the popular children's book, *What Do Animals Do All Day?* In both cases the authors work with mode 2 matrices, in which social types (in Martin's case, represented by animals) are related to attributes or terms of marked symbolic meaning. The final objective of both analyses is to identify the underlying social typifications in the texts analyzed.

Yeung (2005) follows similar lines to those of Mohr and Martin, though the data he analyzes are not the result of the coding or interpretation of any text. Yeung analyzes the responses given by people belonging to different types of urban communes to closed questionnaires[6] asking for a description of their fellow members. Though in this case the terms analyzed are not the result of an interpretative approximation (this is actually one of the recognized drawbacks [Yeung 2005:410] of his data), the author develops a type of structural analysis of the matrices (actor-by-term) that he obtains. The aim is to identify the meaning or "culture" embedded in the terms used by the different communities.

Yeung's use of mode 2 matrices that relate actors and terms used can be rooted in – and considered a methodological sophistication[7] of – the research of authors such as Rogers and Kincaid (1981), Monge and Eisenberg (1987), and Stohl (1993), who take as a basis for the analysis matrices of actors and words (an affiliation matrix), from which one

---

[6] Wuehrer and Kathan (2001) do not give too much importance to the differences between the means used to obtain the terms analyzed. They present a good summary of these means (closed questionnaire, discussion group, in-depth interview, selection from a list, etc.).

[7] Yeung uses Galois lattices to develop his analysis. Breiger (2000:102–106) provides a good explanation of the theoretical and methodological implications of this technique.

can obtain a word-by-word matrix (adjacency matrix) that represents the number of occasions on which each term co-occurs in the same actors.

The general aim of these authors is to obtain groups of actors differentiated according to the content of the communication (what in general we could call the "shared meanings" or "culture"). Monge and Eisenberg (1987), for example, speak of different subcultures (called semantic groups) within the organizations that they analyze, and Stohl (1993) also establishes cultural differences between managers of five countries.

Network Text Analysis

The tools of network analysis and representation can be used not only to identify and relate the main terms in a text, but also as a means of introducing the way in which the different units of the text (not necessarily words or concepts, perhaps longer linguistic sets) are related. This perspective is known as network text analysis. According to Popping (2000:30), "network text analysis originated with the observation that after one has encoded semantic links among concepts, one can proceed to construct networks of semantically linked concepts." In other words – using the language of social networks – in these approaches the meaning of a text is obtained by considering both the nodes and the types of relationships that link them. An example of this type of analysis is presented in Figure 10.2, which shows a network obtained through an analysis based on knowledge graphs (Popping 2003, 2005). The figure shows the relationships among the main concepts of the control theory on labor markets. As can be seen, two main types of relationship are represented: causality (=>) and association (==).

Though there are different ways of developing network text analysis, studies that can be placed under this heading have common characteristics that differentiate them clearly from word-network analysis and structural equivalence analysis. In relation to the first strand, word-network analysis involves a (human) interpretation and a (theoretically guided) reduction of the text, insofar as the terms considered and the relations coded cannot be identified by automated means. In relation to structural equivalence analysis the interpretive role of the analyst is similar, although in network text analysis the semantic relationships that link the terms also have to be encoded. These semantic relationships and the specific procedures of encoding and representation may vary greatly, because they serve the different theoretical goals and methodological interests of the authors.

The approaches of this type are less numerous than those based on word-network analysis and structural equivalence analysis, although some of them have been in development for quite a few years. Kathleen

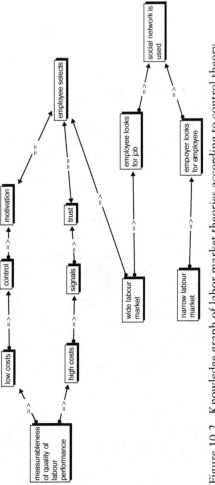

Figure 10.2. Knowledge graph of labor market theories according to control theory

Carley and her colleagues (Carley and Palmquist 1992; Carley 1993, 1994, 1997; Palmquist et al. 1997; Diesner and Carley 2004) perhaps form the core of authors who have worked most on this type of analysis, under the specific name map analysis. The aim of her work is to carry out a formalized analysis of texts going beyond content analysis. Thus, map analysis focuses on "concepts, the inter-relationships among them, and the frequency of concepts and inter-relationships" (Carley 1994:292).

Another variant of network text analysis is the approach that we have called network discourse analysis (Lozares 2000; Lozares et al. 2003; Verd 2005). Network discourse analysis[8] arose as a procedure applied to the analysis of narrative interviews, one of whose main objectives was to use as much contextual information as possible for coding and analyzing transcriptions. It is highly interpretative, with the aim that the reconstruction of the text in the form of a network should be a way to maintain its original unitary nature. In particular, the application that we will present in the next two sections stems from the identification of causal relationships in biographic narratives, and in this sense it is rooted in the work of Abell (1987, 1988) and Heise (1991). By building networks of text, it is possible to reduce the interviews to narrative maps that can be easily analyzed, either quantitatively using the indicators typical of social network methods or qualitatively using the sequence of events.

Though with slightly different objectives, Bearman et al. (1999), Bearman and Stovel (2000), and Smith (2007) use a similar method (coding of the causal relationships present in narrative interviews) as a means of identifying the central events in biographical narrations. Their theoretical orientation is more concerned with inserting the narratives in their historical dimension, which involves a great process of abstraction and translation of the text into concepts or events (the nodes of the network) that will be compared between different narrations. The result is a network representing the causal and temporal ordering of the main events described in the narrative. The procedure produces not only a description of the narrative but also a map of relationships between events that can be analyzed taking into account centrality, intermediation, and the distance between the nodes.

There are other works that fall within the framework of network text analysis (see Kleinnijenhuis et al. 1997; van Cuilenburg et al. 1988; Popping 2003, 2005). As in the other studies that have been reviewed so far, these are procedures that involve not only an identification of the

---

[8] *Network discourse analysis* was developed collectively within the Department of Sociology of the Universitat Autònoma of Barcelona, though in its practical applications some differential elements can be detected according to the purposes and theoretical objectives to which it has been applied (see Lozares 2000, 2006; Martí 2000, 2006; Verd 2002, 2006, 2007).

main words or concepts in a given text but also the coding of the relationships between these words or concepts (i.e., an interpretation of the statements of the text), which are later aggregated to form a network. The analysis carried out by van Cuilenburg et al. (1988) is of particular interest, because it considers four main types of relationships between concepts (similarity, causality, emotional relationship, and association), to which it gives scores of between –1 and 1.

Narrative, Actors, and Ambits of Interaction

In this section we present briefly the theoretical and methodological underpinnings that form the basis of the example of analysis presented in the next section. Let us remember that the objective is to identify the role played by social ambits and the actors connected to them in the development of training and employment biographies. This objective is pursued methodologically by identifying the respondents' personal networks and the relationships among the alteri of the obtained ego networks. These ego networks are not obtained by means of a standard network questionnaire based on name or position generators, but through the coding and analysis of the narratives produced in the interviews, in which ego is the narrator in the interview. The ego networks will be analyzed and placed in relationship with the textual causal narrative initially represented.

The configuration of personal networks has been studied several times in relation to their dynamics and to the social ambits in which the life trajectories of the egos have taken place. For these purposes mainly panel surveys have been used (Wellman 1979; Minor 1983; Suitor et al. 1997; Degenne and Lebeaux 2005; Bidart and Lavenu 2005). In our example, the dynamics and ambits in which the trajectories of the respondents took place were obtained in a different way, by using narrative interviews. The biographical narrative unfolds, presenting – often causally – the links between events and between the narrator and the other actors, thus revealing the social mesh involved in the biographical trajectory of the narrator (Lozares and Verd 2008). This is possible because in the whole biography there is a correspondence between the nature and dynamics of personal networks and the structure of the ambits that encompass them, because they generate each other (Erikson 1982; Gartrell 1987; Bidart and Lavenu 2005).

Whereas White (2009) highlights the interactions between narrative and social networks – the links have a narrative behind them that gives them meaning and leads to the emergence of social networks – we focus on identifying the networks of actors based on the narrative. These networks are in turn obtained by identifying in the text the ambits of interaction – what Degenne and Forsé (1999:54–57) call "social circles."

These three elements – textual narrative networks, ambits of interaction, and personal networks – form the basis of the integrated analysis that we present.

The kind of analysis we have developed is quite similar to that of McKether et al. (2009), whose ultimate aim is also to obtain relationships among actors from narrative data. These similarities would be even greater if we introduced more automation into the coding. Perhaps the main difference is that in our procedure it is important to identify the actors with the ambits of interaction, in order to see the role they play in the textual narrative network and in the whole actor-by-actor network.[9] Thus, by giving importance to narrative networks, we share some of the concerns of the analysis of Bearman and Stovel (2000) and Smith (2007).

The empirical material used for the analysis in the example comes from interviews conducted for the PhD thesis of Verd (2002). This material has been re-analyzed to achieve the previously mentioned objectives, which are different from the original ones of the thesis. In the Appendix to this chapter we present the framework of the original research: the research questions, the kinds of narratives that were produced, and the profiles of the persons interviewed.

An Example of the Procedure

This section explains and illustrates in some detail the procedure applied from the construction of narrative networks to the development and analysis of the networks of actors (ego-centered networks). To facilitate the explanation, we will discuss the different phases separately. We used ATLAS.ti and UCINET to process the data.

To better illustrate the procedure followed and the results obtained, we have used two different interviews as an example. Initially all the verbatims come from a single interview (Miguel's), but from the moment when the narrative networks are built, data from two interviews are presented in order to show the differences between results and their possible explanations.

Processing and Coding the Interviews

The first step in the processing of the interviews was to convert the text into a network of events by coding it. To do this we coded all the units of register of the narrative interview. A textual unit is defined as a unit of register by its meaning in the discourse of the interviewee, in such a

---

[9]   See the section below titled "Establishing the Relationships between Actors."

way that it identifies or relates the actor's objectivizations. Ideally (people do not use perfect sentences, so it is always necessary to reconstruct), a unit of register is a statement composed of a subject and a verb that may be coordinately or subordinately linked to other subjects and other verbs, with any supplements they may have. This initial coding process remains very close to the text and is therefore largely inspired by the principles of Grounded Theory (Strauss and Corbin 1990) and its recommendation not to leave any information out in the initial coding. The coding was performed using the Coding function of ATLAS.ti. Later, in the construction of the relationships among codes, some of the codes were grouped into broader categories to form conceptual hierarchies, as recommended by Strauss and Corbin (1990).

After this initial coding of the units of register, we used the Link Code to Code function to establish the relationships between the initial codes. In the example we present only the causal relationships that were identified, though other types of relationships between codes can be established (see Verd 2002, 2007). As stated in the previous section, a narrative is characterized by the causal relations that form the narrative plot[10] and that are fundamental to understanding the actions taken by the actors. Of course, these are causal relations between events according to the knowledge of the narrators, and they do not necessarily have a truth value. In this regard, we follow the arguments of Maida and Shapiro (1982) and Woods (1975, 1991) in favor of intentional representations, that is, the narrative network represents the reasons that lead from one state to another according to the respondents, rather than universal truths based on formal logic.[11] The interpretative criterion used thus fully agrees with that presented by Bearman and Stovel (2000:76): "Arcs between elements are coded as present if one element 'leads to' another." These causal relationships have been identified by establishing the symbol "=>" between codes A and B (with the meaning "the situation represented by code A influences the situation represented by code B" or "the actor represented by code A leads to the situation represented by code B). These relationships are plotted using the Networks function of ATLAS.ti.

An example of the type of coding performed and the relationships established among codes may be seen in Figure 10.3, which is taken from part of an interview in which the narrator talks about how he got his first job. The symbol $ before the first code indicates that this is an

---

[10] However, it is important to note that in many of the statements of the interviews the narrators merely described a certain state or action without causal links. This fact is important for the analysis (see the section below titled "Establishing the Structural Relationships amoing Textual Units").

[11] The analyst must consider the plausibility of the statements made, but this is an issue that affects any analysis based on interpretive procedures.

> The following excerpt from the interview:
>
> There are always companies that need young kids, of course, they went to the school, they knew there was this course, and there they gave them the name, or phone etc. and then they call you [...] and in my case they telephoned me from the company, I went, I did an interview [...] and then they called me and gave me the contract.
>
> **Is thus coded as :**
>
> $ first company's management => [ego's] first job

Figure 10.3. Example of the coding

actor other than ego (who is the agent or patient subject in most codes and is therefore left implicit).

Establishing the Structural Relationships among Textual Units

In order to recompose the general structure of the narrative and return the inherent character and semantic and syntactic unity to the coded text, a stage of integration of nodes and arcs is needed (Carley 1993). In our case the narrative is reconstructed by representing in a single graph all the codes and relations assigned to the narrator's statements. We thus obtain an isomorphic representation of the original narrative (Bearman et al. 1999; Bearman and Stovel 2000; Lozares and Verd 2008). As an example of this process, Figure 10.4 shows the coding and the subgraph resulting from this integration. At the top of the table are the situations or actors (nodes) and relationships (arcs) that are encoded separately in the text. Represented together, these nodes and arcs form a connected graph sharing the same node (namely the so-called competencies).

The example in Figure 10.4 also shows the importance of placing the codes that represent more specific situations in more general categories during the coding process. Strictly, it is impossible to unify in a single network – by connecting the common nodes – concepts or categories that are situated at different levels of abstraction,[12] because the nodes would not represent the same entities. We agree with Smith (2007:24–25) that the use of hierarchical groupings of events facilitates comparison

---

[12] Specific concepts can be organized into more general types (Carley 1993: 92), and this must be taken into account in the coding process. If it were not, it would be extremely difficult to combine the statements identified into a single graph.

$ first company's management => competencies

competencies => second job

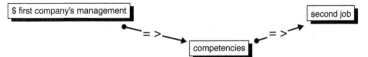

Figure 10.4. Example of the aggregation of codes and relations

across narratives – and also within narratives in the example shown in Figure 10.4, in which the relationship "competencies => second job" includes the respondent's statement that he was recruited for his second job because of his competencies. This statement is connected with the relationship "$ first company's management => competencies" through the shared node "competencies," which actually refers to a whole set of skills and behaviors that are mentioned in the course of the interview. Thus, underlying the concept competencies there are more specific terms such as being reliable, showing interest in the work, responsibility, sacrifice, and working as best as one can, all learned and developed largely due to the high level of demand of the management in his first company.

Once the narrative map has been obtained through the aggregation of nodes and arcs, it is possible to focus on or select a part of the network for a more detailed analysis of the narrative. This can be done by identifying thematic blocks in the original narrative (and analyzing only the corresponding nodes and relationships) or by taking the nodes and relationships that have certain characteristics. This second procedure is carried out by Diesner and Carley (2004) in their analysis of 247 texts designed to detect the organizational structure of covert networks. It is also the one we use. We took all the nodes referring to actors different of ego, whether or not they had a causal influence on the narrative.[13] Figures 10.5 and 10.6 show the graphs resulting from representing these nodes (marked by the symbol $) and their immediate neighbors (nodes that were connected at a distance of 1) in two different interviews (Miguel's and Santi's). Let us recall that the analyzed data came from narrative interviews, and that the actors mentioned are not the result of specific questions but are mentioned spontaneously in association with different contexts in the narrative. At no time did we ask about specific persons, or about the influence that they had on the events

---

[13] Verd (2006, 2007) presents the complete networks to which we refer; herein we present only the subnetworks resulting from the procedure we describe.

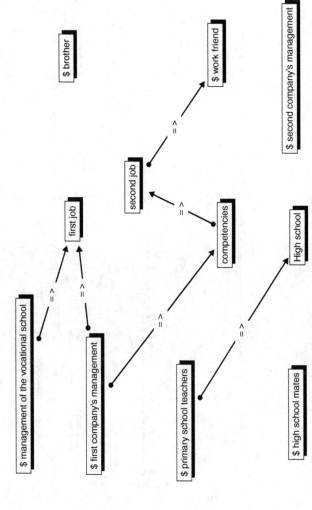

Figure 10.5. Actors mentioned in the narrative of Miguel and causal connections with events in the training and employment pathway

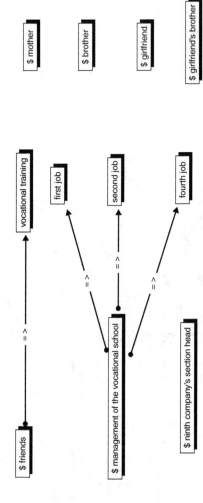

Figure 10.6. Actors mentioned in the narrative of Santi and causal connections with events in the training and employment pathway

described. This could be understood as a sort of qualitative data mining (cf. Gluesing et al., this volume) as we are obtaining relations among actors that are implicit in the narrative. Sometimes the actors appear as protagonists of parallel narratives that the interviewee mentions as a counterpoint to his or her story or simply as secondary figures who have no connection with, or direct impact on, the events described.

Establishing the Relationship between Actors

Having built the narrative subnetworks presented earlier, we built the networks of the actors mentioned in the narrative. As noted earlier, the actors who appear in the narrative are taken as representative of the different ambits of interaction of ego and of the importance of these ambits in training and employment pathways. From the narrative of the interviewee we established four ambits of interaction, which were used to build mode 2 matrices of actors by ambits. These ambits were family, employment, friends, and training. They coincide largely with the life contexts considered by Bidart (2009:182) in her analysis of the "driving forces" that lead to personal networks, although the meaning of the concept used by Bidart is somewhat broader.

Tables 10.1 and 10.2 show examples of the cases of two interviewees: Miguel and Santi. Significant differences can be observed in the presence of actors belonging to different ambits (the fact that the number of actors mentioned is 7 in each case is a coincidence). These mode 2 matrices are built directly on the UCINET spreadsheet, using the same program to obtain the dichotomized mode 1 matrix (presence or absence of a relationship between actors) and the graphical representations and analyses presented in the following.

Unlike the procedure used by McKether et al. (2009), in our case the relationships between actors are defined by the ambit of interaction. That is, the relationships depicted are drawn from the interpretive analysis of the narratives: First we related actors with ambits in the narrative (mode 2 matrices, exemplified by Tables 10.1 and 10.2), and then we obtained actor-by-actor matrices (mode 1) from the mode 2 matrices. The analysis of these actor-by-actor matrices is very robust when it is performed together with that of the narrative networks (Figures 10.5 and 10.6). It is the only way to avoid decontextualizing the relationships between actors from the settings (marked by the narratives) in which they appear. This exercise of joint analysis is performed in the following section.

Figures 10.7 and 10.9 show the ego-centered networks of Miguel and Santi, and Figures 10.8 and 10.10 represent the components of both networks (without taking ego into account). For reasons of space we will not analyze each one separately; in the next section they will be analyzed

Table 10.1. *Matrix of actors by ambits: Interview with Miguel*

	Family	Employment	Friends	Training
Brother	1	0	0	0
High school mates	0	0	1	1
First company's management	0	1	0	0
Second company's management	0	1	0	0
Primary school teachers	0	0	0	1
Management of the vocational school	0	0	0	1
Work friend	0	1	1	0

Table 10.2. *Matrix of actors by ambits: Interview with Santi*

	Family	Employment	Friends	Training
Mother	1	0	0	0
Brother	1	0	0	0
Girlfriend	1	0	1	0
Girlfriend's brother	1	0	1	0
Management of the vocational school	0	0	0	1
Ninth company's section head	0	1	0	0
Friends	0	0	1	0

in conjunction with information from the narrative networks displayed previously. Nevertheless, it is important to note that in our analysis the charts representing relationships between actors must be understood above all as a reflection of the intersection (or absence of intersection) of different ambits. If this information is integrated, in turn, with that provided by the narrative networks in Figures 10.5 and 10.6, we then determine if and how these ambits are connected to the events of the training and employment pathways.

Results of the Integrated Analysis: The Effects of Different Employment Pathways

The reflections presented in the following are intended basically to exemplify the type of results obtained from the whole process to this point in the analysis. They will necessarily be brief for reasons of space[14] and only indicate the interpretative potential of the data set analyzed. They

[14] Although we do not present the results, we have analyzed the structural holes, the cores, and the measures of centrality and centralization (degree, closeness, and betweenness) of the network both with and without ego. These analyses expand on the comments made on the following pages, but not contradict them.

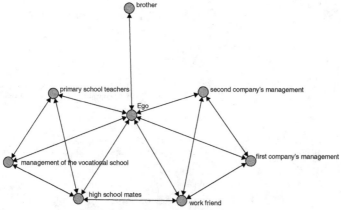

Figure 10.7. Egocentric network of Miguel

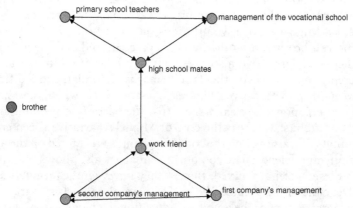

Figure 10.8. Components of Miguel's network without ego

will refer to the two cases that we have been presenting in this chapter; the reader is left to gauge the interest of a comparison among a larger number of cases.

The two cases have the same social profile, increasing the significance of the differences in the narrative networks and networks of actors. The two young men are aged 28 (Miguel) and 26 (Santi), live in the same area (El Vallés County, on the outskirts of Barcelona), are from the same social background (working class origin), and have the same level of education (second-level vocational training). At the time of the interview Miguel was a member of the basic staff in the dying section of a textile finishing company of 50 workers and Santi stocked shelves in a supermarket.

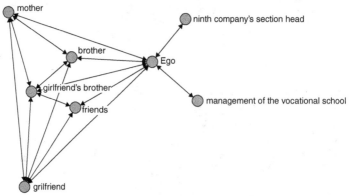

Figure 10.9. Egocentric network of Santi

From the observation of the ego-centered networks the different importances of the family ambit in each narrative are determined. Whereas Miguel's narrative mentions only a brother, Santi's narrative mentions a brother, a mother, and also a girlfriend and the girlfriend's brother – the latter two also forming part of the ambit of friends. The different importance of the family marks a fundamental difference between the two narratives. Figures 10.8 and 10.10, which represent the different components, clearly show that the narratives are built around different ambits: Whereas the core of Miguel's narrative is centered on the ambits of training and the company, Santi's is centered on the ambits of family and friends. The components analysis also shows that in both cases these nuclei are mixed, that is, they have significant intersections (cf. Degenne and Lebeaux 2005). The case of Miguel is characterized by the intersection of the ambits of education, employment, and friends, whereas that of Santi is characterized by the intersection of the ambits of family and friends.

Despite the different narrative frameworks, it is interesting to note from the narrative networks that in both narratives the agents (actors who act causally on the events) are mainly members of the ambit of education and business (more balanced in the case of Miguel and exclusively those of the educational ambit in the case of Santi). This fact may easily be related to the situation of precariousness and insecurity that affects many young people in Spain (and particularly those with a low- or medium-level qualification, like Miguel and Santi). This situation largely prevents young people from taking charge of their own career paths, which are ultimately marked by circumstances external to the individuals. This fact is well reflected in the narrative networks obtained.

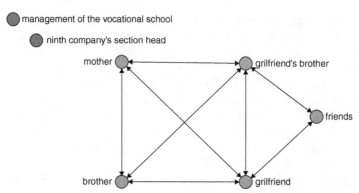

Figure 10.10. Components of Santi's network without ego

This climate of insecurity has affected the pathways we analyze in different ways. In the case of Santi we observe a great lack of focus in the ambit of employment. Friends and family are a world apart from work (they are completely disconnected; see Figures 10.6 and 10.10). This respondent has worked in nine different companies since he finished school, always for short periods of time, and has therefore been unable to identify minimally with the companies or to establish friendships within them (Figure 10.6 is explicit on this). He obtained some jobs through the management of the vocational school where he studied, but no other actors have helped him in his contacts with the world of employment.

Miguel has and maintains friends who come from the ambits (see Bidart 2009) of training or employment (Figure 10.8 clearly shows this intermediary role of the ambit of friends between the other two ambits). In his narrative (see Figure 10.5) the employment ambit is far more central and his friends are not a world apart (the family is, but the narrative shows that this ambit is not central). Why? Possibly because Miguel's path has been far more stable (he has only been in two companies since he finished his training) and this stability has consequences on his life and employment pathways and on the way he experiences and interprets these pathways.

Discussion: Challenges and Benefits of the Method

In the method for analyzing actor networks in narratives that we have just presented, the novel and original aspects lie in the mixed data processing stage, which is not the stage most commonly considered in mixed methods. From a methodological standpoint, we combined a formalized procedure with the continual presence of interpretation. From a purely technical viewpoint, in two different stages we combined the methodology and tools of the analysis of social networks with qualitative procedures, first with an interpretative coding of the text and its relationships oriented toward the construction of narrative networks, and then with a contextualized interpretation of the actor networks that were found. This second contextualized interpretation was possible precisely due to the first stage – the only alternative would have been to go back to the raw interview text.

The use of formalized procedures arouses some reservations among those who favor qualitative approaches. However, we think that formalization is the way to give the analysis transparency and rigor. Opening the "black box" of the analysis can make the findings more vulnerable to criticism, but it also legitimizes the results by exposing them to unrestricted discussion.

Importantly, the integration of the formalized approach with the interpretative approach did not involve "sticking together" quantitative and qualitative information, but was applied at all stages of the process. The different components were thus mutually illuminating, which is the requirement of Bryman (2007:8) for mixed methods to be considered "genuinely integrated."

A second particularity of the approach presented lies in the way it analyzes narrative networks. Usually the analysis is based on measures of centrality of the nodes, and measures of intermediation and nodal distance (see Bearman and Stovel 2000; Smith 2007). In this chapter, in an attempt to answer specific theoretical questions, we have explored a different path of analysis, in which the narrative network has been interpreted vis-à-vis the actor networks drawn from the narrative. Thus, rather than analyzing the importance of different events in the pathways analyzed, we have dealt with the environments and the actors that make up these events, linking them to the pathways described. In a sense, this represents (methodologically) a reverse approach to that explored by Bidart (Bidart and Lavenu 2005; Bidart 2009), in which a combination of panel data and in-depth interviews was used to detect interconnections of the composition of the personal network with events experienced over the years. In our case, the contextualization and narrative integrity offered by stories provided a comprehensiveness and coherence of information that is otherwise difficult to achieve. Personal networks obtained in this way, as an expression of relations between actors located in a specific context and time, were fixed by reference to social spaces, experiences, transitions, key points, and changes in direction.

The most evident drawback of the procedure is the great investment of time needed in order to carry it out. Of the three types of analysis of texts that use social network tools, the one we used requires the greatest presence and interpretive involvement of the researcher. This intervention is carried out at all levels and stages of the analysis process, in both the coding and the re-articulation of the text in the form of a network. This interpretative presence of the analyst prevents the process from being automated and even makes it difficult to outsource the work. Therefore, a large amount of text to be analyzed can involve a heavy workload. This is not particularly distinctive of the analysis we have presented, as it is shared by all analyses that have a strong interpretive component. This feature makes the procedure suitable for intensive rather than extensive analysis.

Appendix

As stated earlier, the interviews analyzed in this chapter come from the doctoral research performed by Verd (2002), which in turn formed part of the "Training and Employment Project" carried out by the Centre d'Estudis Sociològics sobre la Vida Quotidiana i el Treball (QUIT) of the Sociology Department of the Universitat Autònoma de Barcelona. The "Training and Employment Project" was funded by the Spanish Ministry of Education and Science (Directorate-General for Scientific and Technical Research) through contract PB93–0832.

The objectives of the PhD thesis were to identify the training resources used and valued by companies in the everyday work of their employees, and to identify the processes and ambits that had enabled workers to obtain these resources. Training resources were understood to be not only knowledge and skills of individuals but also the abilities, attitudes, and behaviors that they had obtained in education, in work, in their life experiences, and in their interaction within social networks. Since the objective of the research was to link the uses that the companies made of these training resources and the profiles of the employees, the research was designed as a comparative case study of two companies in the same geographical area, the El Vallés county on the outskirts of Barcelona. Both companies were considered representative of the productive structure of Catalonia: One was a small, mainly family-owned textile company of 45 workers and the other was a retailing company (a hypermarket) belonging to a multinational, with 307 workers at the workplace that was studied.

In each of these two companies we identified and contextualized the tasks and work processes. After drawing up an outline of the production processes, tasks, and activities in each company, we carried out a direct observation and a detailed study of four jobs and the activity of the employees who carried them out. Within the structure of the production

Table 10.3. *Respondents and their specific characteristics*

Respondent	Age	Level of education	Company	Post occupied
Cesca	23	BUP (non-vocational secondary education)	Textile	Laboratory Assistant
Miguel	28	BUP (non-vocational secondary education)	Textile	Dyer
Juli	51	Primary education	Textile	Drying supervisor
Enric	52	Primary education	Textile	Dying manager
Tere	24	BUP (non-vocational secondary education)	Hypermarket	Cashier
Santi	26	FP (secondary vocational training)	Hypermarket	Shelf stacker
Mari	32	Primary education	Hypermarket	Pastry assistant
Oscar	36	University degree	Hypermarket	Head of section

process these jobs were considered significant in each company. A total of eight jobs and their occupants were therefore studied (see Table 10.3). The objective of this micro-sociological analysis was to examine the conditions and training requirements of jobs and the demands of the companies with regard to them. The data-collection techniques used were direct observation and narrative-biographical interviews.

As noted, the empirical material used in this chapter comes from the eight narrative-biographical interviews. Using a narrative approach from both a subjective and objective point of view, we asked each of the eight selected workers about their training in all the dimensions addressed, their employment pathway and status at the time of the interview, and their strategies aimed at obtaining training resources with a view to finding and keeping jobs and achieving promotion. The result was a collection of narratives focused on their training and employment pathways.

The eight persons/jobs were chosen according to their position in the production process of each company and their social characteristics such as sex, age, and level of education. For each company one person occupying a middle management position and three people occupying jobs at the base level of production were selected. Of the eight people selected, three were women and five men; six were younger than 40 and two older than 40. One person had a university degree, four had completed secondary education, and the other three had only completed primary education. More important even than these attributive variables was the (always relative) attempt to seek homogeneity in terms of class origin and social pathway of the respondents: All respondents belonged to the working class and had a similar social and cultural background, though their pathways were somewhat divergent. Table 10.3 summarizes the main characteristics of the respondents (the names have been changed).

The sets of questions used in the biographical interviews are presented in the following. These interviews usually took place in two or three different sessions, with at least 15 days between them. Since the interview guideline is very long, it was used openly and flexibly, without strictly following each question, and it was adapted to each case in the course of the interview.

Interview Guideline

A) FIRST SESSION OF THE INTERVIEW

1. FIRST SET OF QUESTIONS

The aim was to determine the extent to which training and employment, or the relationship between them, are threads that influence or establish different stages in life.

– Life pathway?
– Continuity, stages?
– Factors?
– External/internal factors?

2. SECOND SET OF QUESTIONS

The aim was to establish more direct and specific employment stages: what they are, where they took place, the content of the stages, how the respondents got the jobs, and the training content of the jobs.

– Employment pathway?
– Stages, periods, phases?
– Work/no work: experiences, occupations?
– Upward career development?
– Reasons for the progress: planning, chance?
– Training demands in the stages?

3. THIRD SET OF QUESTIONS

The aim here was to determine the whole basic education of the respondent and not just the primary education.

– Compulsory and/or formal education
    – Type of memories
    – Benefit
    – Interest
    – Would you do it again?

– Other interesting training activities carried out
  – Usefulness in your professional life or in general
  – Did you imagine yourself in your current job?

– Extensive aspects of the training or other significant events in this first period

  a. Relationships, family
  – Friends: decisive in your career/employment?
  – Family: decisive in your career/employment?
  – Events: decisive in your career/employment?

  b. Influence of the levels of training acquired at that time
  – Non-academic events that were important for your career/employment
  – Habits, customs, hobbies, leisure

– Questions related to the progress of training
  a. Progress of learning, knowledge acquisition
  – Training pathway after compulsory/formal education
  – Are you concerned? Do you need to keep up to date?
  – Courses? Reading about the profession?

  b. Development of hobbies, tastes, pastimes, entertainment, leisure
  – Hobbies, pastimes?
  – Professional influence?

  c. Development of life experiences, diffuse socialization and in general the creation and development of abilities, skills, etc., that influence professional life
  – Events, experiences of interest that have made you change?
  – Importance in your professional life
  – Important characteristics, qualities, attitudes for professional life

  d. Development of relationships and friendships and their relation with the career, occupation, or job
  – Friendships?
  – Their development?
  – Same level?
  – Same company?
  – Influence on your professional life?

  e. Training on the job and continuing training
  – Learning in life vs learning on the job?
  – Your experience

4. FOURTH SET OF QUESTIONS

The aim was to obtain information on the respondent's assessment of his or her current occupation and training.

- Seeking the current job
    - Same profession, occupation before as now?
    - Time spent seeking this job? How was it? Planned? Easy?
    - Usefulness of initial training? Courses? Offices? Experience? "Labour qualities"?
    - Importance of the family?
    - Importance of relationships?
    - Importance of personal qualities?

- The event or situation of recruitment
    - First and subsequent contacts: How? Tests? By whom? Interview? What do you remember?
    - What qualities and characteristics did they need?
    - What did they value most?
    - Qualified?

- Progress within the company
    - Change of job? Change of contract and qualification?
    - New training demands?
    - Refresher or retraining courses?
    - Mechanisms for promotion? Relationship with training: your case?
    - Does your work facilitate interest in training: your case?
    - Promotion and relationships?

- Current job
    - Description of current job? Qualification, contract?
    - Suited to your qualifications?
    - Training for it?
    - Demands of your job?

B) SECOND SESSION OF THE INTERVIEW (FIFTH SET OF QUESTIONS)

The aim of this second session of the interview was to go deeper into the idea of strategy, i.e., how the respondent has linked training as a resource and employment, job, or occupation as objectives. The aim was to find, from the first interview, thematic channels and threads to make the conversation dynamic. Possible topics to be dealt with were strategies followed in the process of seeking and finding the current job; the link between the available resources and the results; the steps taken and achieved; and development of the strategy over time. The questions within the different subjects may seek information on:

- Training for and in employment
- The limits of training: Is everything training or does only specific training count?
- The influence of training for employment
- The importance of social networks and family influence, etc.

C) SIXTH SET OF QUESTIONS, WHICH MAY CORRESPOND TO A THIRD (OR SECOND) INTERVIEW

The aim of this third section was to explore the symbolic construction of training and employment and the relation between the two. However, the first two sections should give sufficient elements and information for dealing with the question of symbolic construction. The problem is how to talk about something without broaching the subject directly. We therefore tried to choose topics that gave us information indirectly but helped to maintain an interesting conversation.

1. THE FUTURE, THE LIFE PROJECT, MOTIVATIONS

A general question can be used initially to find out how far the profession, job, occupation, and training figure in the respondent's future projects.

- Possible changes in your life? Direction?
- How do you see yourself in 5 years? In 10 years?

Once we have obtained this general reference on their future and projects, we can go more directly to the job, work, occupation, or training.

- Your career project? What do you need for it? Are you preparing?
- How do you see your career in 5 years? In 10 years?
- How do you explain these changes? Do they depend on training?

This thread should be followed to discover the symbolic aspects of the training and career and the strategies of the project.

2. CHILDREN

Children are an important aspect for examining the frustrated or achieved imageries of the projects and the symbolic constructions of training and career: preparation of their future, what the respondents wish them to be.

- Family? How many children? Ages? Are they studying? Are they working?

  If they are studying:

- Would you like your children to be in the future? Why?
- Are they taking the right steps to achieve it? Remedy? Will they manage to do it?
- Problems? Help? What are you unable to do?
- Bleak future? Why?
- What do they want to be? Do you agree with it? Do you encourage it?
- Will it be easier for them than for you?

References

Abell, Peter. 1987. *The Syntax of Social Life*. Oxford: Clarendon Press.
———. 1988. "The 'structuration' of action. Inference and comparative narratives." Pp. 185–198 in *Actions and Structure. Research Methods and Social Theory*, edited by Nigel G. Fielding. London: Sage.
Bazeley, Pat. 2003. "Computerized data analysis of Mixed Methods Research." Pp. 385–422 in *Handbook of Mixed Methods in Social and Behavioral Research*, edited by Abbas Tashakkori and Charles Teddlie. Thousand Oaks, CA: Sage.
Bearman, Peter S. and Katherine Stovel. 2000. "Becoming a Nazi: A model for narrative networks." *Poetics* 27:69–90.
Bearman, Peter S., Robert Faris, and James Moody. 1999. "Blocking the future: New solutions for old problems in historical social science." *Social Science History* 23:501–533.
Bergman, Manfred Max, ed. 2008. *Advances in Mixed Methods Research*. London: Sage.
Bidart, Claire. 2009. "En busca del contenido de las redes sociales: los 'motivos' de las relaciones." *REDES. Revista Hispana para el Análisis de Redes Sociales*, 16, # 7. Retrieved November 30, 2009, from http://revista-redes. rediris.es.
Bidart, Claire and Daniel Lavenu. 2005. "Evolution of personal networks and life events." *Social Networks* 27:359–76.
Boyatzis, Richard E. 1998. *Transforming Qualitative Information: Thematic Analysis and Code Development*. Thousand Oaks, CA: Sage.
Brandes, Ulrik and Steven R.Corman, 2003. "Visual unrolling of network evolution and the analysis of dynamic discourse." *Information Visualization* 2(1):40–50.
Breiger, Ronald L. 2000. "A tool kit for practice theory." *Poetics* 27:91–115.
Brewer, John and Albert Hunter. 2006. *Foundations of Multimethod Research. Synthesizing Styles*. Thousand Oaks, CA: Sage.
Bryman, Alan. 2007. "Barriers to integrating quantitative and qualitative research." *Journal of Mixed Methods Research* 1(1):8–22.
Carley, Kathleen M. 1993. "Coding choices for textual analysis: A comparison of content analysis and map analysis." *Sociological Methodology* 23: 75–126.
———. 1994. "Extracting culture through textual analysis." *Poetics* 22: 291–312.
———. 1997. "Network text analysis: The network position of concepts." Pp. 79–100 in *Text Analysis for the Social Sciences: Methods for Drawing Statistical Inferences from Texts and Transcripts*, edited by Carl W. Roberts. Mahwah, NJ: Lawrence Erlbaum.
Carley, Kathleen M. and Michael E. Palmquist. 1992. "Extracting, representing, and analyzing mental models." *Social Forces* 70(3):601–36.
Corman, Steven R., Timothy Kuhn, Robert D. Mcphee, and Kevin J. Dooley. 2002. "Studying complex discursive systems: Centering resonance analysis of communication." *Human Communication Research* 28(2):157–206.

Creswell, John W. 2003. *Research Design. Qualitative, Quantitative and Mixed Methods Approaches.* 2nd ed. Thousand Oaks, CA: Sage.

Creswell, John W. and Vicky L. Plano Clark. 2007. *Designing and Conducting Mixed Methods Research.* Thousand Oaks, CA: Sage.

van Cuilenburg, Jan J., Jan Kleinnijenhuis, and Jan A. de Ridder. 1988. "Artificial intelligence and content analysis. Problems of and strategies for computer text analysis." *Quality & Quantity* 22:65–97.

Danowski, James A. 1988. "Organizational infographics and automated auditing: Using computers to unobstrusively gather as well as analyze communication." Pp. 385–433 in *Handbook of Organizational Communication,* edited by Gerald M. Goldhaber and George A. Barnett. Norwood, NJ: Ablex.

———. 1993. "Network analysis of message content." *Progress in Communication Sciences* 12:198–221.

Danowski, James Aand David W. Park. 2009. "Networks of the dead or alive in cyberspace: Public intellectuals in the mass and internet media." *New Media & Society* 11(3):337–56.

Degenne, Alain and Michel Forsé. 1999. *Introducing Social Networks.* London: Sage.

Degenne, Alain and Marie-Odile Lebeux. 2005. "The dynamics of personal networks at the time of entry into adult life." *Social Networks* 27: 337–58.

Diesner, Jana and Kathleen M. Carley. 2004. "Using network text analysis to detect the organizational structure of covert networks." *Proceedings of the North American Association for Computational Social and Organizational Science (NAACSOS) 2004 Conference.* Pittsburgh, PA.

van Dijk, Teun A. 1998. *Ideology. A Multidisciplinary Approach.* London: Sage.

Doerfel, Marya L. 1998. "What constitutes semantic network analysis? A comparison of research and methodologies." *Connections* 21(2):16–26.

Erikson, Bonnie H. 1982. "Networks, ideologies and belief systems." Pp. 159–72 in *Social Structure and Network Analysis,* edited by Peter V. Marsden and Nan Lin. London: Sage.

Escobar, Modesto. 2009. "Redes semánticas en textos periodísticos: propuestas técnicas para su representación." *Empiria. Revista de Metodología de Ciencias Sociales* 17:13–39.

Freeman, Cornelia A. and George A. Barnett. 1994. "An alternative approach to using interpretative theory to examine corporate messages and organizational culture." Pp. 60–73 in *Organization Communication. Emerging Perspectives. Volume IV,* edited by Lee Thayer and George A. Barnett. Norwood, NJ: Ablex.

Gartrell, C. David. 1987. "Network approaches to social evaluation." *Annual Review of Sociology* 13:49–66.

Heise, David R. 1991. "Event structure analysis: A qualitative model of quantitative research." Pp. 136–163 in *Using Computers in Qualitative Research,* edited by Nigel G. Fielding and Raymond M. Lee. London: Sage.

Jang, Ha-Yong and George A. Barnett. 1994. "Cultural differences in organizational communication: A semantic network analysis." *Bulletin de Méthodologie Sociologique* 44:31–59.

Jenny, Jacques. 1997. "Méthodes et pratiques formalisées d'analyse de contenu et de discours dans la recherche sociologique contemporaine. Etats des lieux et classification." *Bulletin de Méthodologie Sociologique* 54: 64–112.

Kleinnijenhuis, Jan, Jan A. de Ridder, and Ewald M. Rietberg. 1997. "Reasoning in economic discourse: An application of the network approach to the Dutch press." Pp. 191–207 in *Text Analysis for the Social Sciences: Methods for Drawing Statistical Inferences from Texts And Transcripts*, edited by Carl W. Roberts. Mahwah, NJ: Lawrence Erlbaum.

Leydesdorff, Loet. 2004. "The university-industry knowledge relationship: Analyzing patents and the science base of technologies." *Journal of the American Society for Information Science and Technology* 55(11): 991–1001.

Leydesdorff, Loet and Iina Hellsten. 2005. "Metaphors and diaphors in science communication: Mapping the case of 'stem-cell research'." *Science Communication* 27(1):64–99.

Lozares, Carlos. 2000. "El discurs reticular, més enllà de la classificació." *Revista Catalana de Sociologia* 11: 183–9.

———. 2006. "Las representaciones fácticas y cognitivas del relato de entrevistas biográficas: un análisis del discurso." *REDES. Revista Hispana para el Análisis de Redes Sociales* 10, #8. Retrieved November 30, 2009, from http://revista-redes.rediris.es.

Lozares, Carlos and Joan Miquel Verd. 2008. "La entrevista biográfico-narrativa como expresión contextualizada, situacional y dinámica de la red socio-personal." *REDES. Revista Hispana para el Análisis de Redes Sociales* 15, #6. Retrieved November 30, 2009, from http://revista-redes.rediris.es.

Lozares, Carlos, Joan Miquel Verd, Joel Martí, and Pedro López. 2003. "Relaciones, redes y discurso: revisión y propuestas en torno al análisis reticular de datos textuales." *Revista Española de Investigaciones Sociológicas* 101:175–200.

Maida, Anthony S. and Stuart C. Shapiro. 1982. "Intensional concepts in propositional semantic networks." *Cognitive Science* 6:291–330.

Martí, Joel. 2000. *Formació i ocupació en el discurs dels treballadors. Una proposta metodològica.* Doctoral Thesis. Universitat Autònoma de Barcelona, Departament of Sociology.

———. 2006. "Representación de estructuras argumentativas mediante el análisis de redes sociales." *REDES. Revista Hispana para el Análisis de Redes Sociales* 10, #4. Retrieved November 30, 2009, from http://revista-redes.rediris.es.

Martin, John Levi 2000. "What do animals do all day? The division of labor, class bodies, and totemic thinking in the popular imagination." *Poetics* 27: 195–231.

van Meter, Karl M. 1999. "Social capital research literature: Analysis of key-word content structure and the comparative contribution of author names." *Connections* 22(1):62–84.

———. 2006. "Authors as 'artitsts' or 'heavy weights' in scientific publishing: The sociological analysis of scientific literature and the BMS." *Bulletin de Méthodologie Sociologique* 91:25–39.

van Meter, Karl M. and Mathilde de Saint Léger. 2008. "Co-word text analysis applied to political science: 2006 international political and 'parapolitical' headlines." *Bulletin de Méthodologie Sociologique* 97:18–38.

McKether, Willie L., Julia C. Gluesing, and Kenneth Riopelle. 2009. "From inter-views to social network analysis: An approach for revealing social networks embedded in narrative data." *Field Methods* 21(2):154–80.

Minor, Michael J. 1983. "Panel data on ego networks: A longitudinal study of former heroin addicts." Pp. 89–99 in *Applied Network Analysis*, edited by Ronald S. Burt and Michael J. Minor. Beverly Hills, CA: Sage.

Mohr, John W. 1994. "Soldiers, mothers, tramps and others: Discourse roles in the 1907 New York City charity directory." *Poetics* 22:327 57.

———. 1998. "Measuring meaning structures." *Annual Review of Sociology* 24: 345–70.

Monge, Peter R. and Eric M. Eisenberg. 1987. "Emergent communication net-works". Pp. 304–42 in *Handbook of Organizational Communication. An Interdisciplinary Perspective*, edited by Frederic M. Jablin, Linda L. Putnam, Karlene H. Roberts, and Lyman W. Porter. Newbury Park, CA: Sage.

Onwuegbuzie, Anthony J. and Charles Teddlie. 2003. "A framework for analyz-ing data in mixed methods research." Pp. 351–83 in *Handbook of Mixed Methods in Social and Behavioral Research*, edited by Abbas Tashakkori and Charles Teddlie. Thousand Oaks, CA: Sage.

Palmquist, Michael E., Kathleen M. Carley, and Thomas A. Dale. 1997. "Applications of computer-aided text analysis: Analyzing literary and nonliterary texts." Pp. 171–89 in *Text Analysis for the Social Sciences: Methods for Drawing Statistical Inferences from Texts and Transcripts*, edited by Carl W. Roberts. Mahwah, NJ: Lawrence Erlbaum.

Popping, Roel. 2000. *Computer-Assisted Text Analysis*. London: Sage.

———. 2003. "Knowledge graphs and network text analysis." *Social Science Information* 42:91–106.

———. 2005. "Representation of developments in labour market research." *Quality & Quantity* 39:241–51.

Rogers, Everett M. and D. Lawrence Kincaid. 1981. *Communication Networks. Toward a New Paradigm for Research*. New York: Free Press.

Ryan, Gery W. and Bernard, H. Russell. 2000. "Data management and analy-sis methods." Pp. 769–802 in *Handbook of Qualitative Research*, edited by Norman K. Denzin and Yvonna S. Lincoln. 2nd ed. Thousand Oaks, CA: Sage.

Schnegg, Michael. 1997. *Words as Actors II: Semantic Communities and Their Overlap*. Communication presented at the Qualitative Data Analysis Workshop, July 1997, Geneva University.

Smith, Tammy. 2007. "Narrative boundaries and the dynamics of ethnic conflict and conciliation." *Poetics* 35: 22–46.

Stohl, Cynthia. 1993. "European managers' interpretations of participation. A semantic network analysis." *Human Communication Research* 20: 97–117.

Strauss, Anselm L. and Juliet M. Corbin. 1990. *Basics of Qualitative Research. Grounded Theory Procedures and Techniques.* Newbury Park, CA: Sage.

Suitor, J. Jill, Barry Wellman, and David L. Morgan, eds. 1997. "Change in networks." *Social Networks* 19(1).

Tashakkori, Abbas and Charles Teddlie. 1998. *Mixed Methodology. Combining Quantitative and Qualitative Approaches.* Thousand Oaks, CA: Sage.

Tashakkori, Abbas and Charles Teddlie, C., eds. 2003. *Handbook of Mixed Methods in Social and Behavioral Research.* Thousand Oaks, CA: Sage.

Verd, Joan Miquel. 2002. *Itinerario biográfico, recursos formativos y empleo. Una aproximación integrada de carácter teórico y metodológico.* Doctoral Thesis. Universitat Autònoma de Barcelona, Departament of Sociology.

———.2005. "El uso de la teoría de redes sociales en la representación y análisis de textos. De las redes semánticas al análisis de redes textuales." *Empiria. Revista de Metodología de Ciencias Sociales* 10: 129–150.

———. 2006. "La construcción de indicadores biográficos mediante el análisis reticular del discurso. Una aproximación al análisis narrativo-biográfico." *REDES. Revista Hispana para el Análisis de Redes Sociales* 10, #4. Retrieved November 30, 2009, from http://revista-redes.rediris.es.

———. 2007. "Análisis de narraciones sociobiográficas: una visión reticular, cognitiva y social." Pp. 235–75 in *Interacción, redes sociales y ciencias cognitivas*, edited by Carlos Lozares. Granada, SP: Comares.

Wasserman, Stanley and Katherine Faust. 1994. *Social Network Analysis.* Cambridge: Cambridge University Press.

Wellman, Barry. 1979. "The community question: the intimate networks of East Yorkers." *American Journal of Sociology* 83:1201–31.

White, Harrison C. 2009. "Redes e historias." *REDES. Revista Hispana para el Análisis de Redes Sociales* 16, #1. Retrieved November 30, 2009, from http://revista-redes.rediris.es.

Woods, William A. 1975. "What's in a link: Foundations for Semantic Networks." Pp. 35–82 in *Representation and Understanding. Studies in Cognitive Science*, edited by Daniel G. Bobrow and Allan M. Collins. New York: Academic Press.

———. 1991. "Understanding subsumption and taxonomy: A framework for progress." Pp. 45–94 in *Principles of Semantic Networks*, edited by John F. Sowa. San Mateo, CA: Morgan Kaufmann.

Wuehrer, Gerhard A. and Markus Kathan. 2001. "*Structures of Managerial Decisions in Export Strategies Formulaion. Cognitive Maps of Austrian*

Managers." Communication presented at the XXIst International Sunbelt
Social Network Conference. September 25–29, 2001. Budapest.

Yeung, King-To. 2005. "What does love mean? Exploring network culture in
two network settings." *Social Forces,* 84(1):391–420.

11

Giving Meaning to Social Networks: Methodology for Conducting and Analyzing Interviews Based on Personal Network Visualizations

José Luis Molina, Isidro Maya-Jariego, and Christopher McCarty

I find it convenient to talk of a social field of this kind as a network. The image I have is of a set of points some of which are joined by lines. The points of the image are people, or sometimes groups, and the lines indicate which people interact with each other. We can of course think of the whole of social life as generating a network of this kind. (Barnes 1954)

Introduction

This chapter describes the application of visualization strategies in the context of mixed methods studies. Network visualization is an excellent way to present relational data, and a valuable tool for collecting, exploring, and analyzing data. This chapter focuses mainly on the description of personal networks (Hollstein 2011) with examples of parallel designs. The main contribution for investigating social networks consists in the incorporation of network perceptions and interpretations made by participants in the analysis, which leads to a better understanding of how people are positioned within the social context.

Barnes is recognized as the first one to use the expression "social network" (Barnes 1954). In a footnote next to the word "network" in the quotation at the beginning of this chapter, Barnes says:

> Earlier I used the term web, taken from the title of M. Fortes' book, *The Web of Kinship*. However, it seems that many people think of a web as something like a spider's web, in two dimensions, whereas I am trying to form **an image for a multi-dimensional concept**. It is merely a generalization of a pictographic convention which genealogists have used for centuries on their pedigree charts. Recent modifications of this convention include the tribal "sequences" in W. E. Armstrong, *Rossel Island* (1928), p. 37;

305

"Psychological geography" in J. L. Moreno, *Who Shall Survive?* (1934), pp. 238–47; and "sets" in E. D. Chapple and C. S. Coon, *Principles of Anthropology* (1942), p. 284. [bold added]

So visualizations are, from the very beginning, an essential element of the social network paradigm, not only as a means of representing data but as a tool for theoretical development. This point is echoed by Freeman (2004) in his historical account of network analysis that describes its essential features as (1) the "structural intuition" that confers a significant role to the patterns of relationships, (2) the use of systematic empirical data, (3) mathematic models and software packages, and (4) the importance given to the visual representation.

The important role assigned to visualization in the social network field is apparent. Nevertheless, beyond the aesthetic values of network data visualizations, what are the specific contributions of these visualizations to the research process (both in the collection and analysis phases)? Can we learn something about social reality that cannot be captured by other means?

With these questions in mind we review in this chapter the research projects conducted by the authors (see the Appendix to this chapter) in which visualizations were used, and provide evidences of the unique contributions of network data visualizations in all phases of the research project.

We want to emphasize that the power of visualization lies in the fact that it allows the conversion of quantitative information to qualitative, and vice versa. Thus it is possible to communicate the structural features of social networks to informants, to communicate between researchers with different qualitative/quantitative backgrounds, and to explore new models about the social world. The exploratory power of visualizations has been described widely. Others discuss the explanatory power of network visualizations (see Brandes et al. 2001, 2006; Freeman 2005; and de Nooy et al. 2005).

In this chapter we show how visualizations have allowed us to (1) understand the social world of informants as they see it themselves, (2) compare networks at the individual and community levels, (3) contrast different types of visualizations, and (4) develop new hypotheses.

The first section, "What Do We Mean by 'Visualizing Personal Networks'?", presents personal networks and their visualizations as a measure of the social and cultural world in which informants are embedded. Visualizations can be performed at the individual level, allowing us to ask informants questions about their social world that would otherwise be impossible, as a series or collection of personal networks showing variation or trends, and at the community or aggregated level by collapsing ensembles of personal networks in a simple graph in order to analyze differences between groups or communities using the same layout.

The second section, "Visualizations during the Data Collection," explains the processing of visualizations of personal networks by informants and how and why it is possible to obtain new data that cannot be obtained by other means. After assessing the influence of different types of visualizations of the same data on informants, this section presents the different types of questions that can be crafted with the aid of visualizations and their unique capability of combining compositional and structural variables in order to get new information. One interesting outcome of this combination is the identification of groupings and communities. Also, the comparison between two waves of the personal network of the same informant allows us to obtain information about the reasons given to the changes observed, thus obtaining rich narratives about life events.

The third section, "Visualization during Data Analysis," explains how visualizations allow the construction of typologies or processes and the development of new theoretical models. The power of visualization lies in the fact that the combination of the visual variables color, size, shape, position, and labels (and change if the visualization is dynamic) allows us to simultaneously assess a great amount of information about the substantive topic and to look for patterns or trends that can be related to the current theoretical framework in order to gain new insights about it.

Finally, we discuss the main lessons learned using intensive graphic displays of personal networks during all the research phases and their contribution to the mixed methods literature. As stated in the introduction of this volume, we refer to our approach as parallel design (Creswell, 2003; Johnson and Onwuegbuzie, 2004). In addition, this approach is exploratory and confirmatory, following the typology by Tashakkori and Teddlie (2003), blurring the borders of this dichotomy

Research on personal networks shows how both quantitative and qualitative methods are needed in order to understand not only the worlds of meaning of informants but the often invisible processes and contexts in which they are embedded.

What Do We Mean by "Visualizing Personal Networks"?

Personal networks, defined as the active social contacts of an individual, can be traced in different ways: diaries (Lonkila 1997, 1998; Fu 2007), different types of questionnaires, phone agendas, phone calls (Onnela et al. 2007), and even by social networking platforms.

From the point of view of the people interviewed, drawings represent their current social world, who is in it, and how it is organized structurally. Does everyone tend to be connected or does the informant maintain distinct groups in their life? From the point of view of the researcher, the personal network is a measure of the forces that frame society in a given individual, both macro and micro. We call "composition" the distribution of variables that describe people included in the personal network (percentage of males and females, percentage of kin, percentage of people that provide social support, for instance). Next, the "structure" of the network is the measures that summarize how alters are arranged around the ego (typically without ego included; see McCarty and Wutich 2005).

Composition and structure reflect a given moment in the life of a person within a social structure and a cultural and historical framework. Moreover, people change depending on the life cycle, institutional changes, or by random circumstances. By studying composition, structure, change, and the narratives given by the same individuals, it is possible to assess the different proportions of the factors that make each personal network a unique case and, at the same time, an understandable outcome (cf. Molina et al. 2008).

The visualization of personal networks is, thus, a given combination of compositional and structural features shown through visual variables (position, size, color, shape, connections, labels). By assigning visual variables to compositional or structural variables describing the personal networks, it is possible to interview the informant with different representations of her social world and get her impressions and explanations about them. Figure 11.1 shows an example of two visualizations of the same personal network. In this way, collections of visualizations combining the different information gathered during the interview are shown in order to explore the social world of the informant.

On the other hand, collections of different personal networks are used for data analysis, construction of typologies, and hypothesis generation (see Figure 11.2 for examples of different personal networks).

Apart from collections of the same personal network, or collections of different personal networks, it is possible to use a visual methodology for standardizing and comparing personal networks. This technique is called a "clustered graph" (Brandes et al. 2008) and consists of making a partition of the data with some relevant variables for the study, for instance, "sending country–host country" combinations, thus getting a reduced version of the graph but retaining and showing all relevant information such as density of relationships within a class or relationships among classes.

Figure 11.3, which represents the active contacts of an individual, has four nodes. Each node is a "class" or one of the possible combinations of the pair of variables "sending country–host country." The node in the bottom left represents the proportion of contacts and the density

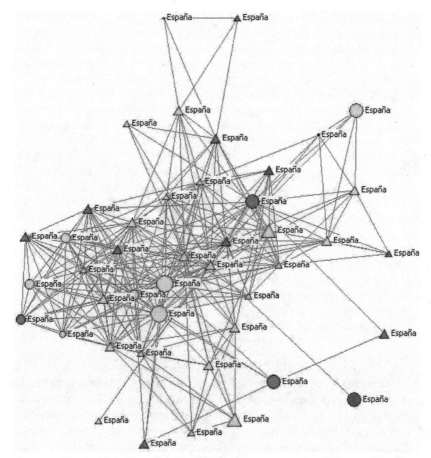

Figure 11.1. Two visualizations of the same personal network (with labels indicating different variables)

of ties corresponding to people born in the sending country and also living in the sending country. The density of ties within each class is represented with the degree of shadow (more darkness, more intra-class density). The number of people born in the sending country and currently living in the host country is represented at the bottom right. The size of the line between the two nodes represents the number of interclass ties (or active contacts across countries among people with the same origin).

At the top there is a node corresponding to "native" people (born and living in the host country). Finally, the number of people who are living in the host country, but who have different origins, are represented in the center. Again, the lines represent the number of interclass ties.

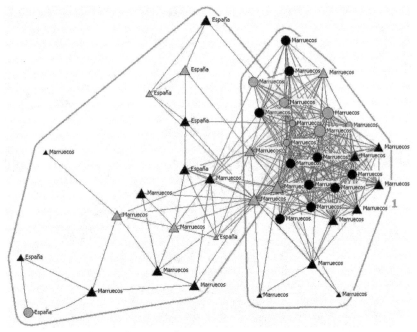

Figure 11.1. (*Continued*)

Moreover, it is possible to aggregate collections of personal networks in a single graph (Lerner et al. 2007, 2008) and compare in this way, for instance, the pattern of relationships between two or more migrant communities (see Figure 11.4).

Visualizations of personal network data are useful both in the data-collection and in the data-analysis phases of the research. During the data-collection phase, the visualization of the personal network allows informants to see a standardized image of their social world, shifting their position from being observed to becoming observers. This shift allows them to obtain new information and insights about themselves (see next section). Such an approach could be used, for instance, for mental health therapists and social workers to work with their patients and/or clients.

In the data-analysis phase, visualizations are used for establishing visual typologies and for, especially in the case of meta-representations, generating new hypotheses about the research problem. This capability for developing new insights about the research problem is due to the fact that standardized visualizations retain a great quantity of information while allowing controlled comparisons. The fixed layout (four nodes laid out in an up triangle with lines connecting them) allows the comparison of the variables represented (country of origin–country of residence in this case) while the changes in size, color, and thickness of the lines

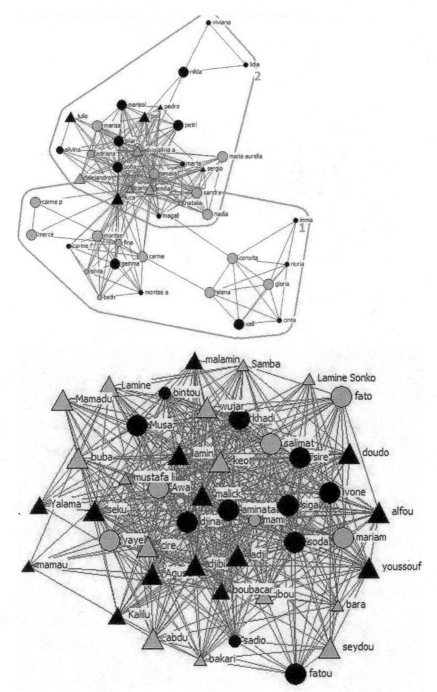

Figure 11.2. Four examples of different personal networks visualizations: Argentinean woman, Senegalese male (mandinga), Moroccan male (amazig), and Dominican male

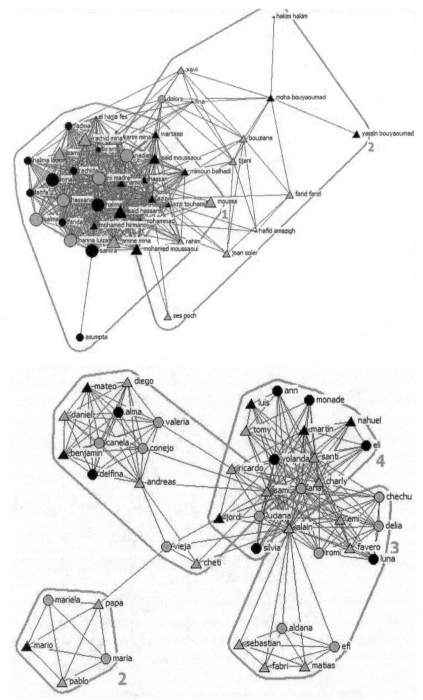

Figure 11.2. (*Continued*)

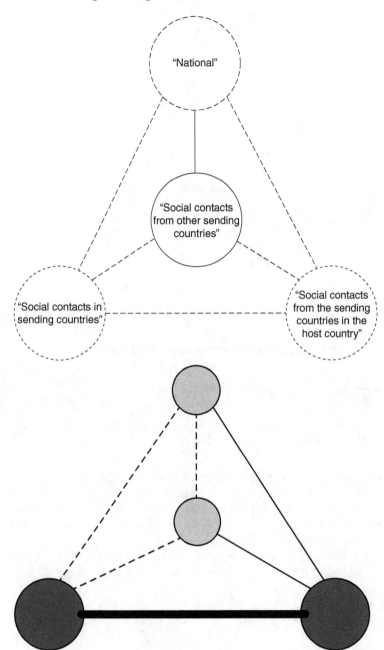

Figure 11.3. Example of a clustered graph representing a migrant personal network. Size represents the number of people living in the sending (left) or host country (top = nationals, right = people from the sending country, center = others). Darkness and strength of lines are proportional to the number of ties in each category or between categories, respectively. Ego is not shown in the figures.

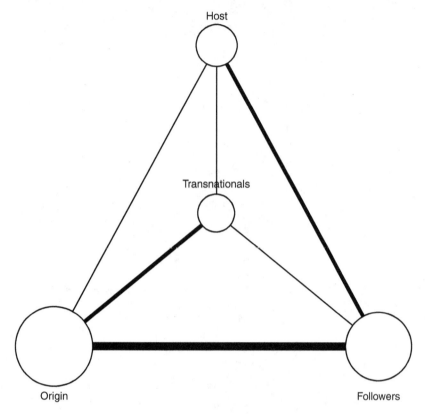

Figure 11.4. Examples of two clustered graphs aggregated: Dominicans in Spain (author: Jürgen Lerner)

represent variation in the data observed. Thus, complex personal networks with 45 nodes and 990 potential lines are reduced to a 4 nodes and 6 lines but showing the same information regarding the variables selected (number of people living in the host country, number of relations among individuals, and so on).

Summarizing the previous paragraphs, Table 11.1 shows the main outcomes of each type of visualization in the research phases of data collection and data analysis.

The next section focuses on the effect that graphic displays of personal networks have on the informants' accounts about their social worlds.

Visualizations during the Data Collection

Although in the social sciences visualizations are not widely used for data collection with some exceptions (see Bernardi et al.; Hollstein and

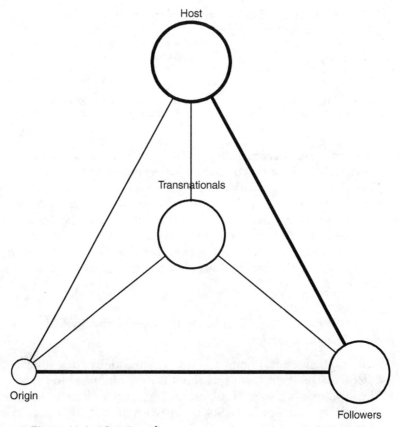

Figure 11.4. (*Continued*)

Wagemann, this volume), visual representations of the personal network are commonly used in counseling psychology and social work (see McCarty et al. 2007). Genograms are techniques used by mental health therapists to capture the relationships, both past and present, surrounding a client (McGoldrick et al. 1999; DeMaria et al. 1999). This technique tends to focus on mostly close family relationships and typically represents the social environment chronologically, including relatives that are both living and dead.

Another approach is the hierarchical mapping technique (Antonucci 1986; Ajrouch et al. 2001), which uses three concentric circles to represent the personal network of the respondent. In the middle of the innermost circle is the word "YOU" and respondents are asked to put close ties first in this place and then less close ties in the outer circle. This technique allows one to get a proxy for the size of the network and the distribution of their network based on closeness.

Table 11.1. *Main outcomes of personal network visualizations*

Research Phase	Collections of Personal Networks Visualizations	Metarepresentations of Personal Networks
Data collection	Narratives	-
Data analysis	Visual typologies	New hypothesis

Recently, Hogan et al. (2007) used a similar approach with four concentric circles. First they asked respondents to free-list alters and then place them on the network map, from the inner circles (close ties) to the outer circles (weak ties). Finally, respondents were asked to draw circles around groups of alters, adding structural features to the drawing.

A new program called Vennmaker (http://vennmaker.uni-trier. de) allows informants to enter their personal network data visually and arrange their alters the way they think of them being arranged in their mind.

What Do Visualizations of Personal Networks Add to the Interview?

First, from an ethical point of view, visualizations are a suitable form of feedback telling respondents about their contribution to the research. This feedback is always recommended in a network or social research (Borgatti et al. 2003, 2005), especially when people will be interviewed some months or years later.

Second, from our experience, respondents like the visual representation we make of their lives; they recognize their social world in the drawings and are able to construct narratives about them. The explanation of this fact is that informants perceive that network drawings do a reasonably good job of capturing the image they have about their social world, independently of the visual variables combined in a given image. Also, the drawings automatically arrange contacts in social settings that make sense for informants. To give meaning to the structures represented we follow a protocol that combines different visual variables in order to explore sequentially the social world of the informant.

Third, informants report errors generated during the survey, errors that normally are solved during the same interview. Those errors are rare in all projects (less than 1% in the case of Alcalá de Guadaíra, for instance; see Maya-Jariego and Holgado 2005; McCarty 2002). So, visualizations are also a tool for controlling and improving reliability.

Last, but not least, the visualizations provide a new context for the interview: Instead of asking the respondent to describe his/her personal relationships as they think of them or would just talk about them using schemas, they are requested to interpret the description previously provided. The interview is then more reflexive and interpretative and reflects the actual content and arrangement of the network that would otherwise be impossible.

Comparing Different Visualizations

McGrath et al. (1997) showed that different renderings of the same data do influence the perception of its structural features. For instance, the importance conferred to an actor in the network grows when she is placed in the center. Likewise, the closeness of actors in the drawing lets you identify groupings. Kennedy et al. (2011) showed that informants may be different in terms of the importance they place on particular structural features.

In order to assess the influence of different visualizations in the informants' accounts, in the Alcalá de Guadaíra study we designed two types of visualizations (Graph type I and Graph type II; see Figure 11.5). The type I visualization shows, among the 25 alters enacted by the respondent, only the strong ties between them. The type II visualization shows all ties reported by the respondent, but the size of nodes is dependent on the number of types of social support provided. One hundred and seventy students evaluated the two types of visualizations of their personal networks.[1]

During the interview respondents were asked about their general impression, groupings, and key people. Also, a Likert-scale questionnaire about different dimensions of graphs was administered. Table 11.2 shows the results of the experience.

Respondents generally preferred the social support–oriented visualization of their personal network (type II), which also allowed the detection of key actors, as it reflected better the position of ego in the network, and was considered an overall better representation of the personal network. On the other hand, the type I visualization allowed the identifications or the detection of clusters and groups.

Discovering New Insights with the Respondents

Personal network visualizations allow respondents to discover new traits of their social world. Similarly, compositional information (depending

[1] Half of them saw in the first place the type I and the others the type II.

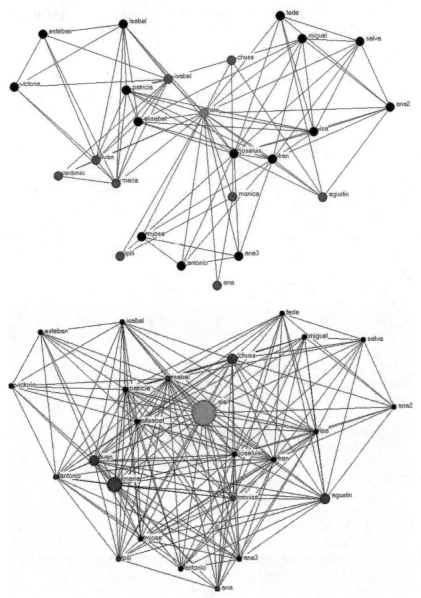

Figure 11.5. Two types of personal network visualizations

on the alter variables) can be elicited without the aid of visualizations. For instance, the following questions could be included in a standard questionnaire:

Table 11.2. *Comparisons of the two types of visualizations (n = 170)*

Dimensions	Type I		Type II		Student's t (gl = 1, 169)	Sig.
	M	DT	M	DT		
Aesthetics	3,35	1.01	3,17	1.15	1.55	0.121
Groupings	3.97	1.08	3.50	1.11	4.31	0.001
Key people	3.14	1.25	4.23	0.92	−9.00	0.001
Novelty	2.05	1.17	2.30	1.40	−3.59	0.001
Biography	3.47	1.14	3.55	1.14	−1.10	0.271
Ego position	3.08	1.35	3.30	1.34	−2.56	0.011
Alters prominence	2.93	1.25	4.20	0.95	−11.40	0.001
Relationship Alcalá/ Sevilla	3.50	1.52	3.41	1.50	1.49	0.136
Utility	2.70	1.26	2.80	1.27	−1.32	0.186
Intimacy	1.76	1.15	1.88	1.25	−1.80	0.073
Global assessment	3.83	1.04	4.01	0.95	−2.51	0.013

- Tell us about people from ... (country of origin).
- Tell us how you communicate with alters abroad (country of residence).
- Tell us about who helped you when you arrived for the first time (degree of proximity).

What we find a unique contribution are questions that include structural (or network) information and the combination of structural and compositional questions. This network dimension aggregated to the questionnaire shows the respondents new images of themselves and triggers justifications or explanations for those new insights. For instance, structural questions could be the following:

- Do you think that this representation of your personal network is accurate?
- Could you identify some groups of people?
- Who are these alters with more centrality?
- Why these are alters isolated?

Examples of compositional and structural questions could be the following:

- Tell us about those central alters living in Spain ...
- This group of Catalan women ... who are they?
- Your group of co-workers ... are they all Cubans?

By combining structural and compositional variables the informant discovers new connections and insights about their social world.

Personal network visualizations are a holistic representation of information obtained analytically. Therefore, the respondent can quickly perceive the information previously provided node by node, and link by link. The analytical approach when obtaining personal network information generates in a second step a constellation (or structure of relationships), which is not necessarily consciously or previously perceived by the informants. The analytical approach is also less influenced by social desirability. The visual representation is a summary of the information previously obtained. In consequence, it is in part new information and facilitates the interpretation and discussion by the respondent.

Eliciting Communities from Personal Network Visualizations

Visualizations assist respondents to elicit groups and cliques in their personal networks (McCarty 2002; Hogan et al. 2007; Maya-Jariego and Holgado 2005), as well as to list communities where they participate (Cachia and Maya-Jariego 2010).

In the psychological literature on sense of community researchers usually ask respondents to express their level of identification with an object. The boundaries are generally defined by formal settings such as neighbourhoods, organizations, or cities. Although researchers sometimes use relationally defined communities (as, for instance, "Moroccans living in Seville"), the boundaries are also defined in advance and then provided to informants to assess their reactions.

However, this approach is often inconsistent with the psychological experience of community. For instance, the limits of communities are frequently open and diffuse; communities may overlap and have a hierarchical or even a conflictive relationship among them; and individuals identify simultaneously with multiple communities.

Cachia and Maya-Jariego (2010) designed a procedure to elicit communities from personal network visualizations. First, respondents were presented with the visualization of their personal networks. They were asked to describe the structure of the graph, identifying groups, and cliques. Second, as groups or cliques in networks tend to be nested in larger communities, visualizations aided the respondents in naming communities which those close-knit ties belonged to.

Following this procedure, individuals mentioned approximately 12 groups and 12 communities on average[2] from their personal networks. The visualization procedure elicited 3 times more communities and 1.5

---

[2] Respondents mentioned 181 groups and 175 communities, with a mean score of 12.1 groups (SD = 3.08) and 11.7 communities (SD = 4.20).

more groups than a spontaneous listing by respondents (Cachia and Maya-Jariego 2010).

Visualizations allow for the identification of more communities, but the procedure is also qualitatively fruitful. The list of communities is derived from the personal network – that is to say, reflecting the dynamics of interaction in which the individual participates – instead of being proposed by the researcher herself. As a consequence, the inventory is less influenced by social desirability and captures a more accurate depiction of the social world of the respondent.

Groups and communities tend to be interrelated, but for respondents it is easier to identify the former than the second. A clique of neighbours may serve to mention the neighbourhood as a community, or a group of friends contributes to the recall of a leisure social setting where they usually socialize among themselves and with others (see, e.g., Figure 11.6). Groups are small sets of people that are able to communicate directly among themselves (not second hand) (Homans 1951), whereas in a community people do not necessarily know each other or interact directly. Through this procedure respondents go from the visualization of social interaction to the identification of concrete groups and then to naming relevant communities. From micro- to meso-social structures.

Communities are mediated social structures that individuals experience less directly and consciously than groups.

Getting Narratives and Reasons About Change

When two or more waves are available the sequential combination of structural and compositional information in visual variables can add temporal dimension. As the number of alters elicited is the same, questions can explore:

- Changes in people (new people)
- Changes in structure (new groupings, new isolates)
- Changes in compositional variables (new values of variables, as, for instance, changes in the country of residence)

To assess change respondents are questioned during the second wave to elicit a list of alters using the same name generator as in the first wave. Once the list is generated, a new variable is added for each alter (repeat? Yes/No). This variable allows interviewers to identify new people and ask questions about them.

From our data, in the two-year period, respondents typically changed about 50 percent of members, but compositional and structural outcomes remained more or less stable (Lubbers et al. 2010). In other words, respondents tend to substitute old alters with new alters of the

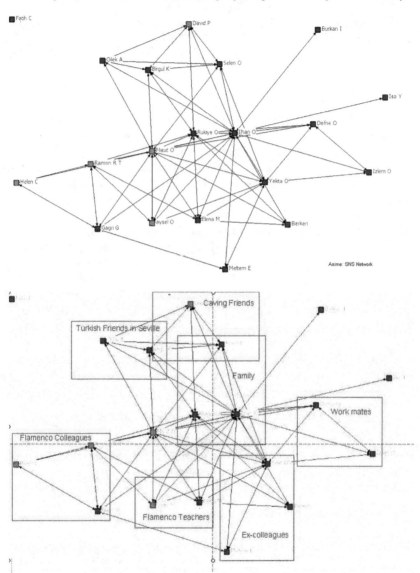

Figure 11.6. Three-step procedure to identify communities from personal network visualizations. The example corresponds to a Turkish woman residing in Seville

same demographics and in the same structural positions (that is, they are structurally equivalent).

The reasons given by informants about change were classified as two types: changes that go in the direction of assimilation to the host country

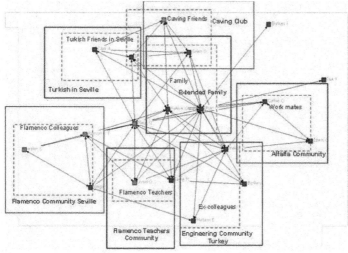

Figure 11.6. (*Continued*)

(Alba and Nee 1997), labeled "evolution," and changes that go in the opposite direction, "involution" (see Table 11.3 for a classification).

In general, informants could explain easily all changes observed (either by changes of residence, getting a new job, marriage with somebody form the host country or from the sending country, the new role of telecommunications and cheap trips in their lives, etc.). Those narratives are rich and give meaning to those social configurations that we call personal networks.

During the data-analysis phase interviews were listened to and transcribed simultaneously with the personal network visualizations. Interviewers were told to list explicit names and groupings during the dialogue with the respondent in order to allow the reproduction of the situation by the analyst. In general, visualizations allow two kinds of tasks: the construction of visual typologies and the development of visual models.

The same approach was developed with Argentinean immigrants residing in Seville, presenting the visualization four years after the first interview, when the name generator was applied. In this context the interview was an opportunity to assess (and to reflect on) the migratory project describing the different phases and social settings of the resettlement in a new country (Maya-Jariego et al. 2008).

Visualization during Data Analysis

If meta-representations of personal networks are available, then the analyst can anticipate information about the interview and thus combine

Table 11.3. *Reasons given by respondents about observed changes in their personal networks classified in "evolution" and "involution"*

	Evolution	Involution
Material life		
Job	* * *	
Housing		* *
Spaces of public interaction		
Training courses	* *	
Associations		* *
Discos	*	
Cult		*
"Ethnic" sport teams		* *
Sports	*	
Lifecycle		
Homophilus marriage		* * *
Heterophilus marriage	* *	
Divorce		* *
Newborn		* *
Death of a relative	*	
Travelling		
Travels		* *
Visits		*
Communications		*

* = slight influence; ** = influence; *** = strong influence.

the narratives with the structural features observed. Figure 11.7 shows an example of two clustered graphs of the same informant. The left graph represents the first wave and the right graph the second one. It is possible to see how new people with the same country of origin appear in the second wave in the host country, maintaining strong relationships with those that remain in the sending country. Thus, the analyst can interpret the explanation of the informant within a large social process and ask about this explanation with other informants in the same situation.

Constructing Visual Typologies of Personal Networks

Each personal network is, like a snowflake, a unique product, as we mentioned in the introduction. Nevertheless, the analyst soon discovers that within the variety of personal networks there are some that resemble each other. Trying to classify networks with the same structural characteristics and then trying to establish a sequence following a

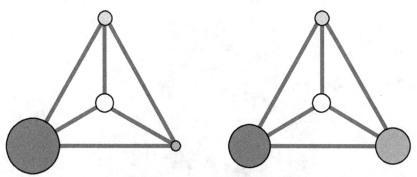

Figure 11.7. Two clustered graphs of the same individual. Left graph shows the first wave; right graph shows the second wave.

given variable is a way followed by different authors (see, for instance, Araya et al. 2005; Araya 2008; Ávila 2008).

Look at the sequence in Figure 11.8. This sequence shows the pattern of change in the personal networks of migrants with different years of residence in the host country (Molina et al. 2006).

Developing Visual Models

Visual models based on meta-representations have the advantage of formulating regularities at a very high level but at the same time are easy to test with the current data available.

If we compare Figure 11.8 and Figure 11.9, we can see that they are trying to show the same process of adaptation of migrants to the host country. The difference is that Figure 11.8 shows empirical cases and Figure 11.9 a general model of change. This mode also has the capability to represent quite accurately current theories about migrant adaptation in the host country (see Figure 11.10).

The power of visualizations for developing typologies and theoretical models is undeniable. Other meta-representations of network data can be developed in order to address other substantive research problems.

Finally, it is worth mentioning here that visualizations and narratives cannot capture by themselves all the effects observed in the data collected. For instance, thanks to the SIENA[3] model (Snijders et al. 2008; Snijders 2005) we found for instance that transitivity between the exiting clusters of acquaintances is an important effect in the alter-alter pattern of change (Lubbers et al. 2010). This effect cannot be directly observed in the personal network visualizations because it is an emergent property of the network beyond the cognition of their actors. Therefore, a mixed methods approach is needed.

[3] http://stat.gamma.rug.nl/siena.html.

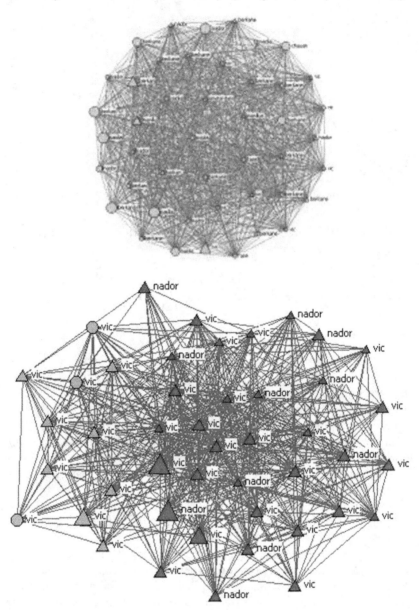

Figure 11.8. Process of acculturation showed through a sequence of personal networks

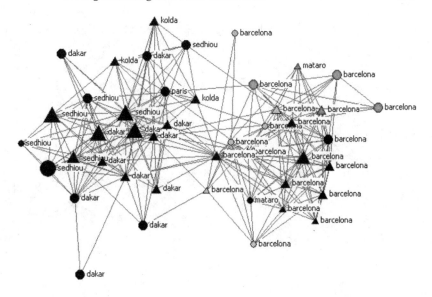

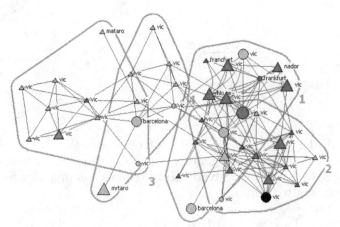

Figure 11.8. (*Continued*)

Discussion: Mixing Methods – Challenges and Benefits

Traditionally, graphic representations have been used to illustrate the structural properties of personal networks. Visualizations are a simple and intuitive manner to communicate research results. As we have shown, they are also tools for data analysis and data collection, and they are particularly well-suited for a mixed methods approach.

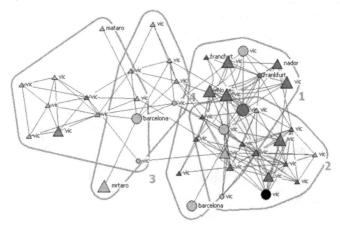

Figure 11.8. (*Continued*)

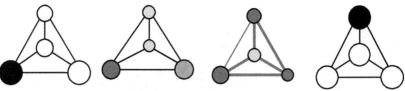

Figure 11.9. General mode of change

Visual images can be used for exploratory research, examining a priori conjectures, validating a model, and deploying post hoc analysis (Freeman 2005). These strategies are also applied during data analysis of personal network information.

Exploratory assessment is probably the most common strategy when using personal network visualizations. The simplest application consists of searching for the structure, looking for distinct patterning of ties. Furthermore, it is common to examine the impact of external variables on the structural patterning of relationships. For instance, the graphics allow for the exploration of the position of alters related to gender or multiplexity of social support. Another example consists in classifying personal networks to formulate new hypotheses (Araya Dujisin and Maya-Jariego 2005; Ávila 2008).

Graphic techniques are also applied for confirmatory analysis. They are tools that look for correlates of structural properties, verifying the role of antecedents and consequences of observed structural patterns. This is the case of the studies that try to point out the association between familiar

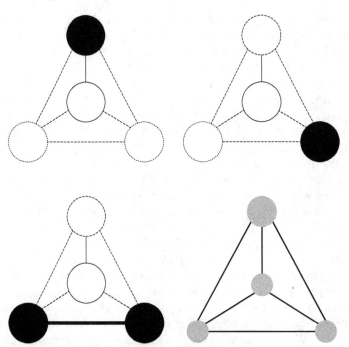

Figure 11.10. Ideal types of adaptation to the host country. Assimilation (top left), ethnic enclave (top right), transnational (bottom left), and mixed (bottom right)

and/or ethnic composition and the structure of the personal networks (see Domínguez and Maya-Jariego 2008; Molina et al. 2008). We have also checked whether mobility and ecological transitions are reflected in a reduction of density and an increase in clustering, based in visual representations.

Graphics can even be used to validate a model, in the same way as we describe the process of acculturation of international immigrants as a function of the time on residence in the host country (Lerner and Brandes 2007; Lerner et al. 2008). Nonetheless visualizations can contribute to the development of new insights and ideas that were not previously anticipated.

As we have shown, visual images can also be used in data collection. Through interviews, respondents are oriented to adopt exploratory, confirmatory, and validating strategies when describing their personal networks. Visualizations contribute to elicit biographical information and to detect groups and cliques that are meaningful for the respondents (McCarty 2002; Maya-Jariego and Holgado 2005). Furthermore, groups and cliques facilitate the identification of relevant communities for the individual (Cachia and Maya-Jariego 2010). When longitudinal network information is available, respondents can also help to explain and interpret the changes (Lubbers et al. 2010).

In both data analysis and data collection, visual display is a fundamental aspect. Although initially visualizations were based in ad hoc strategies – adapted to each data set – some procedures and graphic techniques have been developed to facilitate standardized and replicable representations (Freeman 2005). This is the case of the spatial proximities patterns based in multidimensional scaling (MDS) and principal component analysis. As we have shown, the dimensions and the way of presenting the data influence the perception and interpretations of the respondents (McGrath et al. 1997; Maya-Jariego and Holgado 2005). Mixed methods may contribute to the systematic assessment of the reactions to different visual displays by respondents. This is probably one of the areas in which we will observe significant contributions in next future research.

In the same vein, this is an area open to creativity and innovation. We have shown the use of meta-representations to summarize personal networks' data (Lerner et al. 2007, 2008), contributing to a remarkable potential for theoretical modeling. Diverse visualization tools have been deployed to represent and to detect subsets of actors in cohesive groups in personal networks. On the other hand, more developments are required to capture the structural properties of personal networks, for example, representing actors that occupy equivalent social positions, and so on. We also foresee new tools and strategies in this regard.

Personal network visualizations work as an interface between qualitative and quantitative data analysis and data collection. Respondents collaborate with researchers to interpret the structural properties of their networks and provide a biographical context to network data. Graphic techniques contribute to classifying personal networks and to developing theoretical models. With all this background, network images constitute an active and promising tool for mixed methods research.

Appendix

The empirical basis of our work lies in four research projects developed during the last few years, which are summarized in Table 11.4. All four projects collected the data with the same protocol, although with different tools and emphasis, depending on the substantive questions of each project. The last project introduced a dynamic dimension in the data collected in order to compare networks and narratives over time.

The common protocol[4] for data collection (embedded in EgoNet) is the following:

---

[4] In the Alcalá de Guadaíra study, several name generators exploring the provision of social support were used (derived from the Arizona Social Support Interview Schedule [ASSIS]; Barrera 1980).

Table 11.4. *Research projects in which the protocol for data collection and analysis has been developed and applied*

Projects	Focus	Locations	N	Alters nominated	Software used for aiding interviews	Waves
NSF – 2004–2006	Acculturation	Locations in Barcelona, New York and Miami.	N=294 (Spain)	45	EgoNet[a]	1 wave
Council Alcalá de Guadaíra 2004–2006	Sense of Community	Alcalá de Guadaíra (Seville)	N= 208 undergraduate students	25	Ucinet-Netdraw[b]	1 wave
AGAUR 2008–2009 (undergoing)	Identity, integration	Barcelona and Roses (Girona, Spain)	N= 50 migrants	30	EgoNet + clustered graphs	1 wave
ESF – MICINN 2007–2009 (undergoing)	Identity, patterns of change	Locations in Barcelona and Seville	N= 67 migrants in Barcelona. N= 69 students in Alcalá de Guadaíra	45	EgoNet + clustered graphs	2 waves

[a] http://sourceforge.net/projects/egonet/.
[b] http://www.analytictecnologies.com.

Information about ego. In this module a list of variables describing ego are collected. They may be independent or dependent variables.

> *Flexible name generator.* Instead of using a series of name generators to explore different institutional settings of a personal network, a flexible name generator was used with little variation across projects: Please, give us the names of XX persons you know and who know you by sight or by name, with whom you have had some contact in the past two years, either face-to-face, by phone, mail or e-mail, and whom you could still contact them if you had to.

The *fixed-choice design* was chosen in order to ensure that the respondents nominated not only strong contacts but also weaker ones. For other projects different or multiple name generators may be appropriate.

Information about alters nominated by ego. Variables such as sex, age, location of residence, perceived closeness, and type of support provided were recorded in this module. This part is the most time-consuming because the informants have to provide n variables for each alter nominated previously.

Alter-alter relationship. This module asks for the existence of relations among alters (as perceived by the respondent) with this alter-pair question:

> XX and XX knows each other?

or

> XX and XX would talk independently of you?

Visualization and in-depth interview. In this part a series of visualizations of the personal network of the informant are generated or provided during the interview and the qualitative information is recorded. The details for the different types of visualizations and the protocol for exploring the changes occurring between the two waves will be provided in the following section.

For the data-analysis phase we developed visual typologies of personal networks or meta-representations of the data in order to allow comparisons between informants, between two waves of the same informant, or, once aggregated, between communities (see the section "Eliciting Communities from Personal Network Visualizations"). Along with this qualitative information, the research design allowed us to analyze rich quantitative information, either compositional (the distribution of the attributive variables collected for ego and their alters) or structural (network measures).

References

Ajrouch, Kristine K., Toni C. Antonucci, and Mary R. Janevic. 2001. "Social networks among Blacks and Whites: The interaction between race and age." *Gerontologist* 56B:112–18.

Alba, Richard and Victor Nee. 1997. "Rethinking assimilation theory for a new era of immigration." *International Migration Review* 31(4): 826–74.

Antonucci Toni C. 1986. "Social support networks: Hierarchical mapping technique." *Generations* 10:10–12.

Araya Dujisin, Rodrigo. 2008. "Multitudes y redes en la caída de Milosevic." *REDES-Revista hispana para el análisis de redes sociales* 15(7):126–148. Retrieved April 19, 2012, from http://revista-redes.rediris.es/pdf-vol15/Vol15_7.pdf.

Araya Dujisin, Rodrigo and Isidro Maya-Jariego. 2005. "Los puentes interlocales: las redes personales de los universitarios alcalareños en Sevilla." In *Redes, enfoques y aplicaciones del análisis de redes sociales*. Santiago de Chile: IDEA. USACH – Universidad Bolivariana.

Ávila Molero, Javier. 2008. "Redes personales de africanos y latinoamericanos en Cataluña, España. Análisis reticular de integración y cambio." *REDES-Revista hispana para el análisis de redes sociales* 15(5):61–94. Retrieved April 19, 2012, from http://revista-redes.rediris.es/pdf-vol15/Vol15_5.pdf.

Barnes, John (1954). "Class and committees in a Norwegian Islan Parish," *Human Relations* 7(1):39–58.

Barrera, Manuel. 1980. "A method for the assessment of social support networks in community survey research." *Connections* 3(1):8–13.

Borgatti, Stephen P, and José Luis Molina. 2003. "Ethical and strategic issues in organizational social network analysis." *The Journal of Applied Behavioral Science* 39(3):16–45.

Borgatti, Stephen P. 2005. "Toward ethical guidelines for network research in organizations." *Social Networks* 27(2):107–117.

Brandes, Ulrik, Jörg Raab, and Dorothea Wagner. 2001. "Exploratory network visualization: Simultaneous display of actor status and connections." *Journal of Social Structure* 2(4). Retrieved October 27, 2010, from http://www.library.cmu.edu:7850/JoSS/brandes/index.html.

Brandes, Ulrik, Patrick Kenis, and Jörg Raab. 2006. "Explanation through network visualization." *Methodology* 2(1):16–23.

Brandes, Ulrik, Jürgen Lerner, Miranda J. Lubbers, Chris McCarty, and José Luis Molina. 2008. "Visual statistics for collections of clustered graphs." Pp. 47–54 in *Proceedings of the IEEE Pacific Visualization Symposium (PacificVis'08)*. IEEE Computer Society.

Barnes, John. 1954. "Class and committees in a Norwegian Islan Parish." *Human Relations* 7(1):39–58.

Cachia, Romina and Isidro Maya-Jariego. 2010. "Eliciting communities from personal network visualizations: ties, groups and communities." *XXX International Sunbelt Social Network Conference*. Trento (Italy), June 29–July 4 2010.

Creswell, John W. 2003. *Research Design. Qualitative, Quantitative and Mixed Methods Approaches.* 2nd ed. London: Sage.

DeMaria, Rita, Gerald Weeks, and Larry Hof. 1999. *Focused Genograms: Intergenerational Assessment of Individuals, Couples, and Familes.* New York: Brunner-Routledge.

de Nooy, Wouter, Andrej, Mrvar and Vladimir Batagelj. 2005. *Exploratory Social Network Analysis with Pajek.* Cambridge: Cambridge University Press.

Domínguez, Silvia and Isidro Maya-Jariego. 2008. "Acculturation of host individuals: Immigrants and personal networks." *American Journal of Community Psychology* 42:309–27.

Freeman, Linton C. 2004. *The Development of Social Network Analysis: A Study in the Sociology of Science.* Vancouver: Empirical Press.

———.2005. "Graphic techniques for exploring social network data." Pp. 248–69 in *Models and Methods in Social Network Analysis,* edited by P. J. Carrington, J. Scott and S. Wasserman. New York: Cambridge University Press.

Fu, Yang-Chih. 2007. "Contact diaries: Building archives of actual and comprehensive personal networks." *Field Methods* 19 (2): 194–217.

Hogan, Bernie, Juan Antonio Carrasco, and Barry Wellman. 2007. "Visualizing personal networks: Working with participant-aided sociograms." *Field Methods* 19(2):116–44.

Hollstein, Betina. 2011. "Qualitative approaches." Pp. 404–17 in *The SAGE Handbook of Social Network Analysis,* edited by J. Scott and P. J. Carrington. London: Sage.

Homans, George C. 1951. *The Human Group.* London: Routledge.

Johnson, R. Burke and Anthony J. Onwuegbuzie. 2004. "Mixed methods research: A research paradigm whose time has come." *Educational Researcher* 33:14–26.

Kennedy, David P., Harold D. Green, Jr., Christopher McCarty, and Joan Tucker. 2011. "Nonexperts' Recognition of Structure in Personal Network Data," *Field Methods* 23(3):287–306.

Lerner, Juergen and Ulrik Brandes. 2007. "Comparing networks by their group structure with an application to acculturation networks." *XXVII Sunbelt'07*, Corfu, Greece, May 1–6.

Lerner, Juergen, Ulrik Brandes, Miranda J. Lubbers, José Luis Molina, and Chris McCarty. 2008. "Visualizing tendency and dispersion in collections of attributed networks." *XXVIII Sunbelt'08*, January 24–27, St. Petersburg, FL.

Lonkila, Markku. 1997. "Informal exchange relations in post-Soviet Russia: A comparative perspective." *Sociological Research Online* 2 (2). Retrieved April 19, 2012, from http://www.socresonline.org.uk/welcome.html.

———. 1998. "Continuity and change in social networks of St. Petersburg Teachers, 1993–1996." *Connections* 21(1):62–86.

Lubbers, Miranda J, José Luis Molina, Jürgen Lerner, Ulrik Brandes, Javier Ávila, and Christopher McCarty. 2010. "Longitudinal analysis of personal networks. The case of Argentinean migrants in Spain." *Social Networks* 32(1):91–104.

Maya-Jariego, Isidro and Neil Armitage. 2007. "Multiple senses of community in migration and commuting: The interplay between time, space and relations." *International Sociology* 22(6):741–64.

Maya-Jariego, Isidro and Daniel Holgado. 2005. "Lazos fuertes y proveedores múltiples de apoyo: comparación de dos formas de representación gráfica de las redes personales." *Empiria. Revista de metodología de ciencias sociales* 10:107–27.

Maya-Jariego, Isidro, Daniel Holgado, Daniel Santos, and Enrique Vergara. 2008. "Cuatro grupos de extranjeros en Andalucía: Informe descriptivo de investigación." *Redes. Revista Hispana para el Análisis de Redes Sociales* 15:122–29.

McCarty, Christopher. 2002. "Measuring structure in personal networks." *Journal of Social Structure* 3(1). Retrieved April 19, 2012, from http://www.cmu.edu/joss/.

McCarty, Christopher and Amber Wutich. 2005. "Conceptual and empirical arguments for including or excluding ego from structural analyses of personal networks." *Connections* 26:80–86.

McCarty, Christopher, José Luis Molina, Claudia Aguilar, and Laura Rota. 2007. "A comparison of social network mapping and personal network visualization." *Field Methods* 19(2):145–62.

McGoldrick, Monic, Randy Gerson, and Sylvia Shellenberger. 1999. *Genograms: Assessment and Intervention.* New York: Norton.

McGrath, Cathleen, Jim Blythe, and David Krackhardt. 1997. "The effect of spatial arrangement on judgments and errors in interpreting graphs." *Social Networks* 19(3):223–42.

Molina, José Luis, Miranda J. Lubbers, and Christopher McCarty. 2006. "Acculturation revisited: A model of personal network change." *QMMS*, Groningen (The Netherlands), September 14–15.

Molina, José Luis, Jüergen Lerner, and Sílvia Gómez. 2008. "Patrones de cambio de las redes personales de inmigrantes en Cataluña." *REDES- Revista hispana para el análisis de redes sociales* 15 #4. Retrieved April 19, 2012, from http://revista-redes.rediris.es/pdf-vol15/Vol15_4.pdf.

Onnela, Jukka-P. Jari Saramäki, Jörkki Hyvönen, György Szabó, David Lazer, Kimmo Kaski, Janos Kertész, and Albert L. Barabási. 2007. "Structure and tie strengths in mobile communication networks." *Proceedings of the National Academy of Sciences* 104(18):7332–36.

Snijders, Tom A. B. 2005. "Models for longitudinal network data." Pp. 215–233 in *Models and Methods in Social Network Analysis*, edited by P. J. Carrington, J. Scott, and S. Wasserman. New York: Cambridge University Press.

Snijders, Tom A. B., Christian E. G. Steglich, Michael Schweinberger, and Mark Huisman. 2008. *Manual for SIENA version 3.2.* Groningen: University of Groningen, ICS; Oxford: University of Oxford, Department of Statistics. Retrieved April 19, 2012, from http://www.stats.ox.ac.uk/siena.

Tashakkori, Abbas and Charles Teddlie. 2003. *Handbook of Mixed Methods in Social & Behavioral Research.* London: Sage.

12

Simulating the Social Networks and Interactions of Poor Immigrants

Bruce Rogers and Cecilia Menjívar

Introduction

In social science disciplines the term "mixed methods" usually refers to studies that rely on a mix of qualitative and quantitative methods: on one hand, techniques that rely on small samples and seek to gain an in-depth understanding of a particular situation and the meanings individuals attach to it, and on the other, techniques based on randomized samples that permit the detection of patterns and create generalizable results. In this chapter we propose a different kind of "mixed method" analysis: one that incorporates data generated through qualitative techniques of participant observation and in-depth interviewing with agent-based modeling. The data of interest are the social networks of a local community of Salvadoran immigrants, and we base computer simulations of the networks on an earlier qualitative study by one of the authors. In order to capture the dynamics of the immigrants' social network, describe reciprocity between actors, and understand how information affects access to resources, we use a sequential exploratory design, which, as Hollstein notes in the introduction to this volume, helps to explain conditions under which certain patterns take place and the consequences they can have. We start with qualitative observations that then inform computer simulations that generate data. The qualitative study shows how expectations of reciprocity can weaken social networks in poor communities, and the computer simulations show how adjusting the social cost of failing to reciprocate affects the density of the social networks. Thus, our chapter highlights a fundamental aspect for mixed methods research – that is, the integration of analysis at key stages in the process. As Hollstein (this volume) observes, it is this integration, in contrast to simply combining data or analyses, that is key to mixed methods studies. Also, importantly, the use of computer simulations allows the researcher to conduct experiments in silica that are impossible in the

336

real world, such as changing the economic environment or the weight of social costs. The qualitative study sheds light on social mechanisms, and computer experiments explore those mechanisms in situations other than the ones actually observed.

Menjívar (2000) conducted an ethnographic study to understand the inner workings of the informal social networks among the Salvadoran immigrants in San Francisco. Conducting surveys, ethnographic observations, and in-depth interviews from approximately 1989 to 1994, she found that the networks among this group were fluid, contingent, and changing. It was counterintuitive to find such fluidity in social networks among an immigrant community because studies of immigrant groups usually emphasized the vital place of networks as sources of assistance (Bashi 2007; Massey et al. 1990) particularly among the poor. Scholars from different social science disciplines and in different contexts have found that social networks among immigrants structure their process of assimilation and integration (Portes 1998; Rodriguez and Egea 2006); put jobs within the immigrants' reach (Waldinger and Lichter 2003); facilitate social mobility (Ari 2006) and resettlement (Ilcan 2002); provide companionship, emotional support, and psychological well-being (Jasinkaja-Lahti el al. 2006; Wong et al. 2006); and afford access to a myriad of resources today (Khoo 2003; Piotrowski 2006; Ryan 2007; Tsai 2006) as well as in the past (McCarthy 2005). Indeed, some scholars argue that social networks constitute a key organizing mechanism to understand all aspects of the migration process (Bashi 2007). However, recent scholarship questions some of these assumptions, noting the positive as well as the negative consequences that networks can bring to members (Portes and Sensenbrenner 1993), that social networks at the heart of skilled migration might actually be redundant (Johnston et al. 2006), that networks' centrality does not apply in certain migratory movements (Collyer 2005), or that they might not be as central in promoting migration and might actually be a result and not a cause of migration as it is usually assumed (Aragones and Dunn 2005). Along these lines, as Menjívar noted, social networks can weaken under extreme conditions of poverty, when too many demands are placed on an individual (Menjívar 2000). This finding highlighted the changing, fluid nature of networks and underscored that such ties do not always represent sources of assistance, particularly when people do not have much to share. By presenting a more nuanced picture of how networks among immigrants operate, Menjívar's ethnographic work comes closer to explicating how individuals become members of networks, under what circumstances they do so, how networks might change according to need – as well as how resources and information are channeled through these ties. Thus, we seek to build on her earlier work in order to provide a heuristic tool that can be used in areas beyond immigrant networks.

We aim to capture the essential characteristics of Menjívar's ethnographic study in an agent-based model in order to simulate the social networks among individual actors. Agent-based models use agents to implement social interactions according to a set of rules. The agents are pieces of computer code that act individually in a simulated environment (Griffin 2005). For us, the agents represent the Salvadoran immigrants in a social network. Each agent acts according to a set of rules that are derived from the social interactions witnessed by Menjívar. So there are two parts of the model: the agents' environment and the rules that determine individual behavior. As the agents interact with their environment and each other, they change their environment and their relationships with each other. The model unfolds in time, and at every time-step the agents complete a sequence of tasks that are analogous to the trials and tribulations faced by the Salvadoran population in San Francisco. The agents lose their jobs, get paid and pay rent, acquire information about employment and housing, utilize the beneficial information they acquire, ask network affiliates for aid, exchange information with other agents, and perhaps change their social network. These tasks correspond to different routines (or functions) in the computer code – as explained in more detail in the following sections.

One of Menjívar's main observations was that the social networks of the Salvadoran community were fluid and tended to dissolve. Social ties represent the informal web of family and friends who can provide material, financial, or informational support. In the case of an exchange of material, the people involved in the exchange are expected to reciprocate. However, the immigrants in Menjívar's study were not often in a position to reciprocate material assistance due to the harsh economic conditions of the time which were regularly exacerbated by uncertain legal status. When someone neglects (perhaps repeatedly) requests to fulfill reciprocal obligations, the social ties between the individuals weaken and may disappear – even between close kin. Thus, the main goal of this chapter is to elucidate how reciprocal exchange affects network structure. Since we use computer simulations, we can carefully track the network evolution and study the qualitative dynamic behavior of the social networks. Therefore, we aim to combine Menjívar's qualitative ethnographic work and its perspective on social networks from the sociology of immigration with the rich literature of computational modeling of reciprocity and cooperation.

The model has three components: the economic environment, the reciprocal exchange of resources, and the exchange of information. In the next section we describe the agents' environment. In the third section we discuss the formalization of reciprocal (material) exchange, and in the fourth section the same is done for the exchange of information. In the fifth section, we explain how the three components work together in time, and we discuss the simulation results in the sixth section. Concluding remarks, discussion, and a critique of our methods follow in the final section.

Economic Environment

The economic environment facing Salvadoran immigrants in San Francisco in the early 1990s was poor. The economic recession coupled with a lack of legal status caused a great deal of instability in the immigrants' ability to retain employment. Many worked as day laborers, and even this work was spotty. In this section we describe the computer version of the poor economic environment facing the Salvadoran population. At each time-step, agents are given some amount of resources depending on a "job" state, and they are deducted some amount of expenses depending on the "housing" state of the agent. There are four job states, which by analogy can be thought of as unemployed, spotty part-time employment, regular part-time employment, and full-time employment, which are fairly typical of the employment situations among immigrant newcomers. There are also four housing states corresponding to the job states. Jobs act as a source of resources, and the rent paid for housing acts as a drain on resources. Agents prefer to have a better job state and a housing state that matches their job level. If an agent's expenses outstrip its income, it will seek resource aid from the agents it is connected to in the network.

In order to capture the unstable existence of the immigrants in Menjívar's study, the income levels for jobs and the rent levels for housing are not fixed; they vary from time-step to time-step according to a uniform distribution. However, the variation decreases as the levels increase so that incomes and rents are more stable for the better employed (see Table 12.1).

After resources are distributed according to job type, it is possible, even probable, that an agent will not have enough resources to pay its rent. If this is the case, the agent asks for assistance from affiliates in its social network. In the next section, we describe the details of the exchange process, which turns on the expectation of reciprocity (see Table 12.2).

Modeling Reciprocity

The importance of the concept of reciprocity for the study of social interactions has a long history in the social sciences. For instance, Georg Simmel (1950) observed that all contacts among men rest on the schema

Table 12.1. *Income distribution for each job level*

Housing Level	Rent Distribution
1	0–300
2	200–400
3	600–750
4	950–1000

Table 12.2. *Rent distribution for each housing level*

Job Level	Income Distribution
1	0–300
2	300–500.
3	700–800
4	1200

of giving and returning the equivalence, and L. T. Hobhouse (1951) declared that reciprocity is the vital principle of society. But it was Alvin Gouldner (1960) who would explicate this concept in more depth, suggesting ways in which it could be used to analyze central theoretical problems in sociological theory. According to Gouldner, reciprocity means that "people should help those who have helped them, and ... should not injure those who have helped them." Reciprocity therefore ensures that among parties involved in an exchange, the one who receives will eventually repay, thus providing realistic grounds for trust (Menjívar 2000). However, although reciprocity may be universal, Gouldner warned, it is not unconditional and it imposes obligations contingently. Thus, reciprocity dictates that a person should try to repay, in kind, what another person has provided (Cialdini 1984).

Computational modeling of reciprocity dates back at least to Axelrod's (1984) famous computer tournaments in the 1980s. Axelrod was concerned with how cooperation can come to exist in a world populated by selfish actors. Like most subsequent simulations involving reciprocity and cooperation, these concerns were couched in the language of game theory. The tournament challenged programmers to write computer code to play a repeated game called the Prisoners' Dilemma, where each of the two players must independently decide whether to cooperate with the other or "defect." The winner of the tournaments was a model of reciprocity called Tit-for-Tat. Tit-for-Tat's winning strategy was simple: Always cooperate the first time and then copy the opponent's most recent behavior. If the opponent cooperates, Tit-for-Tat continues to cooperate; however, if the opponent defects, Tit-for-Tat will punish the defection by defecting in the next iteration.

Since Tit-for-Tat, many researchers have conducted computer simulations to determine how cooperation can evolve among self-interested actors (Axelrod 1997; Bowles and Gintis 2004; Zeggelink et al. 2000). These studies are often abstract and game-theoretic with little reference to actual human data or behavior (e.g., Nowak and May 1992), or the authors make references to early human societies where the number of agents is small and everyone can be expected to know everyone else (Bowles and Gintis 2004; Zeggelink et al. 2000). The research most germane to the present chapter focuses on models of reciprocity (or cooperation) that highlight the network structure of exchange (Zeggelink et al. 2000), the effects of poor environmental conditions (deVos et al. 2001), or both (Flache 2001). A common theme of these highlighted works is very minimal modeling of agents' environmental conditions. Other authors (Reynolds et al. 2003; McAllister et al. 2005) make very detailed models of the environment based on observations[1] of specific communities. As discussed in in the second section, we follow the latter tack.

Many of these authors (Nowak and May 1992; Bowles and Gintis 2004; Zeggelink et al. 2000; Flache 2001) also view agents as either "cooperators" or "defectors." The defectors never give assistance to those who ask for help, and cooperators behave almost identically like Tit-for-Tat. However, actual exchange relationships develop over time, and the relationship between two individuals can be characterized by each actor's willingness to put up with defection from the other (Molm 2006). We propose to characterize this willingness to put up with defection as a likelihood, or a probability, to grant assistance when requested. In short, we model reciprocity with the following local rules:

- If Agent Alice receives help from Agent Bob, Alice is more likely to help Bob in the future.
- Conversely, Bob is less likely to help Alice in the future.

Also, we assume there is a social cost for declining to help someone who asks for aid:

- If Agent Alice asks for assistance from Agent Bob – and Bob says no – Alice is less likely to help Bob in the future.

Thus the most important variable for an exchange is the probability for granting aid. The likelihood that Agent Alice (A) will give aid to Agent Bob (B) – if Bob asks – is denoted E_{AB}. Similarly, the probability that Bob will help Alice (when asked) is denoted E_{BA}.

---

[1]　In the case of Reynolds et al. 2003, the observations are archaeological records.

Table 12.3. *Updating exchange probabilities after A asks B for aid*

Outcome	Initial Weight	New Weight
B agrees to help	E_{AB}	$E_{AB} + (1-E_{AB})\beta$
	E_{BA}	αE_{BA}
B declines to help	E_{AB}	αE_{AB}
	E_{BA}	$E_{BA} + (1-E_{BA})\beta$

The question now becomes, after receiving aid, how much does the likelihood to grant assistance change? Because human memories aren't perfect, we propose that more emphasis should be given to the most recent exchanges. A natural way to express this emphasis on recent exchange is to have the likelihoods change geometrically – that is, by a constant factor.

For example, suppose Agent Alice has negative resources, and she asks Agent Bob for assistance. If Agent Bob agrees to help – the probability of which is E_{BA}, then the probability E_{BA} will decrease for the next time Alice asks for help from Bob. The probability E_{BA} decreases by a constant factor α between 0 and 1. So, after the exchange, the probability Bob will aid Alice next time is decreased to αE_{BA}. Also, after receiving assistance from Bob, Alice is now more likely to help Bob than before, so the E_{AB} is increased to $E_{AB} + (1 - E_{AB})\beta$, where β is between 0 and 1.

As expressed in the third bullet above, if Alice asks for assistance from Bob but is denied, the probability Alice will help Bob is similarly decreased by α. If we suppose Agent A asks Agent B for help, the exact mechanism for changing the exchange probabilities is given in Table 12.3.

An interpretation of the exchange rules is that there is a social cost to Agent A for receiving assistance, and on the other hand, there is a social cost to B for refusing to help when asked. This is the exact mechanism Menjívar (2000) posits for the weakening of social ties among Salvadorans in San Francisco. If a person continues to seek assistance without returning the favor, the probability the person receives aid will eventually become negligible. Here, using agents, we make this more precise by expressing exactly how much the probability degrades with each exchange or interaction.

We call the constants α and β reciprocity factors. The constant α determines the amount that exchange probabilities degrade, and β determines the amount that exchange probabilities increase. Much of the discussion that follows involves discerning how different values of α and β affect the evolution of network structure. For example, if we take extreme values $\alpha = 1$ and $\beta = 0$, there will be no change in the probabilities. If instead we set $\alpha = 0$, the weight of some edge will go to 0 after each exchange, and the network quickly becomes disconnected. In the following (see section titled "Changing Reciprocity Factors") we will test more reasonable values of α and β.

For two agents A and B, the exchange probabilities E_{AB} and E_{BA} also provide the model with a means for determining whether A and B are tied together in the social network. If Agent A repeatedly denies B assistance, the probability that B will aid A will approach zero. The decreasing probability E_{BA} corresponds to a weakening of the tie between the two agents. Since every exchange relationship in the model has two probabilities attached to it, we say there is a tie or connection between two agents when both probabilities are above some threshold. Specifically, there is a social bond between A and B if both E_{AB} and E_{BA} are above 0.15.

Strong Ties and Weak: Information Exchange

In addition to the network of material assistance, there is another, weaker (à la Granovetter 1973) network through which agents exchange information about resources – in this case, information about jobs and housing. The information network is weaker than the exchange network in a strict sense; every conduit of material exchange is also a conduit of information exchange. In other words, people are willing to trade information with actors with whom they would not trade material resources.

But besides their partners in material exchange, who else are agents sharing information with? We provide two other possibilities in our model: friends of friends and complete strangers. If two agents are not connected in the affiliation network, the probability that the exchange information with each other (in a given time-step) is the proportion of affiliates they share to the total number of affiliates of each agent. That is, unconnected agents are more likely to share information if they have a large number of "friends" in common. For example, suppose Agent Alice and Agent Bob are not connected in the affiliation network, but they do have 5 affiliates in common. If Alice is connected to a total of 10 agents in the affiliation network and Bob has 20 affiliates, then the probability of Alice and Bob sharing information is $0.25 = 5/25$, the number of common affiliates divided by the maximum number of affiliates between the two.

We also include the possibility that actors with no friends in common can trade information. This represents chance meetings of individuals on the street, at the grocer, and so on. There is a small probability that unconnected actors will trade information. We call this probability ε, and part of the analysis will be to determine how efficiently resources are allocated for different values of ε.

Table 12.4. *Probability of acquiring
information about each job and housing level*

Job State	Job Probability	Housing Probability
1 (Worst)	NA	0.1
2	0.1	0.1
3	0.05	0.1
4 (Best)	0.001	0.1

Now that we know who is likely to share information with whom, we must discuss the process by which actors acquire information. In the model, it is appropriate to think of pieces of information as tokens. At each time-step, each agent has a certain probability of acquiring a token about each job and housing state. The probabilities are given in Table 12.4.

There is no probability of gaining information about a job in state 1 because this state corresponds to unemployment. The probabilities are low to represent the difficulties in finding housing and employment, especially regular, full-time employment. If an actor is fortunate to gain a token for a job or housing state that it prefers to its current state, it "cashes in" the token and transitions to a new preferred state.

If, instead, an agent gains a token about a job state that is not better than its current state, it passes the toke to a random agent in its information network who would find the information beneficial. The receiving agent then cashes in the information token and transitions to the new state. At the end of each time-step, any remaining information that has not been used is wiped out, and new information tokens are generated at the next time-step. This basic setup of treating information as a token to be traded between agent relies heavily on the Jobsearch model (Delany 1988).

Since the information exchange network has random components, it is very contingent and can vary greatly from time-step to time-step. In addition to providing access to resources, these week ties provide our model with a mechanism for the creation of strong ties. If, by chance, a pair of agents are connected in the information network for three consecutive time-steps, a new (strong) material exchange tie is formed between them. The probability that they will assist each other in material exchange is set to 0.75.

The Changing Social Environment: An Overview of the Model

We have developed a rather complicated model in order to capture some of the complexity involved in the lives of the Salvadoran immigrant

Table 12.5. *Probability of becoming unemployed*

Job State:	4	3	2	1
Probability of Unemployment:	0.1	0.15	0.3	NA

population. To implement the model, we used a computer program that executes the economic environment and social interactions of the agents as outlined in the previous sections. In this section, we detail the setup of the model and the execution of a single time-step.

The model is populated with 500 agents, and initially 295 randomly chosen agents are in job state 1 (unemployed); 100 agents are in job states 2 and 3, and 5 are in job state 4. This is the distribution that would occur if the agents were not allowed to share job information (see section titled "Jobs and Housing: Efficient Allocation of Resources"). To start, the agents are given the housing state corresponding to their job state. The initial configuration of the resource exchange is set to be a one degree lattice with average degree 10. One can think of 500 agents arranged in a circle with each agent connected to the 5 agents to its left and the 5 on its right, for a total of 2500 edges. All the exchange probabilities are set to 0.5. Thus, there is a great deal of symmetry in the initial network.

Since rent is paid monthly, each time-step is meant to represent one month. In each time-step, the agents may – in this order – lose their jobs, get paid and pay rent, acquire information about employment and housing, utilize the beneficial information they acquire, ask network affiliates for aid, exchange information with other agents, and perhaps change their social network. An agent "losing its job" means it changes from its current job state to another job state, corresponding to unemployment. The probabilities of becoming unemployed given in Table 12.5 represent the fact that better jobs are more stable (but no jobs are very stable for the immigrant community).

The distributions from which agents get paid and pay rent depend on their job and housing state, respectively, and are given in Table 12.2. The probabilities of gaining information about specific jobs and housing states are given in Table 12.4.

If an agent, say A, has negative resources after being charged rent, it will ask members of its exchange network for assistance. First, all the agents with negative resources are identified. Then, in random order, they request aid from a random member of their exchange network which has positive resources. The probability that an agent who is asked for help, say B, will donate aid is E_{BA}, and then both agents' exchange probabilities are updated according to Table 12.3. If B does provide aid, it gives half of the resources it has available or the amount the requesting agent needs, whichever is less.

It often happens that asking and receiving aid from a single agent is not sufficient to cover the debt an agent has accrued. If this is the case, the agent asks another member of its social network, and another, until the agent breaks even or exhausts its supply of affiliates. After all the agents have had the opportunity to ask for assistance, some of the exchange probabilities may have dropped below the threshold value 0.15. If so, the connection between the two agents is deleted. Also, if two agents that are not connected in the resource exchange network have now traded information for three successive time-steps, a new connection is made between them. In this manner, the structure of the resource exchange network changes every time-step.

Simulation Results

For each choice of parameters described in the following, we run the model 50 times for 136 time-steps each. To compute the date, we average the results of the 50 runs. This allows us to ascertain the average behavior of the model.

Jobs and Housing: Efficient Allocation of Resources

Since the agents trade information, they have access to job and housing resources that they would otherwise have been ignorant of. In other words, exchanging information allows for more efficient allocation of jobs and housing than if the agents were isolated. To determine just how efficient, the initial distribution in the population is precisely the distribution that would result without information sharing.[2] In Figure 12.1 we see that about 300 agents start in job state 1 (unemployed), but rather quickly the system evolves to a point where fewer than 200 agents are in job state 1. So, exchanging information reduces the number of agents in job state 1 by more than 33 percent. Similarly, we can see that the number of agents in job state 2 is increased by about 40 percent and in job state 3 by about 60 percent on average. Because information about job state 4 is so rare, agents receiving the information are likely to have a worse job, so trading information does not change the average number of agents in job state 4. Also, notice the difference in scales in the panels of Figure 12.1.

Clockwise from the upper left is Level 1 (unemployed), Level 2 (spotty part-time work), Level 4 (full-time employment), and Level 3 (regular part-time work). The dotted lines are the job distributions with a high

---

[2] When the agents do not trade information, the process of changing jobs is a Markov chain, and we calculated the stationary distribution.

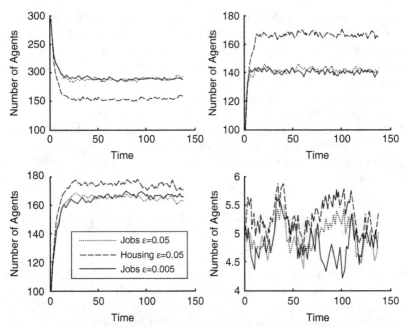

Figure 12.1. The distribution of agents in the four different job and housing levels over time

probability of sharing information with strangers; the dashed lines are the housing distributions corresponding to high information sharing; and the solid lines are the job distributions with a very low probability of sharing information with strangers. Note the different scales on the vertical axes.

Recall from the fourth section that there is some constant probability called ε of an agent exchanging information with a random stranger. For most simulation trials, ε was held constant at 0.05, but as we can see from Figure 12.1, even if we decrease ε by a factor of 10, the distribution of jobs is not affected. So, the information exchanged among affiliates is sufficient to distribute all the jobs available. That is to say, exchanging information with strangers in the simulation may affect which specific agents have access to better job states, but it does not affect the distribution of job states. Additionally, identical distributions are obtained for various choices of reciprocity factors – Figure 12.1 has $\alpha = 0.5$, $\beta = 0.5$ – and the distributions do not change over time. Thus, the structure and sparseness of the resource exchange network do not greatly affect the distribution of jobs (or housing). This is because the economic environment of the model is so poor that agents need to communicate with only very few affiliates to ensure that all the available jobs are taken.

Also, agents try to choose housing states that match their job states, and Figure 12.1 shows that the housing state reaches a stable distribution at roughly the same time as the job states. Housing information is disseminated quickly enough to ensure that a majority of agents can match their housing state to their job state within a couple of time-steps. However, if an agent transitions from a higher job state to a lower, the transition to a lower housing state will lag several time-steps, causing the agent to accrue large amounts of debt, a point that Menjívar captures in her work. This lag is seen in the graphs by the gap between the jobs and housing and is the driving factor behind the lack of resources in the model.

Changing Reciprocity Factors: Effect of Exchange on Network Structure

In the third section we discussed how the exchange probabilities change geometrically based on parameters α and β, the so-called reciprocity factors. In this section we explore how the network evolution varies for four different pairs of α and β.

Since the number of agents in the situation stays constant over time, the simplest way to compare differences in networks is to count the number of edges. Figure 12.2 counts the number of edges in the networks for four pairs of reciprocity factors: (i) $\alpha = .75$ and $\beta = .25$; (ii) $\alpha = .25$ and $\beta = .75$; (iii) $\alpha = .5$ and $\beta = .5$; (iv) $\alpha = .5$ and $\beta = .75$.

The upper left shows the average number of edges deleted at each time; the upper right shows the number of new connections formed; and the bottom is the total number of edges present at each time. The dotted lines correspond to $\alpha = .25$ and $\beta = .75$; the solid lines are for $\alpha = .75$ and $\beta = .25$; the short dashes are for $\alpha = \beta = .5$; and the long dashes are for $\alpha = .5$ and $\beta = .75$ Note the different scales on the vertical axes.

The graph in the upper left corner counts the average number of edges deleted at each time-step. The upper right shows the average number of new connections made, and the bottom graph depicts the mean total number of edges over time for each parameter pair. For larger values of α, the social cost of failing to reciprocate is lower, so the fewer the number of connections severed. For $\alpha = .75$ and $\beta = .25$, the social cost is quite low, so, on average, no more than five edges are deleted in any time-step. On the other hand, for $\alpha = .25$ and $\beta = .75$, the cost of failing to reciprocate (given the initial exchange probabilities of 0.5) is so great that it takes only one interaction to sever a connection. In fact, on average, more than 1000 edges are deleted in the first time-step.[3] For the

---

[3]   The graph goes off the scale.

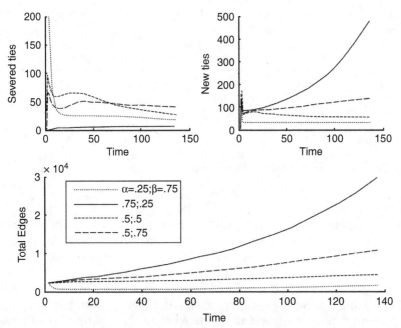

Figure 12.2. The changes in the number of network connections over time for four different simulation runs

other two parameter pairs, the initial deletion of edges is not as severe, and the graph become denser for the higher value of β.

Additionally, there is an interesting connection between the wealth and the connectivity of an agent. An agent's average number of trading partners (with the variance in parentheses) is given in Table 12.6. The average is taken at the end of the simulation run and then averaged over all the simulations for each pair of reciprocity factors.

The first row gives the average degree of all the 500 nodes; the second row averages the number of edges for only the 25 agents with the most resources at the end of the simulation run, and the bottom row gives the average degree for the 25 agents with the least resources at the end of the simulation. There are significant differences in the mean degrees of the population and the wealthiest 5 percent for the parameter pairs $\alpha = .25/\beta = .75$ and $\alpha = .5/\beta = .5$. Notice that these two parameter pairs also produce the least dense networks because many connections are severed in the first couple of time-steps. Apparently, agents who are nearly isolated have few requests to provide aid. Thus, any wealth they accumulate is not likely to be distributed to others.

In the networks where ties are not as easily severed (higher values of α or β), the agents with the most resources ("wealthy") have nearly the same mean degree as the entire population, and they accumulate fewer

Table 12.6. *Average number of exchange partners for each parameter setting*

	α = .25; β = .75	α = .75; β = .25	α = .5; β = .5	α = .5; β = .75
Populaton	5.97	119.88	18.30	43.16
(variance)	(0.29)	(60.43)	(3.54)	(8.23)
Wealthiest 5%	0.7856	119.27	11.03	37.34
	(0.077)	(217.99)	(5.48)	(9.87)
Poorest 5%	8.61	118.11	18.96	42.4
	(0.90)	(212.3)	(7.93)	(18.48)

resources than do the "wealthiest" in the sparser networks. In the denser networks, as soon as an agent has positive resources, many affiliates are requesting aid, so the agent's resources do not stay positive for long – even if it refuses most requests. This is an important observation regarding the dynamics of networks in contexts of poverty.

For example, when α =. 75 and β = .25, there is an average of 33.3 agents with positive resources at the end of the simulation; however, not one agent in any simulation accumulated more than 1 unit of resources, so though they are not in debt, they are still quite poor. This is because as soon as an agent has more than 1 unit of resources, it distributes the resources among its many affiliates. On the other hand, for α =. 25 and β = .75, an average of 62 agents have positive resources, and it is not unusual for agents to accumulate a couple of hundred units of resources or more. In other words, the sparse networks allow some individuals to accrue much more resources.

Conclusion

We have created a model of reciprocity on the likelihood that the two actors will engage in exchange. The resiliency of this likelihood is governed by the factors α and β, which describe the rate that exchange probabilities charge after a request for aid. By choosing appropriate values for the initial probability of exchange and the reciprocity factors, one can describe altruism (100%; α = 1, β = 0), selfishness (0%; α = 1, β = 1), or behaviors in between. This model also provides an easy description for when two actors have a social tie between them: namely, if each will exchange with the other with a probability above some threshold.

In a poor economic environment, like the one facing the Salvadoran immigrants of Menjívar's study, this model of reciprocity – supplemented with a model of information sharing – produces social networks that are fluid and contingent. Furthermore, actors in the model obtain resources from affiliates in a process that unfolds over time, often asking many affiliates to relieve a small portion of their debt. These two qualitative observations about the model match the qualitative observations that Menjívar made about the social networks of the actual immigrant population. However, in formalizing a model of reciprocity, we are also able to make quantitative statements about social networks. For example, since α and β can be interpreted as the social cost of failing to reciprocate – or alternatively, the benefit of reciprocating – their respective values determine the density of the resulting networks. If we hold α = 0.5, increasing β from 0.5 to 0.75 increases the average number of connections by a factor of about two and a half. Thus, the original qualitative study describes the processes that are formalized in the computer model. With more quantitative field data, one could then estimate free parameters (i.e., α and β) in the model for a truly mixed methods approach including qualitative, quantitative, and computational methods.

Now, as with any computational model, the formalization process requires one to make many simplifying assumptions. For example, the initial social network exhibits a high degree of symmetry that is unrealistic for social networks in real life. In some unreported simulations, the initial network used a random graph model. The results were similar to those of the previous section, but new ties were added more slowly. In a random graph, there is significantly less clustering, so there is less opportunity for triadic closure.

Also, we assume that the agents are homogeneous without sex or gender, educational or age differences. In the model all the agents are equally qualified for each type of employment, and everyone is equally likely to hear about a certain level of employment. However, we know that social positions that depend on factors like class, gender, age, race, and ethnicity are key in shaping network dynamics. In the model, the agents are "dumb" – they do not learn from previous experiences, and they do not employ any strategy when asking for aid. But we know that individuals make future decisions based on past experiences. Thus, the present study is a baseline showing how the mechanisms of reciprocity can influence structure in the absence of strategic actors.

However, perhaps the most important questions facing the immigrants of Menjívar's study involve their past experiences: (i) Whom should they ask for assistance? and (ii) When do they agree to grant aid (and how much)? These issues are not emphasized in the present study but are important in network analysis. The issue of whom to ask surely depends on how much information an actor has available. In our model, at least, agents will only ask help of others with positive resources. How much more information should an agent have? If agents are imbued with the ability to determine how likely another agent is to provide aid, they are certainly more likely to obtain assistance by asking those most likely to help. The actual decision process employed by people is a complex question of psychology, and incorporating more realistic decision procedures is the next logical step for this model. As for question (ii), the inherent uncertainty involving this question is why we have chosen to use likelihoods to model exchange relationships. But since every relationship is different, the amount that the likelihood changes after an exchange certainly differs for every pair of actors, especially if the actors are, say, siblings. Thus, a more accurate model of exchange would assign separate values of α and β for each link in the social network.

Our chapter's combination of qualitative ethnographic data and computational modeling seems to be a novel contribution from two methodological perspectives. One, the computational modeling of reciprocity, is rarely based on sociological fieldwork. Instead of drawing information from actual observations of exchange, earlier models relied on laboratory experiments, archaeological data, or idealized hypotheses about the structure of primitive populations. Here we incorporated the actual environmental situation facing the Salvadoran immigrant population in San Francisco with a formalized model of reciprocity informed by actual observations of exchange. The combination of ethnography and computer simulations allows us to address how networks function among the poor by exploring social dynamics that we cannot experiment with in a natural setting. The original ethnography shows that when poor immigrants have multiple demands on their resources from a large number of social ties, they can keep only little for themselves. However rich and in-depth, the observations gathered through this method are restricted to one context. In simulation, on the other hand, by allowing conditions to vary, we see how the same social mechanisms can produce networks with few ties and thus few demands on resources. The various situations created in simulation allow us to see how agents have the opportunity to accumulate resources, and how the wealthiest agents also have the fewest ties.

Secondly, from a mixed methods perspective, quantitative methods are taken solely to mean techniques involving sampling and statistical analysis. While traditional quantitative methods are important, they are unable to describe how individual interactions aggregate to create social phenomena. However, this is precisely what agent-based models do. But of course, an agent-based model can be designed only after qualitative study, and its parameters estimated only with statistical analysis. In the end, no single method has a monopoly on truth, and a research question is answered best by employing several methods, each yielding a different facet that together approximate the real social world.

References

Aragones, Ana Maria and Timothy Dunn. 2005. "Trabajadores indocumentados y nuevos destinos migratorios en la globalización." *Política y Cultura* 23:43–65.

Ari, Lilach Lev. 2006. "Who gains, who loses? Social mobility and absorbtion through emigration to the US, among Israeli men and women." *Social Issues in Israel* 1(2):5–44.

Axelrod, Robert. 1984. *The Evolution of Cooperation.* New York: Basic Books.

———. 1997. *The Complexity of Cooperation: Agent-Based Models of Competition and Collaboration.* Princeton, NJ: Princeton University Press.

Bashi, Vilna Francine. 2007. *Survival of the Knitted: Immigrant Social Networks in a Stratified World.* Stanford, CA: Stanford University Press.

Bowles, Samuel and Herbert Gintis. 2004. "The evolution of strong reciprocity: Cooperation in heterogeneous populations." *Theoretical Population Biology* 75:17–28.

Cialdini, Robert. 1984. *Influence: How and Why People Agree to Things.* New York: William Arrow and Co.

Collyer, Michael. 2005. "When do social networks fail to explain migration?: Accounting for the movement of Algerian asylum-seekers to the UK." *Journal of Ethnic and Migration Studies.* 31(4):699–718.

de Vos, Hank, Rita Samniotto, and Donald Elsas. 2001. "Reciprocal altruism under conditions of partner selection." *Rationality and Society.* 13(2):139–83.

Delany, John. 1988. "Social networks and efficient resource allocation: Computer models of job vacancy allocation through contacts." Pp. 430–51 in *Social Structures: A Network Approach,* edited by Barry Wellman and Stephen D. Berkowitz. New York: Cambridge University Press.

Fehr, Ernst and Simon Gachter. 2000. "Fairness and retaliation: The economics of reciprocity." *Journal of Economic Perspectives* 14(3):159–81.

Flache, Andreas. 2001. "Individual risk preferences and collective outcomes in the evolution of exchange networks." *Rationality and Society.* 13(3):304–48.

Gouldner, Alvin W. 1960. "The norm of reciprocity: A preliminary statement." *American Sociological Review* 25(2):161–78.

Granovetter, Mark. 1973. "The strength of weak ties." *American Journal of Sociology* 78(6):1360–80.

Griffin, William A. 2005. "Using-agent based modeling to simulate the influence of family-level stress on disease progression." Pp. 291–315 in *Handbook of Families and Health: Interdisciplinary Perspectives,* edited by D. Russell Crane and Elaine S. Marshall. Thousand Oaks, CA: Sage Publications.

Hobhouse, L. T. 1951. *Morals in Evolution: A Study in Comparative Ethics.* London: Chapman and Hall.

Ilcan, Suzan. 2002. *Longing in Belonging: The Cultural Politics of Settlement.* Westport, CT: Praeger.

Jasinskaja-Lahti, Inga, Karmela Liebkind, Magdalena Jaakkola, and Anni Reuter. 2006. "Perceived discrimination, social support networks, and psychological well-being among three immigrant groups." *Journal of Cross-Cultural Psychology* 37(3):293–311.

Johnston, Ron, Andrew Trlin, Anne Henderson, and Nicola North. 2006. "Sustaining and creating migration chains among skilled immigrant groups: Chinese, Indians and South Africans in New Zealand." *Journal of Ethnic and Migration Studies* 32(7):1227–50.

Khoo, Siew-Ean. 2003. "Sponsorship of relatives for migration and immigrant settlement intention." *International Migration* 41(5):177–99.

Massey, Douglas S., Rafael Alarcon, Jorge Durand, and Humberto González. 1990. *Return to Aztlan: The Social Process of International Migration from Western Mexico.* Berkeley: University of California Press.

McAllister, Ryan, Ian Gordon, Marco Janssen, and Nick Abel. 2005. "Pastoralists' response to variation of rangeland resources in time and space." *Ecological Applications* 16(2):572–83.

McCarthy, Angela. 2005. "'Bands of fellowship': The role of personal relationships and social networks among Irish migrants in New Zealand, 1861–1911." *Immigrants and Minorities* 23(2–3):339–58.

Menjívar, Cecilia. 2000. *Fragmented Ties: Salvadoran Immigrant Networks in America.* Berkeley: University of California Press.

Molm, Linda. 2006. "The social exchange framework." Pp. 24–40 in *Contemporary Social Psychology Theories,* edited by P. J. Burke. Palo Alto, CA: Stanford University Press.

Nowak, Martin and Robert May. 1992. "Evolutionary games and spatial chaos." *Nature* 359:826–29.

Piotrowski, Martin. 2006. "The effect of social networks at origin communities on migration remittances: Evidence from Nang Rong District." *European Journal of Population/Revue europeenne de demographie* 22(1):67–94.

Portes, Alejandro. 1998. "Social capital: Its origins and applications in modern sociology." *Annual Review of Sociology* 24:1–24.

Portes, Alejandro and Julia Sensenbrenner. 1993. "Embeddedness and immigration: Notes on the social determinants of economic action." *American Journal of Sociology* 98(6):1320–50.

Reynolds, Rober, Timothy Kohler, and Ziad Kobti. 2003. "The effects of generalized reciprocal exchange on the resilience of social networks: An example from the pre-hispanic Mesa Verde region." *Computational and Mathematical Organization Theory* 9(3):227–54.

Rodriguez, Vicente and Carmen Egea. 2006. "Return and the social environment of Andalusian emigrants in Europe." *Journal of Ethnic and Migration Studies* 32(8):1377–93.

Roschelle, Anne. 1997. *No More Kin: Exploring Race, Class and Gender in Family Networks.* Thousand Oaks, CA: Sage.

Ryan, Louise. 2007. "Migrant women, social networks and motherhood: The experiences of Irish nurses in Britain." *Sociology* 41(2):295–312.

Simmel, Georg. 1950. *The Sociology of Georg Simmel.* Translated and edited by Kurt H. Wolff. Glencoe, IL.: Free Press.

Tsai, Jenny Hsin-Chun. 2006. "Xenophobia, ethnic community, and Immigrant Youths' Friendship Network formation." *Adolescence* 41(162):285–98.

Waldinger, Roger and Michael I. Lichter. 2003. *How the Other Half Works: Immigration and the Social Organization of Labor.* Berkeley: University of California Press.

Wong, Daniel, Fu Keung, and He Xue Song. 2006. "Dynamics of social support: A longitudinal qualitative study on Mainland Chinese immigrant women's first year of resettlement in Hong Kong." *Social Work in Mental Health* 4(3):83–101.

Zeggelink, Evelien, Henk de Vos and Donald Elsas. 2000. "Reciprocal altruism and group formation: Degree segmentation of reciprocal altruists who prefer 'old helping partners'." *Journal of Artificial Societies and Social Simulation* 3(3): http://jasss.soc.surrey.ac.uk/3/3/1.html.

Index

Other Books in the Series *(continued from page iii)*